MOUNTAIN BIKE!
Wisconsin

A GUIDE TO THE CLASSIC TRAILS

SECOND EDITION

PHIL VAN VALKENBERG

Menasha
Ridge
Press

Cataloging-in-Publication Data
available from The Library of Congress

Photos by the author unless otherwise credited
Maps by Steven Jones and Jeff Goodwin
Cover and text design by Suzanne Holt
Cover photo by Dennis Coello

Menasha Ridge Press
P.O. Box 43673
Birmingham, Alabama 35243
www.menasharidge.com

All the trails described in this book are legal for mountain bikes. But rules can change—especial
for off-road bicycles, the new kid on the outdoor recreation block. Land access issues and confl
between bicyclists, hikers, equestrians, and other users can cause the rewriting of recreation
ulations on public lands, sometimes resulting in a ban of mountain bike use on specific
That's why it's the responsibility of each rider to check and make sure that he or she rides on
trails where mountain biking is permitted.

CAUTION

Outdoor recreational activities are by their very nature potentially hazardous. All particip
such activities must assume the responsibility for their own actions and safety. The infor
contained in this guidebook cannot replace sound judgment and good decision-makin
which help reduce risk exposure, nor does the scope of this book allow for disclosure o
potential hazards and risks involved in such activities.

Learn as much as possible about the outdoor recreational activities in which yo
pate, prepare for the unexpected, and be cautious. The reward will be a safer and m
able experience.

CONTENTS

AMERICA BY MOUNTAIN BIKE · Map Legend

Ride trailhead

Primary bike trail

Direction of travel

Optional bike trail and trailhead

Other trail

Hiking-only trail

Interstate highways (64)

US routes (51)

State routes (82)

Other paved roads (251B)

Unpaved roads (may be 4WD only)

0 ½ 1
MILES
Scale

True north N

Madison ◉
New Glarus ◉
Cities and towns

726
Forest Service roads

State border

STATE PARK
Public lands*

Ski trails

Ski lift

Lake Dam
River or stream

✈ Airport

🐚 Amphitheatre

♥ Archeological or historical site

🏹 Archery range

⚾ Baseball field

🚣 Boat ramp

▲ Campground (CG)

≡ Cattle guard

✝ Cemetery or gravesite

♠ Church

Ⓢ Drinking water

Fire tower or lookout

Falls or rapids

Food

Gate

House or cabin

Lodging

Mountain pass

△ Mountain summit
3312 (elevation in feet)

✕ Mine or quarry

Ⓟ Parking

Park office or ranger station

Picnic area

Power line or pipeline

Rest rooms

School

Spring

Stable, corral, or ranch

Swimming area

Traffic Light

Transmission towers

Tunnel or bridge

* Remember, private property exists in and around our national forests.

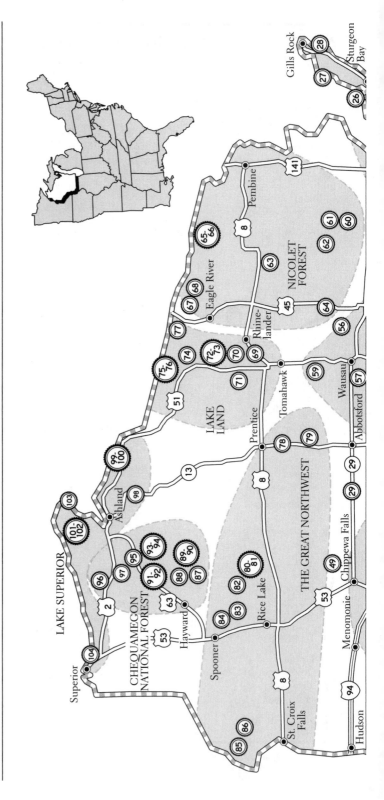

WISCONSIN · Ride Locations

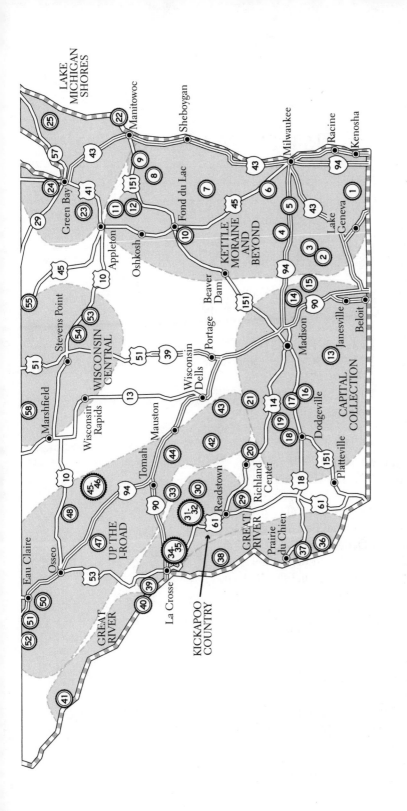

LIST OF MAPS

FOREWORD

Welcome to *America by Mountain Bike*, a series designed to provide all-terrain bikers with the information they need to find and ride the very best trails around. Whether you're new to the sport and don't know where to pedal, or an experienced mountain biker who wants to learn the classic trails in another region, this series is for you. Drop a few bucks for the book, spend an hour with the detailed maps and route descriptions, and you're prepared for the finest in off-road cycling.

My role as editor of this series was simple: First, find a mountain biker who knows the area and loves to ride. Second, ask that person to spend a year researching the most popular and very best rides around. And third, have that rider describe each trail in terms of difficulty, scenery, condition, elevation change, and all other categories of information that are important to trail riders. "Pretend you've just completed a ride and met up with fellow mountain bikers at the trailhead," I told each author. "Imagine their questions, be clear in your answers."

As I said, the *editorial* process—that of sending out riders and reading the submitted chapters—is a snap. But the work involved in finding, riding, and writing about each trail is enormous. In some instances our authors' tasks are made easier by the information contributed by local bike shops or cycling clubs, or even by the writers of local "where-to" guides. Credit for these contributions is provided, when appropriate, in each chapter, and our sincere thanks goes to all who have helped.

But the overwhelming majority of trails are discovered and pedaled by our authors themselves, then compared with dozens of other routes to determine if they qualify as "classic"—showcasing that area's best in scenery and cycling fun. If you've ever had the experience of pioneering a route from outdated topographic maps, or entering a bike shop to request information from local riders who would much prefer to keep their favorite trails secret, or know how trying it is to double- and triple-check data to be positive your trail info is correct, then you have an idea of how each of our authors has labored to bring about these books. You and I, and all the mountain bikers of America, are the richer for their efforts.

Friends, fun, and trails.

You'll get more out of this book if you take a moment to read the Introduction explaining how to read the trail listings. The "Topographic Maps" section will help you understand how useful topos will be on a ride, and will also tell you where to get them. And though this is a "where-to," not a "how-to" guide, those of you who have not traveled the backcountry might find "Hitting the Trail" of particular value.

In addition to the material above, newcomers to mountain biking might want to spend a minute with the Glossary, page 338, so that terms like *hardpack, singletrack,* and *waterbars* won't throw you when you come across them in the text.

All the best.

Dennis Coello
St. Louis

PREFACE

Wisconsin is a terrific state for mountain biking. Wonderful trails are waiting for fun-loving riders in every part of the state. The range of experiences is nearly as great as the number of trails. New mountain bikers, even kids
on training wheels, can get a taste for off-road riding on some of the trails, while
expert riders will also find extreme single-track to make their mouths water.

While the mountain bike wasn't invented in Wisconsin, it found a welcome
here early on. In 1983 the nation's first fat-tire festival, the Chequamegon (Sha-
wa-ma-gun), was begun. This pioneering weekend of fat-tire fun started with 29
riders and grew to a limited entry size of 2,500. It is so popular that recent events
have filled up within 24 hours of the opening of registration—testimony to the
enthusiasm for off-road riding in the state. That means there are lots of people
looking for great places to ride.

If you are one of them, I've collected 104 rides, divided among 12 regions,
where you can have a great time with your mountain bike. They are all 100%
legal places to ride, and each one has some particular appeal. I know your free
time is very valuable. Detailed information on each ride gives you the facts you
need to decide which trail will give you the experience you're looking for.

I know what you need to have a good time. I began off-roading in Wisconsin
in 1974, exploring trails in the Chequamegon National Forest with USGS topographic maps and an old French fat-tire bike. Getting lost can be a pain. I've
chosen rides where those chances are minimized and have told you exactly what
to look for to follow the route. I checked out more than 140 trails for this book.
Many of the rejects were poorly signed.

Families. Bikers have 'em. Bikers love 'em. Bikers are still trying to figure out
how to get a workout with 'em. For families I've included 26 special surface linear trails, usually laid out on abandoned railroad grades, which offer excellent
environments for kids and family members less than enthusiastic about varied-
terrain trails. Along these trails I've noted the locations of playgrounds to give
bike trailer– or child seat–bound kids a fun destination. Many of these trails are
smooth enough for children still on training wheels to ride. Another seven loop
trails are easy enough for families and kids as well.

Sun and shadow
on the trail.

What about that workout? With 17 of the rail-bed trails there are varied-terrain trails associated with the linear trail, and, with six other trails, I've included adjacent road detour options that take in some of the surrounding terrain before rejoining the linear trail.

There are also 46 varied-terrain trails that are all suitable for beginners and novices. These not-too-tough trails are great introductions to off-road riding. More advanced riders can cruise them for a change of pace. This adds up to a lot of miles where nearly anyone can enjoy a wonderful roll through Wisconsin's natural beauty.

This said, I haven't forgotten riders looking for more challenge. Included are 63 rides that can really give you a workout. Among them are 12 trails in the Technical Heaven category, eight of which have sections I've classified as extreme single-track: trails where rough surface, constantly varying terrain, and narrow passage between trees will test your bike handling skills.

Extreme trails differ from others described as single-track in that they've been specially cut for the enjoyment and challenge of mountain bikers. Most other single-track trails are cross-country ski trails narrowed enough to accommodate a single set of ski tracks. These give riders an intimate forest feel, but don't usually present the challenge of the extreme trails.

How about high-speed cruising? You should spend time spinning. It builds endurance, keeps weight down, and makes the muscles supple. You can get just as good a spinning workout in a given period of time on a mountain bike as a road bike if you're on good cruising trails or roads, you just won't go as far as on a skinny tired machine. I've got 39 trails where you can crank up the rpms.

For more rides geared to specific criteria, check out the "Ride Recommendations for Special Interests" section that follows. Whatever the ride you're after, you can head for the trails with this book knowing there's a great time waiting for you.

Family Rides—routes, often rail-trails, where even neophyte riders can have fun; often suitable for kids still on training wheels.

4	Glacial Drumlin State Trail, East	34	LaCrosse River State Trail
6	Bugline Trail	39	Great River State Trail
9	Old Plank Road Trail	42	"400" State Trail
10	Wild Goose State Trail	44	Omaha Trail
11	High Cliff State Park Trails	51	Chippewa River State Trail
13	Sugar River State Trail	52	Red Cedar State Trail
14	Cam-Rock County Park Trails	53	Hartman Creek State Park Trails
15	Glacial Drumlin State Trail, West		
16	Military Ridge State Trail	55	Wiowash Trail
20	Pine River/Bogus Bluff Tour	56	Mountain Bay State Trail, West
23	Mountain Bay State Trail, East	59	Council Grounds State Park Trails
24	Brown County Reforestation Camp Trails	60	Oconto County Recreation Trail
		71	Bearskin State Trail
25	Ahnapee State Trail	76	BATS/Lumberjack Trails
27	Peninsula State Park Trails	79	Timms Hill Spur/Pine Line Trails
30	Kickapoo Valley Reserve Trails	85	Gandy Dancer State Trail
33	Elroy-Sparta State Trail	104	Tri-County/Osaugie Trail

Novice and Beginner—these rides, or portions thereof, offer some challenge but require little technical ability and are fairly easy from an aerobic perspective (note that all of the family rides are also suitable).

1	Bong Recreation Area Trails	40	Perrot State Park Trails
5	Lapham Peak Trails	43	Mirror Lake State Park Trails
7	New Fane Trails	44	Omaha Trail
8	Greenbush Trails	45	Pigeon Creek Trail
11	High Cliff State Park Trails	46	Black River State Forest Trails
13	Sugar River State Trail	47	Perry Creek Trail
15	Glacial Drumlin State Trail, West	49	Lake Wissota State Park Trails
17	Blue Mound State Park Trails	50	Lowes Creek County Park Trails
19	Hyde Mill Tour	52	Red Cedar State Trail
20	Pine River/Bogus Bluff Tour	53	Hartman Creek State Park Trails
22	Point Beach State Forest Trails	55	Wiowash Trail
24	Brown County Reforestation Camp Trails	58	Big Eau Pleine County Park Trails
		61	Lakewood Trails
26	Potawatomi State Park Trails	70	McNaughton Trails
27	Peninsula State Park Trails	71	Bearskin State Trail
28	Newport State Park Trails	75	Escanaba Lake Trails
29	Kickapoo Cowpath Tour	76	BATS/Lumberjack Trails
30	Kickapoo Valley Reserve Trails	77	Langley Lake Trails
33	Elroy-Sparta State Trail	79	Timms Hill Spur/Pine Line Trails
36	Wyalusing Tour		
37	Wyalusing State Park Trails		

Novice and Beginner *(continued)*

82 Tuscobia State Trail
83 Sawmill Lake Tour
88 Frost Pocket Tour
95 Drummond Trails

97 Cisco/Pigeon/Star Lake Tour
99 Gile Falls Tour
103 Apostles Tour

Intermediate and Advanced Short Rides—rides, or portions thereof, under 10 miles that present significant technical challenges and/or a moderate to difficult aerobic challenge.

8 Greenbush Trails
12 Calumet County Park Trails
17 Blue Mound State Park Trails
18 Governor Dodge State Park Trails
21 Devils Lake State Park Trails
24 Brown County Reforestation
    Camp Trails
27 Peninsula State Park Trails
31 Brush Creek Campground Trails
33 Elroy-Sparta State Trail
35 Bluebird Campground Trails
40 Perrot State Park Trails
44 Omaha Trail
54 Standing Rocks County Park
    Trails
55 Wiowash Trail
64 Gartzke Flowage Trails
65 Lauterman/Perch Lake Trails
66 Ridge Trails
67 Anvil Trails

68 Nicolet North Trails
69 Washburn Lake Trails
72 Raven Trails
73 Madeline Lake Trails
74 Razorback Ridges Trails
75 Escanaba Lake Trails
76 BATS/Lumberjack Trails
78 Timms Hill Loop Trails
81 Blue Hills West Trails
84 Nordic Woods Trails
86 Coon Lake Park Trails
87 Trail Descente
89 Winding Pine Trails
92 Esker Trails
93 Rock Lake Trails
98 Copper Falls State Park Trails
101 Valkyrie Trails
102 Teuton Trails
103 Apostles Tour

Intermediate and Advanced Long Rides—rides 10 miles and over that present significant technical challenges and/or a moderate to difficult aerobic challenge.

2 John Muir Trails
3 Emma Carlin & Connector Trails
19 Hyde Mill Tour
20 Pine River/Bogus Bluff Tour
30 Kickapoo Valley Reserve Trails
32 Ice Cave Tour
36 Wyalusing Tour
38 Blackhawk's Stand Tour
41 Maiden Rock Tour
46 Black River State Forest Trails
48 Levis/Trow Mounds Trails

58 Big Eau Pleine County Park Trails
62 Boulder Lake Trails
79 Timms Hill Spur/Pine Line Trails
80 Blue Hills East Trails
90 Lake Helane Tour
91 Short & Fat Trails
94 Namekagon Trails
95 Drummond Trails
96 Delta Hills Trails
100 Pines & Mines Trail #6

Loops—rides that circle an area; these may also include an out-and-back "handle" section.

1	Bong Recreation Area Trails	55	Wiowash Trail
2	John Muir Trails	57	Nine Mile Forest Trails
3	Emma Carlin & Connector Trails	58	Big Eau Pleine County Park Trails
5	Lapham Peak Trails	59	Council Grounds State Park Trails
7	New Fane Trails	62	Boulder Lake Trails
8	Greenbush Trails	63	Ed's Lake Trails
10	Wild Goose State Trail	64	Gartzke Flowage Trails
11	High Cliff State Park Trails	65	Lauterman/Perch Lake Trails
12	Calumet County Park Trails	66	Ridge Trails
13	Sugar River State Trail	67	Anvil Trails
15	Glacial Drumlin State Trail, West	769	Washburn Lake Trails
17	Blue Mound State Park Trails	70	McNaughton Trails
18	Governor Dodge State Park Trails	72	Raven Trails
19	Hyde Mill Tour	73	Madeline Lake Trails
20	Pine River/Bogus Bluff Tour	74	Razorback Ridges Trails
21	Devils Lake State Park Trails	74	Escanaba Lake Trails
22	Point Beach State Forest Trails	76	BATS/Lumberjack Trails
24	Brown County Reforestation Camp Trails	77	Langley Lake Trails
		78	Timms Hill Loop Trails
26	Potawatomi State Park Trails	79	Timms Hill Spur/Pine Line Trails
27	Peninsula State Park Trails	80	Blue Hills East Trails
28	Newport State Park Trails	81	Blue Hills West Trails
31	Brush Creek Campground Trails	83	Sawmill Lake Tour
32	Ice Cave Tour	84	Nordic Woods Trails
33	Elroy-Sparta State Trail	86	Coon Lake Park Trails
35	Bluebird Campground Trails	87	Trail Descente
36	Wyalusing Tour	88	Frost Pocket Tour
37	Wyalusing State Park Trails	89	Winding Pine Trails
38	Blackhawk's Stand Tour	90	Lake Helane Tour
40	Perrot State Park Trails	92	Esker Trails
41	Maiden Rock Tour	93	Rock Lake Trails
43	Mirror Lake State Park Trails	94	Namekagon Trails
44	Omaha Trail	92	Drummond Trails
46	Black River State Forest Trails	96	Delta Hills Trails
48	Levis/Trow Mounds Trails	97	Cisco/Pigeon/Star Lake Tour
49	Lake Wissota State Park Trails	98	Copper Falls State Park Trails
50	Lowes Creek County Park Trails	101	Valkyrie Trails
53	Hartman Creek State Park Trails	102	Teuton Trails
54	Standing Rocks County Park Trails	103	Apostles Tour

Out-and-Backs—linear rides, often rail-trails, you'll most likely want to cover in both directions; these can also, if preferred, be point-to-point rides.

3	Emma Carlin & Connector Trails	9	Old Plank Road Trail
4	Glacial Drumlin State Trail, East	10	Wild Goose State Trail
6	Bugline Trail	13	Sugar River State Trail

Out-and-Backs (*continued*)

14 Cam-Rock County Park Trails	45 Pigeon Creek Trail
15 Glacial Drumlin State Trail, West	47 Perry Creek Trail
16 Military Ridge State Trail	51 Chippewa River State Trail
20 Pine River/Bogus Bluff Tour	52 Red Cedar State Trail
23 Mountain Bay State Trail, East	55 Wiowash Trail
25 Ahnapee State Trail	56 Mountain Bay State Trail, West
27 Peninsula State Park Trails	60 Oconto County Recreation Trail
29 Kickapoo Cowpath Tour	71 Bearskin State Trail
30 Kickapoo Valley Reserve Trails	76 BATS/Lumberjack Trails
33 Elroy-Sparta State Trail	79 Timms Hill Spur/Pine Line Trails
34 LaCrosse River State Trail	82 Tuscobia State Trail
39 Great River State Trail	85 Gandy Dancer State Trail
42 "400" State Trail	99 Gile Falls Tour
44 Omaha Trail	104 Tri-County/Osaugie Trail

Point-to-Points—linear rides best ridden one-way.

30 Kickapoo Valley Reserve Trails	91 Short & Fat Trails
61 Lakewood Trails	100 Pines & Mines Trail #6
68 Nicolet North Trails	

Technical Heaven—places the tech-freaks go to challenge their bike-handling skills.

2 John Muir Trails	57 Nine Mile Forest Trails
3 Emma Carlin & Connector Trails	69 Washburn Lake Trails
15 Glacial Drumlin State Trail West	74 Razorback Ridges Trails
30 Kickapoo Valley Reserve Trails	93 Rock Lake Trails
35 Bluebird Campground Trails	95 Drummond Trails
48 Levis/Trow Mounds Trails	100 Pines & Mines Trail #6

High-Speed Cruising—rides where you can crank on all or a large portion of the trail due to terrain, route configuration, and usage.

1 Bong Recreation Area Trails	25 Ahnapee State Trail
4 Glacial Drumlin State Trail East	29 Kickapoo Cowpath Tour
7 New Fane Trails	32 Ice Cave Tour
9 Old Plank Road Trail	34 LaCrosse River State Trail
10 Wild Goose State Trail	36 Wyalusing Tour
11 High Cliff State Park Trails	38 Blackhawk's Stand Tour
13 Sugar River State Trail	39 Great River State Trail
14 Cam-Rock County Park Trails	41 Maiden Rock Tour
16 Military Ridge State Trail	42 "400" State Trail
19 Hyde Mill Tour	44 Omaha Trail
20 Pine River/Bogus Bluff Tour	49 Lake Wissota State Park Trails
23 Mountain Bay State Trail East	50 Lowes Creek County Park Trails
24 Brown County Reforestation Camp Trails	55 Wiowash Trail
	56 Mountain Bay State Trail, West

High-Speed Cruising *(continued)*

70	McNaughton Trails	88	Frost Pocket Tour
71	Bearskin State Trail	90	Lake Helane Tour
79	Timms Hill Spur/Pine Line Trails	96	Delta Hills Trails
		97	Cisco/Pigeon/Star Lake Tour
82	Tuscobia State Trail	99	Gile Falls Tour
83	Sawmill Lake Tour	103	Apostles Tour
85	Gandy Dancer State Trail		

Wildlife Viewing—exceptional areas due to the types of animals present, frequency of sightings, or on-site information available.

1	Bong Recreation Area Trails	39	Great River State Trail
10	Wild Goose State Trail	41	Maiden Rock Tour
30	Kickapoo Valley Reserve Trails	76	BATS/Lumberjack Trails

Great Scenery—the woods and meadows of Wisconsin are always scenic, but these places are exceptional.

11	High Cliff State Park Trails	41	Maiden Rock Tour
16	Military Ridge State Trail	44	Omaha Trail
20	Pine River/Bogus Bluff Tour	46	Black River State Forest Trails
21	Devils Lake State Park Trails	48	Levis/Trow Mounds Trails
26	Potawatomi State Park Trails	51	Chippewa River State Trail
27	Peninsula State Park Trails	72	Raven Trails
29	Kickapoo Cowpath Tour	90	Lake Helane Tour
30	Kickapoo Valley Reserve Trails	93	Rock Lake Trails
32	Ice Cave Tour	98	Copper Falls State Park Trails
33	Elroy-Sparta State Trail	100	Pines & Mines Trail #6
38	Blackhawk's Stand Tour	103	Apostles Tour
40	Perrot State Park Trails		

Single-Track—traditional cross-country ski trail width, usually 6 to 10 feet wide.

2	John Muir Trails	67	Anvil Trails
3	Emma Carlin & Connector Trails	68	Nicolet North Trails
		72	Raven Trails
12	Calumet County Park Trails	75	Escanaba Lake Trails
15	Glacial Drumlin State Trail, West	76	BATS/Lumberjack Trails
17	Blue Mound State Park Trails	77	Langley Lake Trails
26	Potawatomi State Park Trails	78	Timms Hill Loop Trails
28	Newport State Park Trails	79	Timms Hill Spur/Pine Line Trails
35	Bluebird Campground Trails		
37	Wyalusing State Park Trails	84	Nordic Woods Trails
40	Perrot State Park Trails	89	Winding Pine Trails
62	Boulder Lake Trails	92	Esker Trails
65	Lauterman/Perch Lake Trails	93	Rock Lake Trails
66	Ridge Trails	98	Copper Falls State Park Trails

Extreme Single-Track—rides that are entirely, or (more commonly) contain sections of, exclusive mountain bike trail or narrow hiking trail.

15	Glacial Drumlin State Trail West	57	Nine Mile Forest Trails
30	Kickapoo Valley Reserve Trails	69	Washburn Lake Trails
35	Bluebird Campground Trails	74	Razorback Ridges Trails
48	Levis/Trow Mounds Trails	95	Drummond Trails

Double-Track—usually cross-country ski trails or old logging roads from 10 to 20 feet wide.

1	Bong Recreation Area Trails	58	Big Eau Pleine County Park Trails
5	Lapham Peak Trails	59	Council Grounds State Park Trails
7	New Fane Trails	61	Lakewood Trails
8	Greenbush Trails	63	Ed's Lake Trails
11	High Cliff State Park Trails	64	Gartzke Flowage Trails
18	Governor Dodge State Park Trails	66	Anvil Trails
21	Devils Lake State Park Trails	67	Nicolet North Trails
22	Point Beach State Forest Trails	68	Washburn Lake Trails
24	Brown County Reforestation Camp Trails	69	McNaughton Trails
27	Peninsula State Park Trails	72	Raven Trails
30	Kickapoo Valley Reserve Trails	73	Madeline Lake Trails
31	Brush Creek Campground Trails	74	Razorback Ridges Trails
35	Bluebird Campground Trails	81	Blue Hills East Trails
43	Mirror Lake State Park Trails	82	Blue Hills West Trails
45	Pigeon Creek Trail	86	Coon Lake Park Trails
46	Black River State Forest Trails	87	Trail Descente
47	Perry Creek Trail	88	Frost Pocket Tour
48	Levis/Trow Mounds Trails	89	Winding Pine Trails
49	Lake Wissota State Park Trails	91	Short & Fat Trails
50	Lowes Creek County Park Trails	94	Namekagon Trails
53	Hartman Creek State Park Trails	95	Drummond Trails
54	Standing Rocks County Park Trails	96	Delta Hills Trails
55	Wiowash Trail	100	Pines & Mines Trail #6
57	Nine Mile Forest Trails	101	Valkyrie Trails
		102	Teuton Trails

Roads—tours on, or with significant portions on, roads open to motor vehicle use, usually lightly trafficked gravel or paved roads, or having wide shoulders if moderately trafficked.

6	Bugline Trail	32	Ice Cave Tour
10	Wild Goose State Trail	33	Elroy-Sparta State Trail
13	Sugar River State Trail	36	Wyalusing Tour
19	Hyde Mill Tour	38	Blackhawk's Stand Tour
20	Pine River/Bogus Bluff Tour	41	Maiden Rock Tour
29	Kickapoo Cowpath Tour	44	Omaha Trail
30	Kickapoo Valley Reserve Trails	59	Council Grounds State Park Trails

Roads (*continued*)

60 Oconto County Recreation Trail	90 Lake Helane Tour
68 Nicolet North Trails	91 Short & Fat Trails
79 Timms Hill Spur/Pine Line Trails	92 Esker Trails
80 Blue Hills East Trails	95 Drummond Trails
81 Blue Hills West Trails	96 Delta Hills Trails
83 Sawmill Lake Tour	97 Cisco/Pigeon/Star Lake Tour
88 Frost Pocket Tour	99 Gile Falls Tour
89 Winding Pine Trails	103 Apostles Tour

Special Surface Linear Trails—trails laid out on abandoned railroad beds and usually closed to motor vehicles.

4 Glacial Drumlin State Trail East	39 Great River State Trail
6 Bugline Trail	42 "400" State Trail
9 Old Plank Road Trail	44 Omaha Trail
10 Wild Goose State Trail	51 Chippewa River State Trail
13 Sugar River State Trail	52 Red Cedar State Trail
14 Cam-Rock County Park Trails	55 Wiowash Trail
16 Military Ridge State Trail	56 Mountain Bay State Trail, West
20 Pine River/Bogus Bluff Tour	60 Oconto County Recreation Trail
23 Mountain Bay State Trail East	71 Bearskin State Trail
25 Ahnapee State Trail	79 Timms Hill Spur/Pine Line Trails
27 Peninsula State Park Trails	82 Tuscobia State Trail
33 Elroy-Sparta State Trail	85 Gandy Dancer State Trail
34 LaCrosse River State Trail	104 Tri-County/Osaugie Trail

INTRODUCTION

TRAIL DESCRIPTION OUTLINE

Each trail in this book begins with key information that includes length, configuration, aerobic and technical difficulty, trail conditions, scenery, and special comments. Additional description is contained in 11 individual categories. The following will help you to understand all of the information provided.

Trail name: Trail names are as designated on United States Geological Survey (USGS), Forest Service, or other maps and/or by local custom.

At a Glance Information

Length/configuration: The overall length of a trail is described in miles, unless stated otherwise. The configuration is a description of the shape of each trail— whether the trail is a loop, out-and-back (that is, along the same route), figure eight, trapezoid, isosceles triangle, decahedron...(just kidding), or if it connects with another trail described in the book. See Ride Configurations, page 3, for more details

Aerobic difficulty: This provides a description of the degree of physical exertion required to complete the ride.

Technical difficulty: This provides a description of the technical skill required to pedal a ride. Trails are often described here in terms of being paved, unpaved, sandy, hard-packed, washboarded, two- or four-wheel-drive, single-track or double-track. All terms that might be unfamiliar to the first-time mountain biker are defined in the Glossary.

Note: For both the aerobic and technical difficulty categories, authors were asked to keep in mind the fact that all riders are not equal, and thus to gauge the trail in terms of how the middle-of-the-road rider—someone between the newcomer and Ned Overend—could handle the route. Comments about the trail's length, condition, and elevation change will also assist you in determining the difficulty of any trail relative to your own abilities.

Scenery: Here you will find a general description of the natural surroundings during the seasons most riders pedal the trail, and a suggestion of what is to be found at special times (like great fall foliage or cactus in bloom).

Special comments: Unique elements of the ride are mentioned.

Category Information

General location: This category describes where the trail is located in reference to a nearby town or other landmark.

Elevation change: Unless stated otherwise, the figure provided is the total gain and loss of elevation along the trail. In regions where the elevation variation is not extreme, the route is simply described as flat, rolling, or possessing short and steep climbs or descents.

Season: This is the best time of year to pedal the route, taking into account trail conditions (for example, when it will not be muddy), riding comfort (when the weather is too hot, cold, or wet), and local hunting seasons.

Note: Because the exact opening and closing dates of deer, elk, moose, and antelope seasons often change from year to year, riders should check with the local fish and game department or call a sporting goods store (or any place that sells hunting licenses) in a nearby town before heading out. Wear bright clothes in fall, and don't wear suede jackets while in the saddle. Hunter's-orange tape on the helmet is also a good idea.

Services: This category is of primary importance in guides for paved-road tourers, but is far less crucial to most mountain bike trail descriptions because there are usually no services whatsoever to be found. Authors have noted when water is available on desert or long mountain routes and have listed the availability of food, lodging, campgrounds, and bike shops. If all these services are present you will find only the words "All services available in…"

Hazards: Special hazards like steep cliffs, great amounts of deadfall, or barbed-wire fences very close to the trail are noted here.

Rescue index: Determining how far one is from help on any particular trail can be difficult due to the backcountry nature of most mountain bike rides. Authors therefore state the proximity of homes or Forest Service outposts, nearby roads where one might hitch a ride, or the likelihood of encountering other bikers on the trail. Phone numbers of local sheriff departments or hospitals are hardly ever provided because phones are usually not available. If you are able to reach a phone, the local operator will connect you with emergency services.

Land status: This category provides information regarding whether the trail crosses land operated by the Forest Service, Bureau of Land Management, or a city, state, or national park; whether it crosses private land whose owner (at the time the author did the research) has allowed mountain bikers right of passage; and so on.

Note: Authors have been extremely careful to offer only those routes that are open to bikers and are legal to ride. However, because land ownership changes over time, and because the land-use controversy created by mountain bikes still has not completely subsided, it is the duty of each cyclist to look for and to heed signs warning against trail use. Don't expect this book to get you off the hook when you're facing some small-town judge for pedaling past a Biking Prohibited sign erected the day before you arrived. Look for these signs, read them, and heed the advice. And remember there's always another trail.

Maps: The maps in this book have been produced with great care and, in conjunction with the trail-following suggestions, will help you stay on course. But as every experienced mountain biker knows, things can get tricky in the backcountry. It is therefore strongly suggested that you avail yourself of the detailed information found in the 7.5 minute series USGS (United States Geological Survey) topographic maps. In some cases, authors have found that specific Forest Service or other maps may be more useful than the USGS quads and tell readers how to obtain them.

Finding the trail: Detailed information on how to reach the trailhead and where to park your car is provided here.

Sources of additional information: Here you will find the address and/or phone number of a bike shop, governmental agency, or other source from which trail information can be obtained.

Notes on the trail: This is where you are guided carefully through any portions of the trail that are particularly difficult to follow. The author also may add information about the route that does not fit easily in the other categories. This category will not be present for those rides where the route is easy to follow.

ABBREVIATIONS

The following road-designation abbreviations are used in *Mountain Bike! Wisconsin:*

CR	County Road	I	Interstate
FR	Farm Route	IR	Indian Route
FS	Forest Service Road	US	United States highway

State highways are designated with the appropriate two-letter state abbreviation, followed by the road number. Example: WI 33 = Wisconsin State Highway 33.

RIDE CONFIGURATIONS

Combination: This type of route may combine two or more configurations. For example, a point-to-point route may integrate a scenic loop or an out-and-back spur midway through the ride. Likewise, an out-and-back may have a loop at its farthest point (this configuration looks like a cherry with a stem attached; the stem is the out-and-back, the fruit is the terminus loop). Or a loop route may have multiple out-and-back spurs and/or loops to the side. Mileage for a combination route is for the total distance to complete the ride.

Loop: This route configuration is characterized by riding from the designated trailhead to a distant point, then returning to the trailhead via a different route (or simply continuing on the same in a circle route) without doubling back. You always move forward across new terrain, but return to the starting point when finished. Mileage is for the entire loop from the trailhead back to trailhead.

Out-and-back: On therse rides you will return on the same trail you pedaled out. While this might sound more boring than a loop route, many trails look very different when pedaled in the opposite direction.

Point-to-point: A vehicle shuttle (or similar assistance) is required for this type of route, which is ridden from the designated trailhead to a distant location, or endpoint, where the route ends. Total mileage is for the one-way trip from the trailhead to endpoint.

Spur: This is a road or trail that intersects the main trail you're following.

Ride Configurations contributed by Gregg Bromka

TOPOGRAPHIC MAPS

The maps in this book, when used in conjunction with the route directions present in each chapter, will in most instances be sufficient to get you to the trail and keep you on it. However, you will find superior detail and valuable information in the 7.5 minute series United States Geological Survey (USGS) topographic maps. Recognizing how indispensable these are to bikers and hikers alike, many bike shops and sporting goods stores now carry topos of the local area.

But if you're brand new to mountain biking you might be wondering "What's a topographic map?" In short, these differ from standard "flat" maps in that they indicate not only linear distance, but elevation as well. One glance at a topo will show you the difference, as "contour lines" are spread across the map like dozens of intricate spider webs. Each contour line represents a particular elevation, and at the base of each topo a particular "contour interval" designation is given. Yes, it sounds confusing if you're new to the lingo, but it truly is a simple and wonderfully helpful system. Keep reading.

Let's assume that the 7.5 minute series topo before us says "Contour Interval 40 feet," that the short trail we'll be pedaling is two inches in length on the map, and that it crosses five contour lines from its beginning to end. What do we know? Well, because the linear scale of this series is 2,000 feet to the inch (roughly 2 3/4 inches representing 1 mile), we know our trail is approximately 4/5 of a mile long (2 inches × 2,000 feet). But we also know we'll be climbing or descending 200 vertical feet (5 contour lines × 40 feet each) over that distance. And the elevation designations written on occasional contour lines will tell us if we're heading up or down.

The authors of this series warn their readers of upcoming terrain, but only a detailed topo gives you the information you need to pinpoint your position exactly on a map, steer yourself toward optional trails and roads nearby, plus let you know at a glance if you'll be pedaling hard on them. It's a lot of information for a very low cost. In fact, the only drawback with topos is their size—several feet square. I've tried rolling them into tubes, folding them carefully, even cutting them into blocks and photocopying the pieces. Any of these systems is a pain, but no matter how you pack the maps you'll be happy they're along. And you'll be even happier if you pack a compass as well.

In addition to local bike shops and sporting goods stores, you'll find topos at major universities and some public libraries where you might try photocopying the ones you need to avoid the cost of buying them. But if you want your own and can't find them locally buy them online at http://mapping.usgs.gov or write to:

USGS Map Sales
Box 25286
Denver, CO 80225
(800) ASK USGS (275-8747)

VISA and MasterCard are accepted. Ask for an index while you're at it, plus a price list and a copy of the booklet *Topographic Maps*. In minutes you'll be reading them like a pro.

A second excellent series of maps available to mountain bikers is put out by the United States Forest Service. If your trail runs through an area designated as a national forest, look in the phone book (white pages) under the United States Government listings, find the Department of Agriculture heading, and then run your finger down that section until you find the Forest Service. Give them a call and they'll provide the address of the regional Forest Service office, from which you can obtain the appropriate map.

TRAIL ETIQUETTE

Pick up almost any mountain bike magazine these days and you'll find articles and letters to the editor about trail conflict. For example, you'll find hikers' tales of being blindsided by speeding mountain bikers, complaints from mountain bikers about being blamed for trail damage that was really caused by horse or cattle traffic, and cries from bikers about those "kamikaze" riders who through their antics threaten to close even more trails to all of us.

The authors of this series have been very careful to guide you to only those trails that are open to mountain biking (or at least were open at the time of their research), and without exception have warned of the damage done to our sport through injudicious riding. All of us can benefit from glancing over the following

International Mountain Bicycling Association (IMBA) Rules of the Trail before saddling up.

1. *Ride on open trails only.* Respect trail and road closures (ask if unsure), avoid possible trespass on private land, obtain permits and authorization as may be required. Federal and state wilderness areas are closed to cycling.

2. *Leave no trace.* Be sensitive to the dirt beneath you. Even on open trails, you should not ride under conditions where you will leave evidence of your passing, such as on certain soils shortly after rain. Observe the different types of soils and trail construction; practice low-impact cycling. This also means staying on the trail and not creating any new ones. Be sure to pack out at least as much as you pack in.

3. *Control your bicycle!* Inattention for even a second can cause disaster. Excessive speed can maim and threaten people; there is no excuse for it!

4. *Always yield the trail.* Make known your approach well in advance. A friendly greeting (or a bell) is considerate and works well; startling someone may cause loss of trail access. Show your respect when passing others by slowing to a walk or even stopping. Anticipate that other trail users may be around corners or in blind spots.

5. *Never spook animals.* All animals are startled by an unannounced approach, a sudden movement, or a loud noise. This can be dangerous for you, for others, and for the animals. Give animals extra room and time to adjust to you. In passing, use special care and follow the directions of horseback riders (ask if uncertain). Running cattle and disturbing wild animals is a serious offense. Leave gates as you found them, or as marked.

6. *Plan ahead.* Know your equipment, your ability, and the area in which you are riding—and prepare accordingly. Be self-sufficient at all times. Wear a helmet, keep your machine in good condition, and carry necessary supplies for changes in weather or other conditions. A well-executed trip is a satisfaction to you and not a burden or offense to others.

For more information, contact IMBA, P.O. Box 7578, Boulder, CO 80306; (303) 545-9011.

Additionally, the following Code of Ethics by the National Off-Road Biking Association (NORBA) is worthy of your attention.

1. I will yield the right of way to other non-motorized recreationists. I realize that people judge all cyclists by my actions.

2. I will slow down and use caution when approaching or overtaking another and will make my presence known well in advance.

3. I will maintain control of my speed at all times and will approach turns in anticipation of someone around the bend.

4. I will stay on designated trails to avoid trampling native vegetation and minimize potential erosion to trails by not using muddy trails or shortcutting switchbacks.

5. I will not disturb wildlife or livestock.

6. I will not litter. I will pack out what I pack in, and pack out more than my share if possible.

7. I will respect public and private property, including trail use and no trespassing signs; I will leave gates as I found them.

8. I will always be self-sufficient and my destination and travel speed will be determined by my ability, my equipment, the terrain, and present and potential weather conditions.

9. I will not travel solo when bike-packing in remote areas.

10. I will leave word of my destination and when I plan to return.

11. I will practice minimum impact bicycling by "taking only pictures and memories and leaving only waffle prints."

12. I will always wear a helmet when I ride.

Worthy of mention are the following suggestions based on a list by Utah's Wasatch-Cache National Forest and the *Tread Lightly!* program advocated by the National Forest Service and Bureau of Land Management.

1. *Study a forest map before you ride.* Currently, bicycles are permitted on roads and developed trails which are designated bikes permitted. If your route crosses private land, it is your responsibility to obtain right-of-way permission from the landowner.

2. *Stay out of designated wilderness areas.* By law, all vehicles, including mountain bikes are not allowed.

3. *Stay off of roads and trails "put to bed."* These may be resource roads no longer used for logging or mining, or they may be steep trails being replaced by easier ones. So that the path returns to its natural state, they're usually blocked or signed closed to protect new vegetation.

4. *Keep groups small.* Riding in large groups degrades the outdoor experience for others, can disturb wildlife, and usually leads to greater resource damage.

5. *Avoid riding on wet trails.* Bicycle tires leave ruts in wet trails. These ruts concentrate runoff and accelerate erosion. Postponing a ride when the trails are wet will preserve the trails for future use.

6. *Stay on roads and trails.* Riding cross-country destroys vegetation and damages the soil. Resist the urge to pioneer a new road or trail, or to cut across a switchback. Avoid riding through meadows, steep hillsides or along stream banks and lakeshores because the terrain is easily scarred by churning wheels.

7. *Always yield to others.* Trails are shared by hikers, horses, and bicycles. Move off the trail to allow horses to pass and stop to allow hikers adequate room to share the trail. Simply yelling "Bicycle!" is not acceptable.

8. *Control your speed.* Excessive speed endangers yourself and other forest users.

9. *Avoid wheel lock-up and spin-out.* Steep terrain is especially vulnerable to trail wear. Locking brakes on steep descents or when stopping needlessly damages trails. If a slope is steep enough to require locking wheels and

skidding, dismount and walk your bicycle. Likewise, if an ascent is so steep that your rear wheel slips and spins, dismount and walk your bicycle.

10. *Protect waterbars and switchbacks.* Waterbars, the rock and log drains built to direct water off trails, protect trails from erosion. When you encounter a waterbar, ride directly over the top or dismount and walk your bicycle. Riding around the ends of waterbars destroys their effectiveness and speeds erosion. Skidding around switchback corners shortens trail life. Slow down for switchback corners and keep your wheels rolling.

11. *If you abuse it, you lose it.* Mountain bikers are relative newcomers to the forest and must prove themselves responsible trail users. By following the guidelines above, and by participating in trail maintenance service projects, bicyclists can help avoid closures that would prevent them from using trails.

12. *Know your bicycle handling limitations.*

You get the drift. So that everyone can continue riding our bikes through some of our country's most beautiful places, I urge you to follow the codes above and not be the "one bad apple" that spoils it for the rest of us.

HITTING THE TRAIL

Once again, because this is a "where-to," not a "how-to" guide, the following will be brief. If you're a veteran trail rider these suggestions might serve to remind you of something you've forgotten to pack. If you're a newcomer, they might convince you to think twice before hitting the backcountry unprepared.

Water: I've heard the questions dozens of times. "How much is enough? One bottle? Two? Three?! But think of all that extra weight!" Well, one simple physiological fact should convince you to err on the side of excess when it comes to deciding how much water to pack: A human working hard in 90-degree temperature needs approximately ten quarts of fluids every day. Ten quarts. That's two and a half gallons—12 large water bottles, or 16 small ones. And, with water weighing in at approximately eight pounds per gallon, a one-day supply comes to a whopping 20 pounds.

In other words, pack two or three bottles even for short rides. And make sure you can purify the water found along the trail on longer routes. When writing of those routes where this could be of critical importance, each author has provided information on where water can be found near the trail—if it can be found at all. But drink it untreated and you run the risk of disease.

One sure way to kill the protozoans, bacteria, and viruses in water is to boil it. Right. That's just how you want to spend your time on a bike ride. Besides, who wants to carry a stove, or denude the countryside stoking bonfires to boil water?

Luckily, there is a better way. Many riders pack along the inexpensive and only slightly distasteful tetraglycine hydroperiodide tablets (sold under the names Potable Aqua, Globaline, and Coughlan's, among others). Some invest in portable, lightweight purifiers that filter out the crud. Unfortunately, both iodine *and* filtering are required to be absolutely sure you've killed all the nasties you can't see. Tablets or iodine drops by themselves will knock off the well-known *Giardia*, once called "beaver fever" for its transmission to the water through the feces of infected beavers. One to four weeks after ingestion, *Giardia* will have you bloated, vomiting, shivering with chills, and living in the bathroom. (Though you won't care while you're suffering, beavers are getting a bum rap, for other animals are carriers also.)

But now there's another parasite we must worry about—*Cryptosporidium*. "Crypto" brings on symptoms very similar to *Giardia*, but unlike that fellow protozoan it's equipped with a shell sufficiently strong to protect it against the chemical killers that stop *Giardia* cold. This means we're either back to boiling or on to using a water filter to screen out both *Giardia* and crypto, plus the iodine to knock off viruses. All of which sounds like a time-consuming pain, but really isn't. Some water filters come equipped with an iodine chamber, to guarantee full protection. Or you can simply add a pill or drops to the water you've just filtered (if you aren't allergic to iodine, of course). The pleasures of backcountry biking—and the displeasure of getting sick—make this relatively minor effort worth every one of the few minutes involved.

Tools: Ever since my first cross-country tour in 1965 I've been kidded about the number of tools I pack on the trail. And so I will exit entirely from this discussion by providing a list compiled by two mechanic (and mountain biker) friends of mine. After all, since they make their livings fixing bikes, and get their kicks by riding them, who could be a better source?

These two suggest the following as an absolute minimum:
    tire levers
    spare tube and patch kit
    air pump
    Allen wrenches (3, 4, 5, and 6 mm)
    six-inch crescent (adjustable-end) wrench
    small flat-blade screwdriver
    chain rivet tool
    spoke wrench

But, while they're on the trail, their personal tool pouches contain these additional items:
    channel locks (small)
    air gauge
    tire valve cap (the metal kind, with a valve-stem remover)
    baling wire (ten or so inches, for temporary repairs)
    duct tape (small roll for temporary repairs or tire boot)
    boot material (small piece of old tire or a large tube patch)
    spare chain link
    rear derailleur pulley
    spare nuts and bolts
    paper towels and a tube of waterless hand cleaner

First-aid kit: My personal kit contains the following, sealed in double Ziploc bags:
  sunscreen
  aspirin
  butterfly-closure bandages
  Band-Aids
  gauze compress pads (a half-dozen 4" by 4")
  gauze (one roll)
  ace bandages or Spenco joint wraps
  Benadryl (an antihistamine, in case of allergic reactions)
  water purification tablets / water filter (on long rides)
  moleskin or Spenco "Second Skin"
  hydrogen peroxide, iodine, or Mercurochrome (some kind of antiseptic)
  snakebite kit

Final considerations: The authors of this series have done a good job in suggesting that specific items be packed for certain trails — raingear in particular seasons, a hat and gloves for mountain passes, or shades for desert jaunts. Heed their warnings, and think ahead. Good luck.

Dennis Coello

KETTLE MORAINE AND BEYOND

The words "Kettle Moraine" bring out mountain bikers faster than yelling "free swag." Partly because of its proximity to southeastern Wisconsin and northeastern Illinois population centers and partly because it offers great riding terrain and trails, the Kettle Moraine State Forest has been a mountain biking mecca since the knobby-tired, multi-speed bicycle mutants rolled out of Marin County.

What the glacier did to the land now described as kettle moraine terrain is what the Green Bay Packers want to do to the Dallas Cowboys. Two massive ice sheets ground against each other in a scrimmage that lasted hundreds if not thousands of years. No one knows who won, but what was left over looks like Swiss cheese on a topo map and feels like a roller coaster on a mountain bike.

This collection of rides takes you to the most popular Kettle Moraine State Forest trails and shows you some out-of-the-way ones that will give you a more secluded experience. Two trails beyond the kettles skirt the edge of a 200-foot limestone escarpment. There are four easy family bike trails too.

Wisconsin Off-Road Bicycling Association (WORBA) and Recreation for Individuals Dedicated to the Environment (RIDE) have done a terrific job in the region by putting in countless volunteer hours to make sure we have trails to enjoy. Future efforts will likely include trails in the Milwaukee Metro area. I encourage all riders to become members of one or both of these organizations.

At Bong Recreation Area even the most novice rider can have a fun roll on grassy trails that weave through restored prairie land and stands of oak trees. A nature center at the trailhead tells about the plants and wildlife you'll encounter.

The John Muir Trails and the Emma Carlin & Connector Trails are probably the most popular varied-terrain off-road trails in the state. The high level of aerobic and technical challenge found there attracts advanced-skill riders by the thousands to the Southern Kettle Moraine State Forest.

You can enjoy an easy rail-bed roll on the Glacial Drumlin State Trail-East while visiting an ancient Native American village site and winding through the scenic hills of the Kettle Moraine. Nearby, the Lapham Peak Trails offer a varied-terrain ride that beginners and novices can handle.

Another rail-trail in the area is the Bugline Trail. Tucked in the northwest Milwaukee Metro area, the "Bug" takes visitors through a handful of attractive parks and skirts an active limestone quarry.

In the northern part of the Kettle Moraine State Forest, the New Fane Trails are easy enough for novices and have all the wonderful scenery that attracts riders to this part of the state. The Greenbush Trails have a lot more challenge, but an easy loop will keep novices happy too. Running east out of the historic village of Greenbush to the Lake Michigan city of Sheboygan, the Old Plank Road Trail follows a historic wagon route.

A vast wildlife refuge is the focus of the Wild Goose State Trail. This rail-trail passes along the western boundary of Horicon Marsh, a protected haven for migratory water fowl. Side excursions off the trail can take you into the marsh for a closer look.

The Niagara Escarpment is the most prominent feature in eastern Wisconsin. It is a 200-foot-high ledge of limestone that forms the eastern boundary of Lake Winnebago, the state's largest inland lake. Two trail systems take advantage of the great scenery while offering different riding experiences. At High Cliff State Park families and novice riders can enjoy the trails that wind past mysterious Native American mound groups formed in the shape of panthers overlooking the vast lake waters. There are panther mounds along the Calumet County Park Trails too, but you'll have to scale the escarpment to check them out.

RIDE 1 · Bong Recreation Area Trails

AT A GLANCE

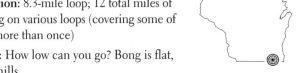

Length/configuration: 8.3-mile loop; 12 total miles of trail allow for riding on various loops (covering some of the same ground more than once)

Aerobic difficulty: How low can you go? Bong is flat, save a few rolling hills

Technical difficulty: Easy; other than a few steep embankments with about 20' of elevation, nothing will challenge your skills

Scenery: Resurgent Midwestern prairie land with some forested spots

Special comments: A good area for novice riders and kids who are old enough to ride without training wheels; signage is fairly good; the surface is mostly grassy and fairly rough

Welcome to your peace dividend—40 years later. Actually, the 4,515-acre parcel of blooming prairie land is a Cold War dividend. Slated to be a supersonic bomber base in the 1950s, Sputnik and the ICBM race nixed the United States' emphasis on planes and the land was spared just before the concrete runways were poured.

Now you can easily cruise the 8.3-mile red trail around the outer boundary with time left over to visit the excellent Molinaro Visitor Center and learn about the native prairie habitat and abundant bird life. Close to the population centers

RIDE 1 • Bong Recreation Area Trails

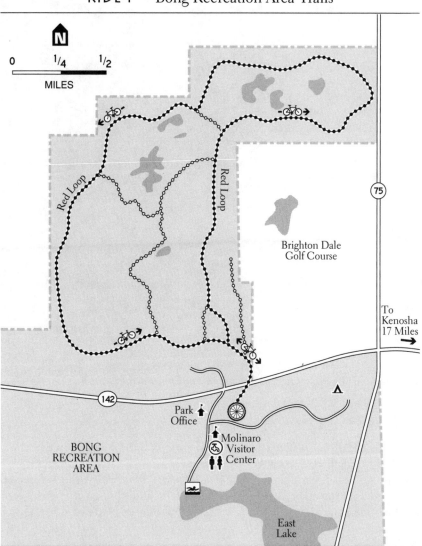

of Chicago and Milwaukee, Bong is far from being overused. In fact, more riders beating down a hardpack track would be nice. You can easily help do that, and no technical skill is required at all.

General location: 14 miles west of the city of Kenosha.

Elevation change: Only about 20'.

Season: April through November.

Services: Water and flush toilets are available at the Molinaro Visitor Center near the trailhead. Camping is available and there are showers.

A prairie oak turns the trail into a tunnel.

Hazards: Trails are well maintained and cleared, but windfalls could occur in the few wooded areas. Busy WI 142, which must be crossed shortly after leaving the trailhead, has deep ditches on each side. Some of the short steep sections up and down the berm ridges have stairs and, though it is possible to climb or descend alongside them, novice riders may be better off walking their bikes.

Rescue index: Help can be summoned on the south side of WI 142 at the park entrance station, Visitor Center, or perhaps at the maintenance building on the north side of the highway on the old road to the west of the trail crossing.

Land status: Wisconsin State Recreation Area. A daily or annual vehicle sticker ($5 daily/$18 annual for Wisconsin residents, $7 daily/$25 annual for out-of-state residents) is required to park in state recreation area lots.

Maps: A park map and information flyer are available at the park entrance station.

Finding the trail: Turn south off WI 142, pass the entrance station, and turn left toward the sunrise campground. The trailhead lot is on the left, you can access all trails from here.

Sources of additional information:

Bong State Recreation Area
26313 Burlington Road
Kansasville, WI 53139
(262) 878-5600

Wisconsin Department of Natural
  Resources
Bureau of Parks and Recreation
P.O. Box 7921
Madison, WI 53707-7921
(608) 266-2621
www.dnr.state.wi.us

Notes on the trail: An annual or day-use motor vehicle sticker is required to park on state land. This fee can be paid at the park entrance station. There is little special signing for mountain biking. A brown mountain bike silhouette sign at the trailhead is about it. The trails are well-signed for travel in a counterclockwise direction with blue cross-country ski trail signs, color-coded posts, and periodic "you are here" map signs.

The gray trail is 1.7 miles; the yellow trail is 4.4 miles; the orange trail is 6.4 miles; and the red trail is 8.3 miles. All mileage is computed from the trailhead. Your only real opportunity to get lost comes shortly after crossing WI 142, when you might mistake a fire break running off to the right for the correct trail. If you find yourself on a very rough surface right next to a golf course, you've gone the wrong way.

RIDE 2 · John Muir Trails

AT A GLANCE

Length/configuration: 10 miles for the John Muir outer (blue) loop; many loop variations are possible

Aerobic difficulty: Some easy riding, but mostly difficult

Technical difficulty: One tough trail system—steep slopes, tight turns, and some sidehill riding make it challenging

Scenery: Deep hardwood forest with lots of athletic-looking mountain bikers

Special comments: Despite heavy use, the Muir trails remain a great place to ride for more gung-ho bikers thanks to trail hardening and a one-way system; riding surfaces vary from grassy with a hardpack track to fine limestone gravel over Geoblock, a plastic grid work placed to slow erosion; trails are easy to follow

When you talk about mountain biking the Kettle Moraine, most riders think of the Muir trails. You can cover ten miles by riding the blue outer trail on this five-loop system. Many variations are possible by combining loops. The single-track cross-country ski trails give an intimate feel in the oak and pine forested area.

Erosion was a real problem on the Muir trails. On any given good-weather riding-season weekend day the trails would be asked to handle more than 2,500 riders, the equivalent of a Chequamegon Fat Tire Festival race. Forest personnel and volunteers have worked to harden the trails by installing a plastic grid work laid under a fine gravel surface. It works pretty well, though you will see the trail worn through to the grid in places.

The narrow trails and one-way travel direction make for an excellent riding experience without a feeling of crowding. You'll pass and get passed occasionally, but until you stop and see the constant flow you won't believe how many bikes are on the trails.

The trails are used for a popular late-September event called the Kettle Moraine Fall Color Festival. A limited-entry event featuring food, awards, and raffles, the festival allows riders to run the trails in time trial fashion.

Popularity has resulted in good privately run services in the area. The General Store at La Grange has long been a favorite for food, rental, retail, and repairs.

The 5-mile one-way Connector Trail at the north end of the loop runs to the Emma Carlin Trail (see Ride 3, page 18). Putting a run on the three trails together you can come up with a very tough 25-mile ride.

General location: Nine miles east of Whitewater.

Elevation change: There are many short steep climbs and several of 80' to 100'.

Season: Trails should be open from April through November.

Services: Food and bike sales and repair are found in La Grange. All services are available in Palmyra. All services, including bike sales and repair, are available in Whitewater, nine miles west.

Hazards: The trails are very well maintained, but watch for windfall trees or branches. The plastic grid placed under the trail surface can become exposed and is very slippery when wet, even from a heavy morning dew.

Rescue index: Aid can be summoned in La Grange and by calling 911 at the pay phone in the Nordic Trails parking lot across CR H from the John Muir parking lot.

Land status: Wisconsin State Forest, Southern Kettle Moraine Unit. A daily or annual vehicle sticker ($5 daily/$18 annual for Wisconsin residents, $7 daily/$25 annual for out-of-state residents) is required to park in state forest lots. Bicycles are not charged for visiting the forest, but a trail pass fee is required of bicyclists age 16 and older for riding the off-road trails ($3 daily/$10 annual). The trail pass also covers usages such as cross-country skiing, horseback riding, and bicycling on railroad-grade bike trails.

Maps: Sheet maps are available at the trailhead and are posted at trail intersections. The 7.5 minute series USGS quads for Whitewater and Little Prairie show the terrain very well, but do not show the trails.

Finding the trail: Trailhead parking lot is on the west side of CR H, 1.5 miles north of the crossroads village of La Grange and US 12. An overflow parking lot is located across CR H.

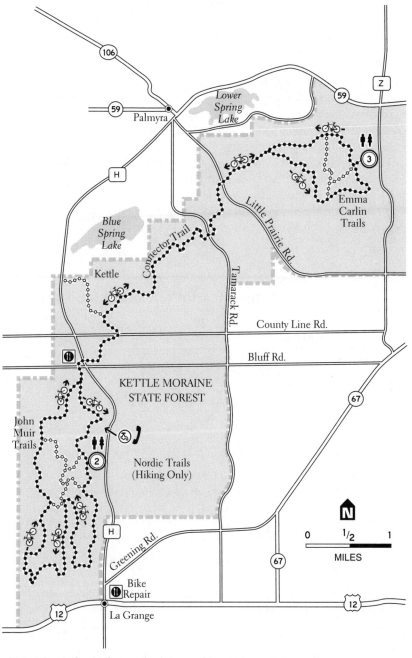

Note: More trails exist than can be shown on this map.

Sources of additional information:

James Wamser (send SASE for map)
1511 South 98th Street
West Allis, WI 53214
(414) 774-7336
www.execpc.com/~jWAMSER

Kettle Moraine, Southern Unit
S91 W39091 Highway 59
Eagle, WI 53119
(414) 594-2135

Notes on the trail: Daily or annual state park vehicle admission and daily or annual trail pass for riders age 16 and older are required (see Land status). There is a self-pay station at the trailhead. There are white and red no-biking signs on hiking trails. Fines apply for riding on hiking-only trails. Always phone ahead to make sure trails are open for riding.

The trails are marked with color-coded signposts that correspond to different loops. Often there will be more than one color at a time. Frequent "you are here" map signs at intersections help keep everything straight. The 1.5-mile red loop is easy and the 4-mile white loop is moderate, while the 5.3-mile orange loop, 6.8-mile green loop, and 10-mile blue loop are challenging.

RIDE 3 · Emma Carlin & Connector Trails

AT A GLANCE

Length/configuration: 4.2 miles for the Emma Carlin outer green loop (several loop variations are possible); 5.5 miles each way for the Connector Trail that leads to the John Muir Trails

Aerobic difficulty: Very high; you'll find sections to max-out on both the Emma Carlin and Connector trails

Technical difficulty: The Emma Carlin has been artificially hardened recently and is merely challenging now; the Connector awaits this treatment and will give you a taste of what the Carlin and Muir trails were like before hardening; lots of loose, egg- to softball-sized rocks plus roots, soft surface, narrow passage, and steep slopes make this one tough trail

Scenery: Hardwood forest of oaks, maples, and pines; scenic overlook at the northwest corner of the Emma Carlin Trail

Special comments: A terrific workout for advanced riders; the recent hardening of the Emma Carlin Trail has made it much easier from a technical perspective

Emma, I hardly know ya. And to my mind, that's good. Recent hardening of the Emma Carlin Trail's steep sections, which was done by laying down plastic grid work and covering it with fine limestone gravel, has made the trail

Downhill switchbacks make the Connector Trail challenging.

much more rideable and, I think, enjoyable. Although some of the technical challenge is gone, the Emma Carlin is now actually a lot more like it was back in the mid-1980s before thousands of tread hours pulverized its surface.

Before hardening, Emma was one of the few places I know where you could take a good fall going uphill, and it had a downhill section I looked at and said "I've got nothing to prove," and walked down. Ride the Connector Trail for a feel of the old Emma.

Palmyra is a pleasant little town to visit. All the roads except the state highways are relatively lightly traveled. Most cars have bike racks on them and give you lots of room anyway.

General location: Three miles east of the town of Palmyra.

Elevation change: Several 120' climbs on the Emma Carlin Trail and many more short, steep ones. The Connector Trail dishes out similar terrain interspersed with moderate, fast-rolling stretches.

Season: Trails should be open from April to November.

Services: Food and bike sales and repair are found in La Grange at the General Store. All services are available in Palmyra. All services, including bike sales and repair, are available in Whitewater at Quiet Hut Sports, 186 West Main Street.

Hazards: The trails are very well maintained, but watch for windfall trees or branches. The plastic grid placed under the trail surface can become exposed and is very slippery when wet, even from a heavy morning dew. Two-way bike traffic on the Connector Trail makes shouting your approach on corners

Going anaerobic is automatic on the Emma Carlin Trail.

essential. Trails are also used by hikers. At Tamarack Road the Connector Trail crosses a horse trail.

Rescue index: Aid can be summoned at La Grange and by calling 911 at the pay phone in the Nordic Trails parking lot across CR H from the John Muir parking lot.

Land status: Wisconsin State Forest, Southern Kettle Moraine Unit. A daily or annual vehicle sticker ($5 daily/$18 annual for Wisconsin residents, $7 daily/$25 annual for out-of-state residents) is required to park in state forest lots. Bicycles are not charged for visiting the forest, but a trail pass fee is required of bicyclists age 16 and older for riding the off-road trails ($3 daily/$10 annual). The trail pass also covers usages such as cross-country skiing, horseback riding, and bicycling on railroad-grade bike trails.

Maps: Sheet maps are available at the trailhead and are posted at trail intersections. The 7.5 minute series USGS quads for Whitewater and Little Prairie show the terrain very well, but do not show the trails.

Finding the trail: The trailhead parking lot is on the west side of CR Z, 0.6 miles south of WI 59, which is 2.5 miles east of the town of Palmyra.

Sources of additional information:

Kettle Moraine, Southern Unit
S91 W39091 Highway 59
Eagle, WI 53119
(414) 594-2135

Whitewater Tourism Council
P.O. Box 34
Whitewater, WI 53190-0034
(414) 473-4005 or (866) 4-WW-TOUR

Notes on the trail: Daily or annual state park vehicle admission and daily or annual trail pass for riders age 16 and older are required (see Land status). There is a self-pay station at the trailhead. There are white and red no-biking signs on hiking trails. Fines apply for riding on hiking-only trails. Always phone ahead to make sure trails are open for riding.

The trails are marked with color-coded signposts that correspond to different loops. Often there will be more than one color at a time. There are "you are here" map signs at intersections. On the Carlin trails the green outer loop is 4.2 miles, the orange loop is 2.4 miles, and the red loop is 2 miles in length. The Connector Trail is 5.5 miles one way to the John Muir Trails.

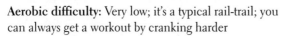

RIDE 4 · Glacial Drumlin State Trail—East (Rail-Trail)

AT A GLANCE

Length/configuration: 18 miles one way from Waukesha to Sullivan

Aerobic difficulty: Very low; it's a typical rail-trail; you can always get a workout by cranking harder

Technical difficulty: Extremely low

Scenery: Great kettle moraine scenery without the effort of pedaling over its hilly terrain; much farmland, marshlands to the west, and burgeoning suburbs to the east

Special comments: A nice family ride with a little playground in the trailside park at Dousman; paved from Waukesha's Fox River Sanctuaty to Dousman, then fine-screen crushed limestone; a wide trail surface makes it good for high-speed cruising even though it is near populous areas

Twisting through the hills of the Kettle Moraine, the section of the Glacial Drumlin Trail between Waukesha and Waterville is probably the most scenic in its 51-mile length (for the western section of the trail see Ride 15, page 56).

Waukesha is a nice small city with a picturesque downtown. It is surrounded by the relentless march to the country of housing developments. Prime farmland turned cul de sac. It's easy to understand why people want to live in this beautiful area, though.

In Wales you'll find a pleasant town green, once the site of that rural community fixture, the feed mill, until a fire took it back in the 1980s.

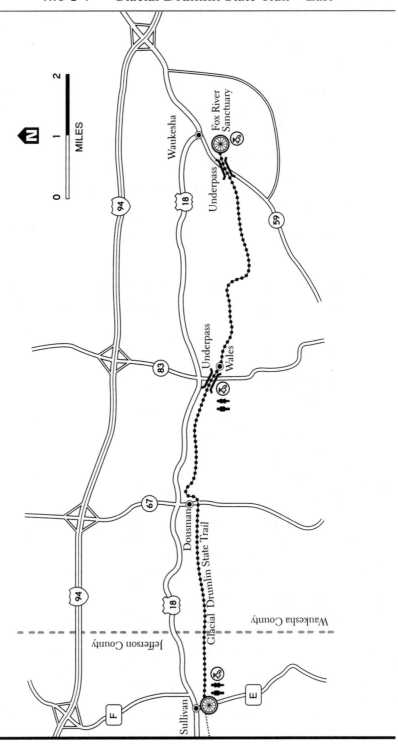

Dousman has a cafe just off the trail. The little store a block north of the trail in Sullivan always makes riders feel welcome. For an aerobic workout you can head one mile north on County Road C to the Lapham Peak Trails (see Ride 5, page 24). The Bicycle Doctor retail, repair, and rental shop is adjacent to the trail.

General location: Two miles south of Interstate 94, running west of the city of Waukesha.

Elevation change: Dead flat.

Season: April through November.

Services: All services are available in Waukesha; bike retail, rental, and repair in Dausman; a cafe and playground in Dousman; and a country store in Sullivan. There are flush toilets at the trailheads.

Hazards: Look out for inattentive riders. Make a full stop at road crossings.

Rescue index: Call 911. Phones are at the trailheads and in towns along the way.

Land status: Wisconsin State Park Trail. A daily or annual vehicle sticker ($5 daily/$18 annual for Wisconsin residents, $7 daily/$25 annual for out-of-state residents) is required to park in state forest lots. Bicycles are not charged for visiting the forest, but a trail pass fee is required of bicyclists age 16 and older for riding the off-road trails ($3 daily/$10 annual). The trail pass also covers usages such as cross-country skiing, horseback riding, and bicycling on railroad-grade bike trails.

Maps: Maps are available at trail pass points of sale.

Finding the trail: In Waukesha start at the Fox River Sanctuary at College Avenue and Prairie Avenue; in Sullivan at the Glacial Drumlin State Trail parking lot, two blocks south of US 18 on County Road E.

Sources of additional information:

Delafield Chamber of Commerce
P.O. Box 171
Delafield, WI 53018-0171
(414) 646-8100

Fox River Sports and Spas
211–213 Madison Street
Waukesha, WI 53188
(262) 544-5557
www.foxriversports.com

Waukesha Area Tourism Council
223 Wisconsin Avenue
Waukesha, WI 53186-4926
(800) 366-8474; (414) 542-0330

Notes on the trail: A daily or annual state trail pass is required for ages 16 and up, except on the city of Waukesha trail segment from the Fox River Sanctuary to McArthur Road.

RIDE 5 · Lapham Peak Trails

AT A GLANCE

Length/configuration: 4-mile outer loop with three shortcut options

Aerobic difficulty: Moderate; terrain is mostly rolling with short climbs that will get your pulse up somewhat; for a harder workout you can always hammer; the frequency of the climbs will make it seem like interval training; you can max-out on a long 380' climb by ascending the paved park road to the observation tower on the east side of County Road C.

Technical difficulty: Low; the ability to shift gears is about all you need; you hardly have to brake on the downhills

Scenery: Mainly open fields; there's a nice view of the forested slopes of Lapham Peak across CR C

Special comments: A good novice or beginner area that is close to Metropolitan Milwaukee; the open land and confined character of the loop make it impossible to get lost, and the wide, grassy trails contain no surprises

I've got to say I felt a bit sad riding the new four-mile loop trail at Lapham (pronounced Laugh-um) Peak. Off to the east I could see the namesake peak, the highest point in southeast Wisconsin at 1,230 feet. The new loop has replaced the cross-country ski trails that used to be open for mountain biking and took in 230 feet of that elevation with several long, steep, heart-in-your-throat climbs. In a state like Wisconsin, where significant relief is hard to come by, I hate to see opportunities like that disappear.

The new loop consists of open, mowed, grassy trails that are also shared with horses. Cleverly, they have routed the bikes and horses in opposite directions. Lapham's big appeal these days is that it is a legal place to ride that is very close to major population centers.

So, the new trail is a mere shadow of the old. Gone too is the opportunity to roll through the deep hardwood and pine forest on the slopes. OK, I'll stop whining. You can still get in a good workout by riding 1.2 miles up the paved park road to the observation tower, a climb of 380 feet. A hike to the top of the observation tower is rewarded by a grand overview of the undulating Kettle Moraine Ridge to the south and the Lake Country to the north.

Delafield is an interesting community, especially if you are into shopping for antiques. Check out the historic Gothic architecture of St. John Chysostom Church at the top of the hill on CR C (Lakeland Drive), or tour Hawks Inn, a restored stage coach stop to the east on County Road DR (Main Street).

General location: 1 mile south of Interstate 94 and the city of Delafield.

Elevation change: Rolling terrain with a number of 20'–30' moderate slopes and several steep 50' climbs.

RIDE 5 • Lapham Peak Trails

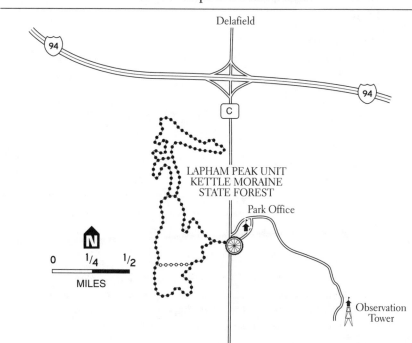

Season: April through November.

Services: A soda machine, warming building with restrooms, and water are located at the trailhead parking area. All services, except bicycle services, are found in Delafield, just north of I-94. For bicycle service there is Wheel & Sprocket to the east at I-94 and WI 83 or the Bicycle Doctor to the west on I-94 and 1.5 miles north on WI 67.

Hazards: Trails are well maintained. They are shared with horses, but, at least at this time, such use is light. You cross busy CR C immediately upon leaving the trailhead parking lot.

Rescue index: Help is available at the park office or by dialing 911 on the phone at the trailhead parking lot.

Land status: Wisconsin State Forest, Southern Kettle Moraine Unit. A daily or annual vehicle sticker ($5 daily/$18 annual for Wisconsin residents, $7 daily/$25 annual for out-of-state residents) is required to park in state forest lots. Bicycles are not charged for visiting the forest, but a trail pass fee is required of bicyclists age 16 and older for riding the off-road trails ($3 daily/$10 annual). The trail pass also covers usages such as cross-country skiing, horseback riding, and bicycling on railroad-grade bike trails.

Maps: A map is available at the park office or fee station.

Finding the trail: From I-94 take the Delafield/CR C exit. Travel south 1 mile to the Lapham Peak Unit entrance on the east side of the road. Take the first park road to Evergreen Grove parking lot, then follow the signs across CTH C.

Sources of additional information:

Lapham Peak Unit
Kettle Moraine State Forest
N846 W329 CTH "C"
Delafield, WI 53018
(262) 646-3025;
(262) 646-4421 for trail conditions

Oconomowoc Convention and
  Visitors Bureau
P.O. Box 27
Oconomowoc, WI 53066-0027
(262) 569-2185
www.ci.oconomowoc.wi.us

Notes on the trail: Trails may be closed due to wet conditions. Call ahead to check. An annual or day-use motor vehicle sticker is required to park on state land as well as an annual or daily per person trail fee (see Land status). These fees can be paid at the park entrance. The trails are marked for one-way travel in a counterclockwise direction except for three east-west, two-way connector trails.

There is a brown sign with a mountain bike silhouette at the trailhead. Otherwise, marking is minimal, but really not needed as the loop is easily followed on the grassy double-track mowed loop. The outer loop is designed for travel one-way in a counterclockwise direction. Horses are supposed to travel the opposite way to minimize surprise encounters. The only spots where you have to make decisions are three two-way connector trails.

RIDE 6 · Bugline Trail (Rail-Trail)

AT A GLANCE

Length/configuration: 13.7 miles one-way from Menomonee Falls to Merton, including the 0.3-mile River trail in Menomonee Falls

Aerobic difficulty: Zilch—well, you could sprint between road crossings; typical rail-trail

Technical difficulty: None, except braking effectively for road crossings

Scenery: Pleasant woodsy feel despite surrounding suburbs; impressive overview of an active limestone quarry

Special comments: An enjoyable family ride with several nice parks along the route—the Menomonee Falls city trail from Millpond Park to the railroad grade is paved, the remaining portion of the city trail and the county Bugline Trail are surfaced with finely crushed limestone

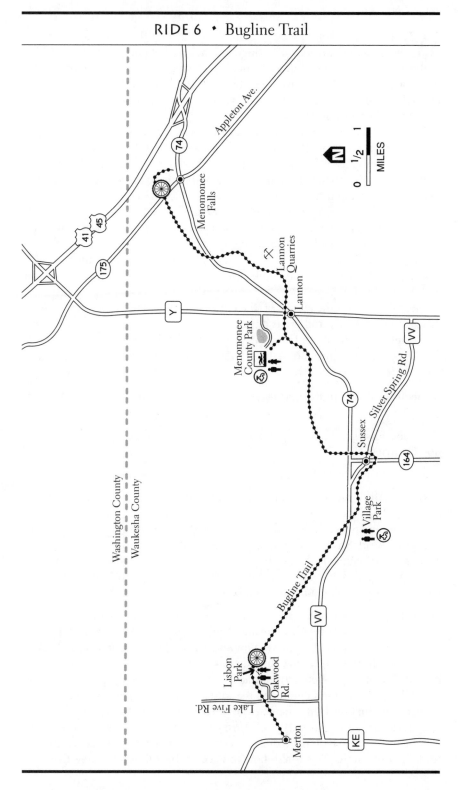

What a name! Appropriate perhaps for a rail bed that twists and turns as much as this one does. The Bugline Railroad that once ran where the bike trail goes today was one of those feeder lines that existed mainly to service the limestone quarries at Lannon. Along the route you'll have an overview of one of the active quarry pits. Lannon Stone has a particular character that makes it very attractive for home construction.

You can make the 13.7-mile one-way ride on the Bugline a pleasant tour of community parks. From the east you begin your ride at the pleasant Millpond Park in Menomonee Falls, following the paved town trail along the Menomonee River for 0.4 miles to the crushed limestone rail-trail. To the west of the Lannon Quarries, a short spur trail runs to Menomonee County Park with a swimming beach and nice playground. On the west side of Sussex, the Village Park just off the trail to the south has a playground. Shortly before the village of Merton is the Lisbon Community Park with spanking new playground facilities.

Merton is minuscule. The old mill just south of the trailhead is still active. It's a great place for a good deal on bulk bird seed, and the stone miller's house is an architectural masterpiece.

Near the east trailhead, just off the city bike trail where the Roosevelt Road bridge crosses the river, there is a classic old bike shop you have to check out. The owner rolls out in front an array of old bikes for display on any sunny day. I found my old Schwinn Spitfire there in mint condition, but, as with the rest of the old bikes, it wasn't for sale.

General location: In the northwest Milwaukee Metro area between US 41/45 and WI 16.

Elevation change: Flat except for a gradual climb of about 50' up to the Lannon Quarries.

Season: April through November.

Services: All services, including bike retail and repair, are found in Menomonee Falls. There are an open shelter, water, and flush toilets at Millpond Park. Lannon has a drive-in right at the County Road Y trail crossing. There is a cafe and grocery in Sussex. All you'll find in Merton are a couple of taverns. Menomonee County Park has a playground, swimming beach, and flush toilets. Sussex Village Park has a playground and flush toilets. Lisbon Community Park has a new playground and clean pit toilets.

Hazards: You must ride a short distance on a residential street, Apple Tree Court, and cross busy Shady Lane and Appleton Avenue (WI 175) to bypass an undeveloped section of trail in Menomonee Falls. At the junction of Apple Tree Court and Shady Lane, follow the sidewalk on the east side of Shady Lane one half block south to Appleton Avenue and cross both streets at the pedestrian cross walks. Then follow the sidewalk on the west side of Shady Lane one half block south to the Bugline Trail. There are no signs guiding you through this intersection. There are also many busy road crossings on the eastern end. To connect the eastern and western parts of the trail, you must ride on several busy streets in Sussex for about a mile. This is also how you access the village's services. Between

Lannon and Sussex, kids are operating a bandit BMX track just off the trail. They can come bombing out of the woods jumping onto the trail. Washouts and loose surface are possible, particularly on the slope near the Lannon Quarries. The trail is often used by walkers.

Rescue index: Call 911. Phones will be found at businesses in Menomonee Falls, Lannon, Sussex, Merton, and at Menomonee County Park.

Land status: Waukesha County Park, Menomonee Falls City Park, and public streets.

Maps: A map is available from the Waukesha County Parks Department.

Finding the trail: At the east end of the trail in Menomonee Falls, park in the public lot one half block off Main Street (WI 74) on Grand Avenue, just behind the Associated Bank. Millpond Park is on the east side of the trail. Central to the trail, park in Menomonee County Park (vehicle fee applies) 1.5 miles north of Lannon on CR Y. On the west end, park on-street on County Road VV in Merton or at Lisbon Community Park, 5 miles west of Sussex on Lake Five Road.

Sources of additional information:

Waukesha County Visitors Bureau
893 Main Street #D
Pewaukee, WI 53072-5812
(262) 695-7903; (800) 366-1961

Waukesha County Parks Department
1320 Pewaukee Road, Room 230
Waukesha, WI 53188
(262) 548-7801

Notes on the trail: There is no user fee for riding the trail, but a motor vehicle parking fee does apply at Menomonee County Park.

RIDE 7 · New Fane Trails

AT A GLANCE

Length/configuration: 3.1-mile outer loop with four shortcut options

Aerobic difficulty: Mostly easy with one moderately steep climb

Technical difficulty: Low; you hardly need to use your brakes; some roots and cobble rocks on steeper slopes

Scenery: Mostly wooded with a few open areas and one nice overview

Special comments: A fun beginner area in an appealing setting; wide, grassy, double-track trails have a mix of distinctive kettle moraine rolling character and some flat, fast-rolling stretches; light usage and a hardpack track allow high-speed cruising; many loop combinations are possible

RIDE 7 • New Fane Trails

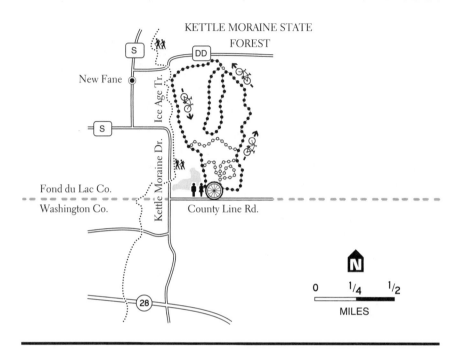

Welcome to the Kettle Moraine. The New Fane Trails are where I'd want to take a neophyte mountain biker knowing they would learn how much fun the sport is without being humbled by the terrain. That doesn't mean more seasoned riders will be bored here. The wide, smooth, grassy, cross-country ski trails invite fast riding. A hardpack track is worn in, and, except for a few roots and cobbles on the hills, there is no need to slow down. There is some terrain, but it's the sort that makes things a bit more exciting. The trails can be challenging if you hammer, but they'll never beat you down. This is an easy, non-technical ride that can really turn a newcomer on to the sport.

Most of the New Fane's trails loop through a forest that is at times hardwood, including oak, birch, and maple, and in other areas pine. In a few spots you will break out into the open for fine overviews of the countryside. Near the end of the ride you will pass near a pond to the right of the trail that is a haven for waterfowl.

General location: 6 miles northeast of the town of Kewaskum.

Elevation change: Terrain varies from flat to rolling. One moderately steep climb and descent of 80' are encountered early on, followed by another more gradual 50' hill.

Season: Trails may be open from mid-April through early November (just before hunting season). The trails are sometimes subject to flooding or damage and may be closed for these reasons. Be sure to call ahead to check their status.

Love those biking allowed signs.

Services: There is water at the trailhead. You will find only a tavern in New Fane, but all services, except bicycle, are available in the small town of Kewaskum.

Hazards: Trails are well maintained, but windfall trees and branches may be found. All trails are open for hiking.

Rescue index: Help can be summoned in the village of New Fane.

Land status: Wisconsin State Forest, Northern Kettle Moraine Unit. A daily or annual vehicle sticker ($5 daily/$18 annual for Wisconsin residents, $7 daily/$25 annual for out-of-state residents) is required to park in state forest lots. Bicycles are not charged for visiting the forest, but a trail pass fee is required of bicyclists age 16 and older for riding the off-road trails ($3 daily/$10 annual). The trail pass also covers usages such as cross-country skiing, horseback riding, and bicycling on railroad-grade bike trails.

Maps: A detailed cross-country ski trail map is available from the forest head-quarters or from the Wisconsin Department of Natural Resources office. The 7.5 minute series USGS quad for Kewaskum shows the terrain but not the trails.

Finding the trail: From the village of Kewaskum on US 45 turn east on WI 28. After 0.4 miles, just after crossing the Milwaukee River, turn north on County Road S while still in the village. Follow CR S for 3.7 miles and go straight east onto Kettle Moraine Drive (indicated by both a street sign and a green Kettle Moraine Scenic Drive sign) at an intersection where CR S turns north into the village of New Fane. Kettle Moraine Drive will bend to the south. Follow it for 1.5 miles to County Line Road and turn to the east. The parking lot for the New Fane Trails is 0.6 miles on the left.

Sources of additional information:

Kettle Moraine State Forest,
Northern Unit
N1765 Highway G
Campbellsport, WI 53010
(262) 626-2116

Wisconsin Department of Natural
Resources
Bureau of Parks and Recreation
P.O. Box 7921
Madison, WI 53707-7921
(608) 266-2621
www.dnr.state.wi.us

Notes on the trail: An annual or day-use motor vehicle sticker is required to park on state land as well as an annual or daily per-person trail fee (see Land status). These fees can be paid by a self-service system at the trailhead. The trails are marked for one-way travel. There is a brown sign with a mountain bike silhouette at the trailhead, but beyond that you will see only color-coded cross-country ski trail signs. Follow the markers for the purple loop throughout. For most of the distance this route also will be the red loop. At 1.8 miles the yellow route separates, dipping to the south before returning to the red loop. Keep a close watch for this sharp intersection, as it comes up suddenly along a fast-rolling section of the trail.

The yellow-signed loop is 3.1 miles; the red is 2.4 miles; the green is 1.5 miles; and the brown is 0.7 miles. At the point where the green trail rejoins the yellow and red loop, a connecting trail runs off to the west to the National Scenic Ice Age Trail , which like other area trails is not open to mountain biking. Marked by a white sign with a mountain bike silhouette with a red slash across it, this is the only trail in the network off limits to bikers.

RIDE 8 · Greenbush Trails

AT A GLANCE

Length/configuration: 5.1-mile loop on the yellow trail; several other shorter loops are options

Aerobic difficulty: Moderate to high—all trails include slopes that will get your heart rate up

Technical difficulty: Mostly moderate with some easy riding on the brown loop; you must be able to shift to the right gear quickly on steep slopes and to handle high-speed downhills

Scenery: Deep hardwood and pine forest with a nice view of a vast marsh and bog on the return leg of the yellow loop

Special comments: Terrific kettle moraine riding—intermediate riders should be able to handle the terrain and have a great time, and the new 0.6-mile brown trail adds a route even beginners can enjoy; the trails are easy to follow; they are wide and grassy with a hardpack track worn in

G et ready for a wonderful off-road tour of classic kettle moraine landscape. The 5.1-mile purple loop on the Greenbush Trails snakes through an inspiring oak and maple forest, skirts the edge of a marsh, and passes a pine plantation. The wide, mowed grass or forest floor cross-country ski trails cover terrain that is typical of kettle moraine terrain: a jumbled landscape that makes for fun mountain biking. A glacier crossed this area just 10,000 years ago, leaving nature relatively little time to smooth over the resulting mess. Cobble-sized rocks, roots, and more rocks make up the riding surface. Downhills are very rough.

Your shifters, brakes, and legs will get a workout on trails that are seldom level or the same grade for very long. A stretch along the southwest segment of the purple loop, where the route runs along a marsh, gives some relief from the up and down, but offers the chance of finding soft or mucky surface. The green loop is most difficult and most sensative to bike impact, so it should only be ridded in dry-trail conditions. Overall, this area is on the high end of the moderate difficulty scale for the average rider. There is some easy riding on the short brown loop.

The Greenbush trails are just a few miles south of the historic village of the same name. Set in the green, rolling hills of the Kettle Moraine, the tiny town looks more like a village in Vermont than one in Wisconsin. Many of the white, clapboard Greek Revival buildings are operated by the Wisconsin State Historical Society, including a carriage museum and the Wade House, a restored stagecoach inn.

General location: 2.5 miles south of WI 23 at the village of Greenbush; 6 miles west of the town of Plymouth.

Elevation change: Much of the terrain is rolling. Steep grades of 50' to 60' are common.

Season: Trails are open for mountain biking from mid-April through early November, though the purple loop shown here typically closes in mid-September due to small-game hunting season. The trails are sometimes subject to flooding or damage and may be closed for these reasons. Be sure to call ahead to check their status.

Services: At the trailhead are a nice shelter building, a water pump, and pit toilets. There is a tavern/restaurant in the village of Greenbush. All services, except bicycle, are available in the town of Plymouth, 6 miles east of Greenbush.

Hazards: Trails are well maintained, but windfall trees and branches are always possible hazards. A horse trail crosses this system at several points. Hiking is allowed on all trails.

Rescue index: Help is available at the village of Greenbush. In case of injury or mechanical difficulty make your way back to the trailhead.

Land status: Kettle Moraine Forest, Northern Unit. A daily or annual vehicle sticker ($5 daily/$18 annual for Wisconsin residents, $7 daily/$25 annual for out-of-state residents) is required to park in state forest lots. Bicycles are not charged for visiting the forest, but a trail pass fee is required of bicyclists age 16 and older for riding the off-road trails ($3 daily /$10 annual). The trail pass covers usages such as cross-country skiing, horseback riding, and bicycling on railroad-grade bike trails.

RIDE 8 · Greenbush Trails

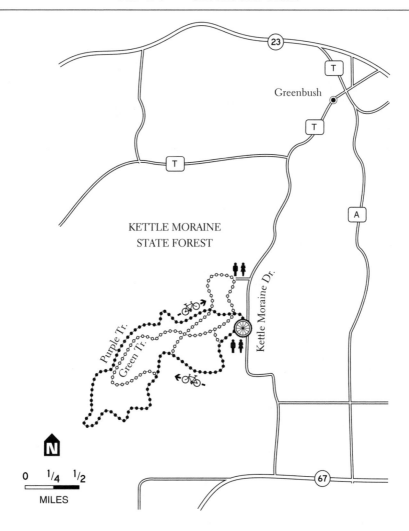

Maps: A detailed cross-country ski trail map is available from the forest head-quarters or from the Wisconsin Department of Natural Resources office. The 7.5 minute series USGS quad for Cascade shows the terrain very well but does not show the trails.

Finding the trail: From WI 23, 6 miles west of the town of Plymouth, turn southeast on County Road T into the village of Greenbush. Follow CR T through the village and after 1.3 miles, turn south (left) onto Kettle Moraine Drive. Travel 1.7 miles to the Greenbush Cross-Country Trails and Group Campground parking lot on the right.

Color-coded posts
make the Greenbush
Trails easy to follow.

Sources of additional information:

Kettle Moraine State Forest,
    Northern Unit
N 1765 Highway G
Campbellsport, WI 53010
(262) 626-2116

Plymouth Chamber of Commerce
P.O. Box 584
Plymouth, WI 53073-0584
(920) 893-0079; (888) 693-8263
www.plymouthwisconsin.com

Wisconsin Department of Natural
    Resources
Bureau of Parks and Recreation
P.O. Box 7921
Madison, WI 53707-7921
(608) 266-2621
www.dnr.state.wi.us

Notes on the trail: An annual or day-use motor vehicle sticker is required to park on state land as well as an annual or daily per-person trail fee (see Land status). More trails exist in the area than can possibly be shown on this map.

The trailhead is signed for mountain biking with a green square featuring a white mountain bike silhouette. The trails are well marked with purple, green, red, and pink color-coded posts en route, with white-and-red no-biking signs on hiking trails. The purple-signed loop is 5.1 miles; the green is 3.6 miles; the red is

2.4 miles; the pink is 1.1 miles; and the brown trail is 0.6 miles. All mileage is computed from the trailhead. Riding is not allowed on the Ice Age Trail, which is marked with yellow and white posts, that crosses the ski trails near the trailhead.

RIDE 9 · Old Plank Road Trail (Recreation Trail)

AT A GLANCE

Length/configuration: 17 miles one way; future plans include on-street and off-road trail routes down to the Sheboygan lakefront

Aerobic difficulty: Moderate; this is not a rail-trail; it follows the natural rolling contours of the land adjacent to WI 23

Technical difficulty: Very low; a smooth, paved surface the entire length

Scenery: Typical Wisconsin farmland on the eastern sections and kettle moraine forest in the west

Special comments: A nice family ride with options to visit interesting small towns; paved surfaces make bike handling easy, even for kids with training wheels

Plank roads were once high-tech transportation routes. A torrent of European immigrants headed west from Lake Michigan ports like Sheboygan in the 1840s. The population in eastern Wisconsin increased twenty-fold during the decade. Dirt roads and boggy lowlands meant axle-deep mud when it rained. But there were plenty of trees around and entrepreneurs soon built plank toll roads to keep wagons, feet, and hoofs high and dry.

WI 23 follows the old plank road route west to the little village of Greenbush, and the 17-mile paved trail runs well off the roadway to its south.

In Greenbush, the Wisconsin State Historical Society maintains the Wade House Stagecoach Inn in the same condition nineteenth century travelers would have found it after a weary day of bumping over the boards. A tour of the inn provides a fascinating look into the past, and includes the Jung Carriage Museum with its incredible collection of buggies and wagons. A reconstructed log cabin with displays from the plank road days serves as the western trailhead.

Spur trails and on-street routes lead into the attractive towns of Kohler, Sheboygan Falls, and Plymouth. By following Sunset Road and Suhrke Road you can ride to the Plymouth City Park where you'll find a swimming pool and playground. Downtown Plymouth, a few blocks further, is an architectural gem. For a varied-terrain off-road ride check out the Greenbush Trails (see Ride 8, page 32).

General location: Between the village of Greenbush and city of Sheboygan, on the south side of WI 23.

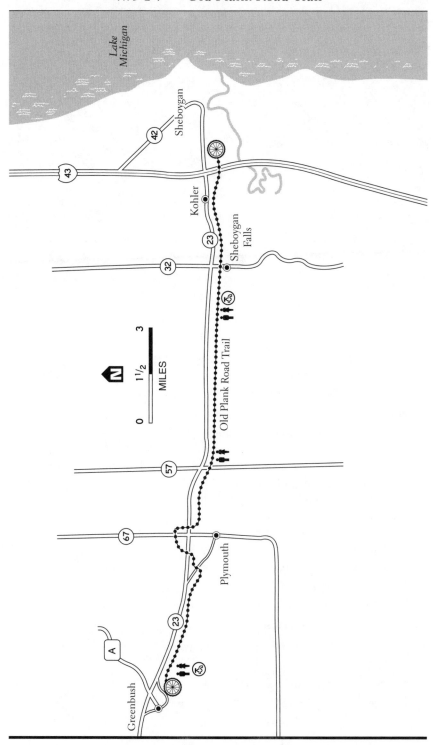

Pavement has replaced boards on Old Plank Road.

Elevation change: This is not a flat trail. While feeling like you are rolling up and down, you will gradually climb 500' in the first 15 miles traveling west. You can really feel the difference heading back east.

Season: Anytime the trail is free of snow and ice.

Services: All services are available in the major towns along the route, including bicycle repair and retail in Sheboygan and Plymouth. Greenbush has a tavern/restaurant and a gas station/convenience store. The western trailhead has a pit toilet. There are flush toilets, a swimming pool, and a playground at Plymouth City Park, and pit toilets and water at the Meadowlark Road crossing.

Hazards: Frequent road crossings are well-designed, but require caution. Moderate your speed just before WI 67 north of Plymouth. The trail runs steeply downhill and there is a fairly sharp right turn into an underpass. There are several short on-road sections between Plymouth and Greenbush.

Rescue index: Call 911. There are phones at town businesses, at the Meadowlark Road crossing, and at the Greenbush trailhead.

Land status: Sheboygan County Resources land.

Maps: Contact Sheboygan County Planning and Resources Department, 615 North 6th Street, Sheboygan, WI 53081; (920) 459-3060.

Finding the trail: Begin in Sheboygan at the west end of Erie Street, 0.5 miles west of Memorial Mall. Near Greenbush at the junction of WI 23 and Plank Road.

Sources of additional information:

Plymouth Chamber of Commerce
P.O. Box 584
Plymouth, WI 53073-0584
(920) 893-0079; (888) 693-8263
www.plymouthwisconsin.com

Sheboygan County Convention and
    Visitors Bureau
712 Riverfront Drive, Suite 101
Sheboygan, WI 53083
(800) 457-9497, ext. 500;
(920) 457-9495

Notes on the trail: No user fee applies for trail riding.

RIDE 10 · Wild Goose State Trail (Rail-Trail)

AT A GLANCE

Length/configuration: 34 miles one way; a 3-mile gravel road loop is a potential midway side trip

Aerobic difficulty: There are no significant grade changes, but you can always pedal faster to get a workout; a typical rail-trail

Technical difficulty: Virtually nil

Scenery: Trailside trees and brush punctuated by farm scenery; several short side trips offer marsh views

Special comments: A pleasant family ride, but one with long distances between services; good potential for viewing wildfowl and raptors; the crushed limestone trail surface is easily ridden by children; since much of the trail sees minimal use, grass encroaches from the sides on some stretches, making riding with training wheels tricky; low use also makes high-speed cruising OK

Marshes are magnets for wildlife. The 32,000-acre Horicon Marsh, the state's largest, is home to hundreds of species of birds. Soaring marsh hawks, red-tailed hawks, and rough-legged hawks are often seen. Canada geese, the signature birds of Horicon Marsh, are frequently spotted honking across the sky in their distinctive chevron formations. Red-winged blackbirds call "o-ka-lee, o-ka-lee" and flare bright orange epaulets to tell other males to keep away.

The 34-mile crushed limestone surface Wild Goose State Trail does not actually go through the marsh, but birds know no boundaries. Several side trips for a better look are possible. In the village of Burnett you can head east on Burnett Ditch Road and penetrate the edge of the marsh, perhaps sighting a great blue heron in the process. Just off the trail south of WI 49, the Horicon "Ternpike" auto route follows a 3-mile loop with several observation points and interpretive

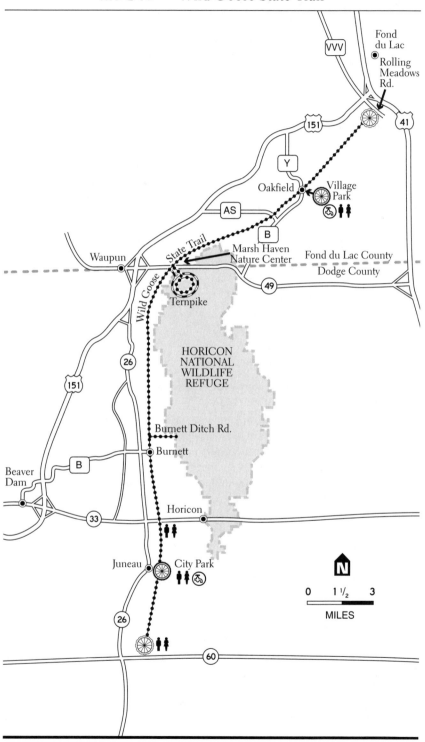

signs. A short spur trail just north of WI 49 leads to a picnic shelter. The Marsh Haven Nature Center is a privately run museum and wildlife gallery devoted to the marsh. An observation tower on their land offers a chance to view the vastness of the marsh.

Juneau and Oakfield are pleasant small towns with nice parks and playgrounds that make good jumping-off points. The trail ends in either direction are merely parking lots. Oakfield was devestated by a tornado that leveled much of the town several years ago. Fortunately, no one was killed, and the lovely oaks in the Village Park were spared.

General location: Parallel to US 151 and WI 26 between Fond du Lac and Clyman Junction.

Elevation change: None.

Season: April through November.

Services: There are cafes in Juneau and Oakfield and flush toilets, water, and playgrounds in their town parks. There is a convenience store at the intersection of WI 33, and there are taverns in Burnett. The Burnett Fireman's Park on the west side of WI 26 has water and a playground.

Hazards: There are numerous road crossings, some across busy highways. You must ride on-street for a few blocks in Burnett and Juneau The southern 14 miles contain a separate equestrian trail, which parallels and occasionally crosses the main limestone trail.

Rescue index: Call 911. Phones can be found at area businesses.

Land status: Wisconsin State Park trail. No user fee is required at this time, but donations are appreciated.

Maps: Maps are available at local information centers, the Wisconsin Department of Natural Resources, and the Dodge County Planning Department in Juneau.

Finding the trail: The trail can be accessed at many road crossings south or east of US 151 or WI 26. The northern trailhead (no facilities) is on Rolling Meadows Road (County Road VVV), off US 151 just southwest of Fond du Lac. Oakfield Village Park is two blocks east of the trail on County Road D in Oakfield. Juneau City Park is at Lincoln and Fair on the southeast side of town. The southern trailhead (portable toilet only) is on the north side of WI 60 near Clyman Junction at Junction Road.

Sources of additional information:

Dodge County Planning and
   Development Department
127 East Oak Street
Juneau, WI 53034
(920) 386-3700

Fond du Lac Convention and
   Visitors Bureau
19 West Scott Street
Fond du Lac, WI 54935-2342
(800) 937-9123; (920) 923-3010

Juneau Chamber of Commerce
P.O. Box 4
Juneau, WI 53039-0004
(920) 386-2424

Wisconsin Department of Natural
   Resources
Bureau of Parks and Recreation
P.O. Box 7921
Madison, WI 53707-7921
(608) 266-2621
www.dnr.state.wi.us

Notes on the trail: No user fee applies for trail riding. To take in the "Ternpike" loop route, ride east on the paved shoulder of WI 49 for 0.1 mile and turn south.

RIDE 11 · High Cliff State Park Trails

AT A GLANCE

Length/configuration: 3.7-mile family loop; 7.2-mile beginner trail consisting of two loops and a two-way connector

Aerobic difficulty: Low; flat terrain with several very short, steep grades

Technical difficulty: Easy; some loose surface on the family loop and some rocky surface on the bridle trail loop

Scenery: Grand overviews of Lake Winnebago, oak forest, and open prairie

Special comments: Pleasant family and novice biking in a scenic setting with historic Native American sites; trails are pretty easy to follow and have a smooth surface for the most part

The "high cliff" at High Cliff State Park is the edge of the 200-foot Niagara escarpment, a sheet of dolomite limestone that stretches all the way east to Niagara Falls. Here it forms the eastern shore of Lake Winnebago, the state's largest inland lake. This makes a scenic setting for an easy mountain bike ride, since all the trails are on top of the escarpment. An observation tower gives a grand overview.

There are two ride choices here. The 3.7-mile loop is fine for anyone, but especially nice for families, and could be ridden by a young child beyond the training wheel stage. The trail is a mix of wood chips, hardpack forest floor, grass, and the bare limestone of an abandoned quarry.

Just south of the trailhead, near the observation tower, is a statue of Red Bird, a Ho-Chunk (Winnebago) warrior. Conflicts with encroaching Americans in southwest Wisconsin caused Red Bird to kill a fur trader and his family at Prairie du Chien in 1827. Using that as a pretext the government forced the tribe to sign over their ancestral lands. At a time when many people believed you could tell a

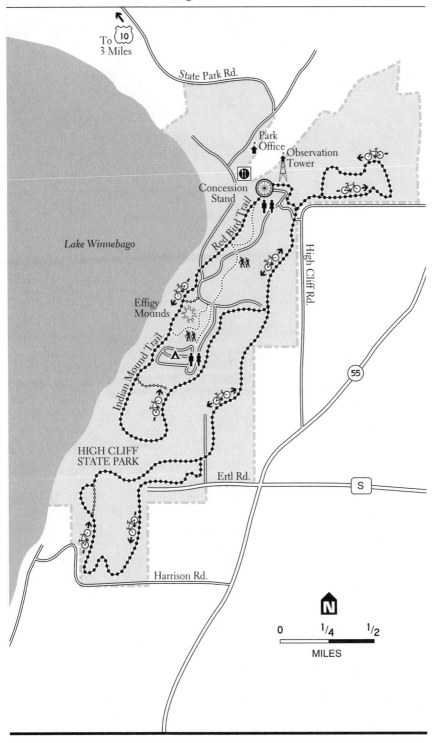

To 10
3 Miles

State Park Rd.

Park Office

Observation Tower

Concession Stand

Red Bird Trail

Lake Winnebago

Effigy Mounds

Indian Mound Trail

High Cliff Rd.

55

HIGH CLIFF STATE PARK

Ertl Rd.

S

Harrison Rd.

N

0   1/4   1/2

MILES

A statue of Red Bird overlooks Lake Winnebago.

person's character by their looks, a man attending Red Bird's trial wrote how shocked he was by his appearance. According to him, Red Bird was one of the most perfect human beings he had ever seen.

Farther south the trail skirts a group of emblematic effigy mounds. These low linear-, conical-, and animal-shaped mounds were constructed one basketful of earth at a time by a mysterious culture that survived in southern Wisconsin from about 600 to 1,200 A.D. The mounds, which do not always contain burials, were clearly ceremonial in nature. Animal shapes include birds, turtles, panthers, and buffalo. The makers left few clues behind them, and little more is known today of the mound's origins and meaning than when they were first described 150 years ago.

The second trail choice is the 7.2-mile bridle trail traversing the east side of the park. It is shared with horses, but such usage is light. The trail consists of two one-way loops and a 1.8-mile, two-way connector. It is mostly in the open, but dips into the woods at several points.

General location: On the northeast shore of Lake Winnebago, 12 miles south of Kaukauna.

Elevation change: Insignificant, one grade of perhaps 20'.

Season: May 1–November 15.

Services: Water and flush toilets at the observation tower parking area; camping, showers, flush toilets, and water at the campground; grocery store and cafe in Sherwood, 2 miles to the northeast.

Hazards: Trails are well maintained, but windfall trees or branches are always a possibility. The bridle trails are shared with horses. The bluff trails are popular with hikers.

Rescue index: Help can be summoned at the park office. There is a phone at the campground shower building.

Land status: Wisconsin State Park. A daily or annual vehicle sticker ($5 daily/$18 annual for Wisconsin residents, $7 daily/$25 annual for out-of-state residents) is required to park in state forest lots.

Maps: A map of all trails is available at the park entrance station. The 7.5 minute series USGS quad for Sherwood shows the terrain very well but does not show the trails.

Finding the trail: High Cliff State Park is located 9 miles east of Appleton on Highway 114. Drive south on Pigeon Road, turn left on State Park Road, and continue to the park entrance. Once in the park, proceed to bridle trail parking area.

Sources of additional information:

Fox Cities Convention and Visitors
Bureau
3433 West College Avenue
Appleton, WI 54914-3919
(920) 734-3358; (800) 2 DO MORE
www.foxcities.org

Wisconsin Department of Natural
Resources
Bureau of Parks and Recreation
P.O. Box 7921
Madison, WI 53707-7921
(608) 266-2181
www.dnr.state.wi.us

Notes on the trail: An annual or day-use motor vehicle sticker is required to park on state land, as is an annual or daily per-person trail fee (see Land status). At present the bluff trails are marked for mountain biking with only a single green-and-white sign at the Red Bird Statue. Beyond that, follow the blue-and-white cross-country skiing signs in a counterclockwise direction. Do not ride on the trails that weave among the effigy mounds. Fines apply for riding on hiking-only trails, even though the signage is poor. The bridle trails are better signed with horseshoe arrows, as well as green-and-white mountain bike signs for travel in a clockwise direction on the south loop and counterclockwise on the north loop.

RIDE 12 · Calumet County Park Trails

AT A GLANCE

Length/configuration: 2-mile loop with several options to combine with other trails

Aerobic difficulty: High; all loops involve at least one long, steep climb

Technical difficulty: Low to moderate; trails are smooth, but steep slopes and some tight turns will be encountered

Scenery: Part forest, part open—nice lake views at the shore and from the old ski slope

Special comments: A fun place to ride for intermediate and advanced riders looking for a bit of a challenge; super-nice people at the park concession

What a find! A real bright spot in the southern Wisconsin mountain biking picture. The park personnel are very enthusiastic about mountain bike use, and the trails are used for an extremely popular Wisconsin Off-Road Series (WORS) race, the Calumet County Sun Run, each mid-August. There isn't a lot of mileage here, the loop I show is only two miles long, but all trails are open for riding and many combinations are possible.

I liked the climb just south of the old ski slope. An evenly graded, steep, gravel trail, it takes you to the top of the Niagara escarpment through a beautiful stand of maples and past fractured blocks of limestone. On top, heading south, the trail takes you past several panther effigy mounds before turning toward the lake, down twisty switchbacks. Let's hope bikers remain respectful of other trail users and don't wear out their welcome here.

General location: 17 miles south of Kaukauna, off WI 55.

Elevation change: Steep 170' climbs on any loop you might choose.

Season: April through November.

Services: The park office building is also a concession stand. Water, flush toilets, and showers are in a building next door. Campsites can be found at the lakeshore and on the bluff top. There is a tavern/restaurant at the entrance to the park.

Hazards: Trails are well maintained, but windfall trees or branches are always a possibility. Trails are shared with hikers.

Rescue index: Help is available at the park office.

Land status: Calumet County Park.

Maps: A map of the trails is available at the park office. The 7.5 minute series USGS quad for Stockbridge shows the terrain very well but does not show the trails.

RIDE 12 • Calumet County Park Trails

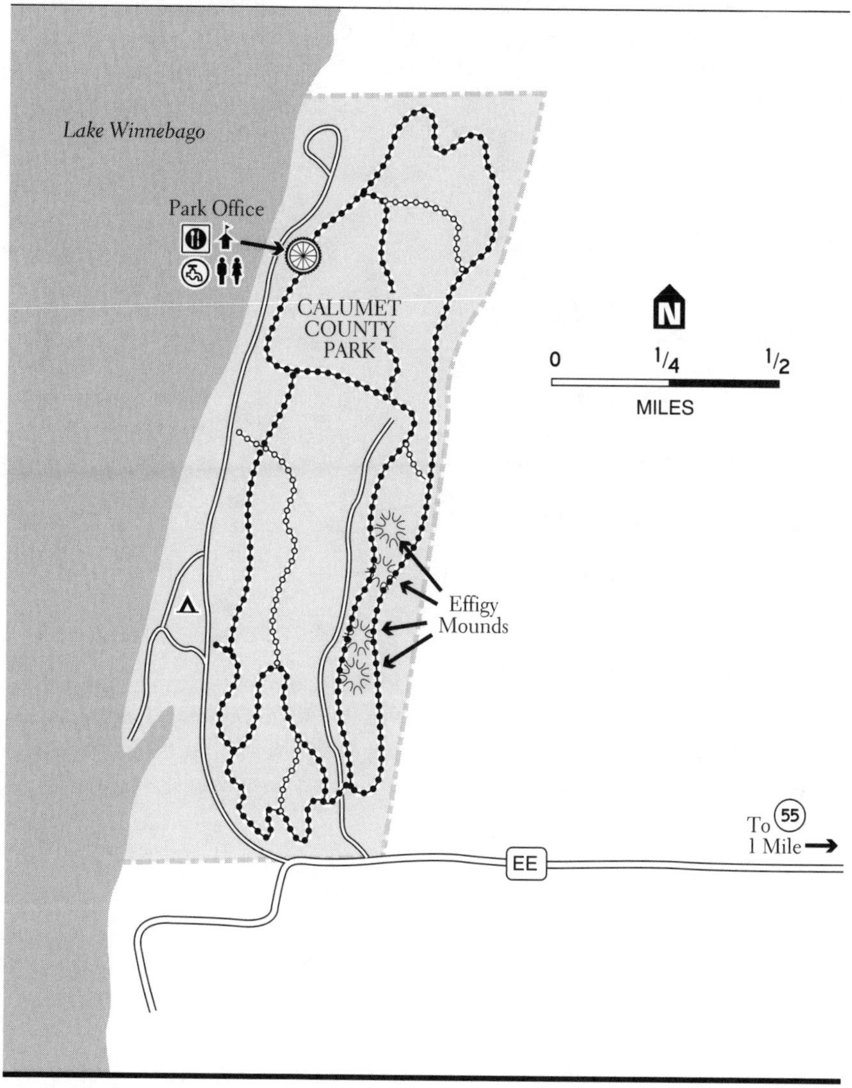

Lake Winnebago

Park Office

CALUMET COUNTY PARK

Effigy Mounds

N

0   1/4   1/2

MILES

To 55
1 Mile →

EE

Finding the trail: Turn west off WI 55 onto County Road EE, 5.5 miles south of Sherwood. CR EE ends at the entrance. Follow the park road to any of the parking areas.

Sources of additional information:

Fox Cities Convention and Visitors
  Bureau
3433 West College Avenue
Appleton, WI 54914-3919

(920) 734-3358; (800) 2 DO MORE
www.foxcities.org

Climbing the Niagara Escarpment is no piece of cake.

Notes on the trail: No user fee is required to ride the trails. Signage for mountain biking is nonexistent at this time, but is in the planning stage. Getting lost is not a problem in such a confined area. Trails can be ridden in either direction. Surfaces vary from gravel to bare forest floor to grassy with a hardpack track.

CAPITAL COLLECTION

Why "capital"? Simply because they ring Madison, the state's capital city, with riding opportunities. These include four rail-trail rides for high-speed cruising or family fun. Three of these trails eventually will connect through Madison, making this beautiful city with a very active biking community even more accessible.

This capital area also marks a zone of transition from the low, rolling, glacial terrain in the east, with its lakes and marshes, to the steep hills of the west, which were untouched by the ice sheet. Known as the "Driftless Area" because of its lack of the rounded glacial boulders so common in the rest of the state, the area west of the capital is marked by striking ridge and valley country.

West of Madison is where the gonzo bikers go. There are climbs that make triple bypass surgery seem painless. The grades at Devils Lake, Governor Dodge, and Blue Mound state parks will do just that. At the same time, you can enjoy the dramatic scenery on a nice high-speed cruise or family ride on rail-trails like the Sugar River, Military Ridge, or Pine River trails. Toss in the Hyde Mill Tour and some on-road options from the rail-trails, and you can take your Driftless experience straight up or on the rocks.

And the east? Cam-Rock Trails may surprise you. Local Wisconsin Off-Road Bicycling Association (WORBA) activists have laid out some challenging single-track in this small park, which offers rolling and hilly double-tracks as well as a short rail-trail. The Glacial Drumlin State Trail takes you on a rail bed through marshes, over streams and rivers, and on a short side trip to one of the state's most significant archaeological sites.

RIDE 13 · Sugar River State Trail (Rail-Trail)

AT A GLANCE

Length/configuration: 23 miles one way, including the on-street segment in Brodhead; an on-road loop option adds 8.3 miles

Aerobic difficulty: Very low on the rail-trail; an on-road loop option takes in several steep hills

Technical difficulty: Easy

Scenery: Wisconsin dairy land, river, and marsh scenery, as well as the Swiss chalet architecture in New Glarus

Special comments: The Swiss character of New Glarus helps make this a fascinating family ride; several trail towns have swimming pools; the southern end of the crushed limestone trail lends itself to high-speed cruising, as it is less traveled

Welcome to Wisconsin's little Switzerland. The people of New Glarus have taken their Swiss heritage to heart, creating an atmosphere that seems straight out of the Alpine foothills. The restaurants, bakeries, and Swiss chalet architecture make any visit an adventure. Off the route, west of Monticello at the junction of County Roads C and N, you can tour the Prima Kase Cheese Factory and see giant wheels of Swiss cheese being made.

The 23-mile-each-way trail visits four towns: New Glarus, Monticello, Albany, and Brodhead. All except Albany have nice town parks with swimming pools and playgrounds. Trail surroundings are sometimes open, often wooded. Views include prime valley dairyland and wild river-bottom areas.

For an aerobic workout you can detour on an 8.3-mile loop by taking the paved bike trail parallel to WI 69 south to New Glarus Woods State Park, then circling back to town on paved roads. Heading west from the park you'll be on the route of the old Lead Road, once a wagon track used to haul ore from the mines to Milwaukee. The loop includes two climbs of 150 feet each, and a nice view of New Glarus as you descend back into the valley.

The New Glarus microbrewery bottles seasonal beers that are guaranteed to tune your yodel. You can tour the brewery or sample beers at just about any local restaurant or tavern. I suggest stopping at Puempel's Tavern (pronounced Pimples), located just a block off the trail on Sixth Avenue, to check out its mural of patriotic Swiss themes, which was painted around the turn of the century.

General location: 24 miles south of Madison on WI 69.

Elevation change: Dead flat for the rail-trail; two 150' climbs on the loop.

Season: April through November.

RIDE 13 • Sugar River State Trail

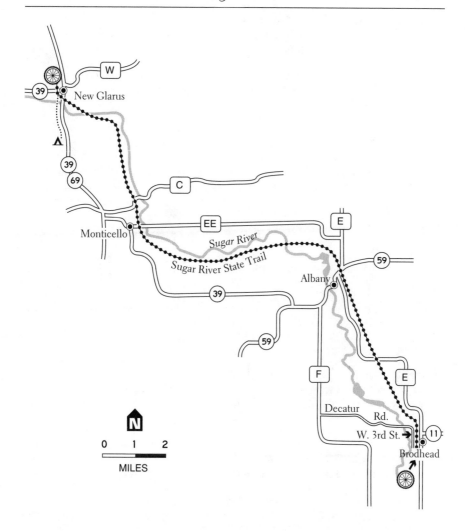

Services: All services, except bicycle, are available in New Glarus, Albany, and Brodhead. There is a cafe in Monticello. Camping is available at New Glarus Woods State Park (no showers), and at the privately run Sweet Minnehaha Camp Ground (with showers) between Albany and Crazy Horse Campground at Brodhead.

Hazards: Inattentive bike riders can be a problem. You must cross busy WI 69 almost immediately if you start in New Glarus, but traffic is light at all other crossings.

Rescue index: Summon help at trail towns by calling 911.

Land status: Wisconsin State Park Trail; public roadways. A trail pass fee is required for the Sugar River State Trail for bicyclists age 16 and older ($3 daily/$10 annual). The trail pass also covers usages such as cross-country skiing, and bicycling on state mountain bike trails.

Maps: A map is available from the trail headquarters in the old New Glarus Depot or from the Wisconsin Department of Natural Resources. The DeLorme book *Wisconsin Atlas & Gazetteer* shows all roads and road names on pages 27 and 28.

Finding the trail: At the trail's north end, turn west off WI 69 onto WI 39 (Sixth Avenue) in New Glarus, then make an immediate right onto Railroad Street to park in the Depot trail headquarters lot. At the trail's south end in Brodhead, park at Exchange Street and West 3rd Street, two blocks west of WI 11 (Center Avenue).

Sources of additional information:

Brodhead Chamber of Commerce
P.O. Box 16
Brodhead, WI 53520-0016
(608) 897-8411

New Glarus Chamber of Commerce
P.O. Box 713
New Glarus, WI 53574-0713
(608) 527-2095

Sugar River State Park Trail
P.O. Box 781
New Glarus, WI 53574
(608) 527-2334

Notes on the trail: A daily or annual state trail pass is required for riders age 16 and older (see Land status), except on the paved trail segment from the town of New Glarus to New Glarus Woods State Park.

RIDE 14 · Cam-Rock County Park Trails

AT A GLANCE

Length/configuration: Two loop trails: 2 miles of double-track at Cam-Rock II, 1.2 miles of double-track and 0.8 miles of extreme single-track at Cam-Rock III. One rail-trail: 1 mile one way of rail-trail between Cambridge and Cam-Rock I

Aerobic difficulty: Low to high; the greatest relief is at Cam-Rock III, where repeating laps will give anyone a workout

Technical difficulty: Low to high; the rail-trail is easy, the double-track cross-country ski trails are moderate, and the extreme single-track will test anyone's skill

Scenery: Wisconsin dairy land, woods, marshes, historic villages, and a fine overview of the land and Kosh Konong Creek at Cam-Rock III

Special comments: The trails are small, but with something for everyone: flat rail-trail and a nice playground at Cam-Rock I, rolling double-track at Cam-Rock II, hilly double-track and technical single-track at Cam-Rock III

Cam-Rock sounds like something out of the Flintstones. Actually, it's a nice little park that draws its hyphenated name from the villages of Cambridge on the north end and Rockdale on the south. There are only 5.8 miles of trails here in total, but the variety and attractions of the area make it well worth a visit.

From Cambridge, the ride menu begins with a two-mile round-trip on an old railroad bed with a nice playground at the south end. At the Cam-Rock II area there is a two-mile loop on double-track cross-country ski trails that have some rolling terrain with fine views of the Kosh Konong Creek.

Cam-Rock has been the site of annual cyclo-cross races for years, but the big news is a new extreme single-track laid out at area III among the already existing 1.2 miles of single-track cross-country ski trails with the help of area WORBA activists. The most difficult section is on the hill between the meadow area and the shelter building. This 0.6-mile trail snakes up and down the hill and is as technical as anything I've seen in the Midwest. If you've ever ridden the race trails in Park City, Utah, you'll be thrilled to find a mini version of the famous "spin cycle" here. This segment switchbacks from one side of a little ravine to the other as it descends the hill's fall line. The other shorter, easier sixth-of-a-mile single-track section splits from the ski trail to the south near the bottom of the hill and comes out near the beer cave.

Yes, there was once a brewery in Rockdale, and the old cave where kegs were stored before mechanical refrigeration is in the process of being restored. There's not much in Rockdale now except a very nice bed-and-breakfast and a tavern with windows overlooking Kosh Konong Creek, which until recently was dammed to create a mill pond. There are fine views of the pioneer mill from the bridge on CTH B.

You'll have to stop in Cambridge to find a good meal or microbrew. The little town has become a center for craft tourism thanks to Rowe Pottery, makers of early-American stoneware. The trade supports some good restaurants, like Graham's Cambridge Mill and Country Inn and Pub, near the north end of the trail.

General location: 20 miles east of Madison on US 12.

Elevation change: None on the rail-trail; several steep 20' climbs at Cam-Rock II; 150' of elevation at Cam-Rock III.

Season: April through November.

Services: All services are available in Cambridge except bicycle service. There is a nice swimming beach at Lake Ripley, 1 mile east of town. Rockdale offers a bed-and-breakfast and a tavern.

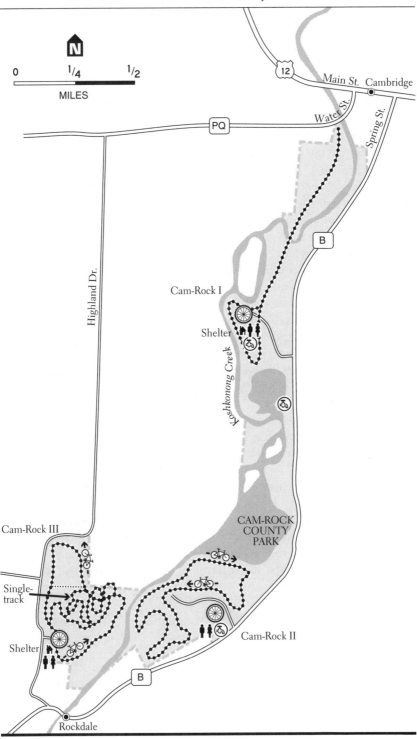

There's something for everyone at Cam-Rock County Park.

Hazards: Windfall trees or branches are always a possibility. Near the end of the rail-trail, at the creek south of the Cam-Rock I playground, there was a low-hanging partially fallen tree over the trail on my last visit. Extreme single-track involves steep grades, rocks, roots, narrow passages, and encroaching brush.

Rescue index: Call 911. Phones can be found at local businesses.

Land status: Dane County Park. A trail fee of $3 per day (except for the rail-trail, which is free) can be paid at self-pay stations at the Cam-Rock II or III parking areas. An annual pass can be purchased for $15 from Dane County Parks.

Maps: Maps are available at the trailheads or from Dane County Parks.

Finding the trail: For the north end of the rail-trail, turn south off US 12 (Main Street) in Cambridge onto County Truck Highway PQ (Water Street) and cross the creek bridge. Park on-street; the trail starts right next to the bridge. For the south end of the rail-trail, turn south off US 12 in Cambridge onto CTH B, and turn west into the Cam-Rock I entrance. For Cam-Rock II, continue south on CTH B to the entrance. For Cam-Rock III, continue south on CTH B into Rockdale, cross the creek bridge, and immediately go straight rather than bearing left on CTH B. This sets you on Jones Street (which becomes Highland Drive) and will take you north to the entrance halfway up the hill on the right.

Sources of additional information:

Cambridge Chamber of Commerce
P.O. Box 572
Cambridge, WI 53523-0572
(608) 423-3780
www.cambridgewi.com

Dane County Parks
4318 Robertson Road
Madison, WI 53714
(608) 246-3896

Notes on the trail: A daily or annual trail pass (see Land status) is required. Trails are marked by brown-and-white bike signs and blue-and-white cross-country ski signs. The rail-trail is two-way except for the short loop near the playground, which is signed for counterclockwise travel. Cam-Rock II trails are signed for clockwise riding and Cam-Rock III for counterclockwise riding. Trail surfaces are mostly grassy or forest floor with a hardpack track.

RIDE 15 · Glacial Drumlin State Trail— West (Rail-Trail)

AT A GLANCE

Length/configuration: 35 miles one way between Cottage Grove and Sullivan, including a 4-mile, on-road connection near Jefferson (part of 51-mile, one-way total length from Cottage Grove to Waukesha; see Ride 4, page 22 for the eastern section)

Aerobic difficulty: Very low; a typical rail-trail (for an aerobic workout on a varied-terrain trail nearby see Ride 14, page 52)

Technical difficulty: None

Scenery: Pleasant mix of farmland, trailside woods, stream crossings, lake views, an ancient Native American mound site, and a buffalo herd

Special comments: A nice family riding experience with an interesting Native American historic site nearby

A trail of surprising isolation despite its proximity to the Madison metro area and Interstate 94. This section of the Glacial Drumlin offers riders a chance to reflect on America's pre-European history at one of Wisconsin's most significant sites, Aztalan State Park. A short, two-mile side trip on paved-shouldered County Road Q, the park sits on the banks of the Crawfish River and contains numerous earthen mounds, including several large, pyramid-shaped ones that characterize them as part of the Middle Mississippian Culture. Aztalan is the northernmost outpost of this vast trade network of fortified towns. It was abandoned before the time of Christopher Columbus.

The 35-mile crushed-limestone trail has even more to offer. Between London and Lake Mills, a rest stop overlooks fields where buffalo roam as they might have hundreds of years ago. You'll cross the impressive Rock and Crawfish rivers on old, stressed-iron bridges and pass over the lazy, meandering Koshkonong Creek five times. The causeway at the south end of Rock Lake is a wonderful spot.

Your best on-trail town stop will be at Deerfield, the only one where the trail passes through the downtown. Future spur trails are being planned into Cambridge and Jefferson.

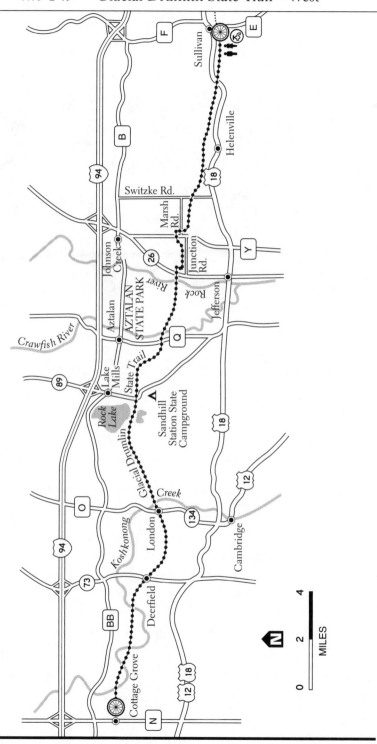

The ancient pyramid mound at Aztalan State Park.

General location: Between Cottage Grove and Sullivan along the route of US 18 and I-94.

Elevation change: Virtually none.

Season: April through November.

Services: There is a cafe and grocery in Cottage Grove north of the trailhead; Deerfield's cafe is just a few blocks south of the trail. There is only a tavern in London; the old depot in Lake Mills has been refurbished as trail headquarters and has flush toilets, water, and area information. The Lake Mills downtown where you'll find the nice Cafe on the Park on Main Street (WI 89) and Joseph Meguan's restaurant and pub; if you venture to Aztalan State Park there are pit toilets, water, and a tavern a few blocks north at County Road B. Helenville has a tavern, but the town isn't accessible from the trail; there is a tavern at WI 26 and Junction Road. Sullivan has several taverns and a country store that always welcomes riders, and has flush toilets and water at the trailhead.

Hazards: The trail bed is very wide, and few hazards exist other than inattentive riders and road crossings. Between Lake Mills and Sullivan there is a 2.1-mile detour on lightly traveled town roads. The trail is also used by hikers. Crop dusting of adjacent fields will sometimes cause the trail to be closed down temporarily between London and Lake Mills.

Rescue index: Dial 911. Phones are found at the trailheads, Lake Mills depot, and at local businesses.

Land status: Wisconsin State Park Trail, public roadways. A trail pass fee is required for bicyclists age 16 and older ($3 daily/$10 annual). The trail pass also covers usages such as cross-country skiing, horseback riding, and bicycling on state mountain bike trails.

Maps: A trail map is available at the Lake Mills Depot or from the Wisconsin Department of Natural Resources.

Finding the trail: At the Glacial Drumlin State Trail parking lot on County Road N in Cottage Grove; in Sullivan at the Glacial Drumlin State Trail parking lot, two blocks south of US 18 on County Road E.

Sources of additional information:

Jefferson Chamber of Commerce
305 South Main Street
Jefferson, WI 53549
(920) 674-4511
www.jefnet.com/jefferson

Lake Mills Area Chamber of
  Commerce
200 Water Street #C
Lake Mills, WI 53551-1632
(920) 648-3585
www.lakemills.org

Wisconsin Department of Natural
  Resources
Bureau of Parks and Recreation
P.O. Box 7921
Madison, WI 53707-7921
(608) 266-2621
www.dnr.state.wi.us

Notes on the trail: A daily or annual state trail pass is required for ages 16 and older (see Land status).

RIDE 16 · Military Ridge State Trail (Rail-Trail)

AT A GLANCE

Length/configuration: 40 miles one way

Aerobic difficulty: Low to moderate; the rail-trail climbs between Riley and Mt. Horeb and rolls over varied terrain on part of the stretch between Ridgeway and Dodgeville

Technical difficulty: Very low

Scenery: Fine ridge-top views of surrounding valleys and the Blue Mounds

Special comments: A good family bike tour with fine scenery, frequent small towns, and interesting natural and historic attractions near the trails

The cone-shaped silhouette of Blue Mound has been a landmark for people traveling this ridge-top route for thousands of years. Rising 400 feet above the trail, the wooded hill appears blue from far away. This easy-riding, 40-mile, one-way trail was once a Native American trail from the Madison area to the Mississippi. Later, it became a military road, a railroad, and then the highway. At some future time the trail will connect through Madison to the Glacial Drumlin State Trail.

Riley is a one-tavern town, but the place jumps on the first Saturday of each month when an informal bluegrass jamboree spills out onto the porch and lawn. Mt. Horeb is a pleasant little town with an attractive Main Street just a block off the trail. For a glimpse of the past check out Little Norway, a reconstruction of an old-world village, or go underground to see the wonders of the Cave of the Mounds. No matter how hot it is outside, it's always 50 degrees in the cave.

Blue Mound State Park, reached via a tough climb on a spur trail, has two observation towers with views over 25 miles in any direction. Mountain bike trails at Blue Mound and Governor Dodge state parks (see rides 17 and 18, pages 62 and 65) offer real aerobic workouts.

General location: Between Verona and Dodgeville, paralleling US 18/151.

Elevation change: Mt. Horeb is 250' higher than Riley, 6.4 miles to the east.

Season: April through November.

Services: All services, except bicycle services, are available in Dodgeville and Mt. Horeb. All services, including bicycle, are available in Verona at Atkins Bicycle Shoppe and Middleton Cycle and Fitness. There are taverns in Ridgeway, Barneveld, the town of Blue Mounds, and Riley. Barneveld and the town of Blue Mounds have playgrounds. There is camping and a swimming pool at Blue Mound State Park, and camping and a beach at Governor Dodge State Park.

Hazards: The trail is well maintained, and major highway crossings are made via underpasses. The trail leaves the rail bed and rolls over natural terrain between Ridgeway and Dodgeville. Some sections may be too steep for small children. There are very steep sections on the spur trails that run into Blue Mound and Governor Dodge state parks. The trail is also used by hikers.

Rescue index: Call 911. Phones are at local businesses and parks.

Land status: Wisconsin State Park Trail. A trail pass fee is required for bicyclists age 16 and older ($3 daily/$10 annual). The trail pass also covers usages such as cross-country skiing, horseback riding, snow-mobiling, and bicycling on state mountain bike trails.

Maps: Trail maps are available in the towns, from the Wisconsin Department of Natural Resources, and online at www.kscon.com/pnp/milridge.htm.

Finding the trail: The east end is at the Military Ridge State Trail parking area on Old PB Road, just west of the US 18/151 and County Road MV interchange (if traveling from the west on WI 23, exit at the County Road PB/M exit and go north 1 mile on Old PB Road). Find the west end at the Military Ridge State Trail parking area on County Road Y2 0.3 miles east of WI 23, just north of the US 18/151 intersection.

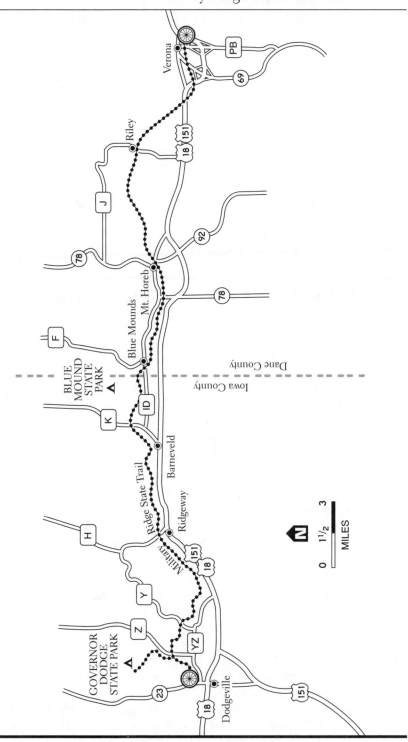

Sources of additional information:

Military Ridge State Trail
Route 1, Box 42, Highway 23 North
Dodgeville, WI 53533
(608) 437-7393

Mount Horeb Area Chamber of
 Commerce
P.O. Box 84
Mount Horeb, WI 53572-0084
(608) 437-5914; (888) TROLLWAY
www.trollway.com

Wisconsin Department of Natural
 Resources
Bureau of Parks and Recreation
P.O. Box 7921
Madison, WI 53707-7921
(608) 266-2621
www.dnr.state.wi.us

Notes on the trail: A daily or annual state trail pass is required for ages 16 and older (see Land status).

RIDE 17 · Blue Mound State Park Trails

AT A GLANCE

Length/configuration: 2 miles on the John Minix Trail/Willow Springs Trail loop with the option of an additional 1.8 miles of narrow single track, 2 miles on the Pleasure Valley Trail loop, and 1 mile one-way on the out-and-back trail connecting the trailhead, campground, and Military Ridge State Trail

Aerobic difficulty: Moderate to high; the Pleasure Valley Trail is moderate, while others will get your heart pumping fast

Technical difficulty: Low to moderate on the cross-country ski trail sections, high on the outer single-track sections; steep grades will require climbing skill on the John Minix Trail and out-and-back trail

Scenery: Gorgeous views from observation towers on top; hardwood forest and open fields on the trails

Special comments: A good place for a workout and a swim afterward; trails are well marked and their hardpack and grassy surfaces stay pretty dry

It looks like an ancient volcano. From any angle, Blue Mound is a perfect, distinctive cone shape with a flat top. No lava flows here though, and the mound owes its shape to a durable cap of limestone. The only flat spot for miles around, it was once used as a horse-racing track.

You'll leave the flat to the horses when you ride the 2-mile John Minix/Willow Springs Trail, 2-mile Pleasure Valley Trail, or the 1-mile trail that connects them with the Military Ridge State Trail (see Ride 16, page 59). You can test

RIDE 17 · Blue Mound State Park Trails

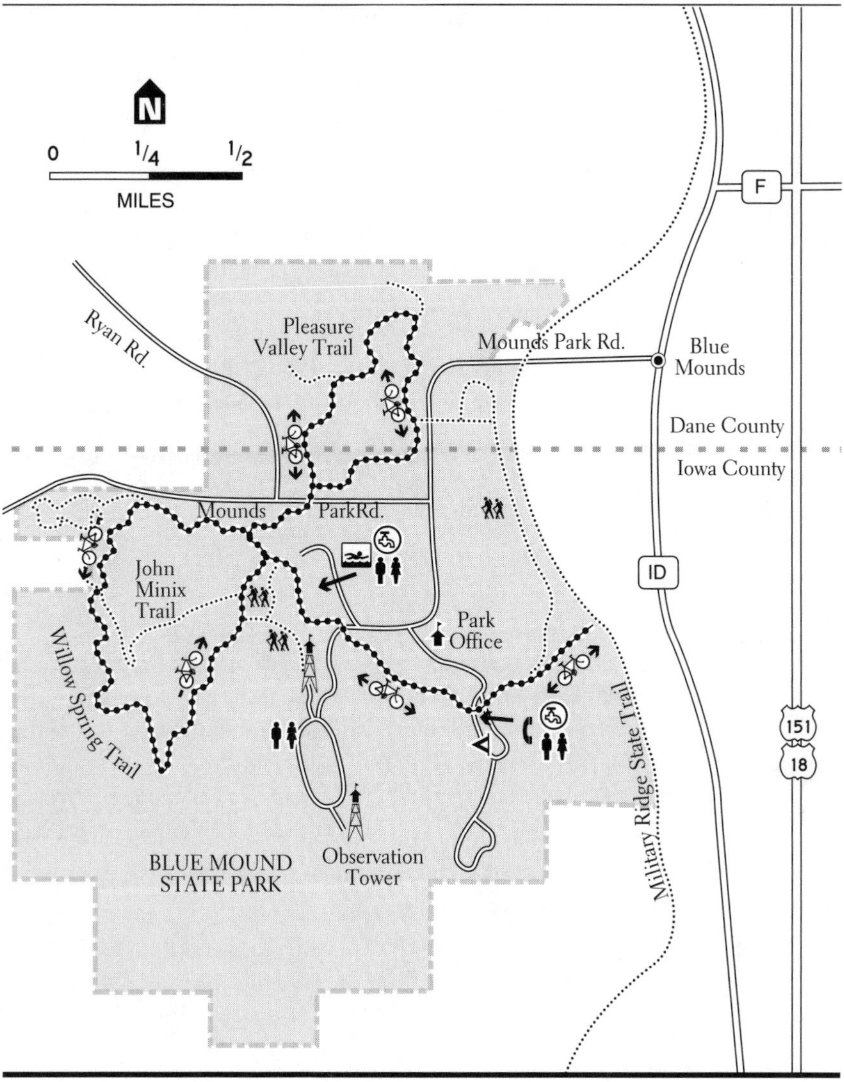

your climbing fiber with a 200-foot grind in areas of various steepness on the Minix, or 280 feet up from Military Ridge on the connector trail, most of it in the first half. The additional 1.8 miles of narrow single track adds technical as well as aerobic challenge to the experience. Still, there could be more. There is 500 feet of relief in the park itself.

You can get a taste of the elevation extremes on-road. From the park entrance to the peak it's 300 feet with an average grade of 1 in 10. The last 100 feet are at 1 in 7. If you want to experience Wisconsin's only true 1,000-foot climb, head down Mounds Park Road and Ryan Road to the County Road F intersection and retrace your route.

You may be ready for some relaxation at the swimming pool after your ride. Check out the views from the observation towers on top of the mound. On a clear day you can see the capitol building in Madison. You can't find a better setting for a ride.

General location: 28 miles west of Madison off US 18/151.

Elevation change: 200' on the John Minix Trail; 280' on the connector trail to the Military Ridge State Trail. You'll roll a lot on the Pleasure Valley Trail, but all in all there is only a 180' change from the low point to the pool parking lot.

Season: April through November.

Services: All services are available in Mt. Horeb, 6 miles to the east. There are taverns in Blue Mounds. Camping, showers, swimming, and water are available at Blue Mounds State Park.

Hazards: Trails are well maintained, but windfall branches are always a possible hazard. Trails are shared with hikers.

Rescue index: Help is available at the park office, swimming pool, or entrance station.

Land status: Wisconsin State Park. A daily or annual vehicle sticker ($5 daily/$18 annual for Wisconsin residents, $7 daily/$25 annual for out-of-state residents) is required in state parks. Bicyclists are not charged for visiting the park, but a trail pass fee is required of bicyclists age 16 and older for riding the off-road trails ($3 daily/$10 annual). The trail pass also covers usages such as cross-country skiing, horseback riding, and bicycling on railroad-grade bike trails.

Maps: Trail maps are available at the entrance station or from the Wisconsin Department of Natural Resources. The 7.5 minute series USGS quad for Blue Mounds shows the terrain very well, but does not show the trails.

Finding the trail: From US 18/151 follow Mounds Park Road north to the park entrance. Pass the entrance station and turn right into the swimming pool parking lot.

Sources of additional information:

Mount Horeb Area Chamber of
  Commerce
P.O. Box 84
Mount Horeb, WI 53572-0084
(608) 437-5914; (888) TROLLWAY
www.trollway.com

Wisconsin Department of Natural
  Resources
Bureau of Parks and Recreation
P.O. Box 7921
Madison, WI 53707-7921
(608) 266-2621
www.dnr.state.wi.us

Notes on the trail: A daily or annual state trail pass is required for bicyclers age 16 and over (see Land status). The trails are well signed with green-and-white mountain bike silhouettes for one-way counterclockwise travel on the Minix

Trail, and for two-way travel on the Pleasure Valley Trail and connector trail. Trails are double-track width and the surface varies from grassy to bare forest floor, with gravel laid down in low spots. In a nice touch, gravel has been laid on the downhill side of wooden water bars on the Minix Trail climb to make them more tractable.

RIDE 18 · Governor Dodge State Park Trails

AT A GLANCE

Length/configuration: 3.3 miles for the Mill Creek loop; 6.9 miles for the Meadow Valley and Gold Mine Trails loop; The Gold Mine Beginner Trail makes a 2.5-mile loop.

Aerobic difficulty: High on all trails; there is no way to avoid steep climbs

Technical difficulty: Moderate; climbing, descending, and dealing with some loose surface are part of the picture

Scenery: Beautiful ridge and valley views of forested slopes punctuated by stone outcrops

Special comments: An excellent aerobic workout on non-technical, well-signed, mostly grassy trails in a beautiful setting—a nice swimming beach makes for a perfect end-of-ride experience

Narrow, twisting, gorge-like valleys and soaring rock sculptures mark this beautiful park named after Henry Dodge, the state's territorial governor. The park brochure glosses over Dodge's career by saying he made peace with Native Americans. It doesn't mention that he did it with a gun. Dodge came up from Missouri and began mining illegally on Ho-Chunk (Winnebago) land in the 1820s. People riding to visit him were warned to approach at a walk, as it was his habit to shoot anyone coming at a gallop. An Indian agent sent out to kick him and other miners off of the land wrote to Washington, D.C., saying it would be easier to get rid of the Indians than the miners.

Good riding here, though, on more than ten challenging miles between two loops with long steep grades on both. The overlook into Lost Canyon is well worth the climb, and there are many more grand views as well. A paved connector runs past the Mill Creek Trail to the Military Ridge State Trail (see Ride 16, page 59).

General location: 4 miles north of Dodgeville and US 18.

Elevation change: 300' between the highest and lowest points. 150' come in one steady climb up from the trailhead to the Meadow Valley Trail and 200' along the Mill Creek Loop.

RIDE 18 • Governor Dodge State Park Trails

Season: May 1 to November 15.

Services: There are flush toilets, showers, swimming, phones, water, and a concession stand at the Cox Hollow Beach trailhead. All services, except bicycle, are available in Dodgeville.

Hazards: Trails are well maintained, but windfall branches are always potential hazards. The trails are also used by hikers, and sections are shared with horseback riders. Stay on the trail, even when letting horses pass, since poison ivy is very common.

Rescue index: Help is available at the Cox Hollow Beach or at the park entrance station.

Land status: Wisconsin State Park. A daily or annual vehicle sticker ($5 daily/$18 annual for Wisconsin residents, $7 daily/$25 annual for out-of-state residents) is required. Bicycles are not charged for visiting the forest, but a trail pass fee is required of bicyclists age 16 and older for riding the trails ($3 daily/$10 annual). The trail pass also covers usages such as cross-country skiing, horseback riding, and bicycling on railroad-grade bike trails.

Maps: A park map is available at the park office or from the Wisconsin Department of Natural Resources. The 7.5 minute series USGS quads for Clyde, Pleasant Ridge, and Jonesdale show the terrain very well, but do not show the trails.

Finding the trail: From the park entrance follow the signs to Cox Hollow Beach.

Sources of additional information:

Dodgeville Area Chamber of
Commerce and Main Street
Partnership
178 ½ North Iowa Street, Suite 201
Dodgeville, WI 53533-1546
(608) 935-9200; (608) 935-5993
www.dodgeville.com

Governor Dodge State Park
4715 Highway 23
Dodgeville, WI 53533
(608) 935-2315

Wisconsin Department of Natural
Resources
Bureau of Parks and Recreation
P.O. Box 7921
Madison, WI 53707-7921
(608) 266-2621
www.dnr.state.wi.us

Notes on the trail: A daily or annual state park vehicle admission and daily or annual trail pass for riders age 16 and older are required (see Land status). The trails are well signed with green-and-white mountain bike signs and frequent "you are here" map signs. White-and-red no-biking signs mark hiking trails. The Meadow Valley and Goldmine trails are signed for travel in a clockwise direction. The paved connector trail to the Mill Creek Trail and Military Ridge Trail is two-way. The Mill Creek Trail is signed for counterclockwise travel. Except for the connector, routes are on grassy, double-track cross-country ski trails with hardpack tracks in places. Rough horse trails, steep rocky slopes, and some soft sand will be found on the north loop.

RIDE 19 · Hyde Mill Tour (On-Road)

AT A GLANCE

Length/configuration: 11-mile loop

Aerobic difficulty: Moderate; one long climb will get your heart rate up

Technical difficulty: Easy

Scenery: Beautiful hill and valley country, and a historic pioneer mill too

Special comments: Low-stress cruising on paved and gravel roads in a rural environment, with a flavor of times long past

This 11-mile loop is a two-wheel-drive gravel road ride with a few paved road sections. It takes you through valley and ridge farmland and wooded hillsides. One steep, 225-foot climb makes it a moderate ride. No technical ability is needed, other than braking and cornering proficiency on gravel surfaces. This is a fine introductory ride for novice mountain bikers or a nice cruise for anyone.

The route winds through the quiet hill and valley country of rural Iowa County. One reward on this tour is a great photo opportunity by the Hyde Mill. This tiny mill was built in 1850, and is well kept under private ownership. You are welcome to stop for a rest and watch the veil of water spill over the mill dam. At times the owners engage the water wheel and let it turn slowly under the weight of the water as it did in days gone by. To get to the mill you cross another remnant of America's past, an old, wood-planked, stressed-iron bridge. Near the mill, at the intersection of County Road T, is the Hyde Chapel and Cemetery. The small, white clapboard structure illustrates how simple the Greek Revival style could be.

The trailhead is at the Hyde Store, another example of a rapidly disappearing feature of rural America. Little country stores once served most of the needs of farm families. What farmers couldn't raise, grow, or make, they could buy there. The Hyde Store is still a friendly place to stop for refreshment.

The scenery is a mix of farmland on the ridge tops and valley bottoms, and dense oak and maple forest on the hillsides. The view is also punctuated by the Knobs, a large sandstone outcrop that rises above the treetops and gives its name to the road that passes nearby. Catch a fine view of the Knobs to the south as you ride near the west end of Erdman Road. Small herds of white-tailed deer are a common sight along the route.

General location: 5 miles north of the village of Ridgeway, 31 miles west of the city of Madison.

Elevation change: Over 460' of elevation are gained and lost. There is a 225' climb on Erdman Road and a long, steep descent on Knobs Road.

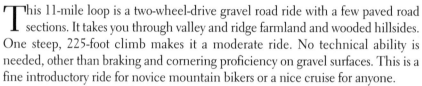

RIDE 19 • Hyde Mill Tour

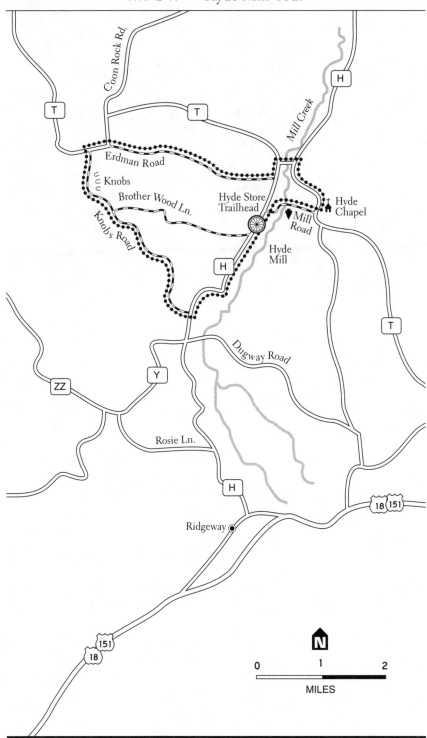

The old iron bridge at Hyde Mill is a great place to rest.

Season: The roads are open year-round, but good riding conditions can be expected March through October. Cool or cold temperatures are likely early or late in the season.

Services: Snacks and drinks are available at the Hyde Store. Gas and food can be found in the village of Ridgeway.

Hazards: All roads are open to motor vehicle traffic. Loose gravel may be encountered. Be careful of deer crossing your path on downhill runs.

Rescue index: Help is available in Ridgeway and at the Hyde Store. Farms are plentiful along the route and farmers are usually friendly and helpful.

Land status: Public roads through private land.

Maps: All of the roads are well marked and the route depiction shown here will be adequate. For the true map freak, the roads are shown on the USGS 15 minute maps for Spring Green and Blue Mounds, but the town roads are not named. The DeLorme book *Wisconsin Atlas & Gazetteer* shows all roads and road names.

Finding the trail: Take County Road H north from US 18/151 from the village of Ridgeway. Look for the Hyde Store on the west side of CR H as you drive through the unincorporated village of Hyde.

Sources of additional information:

An area visitor's guide titled "Southwest Wisconsin's Uplands" is available for $1 from:

Uplands, Inc.
P.O. Box 202
Mt. Horeb, WI 53572-0202
(800) 279-9472

General information is available from:

Wisconsin Division of Tourism
201 West Washington Avenue
Madison, WI 53703
(800) 372-2737

Notes on the trail: Park alongside the road on CR H near the Hyde Store. Be sure to pull well off the pavement. The route can be ridden in either direction. County roads are signed with standard, on-road, white-and-black signs, and town roads are signed with green-and-white street signs. Twisting town road signs 90 degrees is a popular prank, so trust your map.

RIDE 20 · Pine River/Bogus Bluff Tour (Rail-Trail, On-Road)

AT A GLANCE

Length/configuration: 14.3-mile one-way rail-trail with optional 15-mile on-road section which combines with a section of the rail-trail to make a 23.5-mile loop

Aerobic difficulty: Very low to moderate; the rail-trail is perfectly flat, but you can get an aerobic workout by taking to the roads

Technical difficulty: Easy to moderate; no skill is needed for the rail-trail, but you'll find some rough surface on steep grades on the road loop

Scenery: Farm, river, and marsh views on the rail-trail; farm, woods, ridge-top, and Wisconsin River views on the road route

Special comments: This new crushed-limestone rail-trail with several nice town parks makes for a pleasant family ride; or, you can get a workout by taking on the bluffs via the paved and gravel road route

The Pine River Trail traces the course of its namesake stream as it flows south to meet the Wisconsin River. You'll be struck by the contrast between the small, lazy, meandering Pine and the swift-flowing, broad Wisconsin. While there is not much en route in the way of attractions, you'll be in the midst of some of the loveliest scenery in the state.

RIDE 20 • Pine River/Bogus Bluff Tour

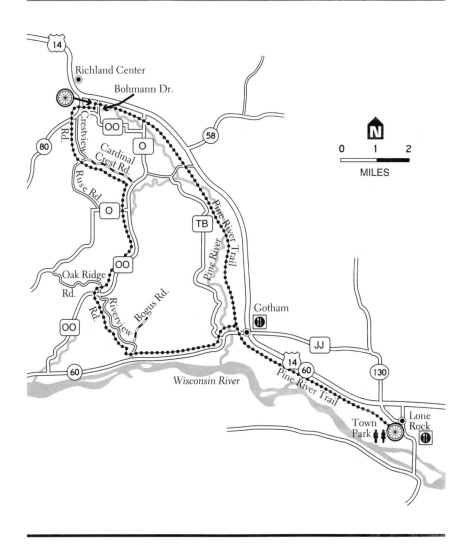

The 14.3-mile trail is laid on an abandoned rail bed, and gives riders a chance to enjoy the beauty of 250-foot river bluffs without having to ride over them. For a challenge you can take on several bluff-top climbs on a 15-mile on-road option which, while mostly on paved roads, features 1.7 miles of primitive gravel through a tunnel of trees on Cardinal Crest Road. Probably the most refreshing stretch is on WI 60 as the road hugs the edge of Bogus Bluff next to the Wisconsin River.

What's so bogus about Bogus Bluff? Well, a hundred years ago an Austrian painter named Paul Seifert settled in the area, and claimed to have found a cave on the bluff face with a burial chamber containing exquisite stone and copper work from a vanished race. A professor from Vienna supposedly confirmed his find before Seifert dynamited the entrance shut. It turns out the University of Vienna knew nothing of the cave or the professor. By the way, a Paul Seifert painting that originally sold for $2.50 is now worth thousands. Honest.

Back down to earth, Richland Center is a pleasant town with attractions including the German Warehouse, one of Frank Lloyd Wright's early designs. There's not much in Lone Rock and Gotham, but small town parks make nice stops on family rides. Hardcore riders can check with the folks at Backroad Bicycle in Richland Center about new single-track riding in the area.

General location: Between Lone Rock and Richland Center, along US 14.

Elevation change: Virtually none on the Pine River Trail. One 180' climb and one 250' climb on the on-road option.

Season: April through November.

Services: All services are available in Richland Center, including bicycle retail and repair at Backroad Bicycle. There are taverns and convenience stores in Gotham and Lone Rock, as well as town parks with playgrounds and pit toilets.

Hazards: The on-road option is shared with motor vehicles. The Pine River Trail is also used by hikers.

Rescue index: Help can be summoned in the three trail towns.

Land status: Richland County Trail. A $2 daily trail fee is required for adult riders; a pass can be purchased at area businesses.

Maps: A trail map is available at trail pass outlets or from Richland County Tourism. All area roads are shown on pages 33 and 34 of the DeLorme *Wisconsin Atlas & Gazetteer.*

Finding the trail: In Lone Rock, go west on Commercial Street off of WI 130 to the trail (bike route signs show on-street routes to a nearby town park which can also be used as a jumping-off point). In Gotham, the town park is a block south of the trail and WI 60 on Fulton Street. In Richland Center, the end of the trail is accessed on Bohmann Drive, two blocks south of US 14 on the south side of town.

Sources of additional information:

Richland Area Chamber of
  Commerce and Main Street
  Partnership
P.O. Box 128

Richland Center, WI 53581-0128
(800) 422-1318; (608) 647-6205
www.richlandchamber.com

Notes on the trail: A $2 daily trail fee is required for adult riders.

RIDE 21 · Devils Lake State Park Trails

AT A GLANCE

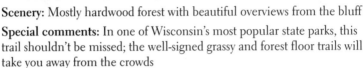

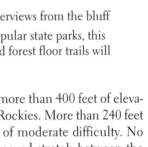

Length/configuration: 5-mile loop with a handle

Aerobic difficulty: High if the north shore trailhead is used; moderate if the bluff top trailhead is used

Technical difficulty: Moderate; steep slopes and some rocks, roots, and loose surface will be encountered

Scenery: Mostly hardwood forest with beautiful overviews from the bluff

Special comments: In one of Wisconsin's most popular state parks, this trail shouldn't be missed; the well-signed grassy and forest floor trails will take you away from the crowds

A five-mile ride at Devils Lake State Park takes in more than 400 feet of elevation and some of the finest views this side of the Rockies. More than 240 feet are gained in one steady climb, making this a ride of moderate difficulty. No great technical skill is needed. Except for a short, paved stretch between the campground and park concession stand, and a short, unpaved section on an access road, the entire distance is on wide, mowed, cross-country ski trails. Mountain biking is allowed only on trails signed for such activity. There are many heavily used hiking trails in the park where riding is prohibited. Leaving your bike and taking a short hike on the CCC Trail or Devils Doorway Trail will lead you to a great overview of the lake gap.

Devils Lake is bottled up between steep, talus-strewn quartzite bluffs that many believe once formed the valley of the Wisconsin River. During the last continental glacier, ice sheets pushed moraines inward from either end of the valley gap, creating a basin for the clear, clean lake. If you ride down to the park concession stand you will get a good view of the gap and a chance to check out the swimming at the North Shore Beach. Although the park is one of the most popular in the state, the area used for the designated mountain bike trails is unlikely to be crowded.

General location: 11 miles south of Interstate 90/94, Baraboo/Wisconsin Dells Exit #92.

Elevation change: For the most part, the trails are rolling with short, moderate climbs. There is a steep 120' climb and descent on the Ice Age Loop. The spur trail to the park concession stand covers 240' of elevation in 0.6 mile.

Season: Depending on trail conditions, the park will be open for mountain biking from late March to early November. Expect cool or cold temperatures at the extreme ends of the season. The swimming beach is open from Memorial Day weekend through Labor Day.

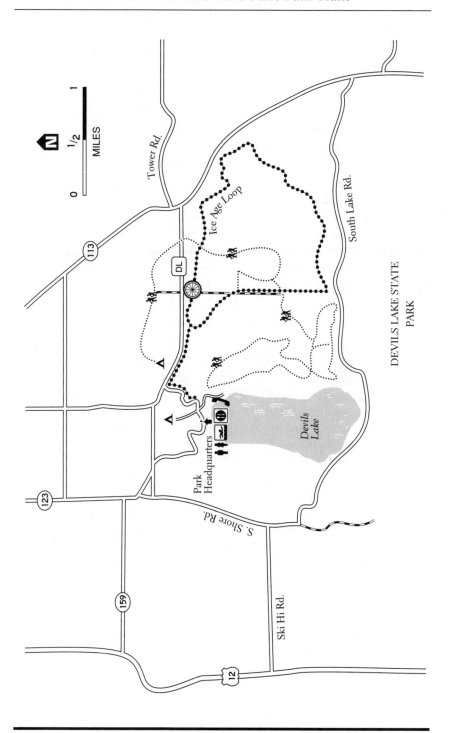

Services: The local WORBA chapter, Off-Road CyclePaths, donated a tool kit and pump to the park, and it is available for loan at the Visitor Center. Snacks are available at the park concession stand at the North Shore Beach. All services, including bicycle retail and repair, are available in the town of Baraboo.

Hazards: Trails are regularly maintained and clear, but fallen trees and branches may be encountered at any time. Hikers may be encountered on all trails.

Rescue index: Help is available at the park headquarters. Although Devils Lake State Park is the most popular in Wisconsin, the mountain bike trails are not, for the most part, in a heavily used area, and the chances of rescue are slim. In case of injury, make for the park headquarters, using bluff edge trails or paved roadways.

Land status: Wisconsin State Park. A daily or annual vehicle sticker ($5 daily/$18 annual for Wisconsin residents, $7 daily/$25 annual for out-of-state residents) is required to park anywhere within the park boundaries. Bicycles are not charged for visiting the forest, but a trail pass fee is required of bicyclists age 16 and older for riding the trails ($3 daily/$10 annual). The trail pass also covers usages such as cross-country skiing, horseback riding, and bicycling on railroad-grade bike trails.

Maps: Maps of the trails are available at Devils Lake State Park Headquarters. The USGS 7.5 minute Baraboo quadrangle map gives excellent information on the terrain, but doesn't show the mountain bike trails.

Finding the trail: To locate the north entrance to Devils Lake State Park when heading south on I-90/94, take US 12 towards Baraboo at Exit #92, Baraboo/Wisconsin Dells. Follow US 12 for 9 miles. Turn east from US 12 onto WI 159. Turn right at the T intersection with WI 123 and follow it to the junction with CR DL. When heading north on I-90/94, take Exit #106 and follow Highway 33 west for 13 miles to Baraboo. Then turn south (left) on WI 123 and follow it to the park, two miles outside Baraboo.

If you need to purchase a park sticker or trail pass, proceed straight at the intersection of WI 123 and CR DL onto the park road and follow it to the park headquarters. If you already have a sticker and pass, turn left on CR DL and drive 1.5 miles to the trailhead parking lot. If you prefer to start at the north shore, ride east from the Visitor Information Station following signs to the Northern Lights Campground and look for the trail across the road and slightly downhill from camp site #165.

Sources of additional information:

Baraboo Area Chamber of
   Commerce
P.O. Box 442
Baraboo, WI 53913-0442
(608) 356-8333; (800) 227-2266
www.baraboo.com/chamber

Devils Lake State Park
S5975 Park Road
Baraboo, WI 53913-9299
(608) 356-8301

Wisconsin Department of Natural
Resources
Bureau of Parks and Recreation
P.O. Box 7921
Madison, WI 53707-7921
(608) 266-2621
www.dnr.state.wi.us

Notes on the trail: An annual or day-use motor vehicle sticker is required to park on state land, as well as an annual or daily per-person trail fee (see Land status). The trails are sometimes subject to flooding or other damage and may be closed for these reasons. Be sure to call ahead to check the status.

The recommended starting point is up on the plateau formed by the bluffs of Devils Lake State Park. You may start below by the lake, but you will face a long 240' climb before you've warmed up. All trails are two-way, but it's advisable to start on top at the parking area (shown as the trailhead on the map) and follow the Steinke Basin and Ice Age loops to the east. This allows you to save the out-and-back, 1.2-mile (total) spur down to the park concession stand for last. If you want to avoid the long climb back up, you can skip the spur and return to the trailhead having covered a total of 3.8 miles. The trails are well marked with green-and-white bicycle silhouette signs. The Ice Age Loop will turn to the south and west where you will face a steep, 120' climb. Riding is prohibited on trails not specifically marked for mountain biking, though these hiking trails aren't marked as such. Assume that riding is not allowed anywhere not specifically marked for the activity.

LAKE MICHIGAN SHORES

L ake Michigan is vast. Its gunmetal blue waters are always good for a cool breeze or, if it decides to get nasty, a stiff, cold wind. Don't let that prospect keep you away though. A good day along its shores is worth many spent elsewhere.

This area is not going to be attractive to the hammer dogs, unless something clicks inside and tells them they don't need to go anaerobic every twenty yards. There is something to be said for kicking back and letting the pleasure soak in. All trails are easy and, except for Reforestation Camp and Mountain Bay, they all have views of the lake.

Get ready for great views of lighthouses and boats. They're never called ships, even the thousand-foot freighters. Point Beach State Forest Trails are a wooded respite from the lure of the nearby crescent-shaped shoreline. At the Sturgeon Bay end of the Ahnapee State Trail after a nice family cruise, you can watch boats—both luxury and utilitarian—being built or repaired across the harbor. Nearby, Potawatomi State Park Trails wind through the woods and lead you to great bay views.

Peninsula State Park is as scenic as any spot you'll ever find. You can take a family ride on the nearly flat Sunset Trail, or take on varied terrain on the mountain bike trails. You'll never be too far from a beach or a fine view. Newport State Park seems isolated in contrast to popular Peninsula. There you can duck off the trail at any one of a dozen spots and soak up the sun and breeze on the warm, smooth, limestone slabs that line the lakeshore.

North of Green Bay, the Reforestation Camp Trails are a popular spot for workouts among local mountain bikers. There is also a small zoo on the grounds, which kids love. Nearby, the Mountain Bay State Trail offers a rail-trail riding experience through picturesque Wisconsin farmland to the resort town of Shawano.

RIDE 22 · Point Beach State Forest Trails

AT A GLANCE

Length/configuration: 3.1-mile outer loop with several possible shortcut trails

Aerobic difficulty: Low; soft surface provides some resistance, but the terrain is gently rolling or flat

Technical difficulty: Easy; skills needed include the ability to power through some soft, sandy spots and handle the same when encountered on short, steep slopes; good for honing a loose riding style that lets the bike take its lead

Scenery: Wonderful Lake Michigan shoreline off the trail; on-trail you'll run through a dense Norway pine plantation

Special comments: A beautiful spot to visit even if you don't bike; the grassy, sometimes sandy but always pine needle–covered trail is well signed and offers a nice off-roading introduction for kids or beginners

Why is a mere 3.1-mile trail in this book? Because I like this place. If life is a beach, you'd better spend some of yours here. This trail is simply a bit of frosting on the cake if you're up for a day of sand and sun or are looking for a nice spot to overnight on your way up north. This loop is easy enough for almost any rider, even kids who want to try off-roading for the first time. The forest personnel are friendly and there is a very nice concession building at the beach.

You'll be riding on old sand dunes that run parallel to the lakeshore. The middle trail is the most rolling. On the northeast section you'll see birch trees and hemlocks and will ride up on a dune ridge. While the sub-surface is always sand and soft spots are common, most of the trail is pretty firm.

So where's the point in Point Beach? Look on a state map and you'll see that it's not very pointy, but it does stick out into Lake Michigan. This made it a death trap for ships both before and after the lighthouse was built. Storms from the east wrecked many hapless vessels on the point.

Wooden sailing ships were used as utilitarian cargo haulers right up until the Great Depression for the simple reason that they were cheap. One of the saddest stories is of the Rouse Simmons, a three-masted schooner that went down off the point with all hands in November of 1912, while loaded with Christmas trees destined for Chicago. In the spring, local fishermen often found their nets clogged with sodden Christmas trees. The Manitowoc Maritime Museum is worth a visit if you are into lake history. There you can tour a WWII submarine that was built at a local shipyard.

General location: 5 miles north of Two Rivers.

Elevation change: The greatest difference in the range is 25', but there are lots of smaller inclines as well.

RIDE 22 • Point Beach State Forest Trails

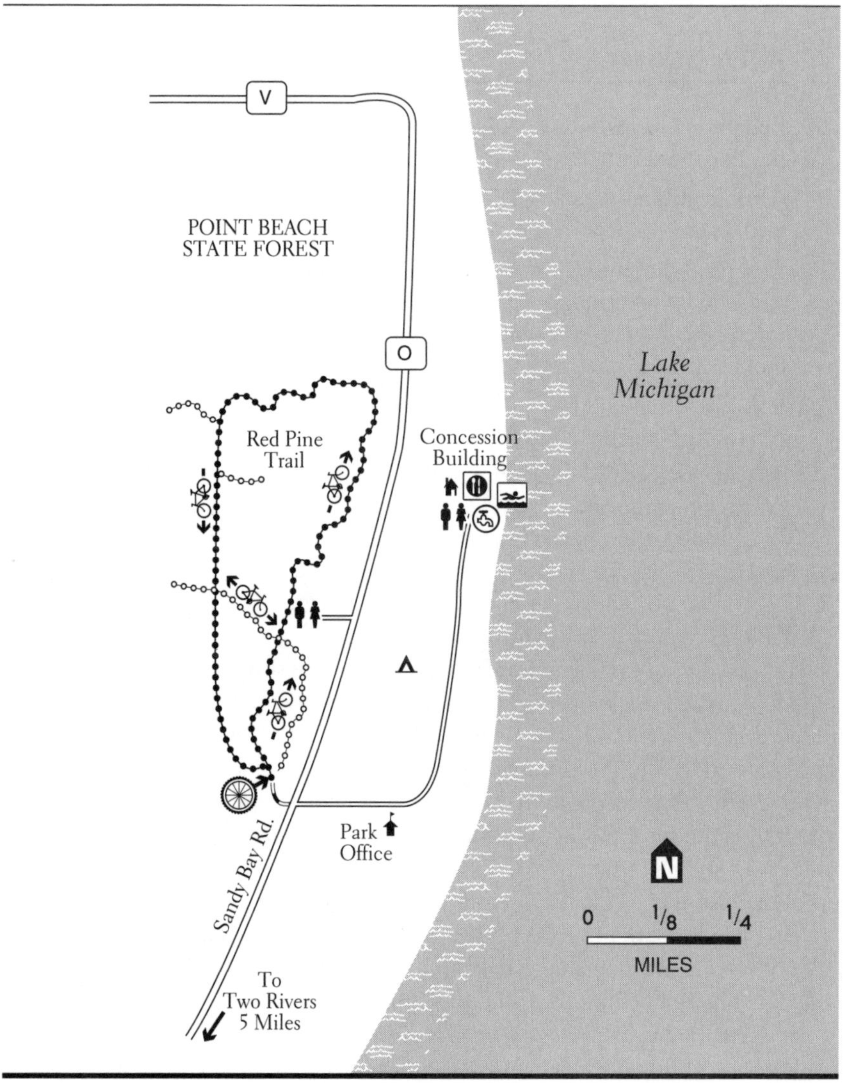

POINT BEACH
STATE FOREST

Red Pine
Trail

Concession
Building

Lake
Michigan

Sandy Bay Rd.

Park
Office

To
Two Rivers
5 Miles

N

0   ⅛   ¼

MILES

Season: April through November.

Services: All services, including bicycle retail and repair, are available in Manitowoc/Two Rivers at Wolf Cyclery, 5 miles south of the forest. There are pit toilets just off the trail at the group campground. The concession stand at the beach has snacks, water, and flush toilets. Camping and showers are nearby.

Hazards: Soft sand and some tree roots will be encountered. Be careful crossing the road from the beach to the trail.

Rescue index: Help can be summoned at the entrance station or concession stand.

Land status: Wisconsin State Forest. A daily or annual vehicle sticker ($5 daily/$18 annual for Wisconsin residents, $7 daily/$25 annual for out-of-state residents) is required to park in state forest lots.

Maps: A map of the forest is available at the entrance station, concession stand, or from the Wisconsin Department of Natural Resources.

Finding the trail: From County Road O, turn west into the trailhead parking lot opposite the road that runs east to the entrance station, family campground, and recreation area.

Sources of additional information:

Manitowoc-Two Rivers Area
  Chamber of Commerce
P.O. Box 903
Manitowoc, WI 54221-0903
(920) 684-5575; (800) 262-7892
www.manitowocchamber.com

Wisconsin Department of Natural
  Resources
Bureau of Parks and Recreation
P.O. Box 7921
Madison, WI 53707-7921
(608) 266-2621
www.dnr.state.wi.us

Notes on the trail: Daily or annual state park vehicle admission is required (see Land status). The Red Pine Trail is double-track width and has a soft, sometimes sandy surface. The route is well marked for counterclockwise riding with green-and-white mountain bike silhouettes and blue cross-country ski signs. Periodic "you are here" map signs are reassuring. Several unmarked trails intersect. CR O can be accessed through the group camp along the east side of the loop.

RIDE 23 · Mountain Bay State Trail—East (Rail-Trail)

AT A GLANCE

Length/configuration: 34 miles one way from Howard to Shawano; this section is part of the complete 83-mile, one-way trail from Howard (near Green Bay) to Weston (near Wausau); see Ride 57, page 186, for the west end of the trail

Aerobic difficulty: Very low; you can always ride faster to get your heart rate up; a typical rail-trail

Technical difficulty: Very low

Scenery: Pleasant central state farm, marsh, and wood lot scenery

Special comments: One of the state's newest trails, it offers a wide crushed-limestone surface, periodic small towns and parks for pleasant family biking, and the option of high-speed cruising. The trail is asphalt paved within the City of Shawano.

Wow. When you look at the Mountain Bay laid out on a state map, it goes nearly halfway across the state. It connects the historic city of Green Bay with the Wisconsin River city of Wausau. If trail development like this keeps up, someday we'll be able to ride practically anywhere in a traffic-free environment.

The attractions of Green Bay are a focus of this 35-mile eastern section of this wide, crushed-limestone rail-trail. The history of the area from the time of European contact is relived at the Heritage Hill State Park. During the 150-year era of the fur trade, Green Bay was the doorway to the west for the French and British. In case you've been living under a cabbage leaf, Green Bay is also the home of the Packers, who are deified in their own Hall of Fame near Lambeau Field, where they play football the old-fashioned way, on natural turf, regardless of the weather.

The trail ride begins in Howard, just west of the city. A nice, short family cruise will take you to the little playground at Spring Green Park just four miles up the trail. Further on at Pulaski, you are at the self-proclaimed polka capitol of the universe. The annual Pulaski Polka Days dance-fest is held during the last weekend of July, but a quarter for the jukebox is all you need to kick up your heels at any local tavern.

There is a nice town park and swimming beach in Bonduel, just off the trail. At the resort town of Shawano (Shaw-no) the trail is discontinuous, but if you can handle the traffic of a few miles of town roads, you can spend some pleasant time among the shade trees at Memorial Athletic Park.

General location: Between Green Bay and Shawano, paralleling WI 29.

Elevation change: Virtually none.

Season: Realistically, May through October.

Services: All services, including bicycle retail and repair, are found in Green Bay and Shawano. There are fast food and convenience stores in Howard and flush toilets and water at Memorial Park. Spring Green Park has a playground and portable toilets. There is a tavern in Zachow. Cedar Park in Bonduel has a swimming beach, flush toilets, water, and a playground. Memorial Athletic Park in Shawano has flush toilets, water, and a playground.

Hazards: Use caution at road crossings. Some on-street riding is necessary to access the trail from either recommended trailhead, or to get into Bonduel. Traffic may be considerable depending on the time of day. The trail is also shared with hikers, motorized wheelchairs, and horseback riders.

Rescue index: Help can be summoned in towns along the way.

Land status: Wisconsin State Park Trail. A trail pass fee is required for the Mountain Bay State Trail for bicyclists age 16 and older ($3 daily/$10 annual). The trail pass also covers all other state trails and usages, such as cross-country skiing, horseback riding, and bicycling on state mountain bike trails.

Maps: A map is available from the Wisconsin Department of Natural Resources. Pages 66 and 67 of the DeLorme book *Wisconsin Atlas & Gazetteer* show the trail and local roads.

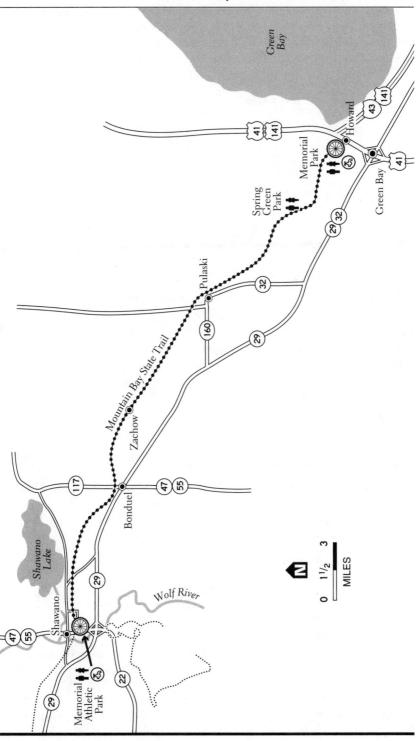

Finding the trail: Exit US 41 at the US 141/Velp Avenue exit. Go northwest 0.5 mile on County Road HS and park at Memorial Park in Howard. Then ride 2 blocks north on Lakeview Drive to the trailhead. In Shawano, park on-street at Memorial Athletic Park at WI 22 (Main Street) and Lieg Avenue and ride a half block north on Main Street to the Mountian Bay Trail.

Sources of additional information:

Brown County Parks Department
P.O. Box 23600
Green Bay, WI 54305
(920) 448-4466; (920) 448-6242

Green Bay Area Visitor and
 Convention Bureau
P.O. Box 10596
Green Bay, WI 54307-0596
(920) 494-9507; (888) 867-3342
www.greenbay.org

Shawano Chamber of Commerce
P.O. Box 38
Shawano, WI 54166-0038
(715) 524-2139; (800) 235-8528

Wisconsin Department of Natural
 Resources
Bureau of Parks and Recreation
P.O. Box 7921
Madison, WI 53707-7921
(608) 266-2621
www.dnr.state.wi.us

Notes on the trail: A daily or annual state trail pass is required to ride the trail for those bicyclists age 16 or older (see Land status). Spring Green Park is a short distance off the trail and there are no signs on-trail pointing it out. Leave the trail at the Glendale Avenue crossing and go north about a block, where you will see a sign directing you west to the park. The trail passes over WI 117 on a high trestle at Bonduel. To get into town, leave the trail at Flambeau Road if you are traveling west or at North Road if traveling east, then ride to WI 117 and turn south into town.

RIDE 24 · Brown County Reforestation Camp Trails

AT A GLANCE

Length/configuration: 7.6-mile loop; many other loop options are possible

Aerobic difficulty: Low to moderate

Technical difficulty: Easy

Scenery: Dense hardwood and pine forest

Special comments: The best place for off-roading in the Green Bay area; a great number of trails offer beginner to intermediate riders a good time; kids will like riding here and visiting the little zoo

Reforestation Camp has been a popular mountain biking destination for years. Just recently the sport has had an official sanction, and a modest trail

RIDE 24 • Brown County Reforestation Camp Trails

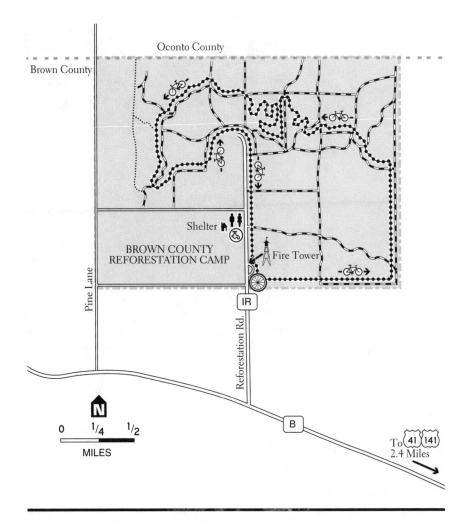

fee is now charged. Countless hours of riding can be yours on its maze of trails. The loop I've shown here offers a variety of terrain that includes gently rolling warmup and cool down sections. Most of the distance is on well-signed old logging roads with hardpack surfaces.

The 7.6-mile loop is easy enough for beginners who have a bit of determination. With all the trail options, you can custom tailor a route for kids. The zoo is always a big hit too.

As you can guess from the area's name, trees are grown here. You'll bike through thick stands of pine, birch, maple, and oak on wide, grassy trails with a hardpack track ridden in.

The Reforestation Camp trails have been Fox Valley favorites for years.

General location: 10 miles northwest of Green Bay.

Elevation change: The greatest climb in one slope will be around 45'. For the most part, the terrain is rolling with climbs in the 10' to 25' range.

Season: May through September.

Services: All services, including bicycle retail and repair, are available in Green Bay. There is a convenience store in Suamico near the US 41/County Road B intersection. Flush toilets and water are available at the zoo Visitor Center.

Hazards: Trails are well maintained, but windfall branches may be present. Trails are also used by horses and hikers.

Rescue index: Help can be summoned at the zoo.

Land status: Brown County Park. A $3 daily fee is required for riders age 16 and older. There is a self-pay station at the trailhead.

Maps: A map is available at the trailhead or from the parks department.

Finding the trail: Take US 41/141 north from Green Bay and turn west on CR B for 2.4 miles to County Road IR (Reforestation Road).

Sources of additional information:

Brown County Park System
P.O. Box 23600
Green Bay, WI 54305-3600
(920) 448-4466

Green Bay Area Visitor and
  Convention Bureau
P.O. Box 10596
Green Bay, WI 54307-0596
(920) 494-9507; (888) 867-3342
www.greenbay.org

Notes on the trail: A daily trail fee is required (see Land status). Double-track trails are well marked for two-way travel with green-and-white mountain bike silhouette signs and frequent "you are here" map signs. Fines apply for riding on unmarked trails.

RIDE 25 · Ahnapee State Trail (Rail-Trail)

AT A GLANCE

Length/configuration: 31 miles total one way: 12 miles from Perry Street in Algoma to Sunset Road south of Casco, 19 miles from Algoma to Sawyer Park in Sturgeon Bay

Aerobic difficulty: Low, but the wind off Lake Michigan can give you a workout; typical rail-trail

Technical difficulty: Easy

Scenery: Mixed farm, marsh, and woods; lake views at Sturgeon Bay and Algoma

Special comments: A good trail for family riding or high-speed cruising; the crushed-limestone surface recently has been redone, making a smooth, wide pathway

When you ride the Ahnapee you'll have a hard time believing it was one of the state's early flops. Following on the heels of the success of the Elroy-Sparta Trail (the nation's first rail-trail), the Ahnapee's planners didn't quite grasp the concept. The Ahnapee didn't start or finish in a town, and without anchors it became an orphan.

Recent efforts have begun to correct the problem. A trail extension is working its way into the interesting boat-building city of Sturgeon Bay, via an underpass. The trail has also been extended into the outskirts of the interesting town of Algoma, where it connects with a new section that runs west through the village of Casco and south to Casco Junction. The new anchor towns create more interest in the trail.

RIDE 25 • Ahnapee State Trail

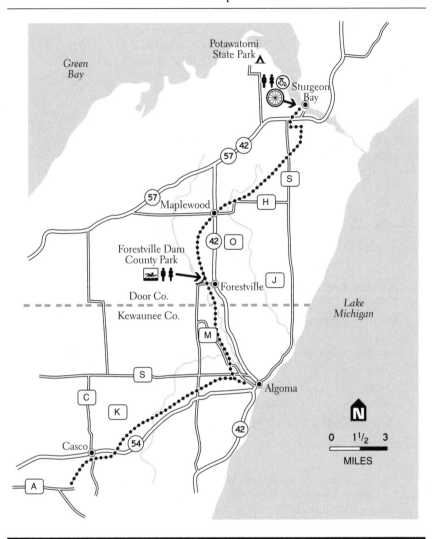

The 31-mile trail is lined with wildflowers for much of its distance. Between Maplewood and Sturgeon Bay it passes through a marsh filled with tamarack trees, the last trees to change color in the fall when they turn a brilliant golden yellow. In and just north of Forestville are nice parks with modern playgrounds for trailer-weary kids. You can connect through Sturgeon Bay to Potawatomi State Park (see Ride 26, page 90) on lightly traveled city streets by staying close to the bay shore.

General location: Between Sturgeon Bay and Casco.

Elevation change: Practically none. Your typical flat rail-trail.

Season: May through October.

Services: All services are available in Sturgeon Bay and Algoma. Bicycle retail and repair are available in Sturgeon Bay at Bay Bikes and Boards. There are cafes, convenience stores, and taverns in Casco and Forestville. Taverns are located in Maplewood and Rio Creek. Sawyer Park at the Sturgeon Bay trailhead has water and flush toilets, as does Legion Park in Forestville. There are pit toilets just north of County Road M near Algoma and at Forestville Dam Park. Playgrounds can be found at Cherry Blossom Park near Sturgeon Bay, at Forestville Dam Park, and at Legion Park.

Hazards: Use caution at road crossings. Between Sturgeon Bay and Maplewood the rail bed is elevated above a marsh, creating a sharp side drop-off of several feet. The trail is also used by hikers and horseback riders. Until the trail extension all the way to Sawyer Park in Sturgeon Bay is complete, it is necessary to ride on Green Bay Road which is wide, but fairly busy.

Rescue index: Call 911. Phones are available at local businesses.

Land status: Wisconsin State Park Trail. Unlike most state trails, no trail pass is required, but donations are requested at the Sturgeon Bay and Algoma parking areas.

Maps: A nicely done map is available from the Friends of the Ahnapee.

Finding the trail: Follow Green Bay Road northeast from WI 42/57 to Sawyer Park in Sturgeon Bay. Take Navarino Street west from WI 42 into Algoma four blocks. Turn north on Mill Street one block, then turn west on Perry Street and park on-street near the CR M and CR S intersection, where the trail junctions. Park on-street on WI 54 in Casco.

Sources of additional information:

Algoma Area Chamber of
  Commerce
1226 Lake Street
Algoma, WI 54201-1300
(800) 498-4888; (920) 487-2041
chamber@itol.com
www.algoma.org

Door County Parks and Recreation
3418 Park Drive
Sturgeon Bay, WI 54235
(920) 743-3636

Door County Chamber of
  Commerce
P.O. Box 406
Sturgeon Bay, WI 54235-0406
(920) 743-4456; (800) 52-RELAX

Friends of the Ahnapee
P.O. Box 82
Algoma, WI 54201
(920) 487-3214
www.alhnapeetrail.org

Notes on the trail: The fine-screen crushed-limestone trail surface is best ridden with medium to wide tires.

RIDE 26 · Potawatomi State Park Trails

AT A GLANCE

Length/configuration: 7-mile outer loop

Aerobic difficulty: Low to moderate; a few short, steep grades will get your heart rate up a bit

Technical difficulty: Easy to moderate; most of the trails are smooth hardpack, but some rocky surfaces will have to be negotiated

Scenery: Superb views of Sturgeon and Sawyer bays—check them out from the top of the observation tower

Special comments: This is one very beautiful state park—the easy-to-follow, grassy and hardpack trails wind through gorgeous stands of pine, maple, and birch, and are fun for riders of any ability

The Door Peninsula has always been an appealing place. The Potawatomi tribe defended it against the Iroquois, who had canoed all the way from what is now the state of New York. Every French explorer of any repute passed through the area. Today it is a popular tourist destination.

The easy-riding 7-mile loop in the park is a good introduction to off-roading for the novice and a nice tour for more advanced riders. Complete newcomers might question how much they will enjoy the sport, judging by the first off-road section that runs next to the park road. It is littered with chunks of limestone cleaved from a rock face, making a very rough ride. The surface soon smoothes out as you climb up on the bluff.

Be sure to take in the sights by riding the paved park road up to the observation tower. The view of the bays is terrific. You can connect to the Ahnapee State Trail (see Ride 25, page 87) by taking the trail off of the park road at the southeast corner of the park and following city streets running close to the bay.

General location: 3 miles northwest of Sturgeon Bay.

Elevation change: Terrain is mostly flat, except for a moderately steep 50' climb on the out-and-back section near the trailhead and an even more moderate 30' climb and descent near the north end of the loop.

Season: May through November.

Services: There are pit toilets and water near the trailhead. Flush toilets and showers are located in the campground. All services, including bicycle retail and repair, are available at Bay Bikes and Boards in Sturgeon Bay.

Hazards: Trails are well maintained, but windfall branches may be encountered. A few rocky surfaces may be unnerving to beginners. Trails are shared with hikers.

Rescue index: Help is available at the park office, and there is a telephone at the shelter near the trailhead.

RIDE 26 • Potawatomi State Park Trails

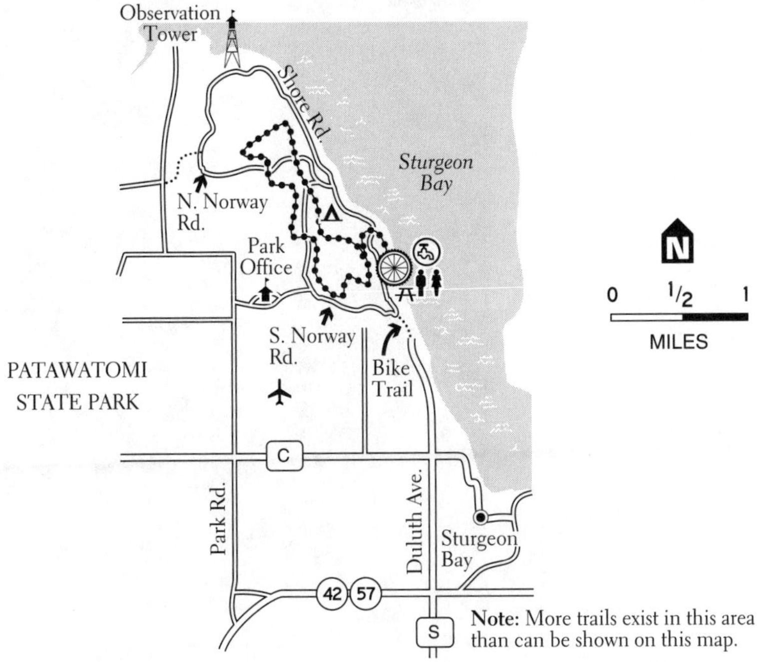

Land status: Wisconsin State Park. A daily or annual vehicle sticker ($5 daily/$18 annual for Wisconsin residents, $7 daily/$25 annual for out-of-state residents) is required in state parks.

Maps: A trail map is available from the park office or the Wisconsin Department of Natural Resources. The 7.5 minute series USGS quad for Sturgeon Bay West shows the terrain very well, but does not show the trails.

Finding the trail: From WI 42/57, go 1.5 miles east of Sturgeon Bay and turn north on Park Road. A large brown sign will direct you to the park. From the entrance station follow South Norway Road southeast, and park at Picnic Area #2. The paved trail section starts at the northeast corner of the parking lot.

Sources of additional information:

Door County Chamber of
 Commerce
P.O. Box 406
Sturgeon Bay, WI 54235-0406
(920) 743-4456; (800) 52-RELAX
www.doorcountyvacations.com-

Potawatomi State Park
3740 Park Drive
Sturgeon Bay, WI 54235
(920) 746-2890

The crazy spiral pine tree on Potawatomi State Park Trail.

Wisconsin Department of Natural
    Resources
Bureau of Parks and Recreation
P.O. Box 7921

Madison, WI 53707-7921
(608) 266-2621
www.dnr.state.wi.us

Notes on the trail: An annual or day-use motor vehicle sticker is required to park on state land (see Land status). Begin at the parking lot for Picnic Area #2 Follow the paved trail at the northeast corner of the parking lot along the bay shore. This is the Hemlock Trail, which is marked with small, square signs depicting a hemlock branch silhouette. Ride around a gate just before the trail junctions with the park drive. Ride onto the unpaved Hemlock Trail directly across the road from the junction. Almost immediately, turn left onto an unnamed trail that is signed with a green-and-white mountain bike silhouette. The Hemlock Trail veers to the right at this point and has a No Mountain Biking sign. From this point on the trails are double-track width, grassy with a hardpack track, and well signed for two-way travel with green mountain bike signs and arrows.

An artist paints the view from the Observation Tower.

RIDE 27 · Peninsula State Park Trails

AT A GLANCE

Length/configuration: 13.8-mile loop route includes the 4.4-mile each-way Sunset Trail, a flat to gently rolling family recreation trail

Aerobic difficulty: Low; only one short, steep grade

Technical difficulty: Easy; although some short sections of rough stone, where fill has been added to low spots, will make beginners a bit uneasy

Scenery: Peninsula is one of the most scenic spots in the state; you'll see bays, harbors, lighthouses, cedar-lined shores, craggy rock faces, bluff-top views of off-shore islands—the list goes on and on

Special comments: A not-to-be-missed ride when visiting Door County; beautiful surroundings make up for any lack of challenge; the Sunset Trail has a crushed-gravel surface, while the mountain bike trails are hardpack forest floor

Peninsula State Park is the essence of the Door County experience. Its wooded bluffs jut out into Green Bay above the small towns of Fish Creek and

Ephraim. Norwegian and Icelandic fishermen settled in this area and made their livings from the lake. The "fish boil," a mix of fish, potatoes, and onions thrown into a cauldron, remains a popular "all you can eat" traditional dinner in the old fishing villages.

The 13.8-mile loop route shown here is a mix of riding experiences. The nearly flat 4.4-mile one-way Sunset Trail is a wonderful family ride with scenery to die for. It does get a bit 'over-familied' on weekends, so it's not a good place for high-speed cruising. There are about four miles of paved park roads too. The mountain bike trails have some rocky and rooted sections, but they will only be difficult if ridden fast.

Why not just take it easy here? A four-mile side trip will bring you to the observation tower, which offers a great view of Green Bay and the villages of Fish Creek and Ephraim.

General location: Just north of the village of Fish Creek, which is 22 miles northeast of Sturgeon Bay.

Elevation change: Terrain is mostly flat to gently rolling. There are several moderately steep climbs of 50' to 80' on the mountain bike trails and paved roads. The difference between the highest and lowest points on the route is 130'.

Season: May through October.

Services: There is water at the trailhead and a concession stand at the Nicolet Bay beach. All services, including bicycle retail, rental, and repair, are available in Fish Creek. Bicycles can be rented just outside the park entrance.

Hazards: Trails are well maintained, but watch for windfall branches. In low spots rough rock fill has been added, which may make bike handling difficult for novices. The Sunset Trail is rather narrow for the high volume of family bike traffic it carries on weekends. Trails are also open to hikers.

Rescue index: Help is available at the park office and the Nicolet Bay beach concession stand.

Land status: Wisconsin State Park. A daily or annual vehicle sticker ($5 daily/$18 annual for Wisconsin residents, $7 daily/$25 annual for out-of-state residents) is required in state parks. Bicyclists are not charged for visiting the park or riding on the Sunset Trail, but a trail pass fee is required of bicyclists age 16 and older for riding the varied-terrain off-road trails ($3 daily/$10 annual). The trail pass also covers usages such as cross-country skiing, horseback riding, and bicycling on railroad-grade bike trails.

Maps: A trail map is available from the park office or the Wisconsin Department of Natural Resources. The 7.5 minute series USGS quad for Ephraim shows the terrain very well, but does not show the trails.

Finding the trail: Follow WI 42 through the village of Fish Creek, and turn north into the park at the eastern village limits. Just past the park office, where the inbound drive rejoins the outbound drive, turn left into the parking lot for the Sunset Trail. The trail begins on the south side of the parking lot.

RIDE 27 • Peninsula State Park Trails

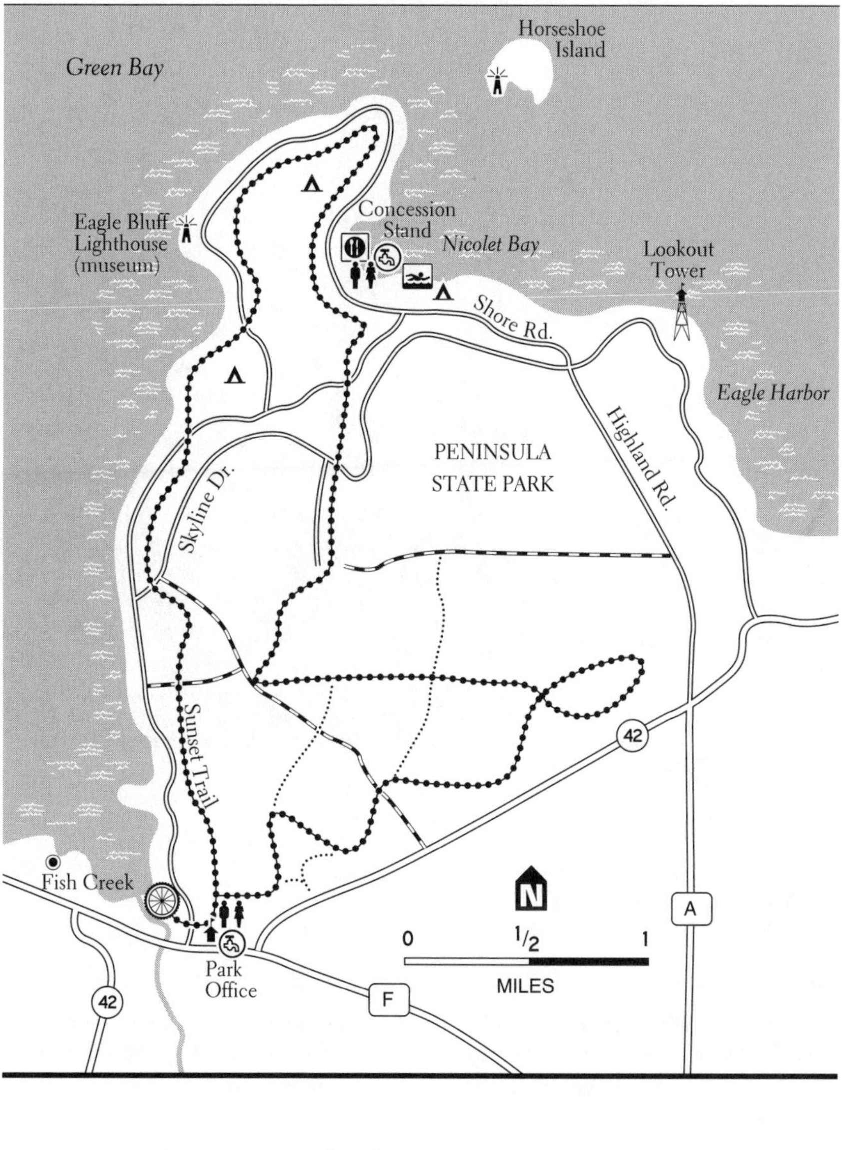

Sources of additional information:

Door County Chamber of
  Commerce
P.O. Box 406
Sturgeon Bay, WI 54235-0406
(920) 743-4456; (800) 52-RELAX
www.doorcountyvacations.com

Peninsula State Park
Box 218
Fish Creek, WI 54212
(920) 868-3258

The woods are deep and fragrant at Peninsula State Park.

Wisconsin Department of Natural Resources
Bureau of Parks and Recreation
P.O. Box 7921

Madison, WI 53707-7921
(608) 266-2621
www.dnr.state.wi.us

Notes on the trail: An annual or day-use motor vehicle sticker is required to park on state land, as well as an annual or daily per-person trail pass for riding the varied-terrain off-road trails (see Land status). The varied terrain trails are well marked for two-way travel with green-and-white mountain bike silhouette signs and periodic "you are here" sign maps. Trails where mountain biking is not allowed are marked by signs with a red slash on a white background.

From the south side of the trailhead parking lot, follow the crushed-gravel Sunset Trail to the southeast, across the park road and around to the north. Trails can be ridden in either direction, but these cues describe counterclockwise travel. Watch very carefully for the right-angle turn off of the Sunset Trail onto the unsurfaced, single-track cross-country ski trail that is marked "difficult trail." After a fairly steep climb you will come to an intersection where both the left and right double-track trails are signed for mountain biking. Go left here; the right trail will take you out to the highway.

At the next intersection turn right onto the remaining pavement of an abandoned road. This section is also signed with orange snowmobile diamonds. Watch closely for the next turn to the left, one-half mile farther. If you reach the highway you have gone too far. The rest of the route is easy to follow with periodic "you are here" map signs at each intersection. Eventually you will junction with Hemlock Road, a paved road that you will take north. Follow it until you reach Bluff Road. Turn right on Bluff Road and, a short distance later, turn left (west) on Shore Road. For an interesting side trip, follow Shore Road east to Eagle Tower, an observation platform with a great view of the bay and neighboring towns.

Just beyond the Nicolet Bay beach on Shore Road, a sign will direct you to Sunset Trail on the east side of the road. Follow the Sunset Trail back to the trailhead.

RIDE 28 · Newport State Park Trails

AT A GLANCE

Length/configuration: 10.9-mile loop and out-and-back route

Aerobic difficulty: Low, terrain is flat to gently rolling

Technical difficulty: Easy

Scenery: Pristine Lake Michigan shoreline and hardwood forest

Special comments: A great place for riders of all abilities to enjoy the beauty of Door County without the crowds; the easy-to-follow, grassy cross-country ski trails are nearly always close enough to the lakeshore that you can slip over to take a break and enjoy some solitude by the water

Door County gets a lot quieter the farther north you go. And you can't get much farther north than Newport State Park. Nearby, Port des Morts Passage (Death's Door) separates the mainland from Washington Island. The passage was named for the havoc it wreaked on sailing ships; the county was named after the channel. The highest concentration of wrecks in the country lie beneath its waters, and it has become a real mecca for scuba divers. A small maritime museum in the nearby village of Gills Rock (where you can take a fast passenger/bike ferry to Washington Island) displays artifacts from many wrecks.

Your 10.9-mile loop and out-and-back ride at Newport will be much less menacing. The easy, quiet, hiking and cross-country ski trails can be handled by even the most inexperienced rider. The terrain is almost dead flat, and the grassy and forest floor surfaces of the trail offer little rolling resistance, except for some swampy sections in the southwest loops. But riding is hardly the whole story at Newport. There are many opportunities to get off your bike and walk out to the more than 11 miles of lakeshore and enjoy the tranquillity of this unique park.

RIDE 28 · Newport State Park Trails

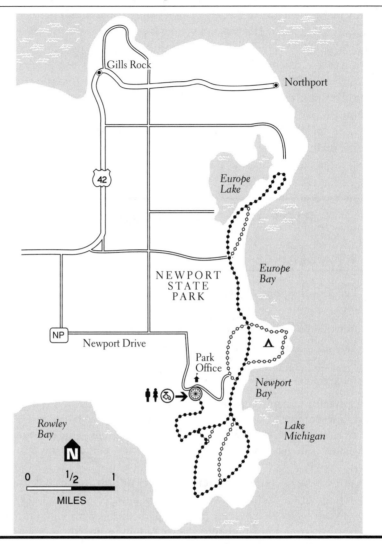

General location: 4 miles east of the village of Ellison Bay, which is 36 miles northeast of Sturgeon Bay.

Elevation change: No significant change.

Season: May through October.

Services: Water is available along the trail at Newport Bay. All services, except bicycle services, are available in the small villages of Gills Rock and Ellison Bay.

Bicycle retail, rental, and repair are available in Fish Creek, 17 miles south on WI 42.

Hazards: Keep an eye out for windfall trees and branches. Trails are shared with hikers.

Rescue index: Help is available at the park office.

Land status: Wisconsin State Park. A daily or annual vehicle sticker ($5 daily/$18 annual for Wisconsin residents, $7 daily/$25 annual for out-of-state residents) is required in state parks.

Maps: A hiking or biking trail map is available at the park office or from the Wisconsin Department of Natural Resources.

Finding the trail: From the village of Ellison Bay, travel 2 miles east on WI 42 and turn south on County Road NP (Newport Drive). Follow it 3 miles to the park office.

Sources of additional information:

Door County Chamber of
  Commerce
P.O. Box 406
Sturgeon Bay, WI 54235-0406
(920) 743-4456; (800) 52-RELAX
www.doorcountyvacations.com

Newport State Park
475 County Highway NP
Ellison Bay, WI 54210
(920) 854-2500
www.dcty.com/newport

Wisconsin Department of Natural
  Resources
Bureau of Parks and Recreation
P.O. Box 7921
Madison, WI 53707-7921
(608) 266-2621
www.dnr.state.wi.us

Notes on the trail: An annual or day-use motor vehicle sticker is required to park on state land (see Land status). There is no special signage for mountain biking, but the trails are well marked for cross-country skiing with frequent "you are here" sign maps. The small confines of the park make getting lost unlikely. This route features a loop and an out-and-back section. Trails can be ridden in either direction, but these cues apply to riding counterclockwise. Begin riding at Parking Lot #1 near the park office and head south on the blue trail. At a T intersection turn left, then turn right on Rowley's Bay Trail. Continue north following the Europe Bay/Hotz Trail along the out-and-back stretch. When you return, heading southward, veer left to take the loop portion of the ride.

KICKAPOO COUNTRY

What a funny name! Come on, if you're not from Wisconsin, or maybe even if you are, that's what you're thinking. Well, it's one of those Native American names so common in the state. The Kickapoo are an Algonquian-speaking tribe that found refuge in the area's deep, twisting valleys before being forced to the southwestern United States and Mexico.

Today, it's a great place for bikers to get away from it all. Scenery is superb and riding ranges from easy to very challenging. On the nation's first railroad-bed bike trail you can explore three 125-year-old tunnels. Though not a real touristy area, there are enough services and interesting diversions to occupy the non-riding hours. You can visit the world's first solar village, canoe the meandering Kickapoo, camp in beautiful settings, lodge at a Victorian inn with a superb restaurant, and shop for local crafts ranging from quilts to handmade guitars.

Kickapoo country is a bucolic backwater that appeals to the Amish folk, many of whom have migrated from Pennsylvania to practice their simple agrarian lifestyle here—so fitting in a region little changed since the horse and buggy days. They enjoy seeing bicyclists and don't mind you taking photos of them, as long as it's not of their faces (as that is considered vanity in their culture). The area also attracted counterculture types seeking a gentler lifestyle back in the 1970s. They are now a solid part of local communities.

The Kickapoo Valley is Wisconsin's Grand Canyon—albeit on a one-tenth scale. It's just as precious a natural feature though, and much more intimate than the world's greatest gorge. The same factors created the Kickapoo—time and water. It's smack in the heart of the Driftless Area, a unique part of the Midwest that the glaciers never touched. Spared the bulldozing of ice sheets that pressed in from all four sides at one time or another, the waters of the Kickapoo cut deeper and meandered more wildly, creating 400-foot-high bluffs where buff-colored stone cliffs pop out of the hardwood forest here and there.

The recently created 8,400-acre Kickapoo Valley Reserve between La Farge and Wildcat Mountain State Park was the longtime orphan of the three. An early 1970s environmental effort stopped the Army Corps of Engineers from damming the Kickapoo, one of the state's most scenic canoe rivers. Just mentioning the subject still stirs local controversy. Lakes mean summer tourism in many parts of Wisconsin, and lakes are one thing the Driftless Area naturally lacks. No matter that the lake the dam at La Farge would have created would have been too narrow for safe power boating, or that flood control benefits were very questionable, the Corps was ready to charge ahead and some locals could only see dollar signs.

Parts of these lands are now being turned over to the state, while parts that have cultural significance will be under the control of the Ho-Chunk Nation (Winnebago tribe). At this point, nearly all of the lands are expected to be open for recreation. The area could certainly use some tourism, at least on a scale that won't destroy its character. While there are many prosperous looking farms in the valleys and on ridge tops, signs of rural poverty are also common. The leap from the log cabin to the mobile home seems to have been made about thirty years ago. Now you'll see some of the old cabins being fixed up—an encouraging sight.

It's your choice when it comes to types of riding experiences in this beautiful region. The Kickapoo Cowpath Tour shows you the best of valley scenery on an easy gravel road, with high-speed cruising connecting little towns. On the Kickapoo Valley Reserve Trails, you get to attack the terrain you only looked at on the gravel road tour. Challenging double-track and single-track lead you to marvelous places.

If you like the idea of unique camping or lodging, check out Brush Creek Campground. The friendly people who run this private recreation area will give you a map of the hilly trails on the property, and invite you for a swim in the pond when you're done. From the campground, you can also take on a scenic, hilly on-road cruise to a secluded spot called the Ice Cave.

Rail-trails are a blessing in this area for riders who love the scenery but hate the steep climbs. The Elroy-Sparta State Trail lies at the headwaters of the Kickapoo and passes through three old railroad tunnels. The La Crosse River State Trail heads west from Sparta to the city of La Crosse. Just off the rail-trail are the Bluebird Campground Trails, where local riders go to take on the challenging climbs and descents dished out by the steep ridges.

RIDE 29 · Kickapoo Cowpath Tour (On-Road)

AT A GLANCE

Length/configuration: 24.7-mile one-way point-to-point

Aerobic difficulty: Low to moderate; while the ride is mostly flat, some grades on the southern section will get your heart rate up

Technical difficulty: Easy; the ability to handle some loose surface is all you need

Scenery: Beautiful views of valley farmland and wooded bluffs with stone outcroppings

Special comments: Soak up all the beauty the winding Kickapoo Valley offers while rolling on gentle gravel roads that parallel the river; a great ride for high-speed cruising or initiating novice mountain bikers

I don't know how it got its name, but cowpath isn't far off as a description. I mean, if the cows wanted to get from La Farge to Soldiers Grove, they wouldn't take the highway. The cowpath links mostly gravel roads that run on the opposite side of the Kickapoo from WI 131. Your reward is a major dose of the peace and quiet that makes the valley so attractive.

The 24.7-mile one-way route can be ridden as a point-to-point ride, or if you're ambitious, an out-and-back. It's a fine high-speed cruise, and none of the few grades you'll encounter will seem serious compared to the steep valley slopes around you, though there is a serious climb on Hankins Road. Along the way you'll visit the tiny towns of Viola, Readstown, and Soldiers Grove. The latter has an excellent restaurant, as well as lodging at a buffed out Victorian mansion called the Old Oak Inn.

On a much more modern note, the town has what it claims to be the world's first solar village. To deal with the frequent flooding of the Kickapoo, in 1975 businesses were offered the option of relocating to higher ground in energy-efficient solar-heated buildings. Today there is a grocery, hardware, bank, motel, and a nice little tavern/restaurant with a mirror-mural depicting the old store-fronts of the downtown.

General location: Between La Farge and Soldiers Grove, running parallel to WI 131.

Elevation change: Flat to gently rolling.

Season: April through October.

Services: There are taverns, groceries, and cafes in La Farge, Viola, Readstown, and Soldiers Grove.

Hazards: All roads are shared with motor vehicle traffic. There may be moderate traffic on WI 131 for the first couple of miles south of La Farge.

Rescue index: Help can be summoned in towns along the way.

Land status: Public roadways.

Maps: Pages 33 and 41 of the DeLorme book *Wisconsin Atlas & Gazetteer* show all local roads.

Finding the trail: Park on WI 131/82 (Main Street) in La Farge and ride east, turning south on WI 131 (Park Street). In Soldiers Grove, park at the Solar Village just east of WI 131 on US 61.

Sources of additional information:

Crawford County University of
    Wisconsin Extension (UWEX)
    Office

111 West Dunn Street
Prairie du Chien, WI 53821
(608) 326-0223 or (608) 326-0224

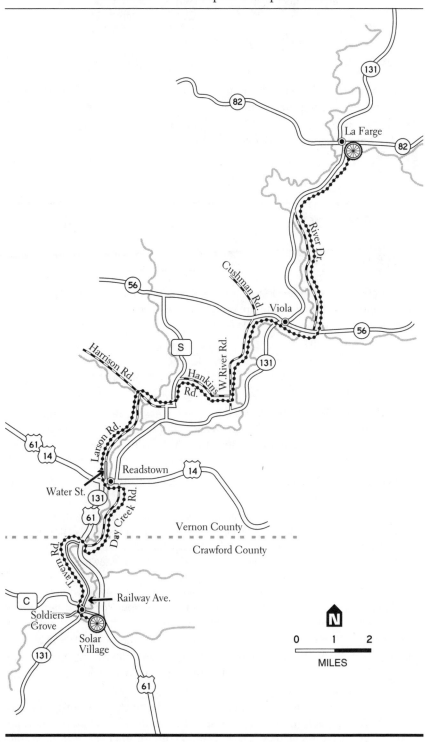

Prarie du Chien Chamber of
  Commerce
P.O. Box 326
Prarie du Chien, WI 53821-0326
(608) 326-8555; (800) 732-1673

Vernon County Viroqua Partners
220 South Main Street
Viroqua, WI 54665-1650
(608) 637-2575
www.viroqua-wisconsin.com

Notes on the trail: The route is entirely on public roads. Road signs are sometimes vandalized or may be missing. And they do not always have the same name at each end, as is the case with Dry Creek Road/Olson Road. At the Readstown end, the road is signed as Dry Creek Road; near Soldiers Grove, it is signed as Olson Road.

RIDE 30 · Kickapoo Valley Reserve Trails

AT A GLANCE

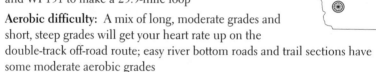

Length/configuration: 13.9 miles one way (27.8 miles out-and-back) or you can return on Hay Valley Road and WI 131 to make a 23.9-mile loop

Aerobic difficulty: A mix of long, moderate grades and short, steep grades will get your heart rate up on the double-track off-road route; easy river bottom roads and trail sections have some moderate aerobic grades

Technical difficulty: No special skills besides braking and shifting are needed. There is easy riding on roads and valley-bottom trail sections; the double-track, forested trails pose little technical challenge, except on steep grades and eroded spots.

Scenery: Breathtaking ridge and valley route, mostly in a deep hardwood forest but with periodic open fields

Special comments: A beautiful and captivating part of the world, there is a time-forgotten character to the Kickapoo Valley. The trail is evenly graded, with a standard width for off-road vehicle trails; the riding surface is grassy in the open areas and grassy to bare hard-packed forest floor elsewhere

The Kickapoo Valley Reserve, an 8,569-acre parcel of land, once slated to be flooded by a dam on the Kickapoo River, is now open for mountain biking fun. The Army Corps of Engineers transferred the land to the Wisconsin Department of Natural Resources and the Ho-Chunk Nation (the Native American tribe once known as the Winnebago). Now it is administered by a local organization, the Kickapoo Valley Reserve. Mountain biking is an integral part of the recreation picture, and no motorized uses are planned except for snowmobiles.

What this all means is a vast mountain-biking playground is waiting for you in one of the most beautiful, unspoiled parts of the state. If quiet scenic trails are what you like, Kickapoo Valley is well worth a visit. Future plans call for placing

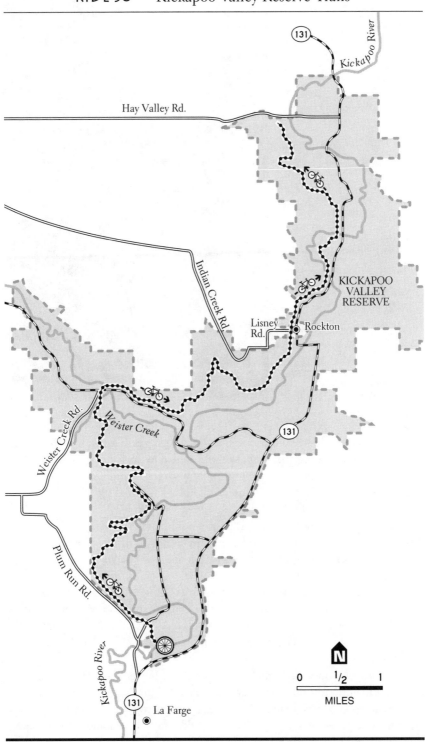

Tall corn makes a narrow passage at the north end of the trail.

bike/pedestrian bridges at old bridge sites along the river. This will create a valley bottom system of very easy trails that should appeal to novice riders and families.

The present 13.9-mile one-way route goes from the abandoned Army Corps of Engineers dam construction site, just north of La Farge, to Hay Valley Road near Wildcat Mountain State Park. This route is easy to follow and well marked with special brown and yellow signs. It is a fun double-track trail that could easily be driven by a four-wheel drive vehicle. At one point you'll ride along the edge of the Kickapoo River. Most of the ride is in a dense forest of oak, pine, and sumac, except for occasional farm fields.

Much of the trail length is shared with horses. Equestrians love this area for its challenging terrain, but the amount of use is causing severe erosion on steep sections. In their ongoing effort to deal with these effects, reserve staff seem to be fighting a losing battle. The worst horse impact occurs at stream edges and low soft spots.

Examples of erosion are found in the combined horse/bike sections, adding to the challenge. Be careful of wooden waterbars and drainage channels that cross the trail at sharp angles. Don't get me wrong, the riding is wonderful despite the erosion. Along the way I encountered sandhill cranes. It's wonderful to see these giant birds and to hear their croaking call.

General location: Between La Farge and Ontario, paralleling WI 131.

Elevation change: About 400' at the extreme, but 200' to 300' climbs are more common.

Season: May through October.

Services: La Farge has taverns, a convenience store, motel, and a cafe. The water is good to drink at the artesian well at the Weister Creek Road parking lot and there are portable toilets in the trail parking lot. There is a tavern with good food in Rockton.

Hazards: Rough surface, steep grades, and soft, mucky low spots are common. Most trails are shared with horses. These sections are often rough from the hoofs and frequently have severe erosion on steep sections. When you encounter horses, it is best to stop riding until they pass. Some riding on public roadways is necessary to connect up trail segments.

Rescue index: Help can be summoned in La Farge or Rockton.

Land status: Wisconsin Department of Natural Resources and Ho-Chunk Nation land. A special $3 daily or $10 annual trail fee is required for persons age 16 and over. The Wisconsin State Parks trail pass is not honored here. The special pass can be purchased at the Kickapoo Valley Reserve office along WI 131, on the north side of La Farge, and there are self-pay stations at the southern trailhead and at Rockton.

Maps: A good topographic map of the trails is available a the Kickapoo Valley Reserve office. The 7.5 minute series USGS quads for Dell, Ontario, La Farge, and West Lima show the terrain very well, but do not show the trails.

Finding the trail: The best spot to start is at the old damsite just north of La Farge. Take WI 131 north from town and turn left on Seeleyburg Road, then right after a half mile onto Corps Road. You'll pass an open gate and you can park anywhere along the road after it. On the left, you will see a low, modern-looking building. Ride past it, staying on the left, into a grassy field. There you will begin to see small brown and yellow signs marking the trail.

Sources of additional information:

Kickapoo Reserve Management Office
505 N. Mill Street
La Farge, WI 54639
(608) 625-2960

Vernon County Viroqua Partners
220 South Main Street
Viroqua, WI 54665-1650
(608) 637-2575
www.viroqua-wisconsin.com

Notes on the trail: A daily or annual trail fee is required (see Land Status). The following directions are for the double-track trail from Corps Road trailhead to Hay Creek Road. The trail is well marked with small brown signs with yellow bike silhouettes and arrows. The first off-road section starts at the Corps Road trailhead and goes 5.5 miles to a small parking lot and the artesian well on Weister Creek Road. From there you travel 1.2 miles on Weister Creek Road and CR P to an unnamed dirt road. There is a trail sign at this point. After 0.2 mile on the dirt road, you begin climbing on a steep eroded double-track trail.

After 2.6 miles, you arrive at Rockton. The Rockton Bar is the only services option you'll find along the route. Riding north you'll travel 1.2 miles on WI 131 before turning onto the off-road trail, which seems actually to be a 0.6-mile long remnant of the old highway. Another 0.4 miles on WI 131 takes you to the 2.2 mile Hay Valley off-road section. Keep an eye open for this one. There is a sign, but it is easy to miss. The trail begins as the highway climbs and looks like an opening into a farm field. In fact, you'll cross about a quarter mile of open field before the trail goes into the woods. There is a wonderful overview of the valley along the way. At Hay Valley Road you have the option of riding the trail back or going east on the road to WI 131 and turning south for a 10-mile ride back to the trailhead.

RIDE 31 · Brush Creek Campground Trails

AT A GLANCE

Length/configuration: 3.9-mile loop including an out-and-back stretch to Lookout Point; several other loop combinations are possible

Aerobic difficulty: Very high; you will either be climbing or descending steeply

Technical difficulty: Pretty challenging; with very steep climbs, loose surface, and occasional washouts

Scenery: Deep hardwood forest with overviews of ridge-and-valley country

Special comments: A real find for riders interested in camping or lodging mixed with some challenging riding; the owners, Bud and Sis Kalb, are super-nice people who focus on nonmotorized recreation. Trails vary from gravel roads to dirt forest floor to grassy; the confines of the area make getting lost difficult

Friends told me for years about the nice camping and fun riding at Brush Creek. My visit proved them right. I found a wonderful little bike playground in the confines of a side valley of Brush Creek. Campsites come in various forms, many up and out of the way. There is lodging now too, in the form of a beautiful new log cabin with a terrific view of the valley. Brush Creek is a great place to base your exploration of Kickapoo Country.

The four-mile loop shown here is a mix of gravel road and double-track trails that can be recombined to produce many variations. The one common factor is that the trails are always up or down, except for on the out-and-back run to Lookout Point and in the campsite area. Lots of hard riding in a small area, but your tent or cabin will be nearby, and there's even a swimming hole for a cool dip after your ride.

RIDE 31 • Brush Creek Campground Trails

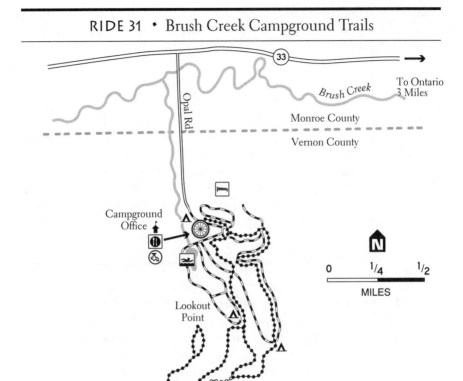

General location: 3 miles west of Ontario.

Elevation change: 250' maximum elevation difference from the lowest to highest spots. Any trail will include steady, steep climbs of 200'.

Season: May through September.

Services: Camping, lodging, laundry, hot showers, flush toilets, recreation room, snacks, groceries, and swimming are available on the property. Pit toilets are located in the campgrounds.

Hazards: Loose surface on steep slopes, windfall branches, and washouts may be encountered. Trails are open to hikers.

Rescue index: Help is available at the campground office.

Land status: Private campground.

Maps: The campground map available at the office is useful for navigating. The 7.5 minute series USGS quad for Dell shows the terrain very well, but does not show the trails.

Finding the trail: Travel west on WI 33 from the village of Ontario for 3 miles, and turn south on Opal Road to Brush Creek Campground. Ride east from the office on the steep road to the I 90-94 campsite.

Sources of additional information:

Brush Creek Campground
Route One, Box 26
Ontario, WI 54651-9708
(608) 337-4344

Vernon County Viroqua Partners
220 South Main Street
Viroqua, WI 54665-1650
(608) 637-2575
www.viroqua-wisconsin.com

Notes on the trail: Trail riding is free for campers and lodgers. Check trail conditions at the office before riding. Navigating the trails is best done with a campground map showing the site numbers. Though there is no special signing at present, the confines are small, making getting seriously lost impossible. From the office, ride east on the gravel road, make an immediate right, then left onto a gravel road that rises steeply to site I 90-94. Just after the site, make a sharp right turn off the road onto a double-track trail and continue climbing. After switchbacking and passing a barricade, the trail becomes a gravel road through the Creek Sites campground. At site number 33 head down the double-track trail into the woods. You'll soon have the option of going sharply right and descending to the valley bottom or, as the map shows, going straight, descending, and climbing to join the out-and-back trail to Lookout Point. On the way you'll pass a trail coming in from the right that you will take on your return trip back down into the valley. This trail meets the Hidden Valley sites at numbers 9 and 11. Cross the gravel road and climb sharply on the grassy double-track trail. Make an immediate left at a **T** intersection to return to the office via a steep switchback descent.

RIDE 32 · Ice Cave Tour (On-Road)

AT A GLANCE

Length/configuration: 23-mile loop; if you base your ride out of Brush Creek Campground or Wildcat Mountain State Park add 2.4 miles

Aerobic difficulty: High; 4 long climbs (5 if you use Wildcat Mountain State Park as a base) will get your heart rate up

Technical difficulty: Easy; route is on paved roads except for one flat gravel stretch

Scenery: Lots of the gorgeous ridge-and-valley views that make Kickapoo Country famous

Special comments: A fine high-speed cruise or leisurely tour with enough climbing to give anyone a workout; entirely on-road, almost all of the route is paved except for a stretch on County Road F

RIDE 32 • Ice Cave Tour

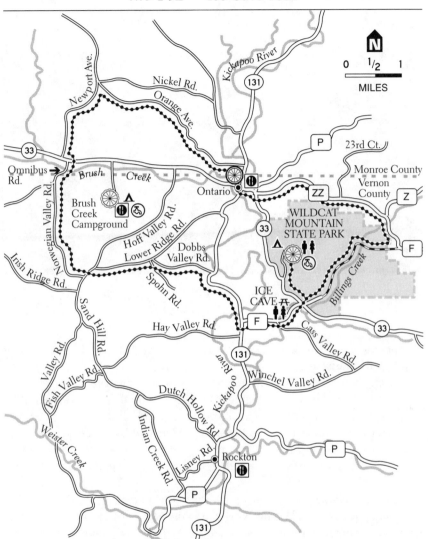

Want to take a ride back into a quieter, more peaceful time? Well, this is it. The Amish, a religious sect that rejects the use of modern machinery, have come to the area over the past few decades to get away from high land prices in the eastern United States. You'll see them plowing the land with work horses or traveling the backroads in plain black buggies drawn by their prize trotters.

The "plain people," as they are called, seem straight out of nineteenth century agrarian America. Their look is simple: bonnets for the women, straw hats and beards for the men (if a man doesn't have a beard, it means he's single). You can

The Amish farmers gather their corn in shocks.

take photos of their farms, buggies, animals, and of the Amish themselves, as long as you don't photograph their faces—this smacks of vanity to them.

Check out the Ice Cave, a short walk from a gravel side road. This lovely little rock overhang will have ice hanging from it, even into the early summer. It's a nice spot to take a break and decide if you want to add a fifth climb to your ride, by making a side trip up to Wildcat Mountain State Park. If you do, keep in mind that the grade as you turn into the park is about as steep as anything you'll find off-road. The view in the park is worth it, by the way (note that mountain biking is not allowed on park trails).

If that isn't enough to lure you onto this 23-mile on-road route, let me say that you should do more road riding. A big part of the success of Euro mountain bike racers in recent years has been on-road miles. You need to get out there and spin to build endurance and make those muscles supple.

Get the new tires with no knobs in the center, like the ones by Ritchy or Corratec. They can be pumped up to 80 pounds pressure and roll great on the pavement or hardpack. Their only downside is in real mud, and you should stay off the trails when they're that bad anyway. Add bar-end extensions to get a low aerodynamic riding position and you're ready to enjoy the fun and benefits of on-road riding. What better place to start than Kickapoo Country?

For off-roading in the area, try Brushwood Creek Campground (see Ride 31, page 108) or the Kickapoo Valley Reserve Trails (see Ride 30, page 104), which can be accessed from this route on CR F or via town roads south of the route.

General location: West, south, and east of the village of Ontario.

Elevation change: There are 4 significant climbs, 5 if you take a side trip to Wildcat Mountain State Park. Northwest of Ontario on Orange Avenue there is a gradual 370' climb. South of WI 33 on Norwegian Valley Road there is a moderate-to-steep 250' climb. Riding south on WI 131, you'll encounter a steep 150' climb. Going west on County Road ZZ there is a moderate-to-steep 370' climb. If you ride to Wildcat Mountain State Park, the 400' climb is steep to very steep.

Season: April through October.

Services: Ontario offers a cafe, convenience store, grocery, and taverns. Camping, lodging, laundry, hot showers, flush toilets, a recreation room, snacks, groceries, and swimming are available at Brush Creek Campground. There's camping, water, flush toilets, and showers at Wildcat Mountain State Park. There are pit toilets at the Ice Cave picnic area.

Hazards: All roads are shared with motor vehicle traffic. Expect light traffic on all roads.

Rescue index: Help is available in Ontario or at Wildcat Mountain State Park.

Land status: Public roadways.

Maps: All roads are shown on page 41 of DeLorme's *Wisconsin Atlas & Gazetteer*. The 7.5 minute series USGS quads for Dell and Ontario show the terrain and roads in high detail.

Finding the trail: Park on WI 131 (Broad Street) in Ontario, or base your ride at Wildcat Mountain State Park, off of WI 33 south of Ontario, or Brush Creek Campground, off of WI 33 west of Ontario.

Sources of additional information:

Vernon County Viroqua Partners
220 South Main Street
Viroqua, WI 54665-1650
(608) 637-2575
www.viroqua-wisconsin.com

Notes on the trail: Obey all general traffic regulations and those that apply specifically to bicycling. In Wisconsin, you may ride two abreast as long as you do not impede traffic, so fall to single file as vehicles approach. Roads are paved with the exception of a two-and-a-half mile section of CR F. The route can be ridden in either direction.

RIDE 33 · Elroy-Sparta State Trail (Rail-Trail, On-Road)

AT A GLANCE

Length/configuration: 34 miles one-way between Elroy Commons and the Sparta Depot

Aerobic difficulty: Low, if only the rail-trail is ridden; high, if the on-road loop is added

Technical difficulty: Easy on the rail-trail and paved roads; Gravel Summit Road is very steep and requires climbing skill and descending confidence

Scenery: Beautiful ridge and valley scenery plus 3 railroad tunnels

Special comments: A family riding experience that's hard to match; kids — adults too — will find walking through the tunnels (riding isn't allowed) a real adventure; the crushed-limestone rail-trail is punctuated with pleasant towns

Don't miss this trail. The Elroy-Sparta is the nation's original rail-trail. The state purchased the abandoned rail bed and surfaced it for bike travel in the early 1970s when they perceived a burgeoning interest in bicycling. The trail was an immediate hit. Big factors in its popularity were the traffic-free riding environment, the spirit-lifting scenery, the adventure of traveling through the three tunnels (the longest is over three-quarters of a mile), and the string of pleasant small towns en route .

The 34-mile one-way crushed-limestone trail isn't exactly dead flat either. The grade isn't steep, but you'll go up 150 feet between Norwalk and Tunnel 3. You'll really feel it heading away from the tunnel. For a real workout you can take a side trip just before the tunnel and climb another 190 feet on a steep gravel road, and then rejoin the trail by taking paved roads toward Sparta or looping back to Norwalk. Either way, you'll be surmounting the ridge Tunnel 3 goes through. As you grind up the slope imagine how hard it would be to get a train over this incline.

The trail is one of the most popular in the state. It's sure to be busy on nice summer weekends. The mix of riders of all types is a sign that you've come to the right place to celebrate the joys of bicycling.

General location: Between Sparta and Elroy, paralleling WI 71.

Elevation change: The rail-trail is basically flat, but there is a 150' very gradual climb to Tunnel 3. If you opt to try the on-road loop, you will climb 190' in just 0.8 mile.

Season: May through October.

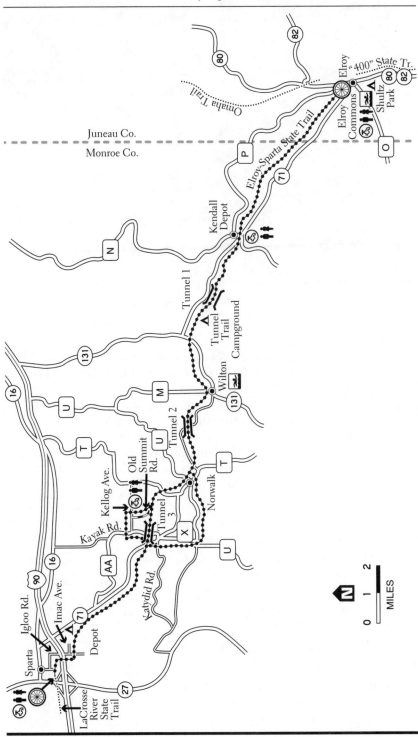

There are plenty of cool, shady spots on the Elroy-Sparta Trail.

Services: All services are available in Sparta, Wilton, Kendall, and Elroy. Bicycle retail and repair are available in Sparta at Speed's Bicycle Sales and Service and in Elroy at Tom's Bicycle Shop. Norwalk has a nice cafe right on the trail, a grocery, and taverns. Public campgrounds are near Sparta and at Wilton, Kendall, and Elroy. The private Tunnel Trail Campground between Wilton and Kendall has showers and swimming. There are swimming pools in Sparta, Wilton, and Elroy. Playgrounds are at Norwalk, Wilton, and Elroy. Water and flush toilets are at the Sparta and Kendall depots, Wilton Town Park, and at Elroy Commons.Water and pit toilets are at the east end of Tunnel 3.

Hazards: Road crossings and inexperienced riders. A short on-road section must be ridden to connect into Sparta. The optional loop route is on public roads shared with motor vehicles. The trail is also used by hikers.

Rescue index: Help is available in towns along the way.

Land status: Wisconsin State Park Trail. A trail pass fee is required for bicyclists age 16 and older ($3 daily /$10 annual). The trail pass also covers usages such as cross-country skiing, horseback riding, and bicycling on state mountain bike trails and other rail-trails.

Maps: Trail maps are available from local businesses, information contacts, or the Wisconsin Department of Natural Resources.

Finding the trail: For the east end, park at Elroy Commons, located at Main and Franklin Streets in Elroy. For the west end, park at the Sparta Depot at 111 Milwaukee Street and South Water Street in Sparta.

Sources of additional information:

Elroy-Sparta State Park Trail
  Headquarters
Kendall Depot
P.O. Box 297
Kendall, WI 54638
(608) 463-7109

Elroy Commons Bike Trails and
  Tourist Information
303 Railroad Street
Elroy, WI 53929
(608) 462-BIKE

Sparta Area Chamber of Commerce
111 Milwaukee Street
Sparta, WI 54656-2576
(608) 269-4123
www.spartachamber.org

Sparta Area Convention and Visitors
  Bureau
123 North Water Street
Sparta, WI 54565
(800) 354-BIKE

Notes on the trail: A trail pass fee is required for bicyclists age 16 and older (see Land status). You must walk through the tunnels. Bike lights and a windbreaker are recommended.

To take the on-road side trip, leave the trail at Summit Station (where the water pump and tunnel tender's shack are near the east end of Tunnel 3), by riding up on the berm on the north side of the trail and following it a short distance to the west. You will see a deep, stone channel called a flume alongside the berm. Cross the flume on the wooden foot bridge and turn west. You are on Old Summit Road (gravel), which will take you up to St. John's Church on the ridge top. At the church, turn west onto Kellogg Avenue. When you reach the **T** intersection with Kayak Road 0.9 mile later, you have the option of turning right to follow roads to the west and rejoin the trail toward Sparta, or left to follow roads to Norwalk.

RIDE 34 · La Crosse River State Trail (Rail-Trail)

AT A GLANCE

Length/configuration: 21 miles one way between the Sparta Depot and the trailhead parking lot at Medary

Aerobic difficulty: Low; typical flat rail-trail

Technical difficulty: Easy

Scenery: A broad, farmed valley with high bluffs in the distance; the adjacent active rail line makes watching the trains and waving at the engineers frequent fun. Prarie remnants and wetlands are found along the trail

Special comments: A nice family ride with pleasant small towns and parks en route; the crushed-limestone surface is well packed for a smooth roll

The La Crosse River State Trail forms a link in a nearly continuous system of motor vehicle–free state rail-trails, stretching over 100 miles from the Mississippi River to Reedsburg in the south-central part of the state. A brand-new trail bridge at Medary overpasses an active rail line for an easy connection to the Great River State Trail (see Ride 39, page 132). You can connect to the famous Elroy-Sparta State Trail (see Ride 33, page 114) through Sparta.

Between the town of Sparta and Medary, on the outskirts of the city of La Crosse, the 21-mile, crushed-limestone rail-trail passes through three pleasant little towns on the way to Sparta. The Village Park in Bangor has a nice playground. The busy Soo Line railroad makes train watching part of the fun of riding the trail. A spur trail links the ride to Veteran's Memorial County Park, 2 miles west of West Salem. Camping is available at the park.

In Sparta you can visit the Monroe County Museum where unique historic bicycles are displayed, including the mountain bike that local bicycling legend Olga McNulty used to win the women's division of the famous Idita bike race in Alaska. For your own mountain bike challenge, check out the trails at Bluebird Campground (see Ride 35, page 120) near the Medary trailhead.

General location: Between La Crosse and Sparta, paralleling I-90.

Elevation change: None, typical flat rail-trail.

Season: May through October.

Services: All services are available in La Crosse and Sparta. Bicycle retail and repair are available in La Crosse at Bikes Limited and in Sparta at Speed's Bicycle Sales and Service. Cafes, groceries, and taverns are in West Salem and Bangor. There is a grocery in Rockland. Bangor has a village park, accessible via a short spur trail, with flush toilets, water, and a playground. There are flush toilets and water at the Medary trailhead parking lot, Veterans Park between Medary and West Salem and at the Sparta Depot. Camping is available at Veterans Park between Medary and West Salem and at a private campground on Neshonoc Lake near West Salem.

Hazards: Road crossings and inexperienced riders. A short on-road section must be ridden from the east side of Sparta if you wish to connect with the Elroy-Sparta State Trail (see Ride 33, page 114). The trail is also used by hikers.

Rescue index: Help is available in towns along the way.

Land status: Wisconsin State Park Trail. A trail pass fee is required for bicyclists age 16 and older ($3 daily /$10 annual). The trail pass also covers usages such as cross-country skiing, horseback riding, and bicycling on state mountain bike trails and other rail-trails.

Maps: Trail maps are available from local businesses, information contacts, or the Wisconsin Department of Natural Resources.

Finding the trail: On the trail's east end, park at the Sparta Depot at 111 Milwaukee Street and South Water Street. On the west end, park in Medary at the trail parking lot located 0.5 mile east of the WI 16/County Road B intersection.

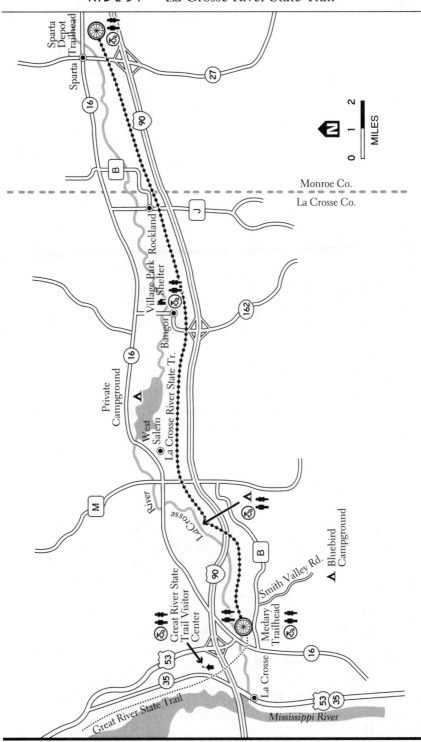

Sources of additional information:

La Crosse Area Convention and
   Visitors Bureau
410 East Veterans Memorial Drive
La Crosse, WI 54601-4990
(608) 782-2366; (800) 658-9424
www.explorelacrosse.com

La Crosse River State Trail
P.O. Box 99

Ontario, WI 54651
(608) 337-4775

La Crosse River Trail headquarters
123 North Water Street
Sparta, WI 54656
(800) 354-BIKE
www.lacrosserivertrail.org

Notes on the trail: A trail pass fee is required for bicyclists age 16 and older (see
Land status).

RIDE 35 · Bluebird Campground Trails

AT A GLANCE

Length/configuration: 8-mile loop (can be divided
into 3 roughly equal loop segments)

Aerobic difficulty: High; long, steep climbs in every
direction

Technical difficulty: Challenging; steep slopes test
climbing skills and descending confidence, while single-track sections mix
rocks, roots, steep slopes, and narrow passage

Scenery: Hardwood and pine forest trails with superb ridge and valley
views

Special comments: This is the place La Crosse–area riders go for a real
off-road workout

Mountain bike races have been held at Bluebird Campground since the
early 1980s. Its gut-busting four-hundred-foot climb separates the super fit
from the rest of us. Each May it is the site of the Crusty Bluff Hunker Down, a
prominent race venue on the Wisconsin Off-Road Series (WORS) calendar.

The eight miles of trails include several monster climbs and numerous lesser,
but no-nicer ones. New single-track trail on the northeast side of the campground road will test any rider's mettle. The switchback descent is as tough as off-
roading gets in the Midwest.

One of the nice aspects at Bluebird—besides being able to take a swim and get
a beer when you're done—is that three roughly equal-distance trails run up side
valleys and come back to the campground area, so you can mix and match rides to
suit your taste. In addition to the single-track, a tough double-track loops off to the
southwest, and an easier, but not easy, double-track goes to the southeast.

RIDE 35 • Bluebird Campground Trails

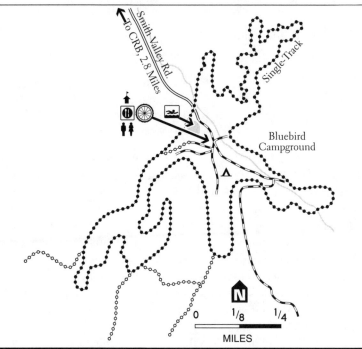

For a rail-trail riding experience to spin the kinks out of your quads, head for the nearby La Crosse River or Great River state trails (see Ride 34, page 117, and Ride 39, page 132).

General location: 5 miles east of La Crosse.

Elevation change: 400' from the low to high point. Climbs take in all of this on the southwest double-track and northeast single-track.

Season: May through September.

Services: All services, including bicycle retail and repair (at Bikes Limited), are available in La Crosse. Camping, swimming, water, showers, snacks, groceries, and a recreational room are available on the grounds.

Hazards: Trails are not always well cleared of windfall trees and branches. Trails are shared with hikers.

Rescue index: Help is available at the campground office.

Land status: Private campground. A $1 fee is charged to ride the trails or swim.

Maps: The 7.5 minute series USGS quads for La Crosse shows the terrain, roads, and some of the trails in high detail.

Finding the trail: From WI 16 south of I-90, turn east on County Road B. Go 1.2 miles, then turn south on Smith Valley Road and go 2.8 miles to the campground.

Sources of additional information:

Bluebird Campground
N2833 Smith Valley Road
La Crosse, WI 54601
(608) 781-2267

La Crosse Area Convention and
 Visitors Bureau
410 East Veterans Memorial Drive
La Crosse, WI 54601-4990
(608) 782-2366; (800) 658-9424
www.explorelacrosse.com

Notes on the trail: A daily trail fee is required to ride at Bluebird Campground (see Land status). The double-track and single-track trails can be ridden in either direction, but these cues are for riding clockwise. There is little or no signage on the trails, but it's hard to get lost since they remain within the confines of the valley and side valleys. Also, the trails get enough usage so that there is always a worn-in hardpack track on the correct trails. From the campground office, cross the little bridge over the small creek toward the open field to the northeast. Immediately turn right heading southeast on the double-track access road. This will lead you to a double-track trail into the woods. There is a shortcut option to the right on a flood control dike that takes you to the return leg of the trail. As you near the campground, make a sharp left turn to head out on the southwest double-track loop. As you return to the valley again, cross the road to head northeast onto the single-track loop.

GREAT RIVER

It really is a great river, you know. The Mississippi is North America's longest. Long before European explorers plied its 2,470-mile length, it was the river highway of Native Americans who spread sophisticated trading cultures along its shores. Today the bounty of the nation's prairie farms goes downstream and the Midwest's energy needs go upstream in huge barges pushed by mighty-mite tugboats. As many as forty trains, each pulling more than a hundred cars, blast daily along railroads on the Wisconsin shore. In contrast, most of the river's quiet, lush, and green backwaters are protected as wildlife refuges, and they are teeming with all types of wonderful birds.

All of this makes for great scenery. The valley and side valleys of the river make for great riding. The Wyalusing Tour is a moderate gravel-road route that visits sleepy river towns, follows scenic side valleys, and skirts the very edge of the Mississippi River. In the state park of the same name, easy and moderate off-road trails will lead you to fantastic views five hundred feet above the river.

Further north you can tackle an on-road ride with a monster climb through the area where Sauk warrior Black Hawk made his last stand. Things get much more challenging, but no less scenic, on the tough off-road ride at Perrot State Park, where a ski trail system takes riders up long, steep climbs to grand overviews of the Mississippi. Nearby, the Great River State Trail gives riders a chance to enjoy the river valley on an easy, rolling rail-trail.

On the moderately difficult Maiden Rock Tour, a network of paved and gravel roads lead riders through picturesque side valleys and along the towering limestone palisades that line the shore of scenic Lake Pepin, a lake within the course of the Mississippi.

In all, you'll get a big dose of the best riding the Mississippi has to offer, a shot that will make you return for more.

RIDE 36 · Wyalusing Tour (On-Road)

AT A GLANCE

Length/configuration: 23.4-mile loop with an out-and-back handle

Aerobic difficulty: Moderate; one long, gradual climb

Technical difficulty: Easy; loose surface possible on gravel roads

Scenery: Fantastic view of the Mississippi on Dugway Road, with intriguing runs up side valleys on this paved- and gravel-road route

Special comments: A fine, leisurely tour or high-speed cruise that showcases some of the best scenery the Mississippi River and its tributary valleys offer

Anyone with a sense of adventure and the ability to make it up one moderate 450-foot climb can take on this easy 24.5-mile tour. A combination of well-maintained, hardpack gravel roads and paved roads will take you through narrow, winding hollows and sleepy Mississippi River settlements. There is a total of 6 miles of pavement, 3 miles of which you cover twice.

Your refreshment options en route have a bucolic air. In the village of Bagley are the Bagley Bottoms Inn, Hotel Bagley Dining Room, Oswald's Tavern ("1912" it says on the store front), and Grampa's General Store. Don't count on modern financial services at the Prairie City Bank; it's been closed for years. Riding the northern loop will take you 450 feet up Ready Hollow to the open farmland up on Military Ridge, and to the Dew Drop Inn at the junction of County Road X and County Road C.

The out-and-back route south of Bagley leads along a narrow track called Dugway Road, which clings so closely to the towering limestone river bluffs that at one point it actually passes under the rock. The road will take you above the lush green backwater that is part of the Upper Mississippi National Wildlife and Fish Refuge, and the home of graceful white egrets and great blue herons. The Burlington Northern, one of the nation's busiest railroads, runs as many as forty freight trains a day along the shore. At the village of Glen Haven, the river channel runs smack up against the Wisconsin shore.

For a varied-terrain off-road ride in the area, check out the trails at nearby Wyalusing State Park (see Ride 37, page 127).

General location: 17 miles south of the town of Prairie du Chien.

Elevation change: Generally flat to gently rolling with one moderate 450' climb and descent.

Season: Roads are likely to be clear of snow and ice from March through November. Cold temperatures are likely at the extremes of this season, while heat and humidity can be oppressive in July and August.

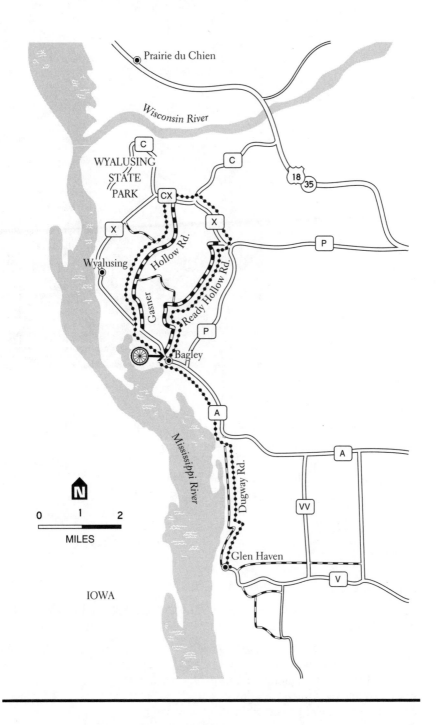

Prairie du Chien

Wisconsin River

C

C

18 35

WYALUSING
STATE
PARK

CX

X

X

P

Wyalusing

Hollow Rd.

Casner

Ready Hollow Rd.

P

Bagley

A

A

Dugway Rd.

VV

N

0   1   2
MILES

Mississippi River

Glen Haven

V

IOWA

Wonderful river views
are part of the appeal
at Wyalusing.

Services: All services, except bicycle, are available in the village of Bagley. There are several taverns in the village of Glen Haven and a tavern/restaurant at the junction of CR X and CR C. In Prairie du Chien there are many dining and lodging choices, as well as bicycle repair by arrangement at (608) 326-8787.

Hazards: All roads are open to two-way motor vehicle traffic. Gravel roads are periodically maintained with fresh coverings of loose gravel. Rattlesnakes are common in rocky crevasses.

Rescue index: Help is available in Bagley, Glen Haven, and Wyalusing State Park.

Land status: Public roadways through private land.

Maps: The DeLorme book, *Wisconsin Atlas & Gazetteer*, shows all roads and road names on page 24.

Finding the trail: From the junction of US 18/WI 35 and CR C, on the south side of the Wisconsin River, turn west on CR C. After 3 miles, turn right on CR CX at a **T** intersection (across from the Dew Drop Inn). After one mile CR C splits off to the right toward Wyalusing State Park. At this point follow CR X for 6 miles to the village of Bagley, and park on any street.

Sources of additional information:

Prarie du Chien Chamber of
   Commerce
P.O. Box 326

Prarie du Chien, WI 53821-0326
(608) 326-8555; (800) 732-1673

Notes on the trail: The route is well signed with standard county road signs and street-type town road signs. The northern loop can be ridden in either direction, but the following cues are for riding counterclockwise. From the village of Bagley, ride northwest on County Road X a half-mile and turn right on Ready Hollow Road (gravel), which heads northeast into the first side valley off the Mississippi north of Bagley. At a **T** intersection with a paved road (CR X), turn left. At the junction with CR C, at the Dew Drop Inn, proceed straight on CR CX. After one-half mile, take the first left onto Gasner Hollow Road (gravel). At a **T** intersection with a paved road (CR X), turn left and follow it back to Bagley. To ride the southern route, continue southwest through Bagley where CR X becomes CR A. After about 3 miles turn right onto Dugway Road (gravel) just before CR A begins to climb steeply and follow it to the village of Glen Haven. If you begin to climb on CR A, you have missed Dugway Road. Return from Glen Haven by the same route.

RIDE 37 · Wyalusing State Park Trails

AT A GLANCE

Length/configuration: 10.2 miles total for a complete run on this out-and-back/loop/out-and-back combination

Aerobic difficulty: Low to moderate; the Mississippi Ridge, Whitetail Meadow, and the portion of the Walnut Springs Connector leading to the park office are low; the Turkey Hollow Trail is moderate

Technical difficulty: Easy to moderate; the Turkey Hollow Trail provides some challenge with moderately steep climbs and descents; there are some roots and a sharp drop-off into a little ravine on the Mississippi Ridge Trail

Scenery: Grand views along the course of the Mississippi at the southernmost point on the Mississippi Ridge Trail and northeast of the park office, where you can see the confluence of the Wisconsin and Mississippi Rivers

Special comments: A park not to be missed, for its natural beauty alone; trails are easy to follow, generally grassy or hardpack, and segmented into 4 sections, so riders from novice to expert can make a variety of combinations

Wyalusing State Park overlooks the confluence of the Wisconsin and Mississippi Rivers. Numerous Indian mounds testify to the timeless attraction of this spot. The mountain biking trails generally roll around on the bluff top. To my

RIDE 37 · Wyalusing State Park Trails

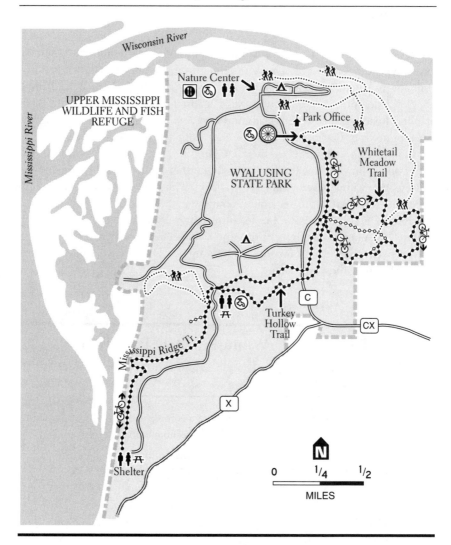

mind, this is unfortunate, since the park has five hundred feet of scenic, challenging terrain and a great many miles of seldom-used trails. For instance, combining the Walnut Springs and Old Wagon Road trails would create a three-mile loop all the way down to the Wisconsin River bottom and back—one tough trip. Mention your interest in some tougher routes at the park office.

The 10.2-miles of double-track shown here mix four types of trails. The short out-and-back section of the Walnut Springs Trail where riding is allowed runs from the park office to the parking lot for the Whitetail Meadow Trail. It rolls gently and usually has a hardpack track on its otherwise grassy surface. The Whitetail Meadow Trail is probably the least interesting, as it circuits the edge of a field and its mown grassy surface is rough. The Turkey Hollow Trail loop presents a bit of interesting terrain, and garners a moderate difficulty rating, as it dives down into a little hollow. The Mississippi Ridge Trail is rather flat, but goes through a lovely hardwood forest and leads to a wonderful overview of the great river.

General location: 11 miles south of the town of Prairie du Chien.

Elevation change: 120' on the Turkey Hollow Trail; maximum changes on the Whitetail Meadow and Mississippi Ridge trails are 30' to 40'. To take advantage of the full 500' of elevation in the park, ride on-road down to the boat landing and back.

Season: May through October.

Services: All services are available in Prairie du Chien. Camping, flush toilets, showers, and a concession stand with snacks are located in the park.

Hazards: Watch for windfall branches. On the Mississippi Ridge Trail a sharp drop into a small ravine may surprise you on this otherwise flat trail.

Rescue index: Help is available at the park office or from the park patrol.

Land status: Wisconsin State Park. A daily or annual vehicle sticker ($5 daily/$18 annual for Wisconsin residents, $7 daily/$25 annual for out-of-state residents) is required to park in state forest lots.

Maps: A trail map is available at the park office or from the Wisconsin Department of Natural Resources. The USGS 7.5 minute Clayton Iowa-Wisconsin and Bagley Wisconsin-Iowa quadrangle maps give excellent information on the terrain, but show few mountain bike trails.

Finding the trail: From the junction of US 18/WI 35 and County Road C, on the south side of the Wisconsin River, turn west on CR C. After 3 miles turn right on County Road CX at a T intersection (across from the Dew Drop Inn). After 1 mile, CR C splits off to the right toward Wyalusing State Park. This becomes the park road and will lead to the park office and the start of the ride.

Sources of additional information:

Wisconsin Department of Natural Resources
Bureau of Parks and Recreation
P.O. Box 7921
Madison, WI 53707-7921
(608) 266-2621
www.dnr.state.wi.us

Wyalusing State Park
13081 State Park Lane
Bagley, WI 53801
(608) 996-2261; (888) 947-2757

Notes on the trail: A daily or annual vehicle sticker is required (see Land status). The double-track trails are well signed for two-way travel with green-and-white mountain bike silhouette signs, except for the Whitetail Meadow Trail, which is one-way in a clockwise direction. At the west end of the Turkey Hollow Trail, it's necessary to turn south out of the parking lot and travel the paved road for one third of a mile to meet the Mississippi Ridge Trail.

RIDE 38 · Black Hawk's Stand Tour (On-Road)

AT A GLANCE

Length/configuration: 35-mile or 17-mile loops

Aerobic difficulty: High due to one long, steep climb on either loop

Technical difficulty: Easy; entirely on paved or gravel roads

Scenery: Wonderful views of the Mississippi River and its side valleys and ridge tops

Special comments: A great on-road tour for high-speed or leisurely cruising; one monster climb will keep things from getting too leisurely, but all riders can take on this ride if they have the will for the hill

The spectacular stretch of the Mississippi between La Crosse and Prairie du Chien offers fantastic scenery but few off-road riding opportunities. This paved and gravel on-road tour makes a terrific break during a drive along the Mississippi and takes in some of the fascinating history of the valley.

Black Hawk had two strikes against him. First, he was proud; second, he'd never been taken to Washington. It was the government's practice with influential warriors to take them east and show them the power of the United States. Instead, Black Hawk remembered the traditions of his Sauk nation, how they had stopped the French from destroying their Fox (Mesquakie) brothers and taught the British a lesson during Pontiac's Rebellion. He knew that the Americans had taken their lands by trickery.

In 1832, after a prophet told Black Hawk the British in Canada would aid his people in pushing back the Americans, he and 2,000 followers crossed the Mississippi to ancestral lands in central Illinois. As they advanced they found the prophecy had been false, but the forces that would ultimately destroy them were already in action. What followed was a retreat punctuated by futile attempts to surrender, culminating here, as his people were massacred trying to get back across the Mississippi. Sixty-five-year-old Black Hawk was captured and paraded through eastern cities, including Washington. Seven historical markers on this route tell the story of the leader's last days.

Riding the 35- or 17-mile, aerobically challenging on-road route is a good way to reflect on these events. You'll face your own trial in the form of a steep 500-foot climb from the river bottom to the bluff top.

General location: 18 miles south of La Crosse.

Elevation change: 500' from the valley bottoms to the ridge top.

Season: Any time the roads are free from snow and ice. May through October will be best.

RIDE 38 • Black Hawk's Stand Tour

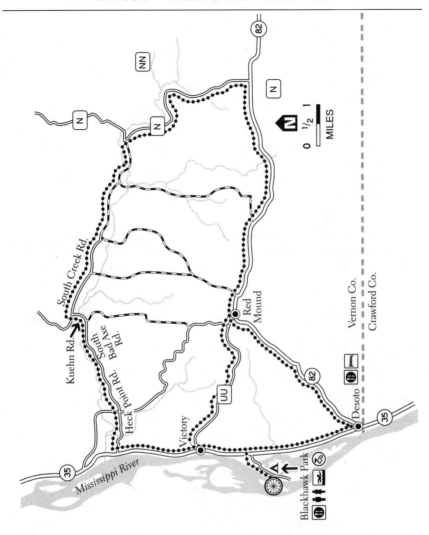

Services: Desoto has a cafe, grocery, motel, and taverns. There is a tavern in Victory and a country store at Red Mound. Camping, swimming, flush toilets, showers, and a concession stand are at Blackhawk Park.

Hazards: The entire route is on public roadways shared with motor vehicles. The rail line between Blackhawk Park and WI 35 is very busy.

Rescue index: Help is available at the park and towns en route.

Land status: Public roadways.

Maps: The DeLorme book, *Wisconsin Atlas & Gazetteer*, shows all local roads on pages 32 and 40.

Finding the trail: Turn west off WI 35 into Blackhawk Park and park in the swimming beach lot.

Sources of additional information:

U.S. Army Corps of Engineers
Blackhawk Park
Route 1
Desoto, WI 54624
(608) 648-3314

Vernon County Viroqua Partners
220 South Main Street
Viroqua, WI 54665-1650
(608) 637-2575
www.viroqua-wisconsin.com

Notes on the trail: Roads are well signed and easy to follow except for the eastern part of gravel South Creek Road. Just make sure to stay in the main valley. The route can be ridden in either direction. Traffic is light on all roads except for WI 35, which has a paved shoulder.

RIDE 39 · Great River State Trail (Rail-Trail)

AT A GLANCE

Length/configuration: 24 miles one way, from the La Crosse River State Trail parking lot in Medary to the Great River State Trail parking lot at Marshland

Aerobic difficulty: Low; typical flat rail-trail

Technical difficulty: Easy

Scenery: Woods and marshland of the Mississippi River flood plain

Special comments: Many crossings of backwater streams provide great opportunities to spot wildlife; the crushed-limestone trail passes by Perrot State Park and through the attractive towns of Trempealeau and Onalaska

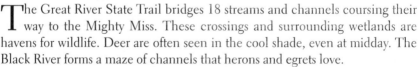

The Great River State Trail bridges 18 streams and channels coursing their way to the Mighty Miss. These crossings and surrounding wetlands are havens for wildlife. Deer are often seen in the cool shade, even at midday. The Black River forms a maze of channels that herons and egrets love.

In the sleepy river town of Trempealeau you can watch tugboats finesse 400-foot-long barges through the Army Corps of Engineers locks. Nearby, Perrot State Park is a scenic wonder. In ancient times, its soaring bluffs were isolated from those on the western shore when torrents of glacial meltwater changed the river's course. It became a natural landmark for people from the sophisticated Native American Hopewell culture of 2,000 years ago, and to the French explorer Nicholas Perrot in 1685. See Ride 40, page 135, for a varied-terrain ride in the park.

RIDE 39 • Great River State Trail

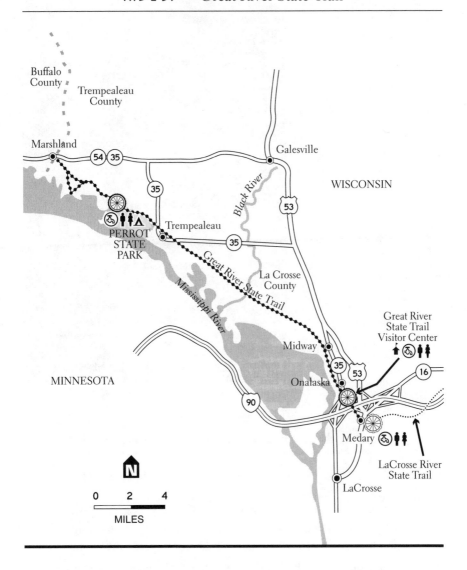

General location: Between Onalaska and Marshland, paralleling WI 35.

Elevation change: None; dead-flat rail-trail.

Season: May through October.

Services: All services, including bicycle retail and repair, are available in Onalaska and La Crosse. There are cafes and motels in Trempealeau. There is a tavern in Midway. Camping, flush toilets, and showers are available in Perrot State Park.

The Great River Trail
crosses a labyrinth
of streams.

Hazards: Don't let the infrequency of road crossings make you careless. The trail is also used by hikers.

Rescue index: Help is available in town, along the trail, and at Perrot State Park.

Land status: Wisconsin State Park Trail; public roadways. A trail pass fee is required for the Great River State Trail for bicyclists age 16 and older ($3 daily/$10 annual). The trail pass also covers usages such as cross-country skiing, horseback riding, and bicycling on state mountain bike trails and other rail-trails.

Maps: A trail map is available at Perrot State Park, at the Visitor Center in Onalaska, or from information contacts.

Finding the trail: The southeastern trailhead is at the junction with the La Crosse River State Trail in Medary, at the trail parking lot 0.5 mile east of the WI 16/CR B intersection. An alternative trailhead in Onalaska is near the Great River and the Onalaska Center for Commerce and Tourism, where trail passes can be purchased (address below). You can locate the trail in Trempealeau, at the WI 35 trail crossing. If you wish to start at the northwesternmost point, look for the Wildlife Refuge road just east of the railroad tracks along WI 35 near Marshland.

Sources of additional information:

Onalaska Center for Commerce and
  Tourism
800 Oak Forest Drive
Onalaska, WI 54650
(608) 781-9570; (800) 873-1901

Trempealeau Chamber of
  Commerce
P.O. Box 212
Trempealeau, WI 54661-0212
(608) 534-6780

Notes on the trail: A trail pass fee is required (see Land status).

RIDE 40 · Perrot State Park Trails

AT A GLANCE

Length/configuration: 5.1- or 2-mile loops with pan-handles

Aerobic difficulty: High for the long loop; moderate for the short loop

Technical difficulty: Challenging for the long loop; steep slopes will test climbing skills and descending confidence; easy for the short loop

Scenery: Wonderful forest and bluff-top scenery

Special comments: About as tough as anyone could want if you take the bluff trails; you can opt for an easy loop by following Wilber's Trail, but you'll miss the great views of the Mississippi up on the bluff; all trails are easy to follow, double-track, and grassy with a hardpack track

As you enter Perrot State Park, a historical marker will tell you that trader and explorer Nicholas Perrot wintered in the park in 1685–86, around the time he claimed all of the lands of the Mississippi and its tributaries for the King of France. A look at the Indian mounds around the corner might have given him a clue that if it belonged to anyone it should have been the people who had been there for thousands of years, but he got the land for the king, and eventually the park name for himself.

The 5.1-mile route shown here will give you a good idea of why people wanted this land. The hardwood forest is glorious and white-tailed deer abound. The views of the Mississippi are unforgettable. The river valley is narrow here because the channel, less than a mile wide, is new. It was formed when the last continental glacier melted and the river was forced away from its old course in the four-mile-wide valley to the north of the park.

Such grandeur has its price. Steep sections test your ability to continue moving and keep the front wheel on the ground at the same time. The downhills require different, though no less important, technical skills. On the plus side, the cross-country ski trails are fairly wide and the surfaces are mostly smooth with a

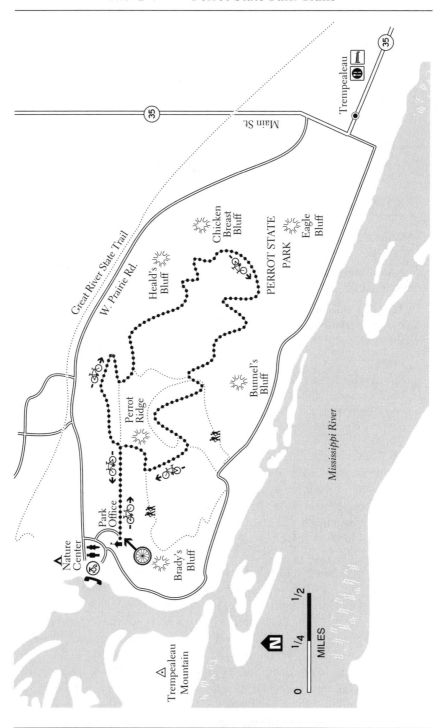

The view of the Mississippi is worth the climb.

few rocks and roots. You will find some soft sand on the bluff trails that make climbing impossible or descending squirrelly.

For a relatively easy ride, stick to the 2.0-mile Wilber's Trail or hop onto the Great River State Trail (see Ride 39, page 132), a rail-trail you can access via a spur from the campground.

General location: Just outside Trempealeau, 23 miles north of LaCrosse.

Elevation change: The terrain varies from constantly rolling to extremely steep. There is a 250' variation between the trailhead and the highest point. There are two steady 200' climbs and a large number of 50' to 80' climbs.

Season: May through October. The park management is very sensitive to potential erosion, and trails may be closed at any time due to wet conditions. Be sure to call ahead to check trail status.

Services: Some services, including bicycle rental, gas, lodging, food, and beverages, are available in the village of Trempealeau. All services, including bicycle retail and repair, are available in the city of LaCrosse.

Hazards: Expect to find extremely steep slopes and some rough surface. Soft sand can cause bike handling difficulty. Deep, narrow washout gullies will be found on steep sections. On these sections rubber waterbars are laid across the trails at angles to prevent erosion.

Rescue index: Help is available at the park office. Few people will be encountered on the trails, so if you are injured or have mechanical trouble, you should make your way to the trailhead or follow a hiking trail to the paved road.

Land status: Wisconsin State Park. A daily or annual vehicle sticker ($5 daily/$18 annual for Wisconsin residents, $7 daily/$25 annual for out-of-state residents) is required to park in state parks. Bicyclists are not charged for visiting the park, but a trail pass fee is required of bicyclists age 16 and older for riding the trails ($3 daily/$10 annual). The trail pass also covers usages such as cross-country skiing, horseback riding, and bicycling on railroad-grade bike trails like the Great River State Trail (see Ride 39, page 132), which skirts the north boundary of the park.

Maps: A cross-country ski trail map is available at the park office. The 7.5 minute USGS Trempealeau quad map does an excellent job of showing the terrain, but does not show any of the trails.

Finding the trail: From I 90, take Highway 53, Exit #4, north 8 miles. Then exit onto WI 35 North and continue 8 miles to the village of Trempealeau, where WI 35 is Main Street in its north/south direction and Third Street in its east/west direction. From the junction of Main Street and Third Street, go south on Main Street two blocks, and turn west on First Street (unmarked) just before crossing the railroad tracks. A large sign will direct you to Perrot State Park. Follow First Street (it becomes a paved road) three miles to the park office.

Sources of additional information:

Perrot State Park
Route 1, Box 407
Trempealeau, WI 54661
(608) 534-6409

Trempealeau Chamber of
  Commerce
P.O. Box 212
Trempeleau, WI 54661-0212
(608) 534-6866
www.trempealeau.net

Wisconsin Department of Natural
  Resources
Bureau of Parks and Recreation
P.O. Box 7921
Madison, WI 53707-7921
(608) 266-2621
www.dnr.state.wi.us

Notes on the trail: The trails are sometimes subject to damage from periods of wet weather and may be closed for this reason. Be sure to call ahead to check the status. A daily or annual Wisconsin Trail Pass fee is required to ride on the park off-road trails (see Land status). The trails are mostly one-way, with some two-way connectors. They are well signed with green squares with white mountain bike silhouettes, trail name signs, and "you are here" sign maps at trail intersections. Trails where riding is not allowed have white squares with red slashes through the mountain bike silhouette.

From the trailhead at the park office, follow the two-way trail signed as the Brady's Bluff Trail. After a short distance, the Brady's Bluff Trail turns to the right and is signed for hiking only. At this point continue straight on the unmarked trail. After a similar distance, turn left on the Wilber Trail, which will lead you through the White Pine Run. At the next signed trail intersection, turn left up the Tow Rope Hill (black diamond rated) to the Cedar Glade Trail and Prairie Trail. At around 3.5 miles you will climb to a trail junction where the trail to the right falls away sharply. Turn left to complete the route shown here and follow Perrot Ridge around. If you turn right you can return to the trailhead by a slightly shorter route that will save a considerable amount of climbing.

RIDE 41 · Maiden Rock Tour (On-Road)

AT A GLANCE

Length/configuration: 21.5- or 14.2-mile loops

Aerobic difficulty: High; there is no way you can get to the top without a workout

Technical difficulty: Easy to moderate; some of the gravel roads may be rutted or have washouts after periods of stormy weather

Scenery: One of the most beautiful stretches along the entire length of the Mississippi

Special comments: Soak up the wonderful scenery on this paved and gravel road tour, and ride past the reconstructed log cabin on the site where the much-loved children's book writer Laura Ingalls Wilder was born

Mississippi River scenery is the big payoff on this combination paved- and gravel-road tour. You have a choice of 14.2- or 21.5-mile routes that have 5.6- or 10.5-miles of paved surface, respectively. Grades are sometimes steep on the gravel roads, but no great technical skill is needed except for braking proficiency. The short and long loop are of moderate difficulty due to the steep grades.

Starting along the Mississippi you will have a chance to warm up before taking on the 400-foot climbs that wind up narrow valleys. This part of the river is called Lake Pepin. The Mississippi fills up the valley from bluff to bluff for a 22-mile stretch, creating one of the most beautiful expanses along North America's greatest river. The towering 300-foot limestone bluffs were noted by early French explorers. A historical marker near the village of Stockholm commemorates the Dakota Sioux tale of a young woman who jumped off a jagged outcropping rather than marry a man she didn't love. This outcropping has been known since as Maiden Rock.

The gravel road sections follow narrow, wooded valleys that lead to bluff-top farmland. Pine Creek Road (signed as 20th Avenue) has been protected from development by designation as a Wisconsin Rustic Road. There are several small stream fords to splash through as you follow its one-lane gravel surface. All gravel roads are open to traffic and are negotiable by two-wheel-drive vehicles. Along County Road CC you will pass the Little House Wayside Park, the homestead site of which Laura Ingalls Wilder wrote in *Little House in the Big Woods*. Stockholm is an artist's community with several attractive cafes. A few miles off the route, in

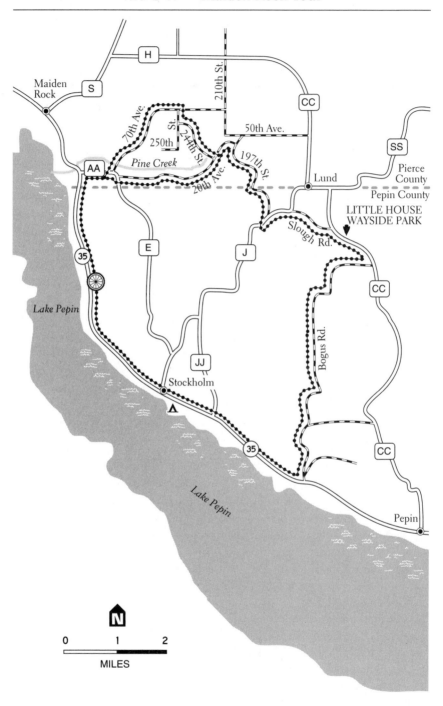

Maiden Rock

H

S

210th St.

CC

70th Ave.

50th Ave.

St.

244th St.

250th

SS

Pine Creek

197th St.

20th Ave.

Pierce County

AA

Lund

Pepin County

LITTLE HOUSE WAYSIDE PARK

E

J

Slough Rd.

Lake Pepin

35

CC

JJ

Bogus Rd.

Stockholm

35

CC

Lake Pepin

Pepin

N

0   1   2

MILES

Quiet, wooded valleys branch off the Mississippi.

the village of Pepin, is an excellent restaurant called the Harbor View. Be prepared and be patient. A posted sign says: No Reservations, No Credit Cards, No Whining. Kick back at the bar while you wait and sip one of the fine microbrews.

General location: On WI 35 between the villages of Maiden Rock and Stockholm, 79 miles north of the city of LaCrosse.

Elevation change: On the short loop you will gain and lose 480'. Riding the long loop involves 700' of climbing and descending. Each loop has a moderately steep 400' climb.

Season: Late March through early November, though the temperatures will be cool or cold at the extremes of this period.

Services: Food, lodging, and gas are available in Stockholm, Maiden Rock, and Pepin. There is a water pump at the trailhead. A soft drink machine is all you will find in Lund. All services are available in Red Wing, Minnesota, 25 miles northwest, and in Wabasha, Minnesota, 21 miles southeast of the trailhead. Bicycle rental, retail, and repair services are available in Red Wing at the Outdoor Store.

Hazards: Loose gravel may be present on any of the unpaved roads. Stream fords can be deep in the spring or during rainy periods. Washouts may be encountered on gravel roads. Two-wheel-drive motor vehicle traffic may be significant on all roads during the summer months and fall-color period in mid-October.

Rescue index: Help can be summoned at Stockholm. The bluff top sections of the route are lined with farms, and farmers are usually friendly and willing to help.

Land status: Public roadways through private land.

Maps: Good signage on all roads make additional maps unnecessary, unless you are a lover of topo maps. If so, the short route can be found on the Maiden Rock and Nerike Hill USGS 7.5 minute quadrangles. The long route is on these and the Stockholm and Pepin quadrangles. The DeLorme book, *Wisconsin Atlas & Gazetteer*, still shows the old road names in Pierce County instead of the current numbering system.

Finding the trail: The scenic overlook wayside starting point is located on WI 35, 3.5 miles south of the village of Maiden Rock and 2.8 miles north of the village of Stockholm.

Sources of additional information:

Red Wing Area Chamber of
  Commerce
420 Levee Street
Red Wing, MN 55066
(651) 388-4719

Mississippi Valley Partners
c/o John Hall, Anderson House
333 West Main Street
Wabasha, MN 55981
(651) 565-4524

Wisconsin Department of
  Transportation
Rustic Roads Board, Room 901
P.O. Box 7913
Madison, WI 53707
(608) 266-3661
Request: "Wisconsin's Rustic
Roads…A Positive Step Backward"

Notes on the trail: The routes are easy to follow due to good highway and town road signage. You can ride both routes in either direction. On the short route, you begin by riding north on WI 35 to County Road AA and return by the same roads. There is a wide paved shoulder along WI 35. Other roads should be lightly traveled.

In Pierce County the town road names were recently changed to a numerical system, but the locals continue to know them by the old names. Pine Creek Road (20th Avenue.) and Willow Road (50th Avenue) are Wisconsin Rustic Road (R-51). The town roads are signed with standard green-and-white street signs. A common rural prank is to twist these signposts 90 degrees, so check your map closely. Someone once even went to the extra effort of unbolting the arrow for the Rustic Road sign and turning it 180 degrees. In Pepin County, at the intersection of Bogus Road and CR CC, the street-type sign still indicates that CR CC is State Highway 183, its former designation.

Your choice of direction of travel will determine whether you climb or descend Pine Creek Road (20th Avenue). I can't say which way of covering this lovely road you'll enjoy most, but, if you ride clockwise, splashing through the fords on a downhill run is always fun.

UP THE I-ROAD

That ribbon of highway, the I-Road—the fastest way to get from Madison to Minnesota's Twin Cities on wheels. Time was when you could make about the same time on streamlined passenger trains, including stops. While those days are long gone, some of the old rail lines have become bike trails. Among them is the "400" State Trail, named after the famous train that once raced along its grade.

All of the trails in this section are easily accessible from Interstate 94 (I-90/94 in places), making them easy to reach. They can be destinations or just convenient breaks from a long day of driving.

You don't have to stray far off the four lane to ride the Mirror Lake State Park Trails. The pleasant, unchallenging loops are just a few miles south of the I-road and close to the "400" State Trail and the state's perennial, attraction-filled tourism mecca, Wisconsin Dells.

The north end of the Omaha Trail is less than a quarter mile from the Camp Douglas exit, if you don't miss it gawking at the picturesque sandstone bluffs along the I-Road. This hard-surfaced rail-trail features a tunnel and great ridge and valley scenery as it heads south to Elroy and connects with the "400" and Elroy-Sparta state trails.

There is a real treasure of trails farther up the I-Road in Black River State Forest. At Millston you can exit to the easy Pigeon Creek Trail or the challenging Smreaker, Red Oak, Norway Pine, and Wildcat Trails. The former starts at a nice swimming beach, and the other four trails take you up 200-foot climbs to fantastic overviews of the forest. Also in the state forest is the easy-riding Perry Creek Trail, just south of the town of Black River Falls.

In the same area, a bit farther off the I-Road, are the Levis/Trow Mounds Trails. Similar in some way to the challenging trails in the state forest, they have the added attraction of being some of the toughest single-track riding in Wisconsin.

Also a bit out of the way but well worth the trip are the Wissota State Park Trails near Chippewa Falls. These easy trails will be attractive to beginners and families who are as interested in the swimming beach as the riding. A new state rail-trail is slated to open soon nearby.

Much more accessible and more interesting for beginner riders are the Lowes Creek Trails just south of Eau Claire. There is enough variety there to get a newcomer really excited about the sport. Nearby is the Chippewa River

State Trail, a rail-trail that connects via short city trails to the attractions of Carson Park.

The next city to the west is the college town of Menomonie, the jumping-off point for the scenic Red Cedar State Trail. Running close to the swift-moving Red Cedar River, the rail-trail visits the distinctive village of Downsville.

RIDE 42 · "400" State Trail (Rail-Trail)

AT A GLANCE

Length/configuration: 22 miles one way from the Reedsburg Depot to Elroy Commons; a 4-mile one-way spur trail goes from Union Center to Hillsboro

Aerobic difficulty: Very low; typical flat rail-trail

Technical difficulty: Easy

Scenery: Views of the hills and stone outcroppings that line the valley of the Baraboo River

Special comments: A pleasant family ride or high-speed cruise; frequent small towns and parks with playgrounds segment this easy crushed-limestone rail-trail

When the "400" went through on its Minneapolis/Chicago run, you can bet it wasn't picking any daisies. In the era when everyone traveled by train, its reputation depended on covering 440 miles in less than 400 minutes. Where the line ran straight and smooth the engineer cranked it to 100 miles per hour or more.

Your ride on the bike trail that replaced the rails can be much more leisurely. The 22-mile trail is punctuated by six pleasant little towns. Between Reedsburg and La Valle you can make a short side trip to Lake Redstone County Park for a relaxing swim or to let the kids burn off some energy on the playground. Also, there are swimming pools and playgrounds in Reedsburg, Wonewoc, Hillsboro, and Elroy. There are few road crossings along the trail, but you'll cross the lazy, meandering Baraboo River 11 times.

You'll feel as though you've taken a step back into America's rural past as you ride the "400." For a look at the images of the past that charmed the nation for generations, visit the Museum of Norman Rockwell Art in Reedsburg, where more than 4,000 of his works are featured. For family fun of a less cerebral sort, check out nearby Wisconsin Dells, the prototypical tourist town where you'll find amusements at every turn, including the world's largest water theme park.

The "400" Trail is the easternmost link in a system of one county and four state trails that make an almost continuous motor vehicle–free riding environment over 100 miles in length (see Rides 33, 34, 39, and 44). For a varied-terrain ride in the area, visit nearby Mirror Lake State Park (see the following ride, 43).

General location: Between Reedsburg and Elroy, paralleling WI 33 and WI 82.

RIDE 42 • "400" State Trail

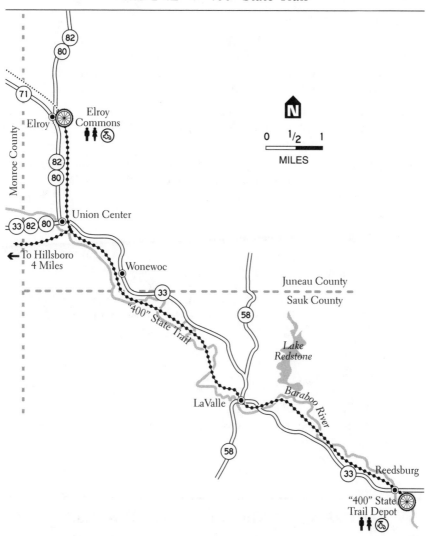

Elevation change: Virtually none; typical, flat rail-trail.

Season: May through October.

Services: All services are available in Elroy and Reedsburg. Hillsboro, Union Center, Wonewoc, and La Valle have cafes, groceries, and taverns. Swimming beaches or pools are at Webb Park in Reedsburg, at Redstone County Park, Legion Park in Wonewoc, and at Schultz Park in Elroy. All except Lake Redstone have flush toilets. There are flush toilets and water at the Elroy Commons, Hillsboro trailhead, and the "400" Trail Depot in Reedsburg. Camping and showers are at Schultz Park in Elroy.

Hazards: Use caution at road crossings. The trail is also used by hikers, and a horse-riding trail parallels the route between La Valle and Wonewoc.

Rescue index: Help is available in trail towns.

Land status: Wisconsin State Park Trail. A trail pass fee is required for the "400" State Trail for bicyclists age 16 and older ($3 daily/$10 annual). The trail pass also covers usages such as cross-country skiing, horseback riding, and bicycling on state mountain bike trails and other rail-trails.

Maps: A trail map is available from local information contacts and from the Wisconsin Department of Natural Resources. The DeLorme book, *Wisconsin Atlas & Gazetteer*, shows all roads and road names on page 42.

Finding the trail: Locate the east end in Reedsburg at the Depot Visitor Center, at Railroad Street and Walnut Street, one block south of WI 33/23. For the west end, start in Elroy at the Elroy Commons, at Main Street (WI 80) and Franklin Street.

Sources of additional information:

Elroy Commons Bike Trails and
   Tourist Information
303 Railroad Street
Elroy, WI 53929
(608) 462-BIKE

The Depot
240 Railroad Street
P.O. Box 142
Reedsburg, WI 53959
(800) 844-3507; (608) 524-2850

Wisconsin Dells Visitors and
   Convention Bureau
701 Superior Street
Wisconsin Dells, WI 53965
(608) 254-4636; (800) 22-DELLS
www.wisdells.com

Notes on the trail: A trail pass fee is required for bicyclists age 18 and older (see Land status).

RIDE 43 · Mirror Lake State Park Trails

AT A GLANCE

Length/configuration: 8.7-mile loop; many loop variations are possible

Aerobic difficulty: Low; flat to gently rolling terrain

Technical difficulty: Easy; some soft sand is the toughest challenge

Scenery: Mixed hardwood and pine forest interspersed with open spaces

Special comments: A fun, easy area for novice riders—the easy-to-follow multiple loops of its double-track trail system offer many options

The deep hardwood
forest at Mirror Lake.

Just down the road from one of the Midwest's most popular tourist traps lies
Mirror Lake State Park. The hype and clutter of the "attractions" at the
nearby town of Wisconsin Dells comprise a mecca to some and a mishap to others. Mirror Lake is a vastly different experience. The pleasant oak and pine forests
and open fields of the park are the backdrop for 8.7 miles of trails open for mountain biking. The grassy and bare forest floor cross-country ski trails offer an easy
riding experience for the average cyclist. Three loops are pieced together to form
a system that rolls gently over the terrain. The biggest challenge will come on a
few soft, muddy low spots and exposed sandy stretches.

General location: 3 miles south of the town of Lake Delton.

Elevation change: The terrain is sometimes flat, but mostly is gently rolling to
rolling. Moderate climbs of 50' will be found on the Turtleville and Fern Dell
loops. There are steeper climbs on the Hastings loop with gains of 70'.

Season: Mirror Lake trails are open for mountain biking from May 1 through
November 1. The trails are sometimes subject to flooding or damage and may be
closed for these reasons. Be sure to call ahead to check on the status.

Services: Water is available at the campground parking lot, to the northeast of
the park office. All services, except bicycle, are available in the towns of Lake

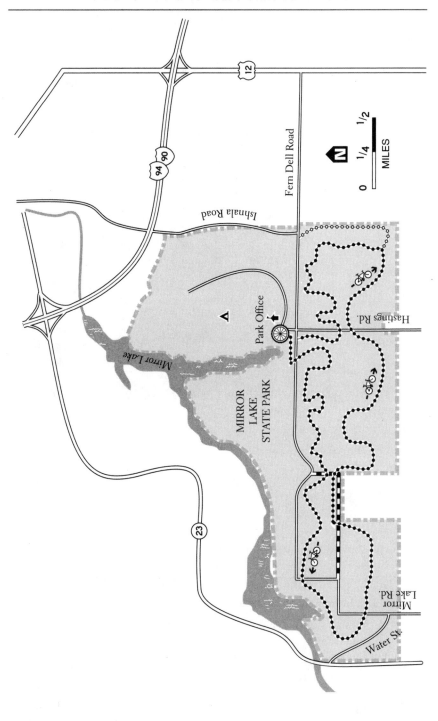

Delton and Wisconsin Dells. Bicycle retail and repair are available in Baraboo, 8 miles to the south.

Hazards: Although the trails receive regular maintenance, fallen trees or branches may be encountered at any time. The trails are open to hikers.

Rescue index: Help is available at the park office. Trails are not heavily used, but you are never far from a well-traveled road.

Land status: Wisconsin State Park. A daily or annual vehicle sticker ($5 daily/$18 annual for Wisconsin residents, $7 daily/$25 annual for out-of-state residents) is required to park in state parks. Bicyclists are not charged for visiting the park, but a trail pass fee is required of bicyclists age 16 and older for riding the trails ($3 daily/$10 annual). The trail pass also covers usages such as cross-country skiing, horseback riding, and bicycling on railroad-grade bike trails.

Maps: A detailed trail map is available at the park office or from the Wisconsin Department of Natural Resources. The 7.5 minute series USGS quad for Wisconsin Dells South shows the terrain very well, but only shows some of the trails.

Finding the trail: Exit Interstate 90/94 onto east US 12 at the Lake Delton interchange and travel 0.5 mile south on US 12. Turn west at Fern Dell Road and follow it 1.5 miles to the park office parking lot on the right.

Sources of additional information:

Baraboo Chamber of Commerce
P.O. Box 442
Baraboo, WI 53913-0442
(608) 356-8333; (800) 227-2266
www.baraboo.com/chamber

Mirror Lake State Park
E10320 Fern Dell Road
Baraboo, WI 53913
(608) 254-2333

Wisconsin Department of Natural Resources
Bureau of Parks and Recreation
P.O. Box 7921
Madison, WI 53707-7921
(608) 266-2621
www.dnr.state.wi.us

Notes on the trail: An annual or day-use motor vehicle sticker is required to park on state land as well as an annual or daily per-person trail fee (see Land status). The trails are well marked for mostly one-way travel by green signs with white mountain bike silhouettes and cross-country ski signs. Trails where riding is not allowed have white signs with a red slash through the bike silhouette.

From the trailhead, ride out to Fern Dell Road and turn right. After a short distance, just before the narrow old bridge, turn left off the pavement onto a grassy cross-country ski trail that is signed for mountain biking, and follow it as it loops around a beaver pond. You are on the Fern Dell Loop. At the junction with a gravel road (Turtleville Road), go straight across onto the Turtleville Loop. The loop will cross a paved road (Fern Dell Road) twice and a gravel road (Turtleville Road) once before returning to this intersection. Cross the road back onto the Fern Dell Loop and follow it to the south. At the junction with a paved road (Hastings Road) cross onto the Hastings Loop. When the loop returns to this intersection, turn right onto Hastings Road and return to the trailhead.

RIDE 44 · Omaha Trail (Rail-Trail, On-Road)

AT A GLANCE

Length/configuration: 13 miles one way from Camp Douglas to Elroy Commons

Aerobic difficulty: Low to moderate; the Omaha is a typical rail-trail, but the on-road option will tax your cardiovascular system with one steep climb

Technical difficulty: Easy; some shifting and high-speed confidence are needed for the on-road option

Scenery: Beautiful ridge and valley views; the Camp Douglas area is famous for its striking tower rock formations

Special comments: What a nice little trail—a fun family ride or high-speed cruise with a short tunnel thrown in

Counties have gotten on the rail-trail bandwagon too. One of the nicest is the Omaha Trail in Juneau County. Running from Camp Douglas, the little town on Interstate 90/94 surrounded by fantastic rock formations, to Elroy, where it junctions with the Elroy-Sparta and "400" state trails (see Rides 33 and 42), it passes through an 875-foot-long tunnel that will have a buildup of ice at its center, even into the summer months.

The trail's 12-mile length (the ride requires one additional on-street mile to connect to Elroy Commons) is hard surfaced. It dries out faster after a rain than its neighboring crushed-limestone trails. Anyone needing an aerobic workout can take a parallel gravel road over the top of the tunnel. The adjacent road is a great place for photo opportunities of the rest of the group cruising the rail-trail. Be sure to get a shot of them crossing the high trestle over County Road H.

General location: Between Camp Douglas and Elroy, south of I-90/94.

Elevation change: The rail-trail climbs gradually 120' from either end to the tunnel. The on-road option rolls over adjacent terrain and climbs the 110' ridge over the tunnel.

Season: May through October.

Services: All services are available in Camp Douglas and Elroy. There is a restaurant at the Camp Douglas trailhead and water and flush toilets at the Elroy Commons trailhead. There are flush toilets and a playground at the trailside park in Hustler, and a convenience store and taverns on Main Street. Water and clean pit toilets are at the north end of the tunnel. Camping is available at Mill Bluff State Park 3 miles west of Camp Douglas, as well as just south of Elroy at Schultz Park, where you'll also find flush toilets, showers, and swimming.

Hazards: Use caution at road crossings. A 1-mile on-street section must be ridden if you want to connect to Elroy Commons and the state trails in downtown Elroy.

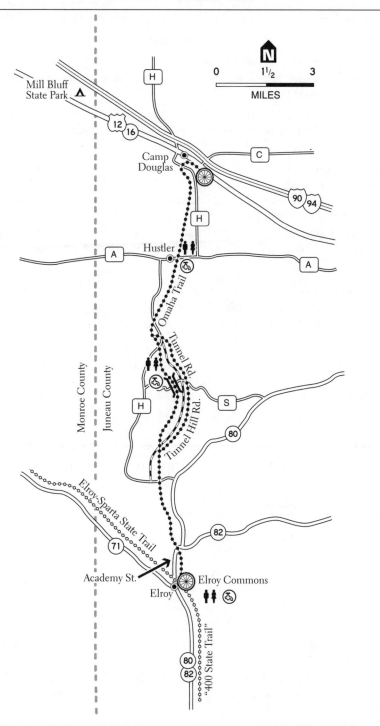

Walk through the tunnel. Ice builds up in the center and usually stays well into the summer. Where it flows over the tunnel floor there is typically enough sand for good traction, but caution is advised. The trail is also shared with hikers.

Rescue index: Help is available in towns along the trail.

Land status: Juneau County Parks trail. A $1 daily or $5 annual trail pass fee is required for adult bicyclists. Note: This is a specific Juneau County pass and the state trail pass is not valid.

Maps: A map of the trail is available from local businesses or information contacts. The 7.5 minute series USGS quads for Camp Douglas and Kendall East show the terrain and trail.

Finding the trail: At the north end in Camp Douglas, the trail starts next to the Target Bluff store/restaurant on US 12/16 — 0.2 mile east of the I-90/94/CR C and Camp Douglas/Volk Field interchange. At the south end in Elroy, the recommended trailhead is at the Elroy Commons at Main (WI 82/80) and Franklin Streets. You must then ride 1 mile on-street to get to the trail, or you can park on-street at the beginning of the trail on Crandon Street, 1 block east of Academy Street (WI 82/80).

Sources of additional information:

Elroy Commons Bike Trails and
   Tourist Information
303 Railroad Street
Elroy, WI 53929
(608) 462-BIKE

Omaha Trail
Juneau County Land, Forestry, and
   Parks
Mauston, WI 53948
(608) 847-9389

Notes on the trail: A trail pass fee is required for adult bicyclists (see Land status).

RIDE 45 · Pigeon Creek Trail

AT A GLANCE

Length/configuration: 4.2 miles out-and-back (2.1 miles each way)

Aerobic difficulty: Very low; some resistance comes from the slow roll on the grassy surface

Technical difficulty: Easy; occasional or seasonal soft surface is the only challenge

Scenery: Pine and hardwood forest with occasional views of surrounding mound ridges

Special comments: A nice, easy-to-follow beginner ride on grassy trails; camping, swimming, and nearby challenging trails add to the attraction

The Black River State Forest has attracted mountain bikers to its trails since the early days, mostly to take on the steep, challenging mound trails (see Ride 46, page 154). That didn't leave much for the casual rider. Eventually the forest planners created the Pigeon Creek Trail, connecting the pleasant campground and swimming area of the same name with the mound trails, making a great area even greater with something for everybody.

The easy 4.2-mile trail consists of a 3-mile eastern segment that runs to Smreaker Road in the direction of the mound trails, and a 1.2-mile western leg leading out to North Settlement Road. You can ride the trail out-and-back or make your return trip a road cruise on Smreaker and North Settlement roads.

General location: 2 miles east of the Millston/County Road O exit on Interstate 94.

Elevation change: Virtually dead flat.

Season: May through October.

Services: Millston has a motel, cafe, and convenience store/gas station. Camping, water, pit toilets, swimming, and a playground are at the trailhead.

Hazards: Trails are well maintained, but watch for windfall branches.

Rescue index: Help is available at the campground office or by contacting the Jackson County Sheriff's Department.

Land status: Wisconsin State Forest. A daily or annual vehicle sticker ($5 daily/$18 annual for Wisconsin residents, $7 daily/$25 annual for out-of-state residents) is required to park in state forests. A trail pass fee is required of bicyclists age 16 and older for riding the off-road trails ($3 daily/$10 annual). The trail pass also covers usages such as cross-country skiing, horseback riding, and bicycling on railroad-grade bike trails in other forests and parks.

Maps: A detailed map is available at the Pigeon Creek Campground office. The 7.5 series USGS quad for Millston shows the terrain but not the trails.

Finding the trail: Exit I-94 at the CR O/Millston exit. Travel northeast 0.1 mile and turn left on North Settlement Road. Travel 2 miles to the Pigeon Creek Campground entrance on the right. Park in the picnic area parking lot.

Sources of additional information:

Black River Area Chamber of
   Commerce
120 North Water Street
Black River Falls, WI 54615-1315
(715) 284-4658; (800) 404-4008
www.blackrivercountry.com

Black River State Forest
910 Highway 54 East
Black River Falls, WI 54615
(715) 284-4103

Wisconsin Department of Natural Resources
Bureau of Parks and Recreation
P.O. Box 7921

Madison, WI 53707-7921
(608) 266-2621
www.dnr.state.wi.us

Notes on the trail: The trails are sometimes subject to flooding or damage and may be closed for these reasons. Be sure to call ahead to check on the status. An annual or day-use motor vehicle sticker is required on state land, as well as an annual or daily trail fee (see Land Status). These can be paid at the Pigeon Creek Campground office on any day of the week through self registration or Monday through Friday at the Black River DNR service center just south of the interchange of I-94 and WI 54.

The two-way trail is well marked with brown signs with white mountain bike silhouettes. From the trailhead at the Pigeon Creek Campground picnic area, follow the unimproved road on top of the earthen dam along the swimming pond. After 0.3 mile stay left (east) on the Pigeon Creek Trail and follow it to the junction with an improved gravel road (Smreaker Road), or turn right to take the leg out to North Settlement Road.

RIDE 46 · Black River State Forest Trails

AT A GLANCE

Length/configuration: 19.4-mile loop with many short-cut and combination options

Aerobic difficulty: High, most loop combinations include long, steep climbs; the North Ridge Trail, Norway Pine Trail, and Wildcat Trail sections are toughest

Technical difficulty: Moderate to challenging, climbing skills and confidence on steep downhills are needed; soft sand and washouts are often encountered on downhills

Scenery: Fantastic overviews of the forest from ridge-top overlooks

Special comments: A day on the Smreaker, Red Oak, and Wildcat trails makes you remember why you love this sport; a real treat for riders with some experience under their belts

The Smreaker, and Wildcat trail loops are great for riders looking for some challenging climbing. Once you're on top of the 200-foot mounds you can stop at scenic overlooks and view the vast, flat expanse of the Black River State Forest. The tops of the pine trees look like waves on a windy day. Ten thousand years ago the mounds looked out on a vast inland sea formed from meltwater as the continental glacier receded to the north.

RIDE 45 • Pigeon Creek Trail
RIDE 46 • Black River State Forest Trails

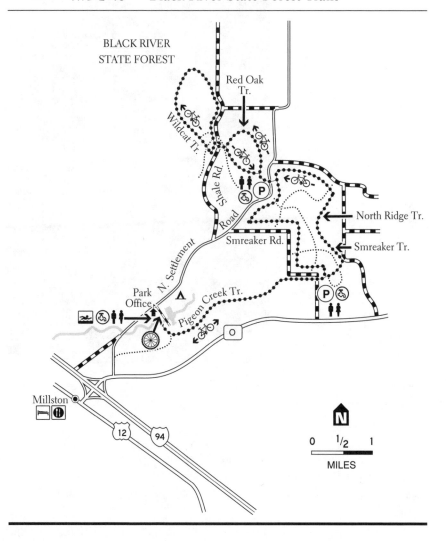

BLACK RIVER
STATE FOREST

Red Oak
Tr.

Wildcat Tr.

Shale Rd

Road

P

North Ridge Tr.

Smreaker Rd.

Smreaker Tr.

N. Settlement

Park
Office

Pigeon Creek Tr.

P

Millston

12   94

N

0   1/2   1

MILES

There are many shortcut options on this 19.4-mile ride. All trails are challenging for the average rider. It's not just the steep climbs on the 6.4-mile Smreaker, and 6.6-mile Wildcat trail loops that make them difficult, it's the technical skill needed to handle loose surface and soft sand on the fast downhills. The route is entirely in the woods, with pines predominant in the low areas and oaks on the ridges.

The route is on grassy or forest-floor double-track cross-country ski trails. All of the mound trails are well drained thanks to the sandy base that also creates a fair amount of rolling resistance in low areas.

Trails are either up
or down on the
Wildcat Trail.

General location: 2 miles northeast of the County Road O exit on Interstate 94 at the small village of Millston.

Elevation change: The terrain is a mix of flat to gently rolling in the lowland and very steep to rolling on the mounds. There are seven climbs and descents in the 120' to 200' range on a complete circuit.

Season: Black River State Forest trails are open for mountain biking from May 1 through November 1.

Services: Water is available at the Pigeon Creek trailhead. Food, lodging, and gas are available in of Millston. All services, including bicycle retail and repair, are available in the city of Black River Falls, 12 miles to the northwest on I-94.

Hazards: Although the trails receive regular maintenance, fallen trees or branches may be encountered at any time. The trails are open to hikers, and are heavily used during the fall. Rough, loose surface on the downhills and soft sand washouts at the bottom can be hazardous to the unskilled.

Rescue index: Help is available at the Pigeon Creek Campground office or in the village of Millston.

The view from the top of North Ridge Trail.

Land status: Wisconsin State Forest. A daily or annual vehicle sticker ($5 daily/$18 annual for Wisconsin residents, $7 daily/$25 annual for out-of-state residents) is required to park in state forests. Bicycles are not charged for visiting the forest, but a trail pass fee is required of bicyclists age 16 and older for riding the off-road trails ($3 daily/$10 annual). The trail pass also covers usages such as cross-country skiing, horseback riding, and bicycling on railroad-grade bike trails in other forests and parks.

Maps: A detailed map is available at the Pigeon Creek Campground office and at each trailhead. The 7.5 series USGS quads for Millston and Hatfield SE show the terrain very well, but do not show the trails.

Finding the trail: Exit I-94 at the CR O/Millston exit. Travel northeast 0.1 mile and turn left on North Settlement Road. Travel 2 miles to the Pigeon Creek Campground entrance on the right if you need to purchase a trail pass or vehicle sticker. Otherwise, continue on North Settlement Road another 1.7 miles, turn right (east) on Smreaker Road, and travel 2.2 miles to the Smreaker Trail parking area.

Sources of additional information:

Black River Area Chamber of
  Commerce
120 North Water Street
Black River Falls, WI 54615-1315
(715) 284-4658; (800) 404-4008
www.blackrivercountry.com

Black River State Forest
910 Highway 54 East
Black River Falls, WI 54615
(715) 284-4103

Wisconsin Department of Natural
  Resources
Bureau of Parks and Recreation
P.O. Box 7921
Madison, WI 53707-7921
(608) 266-2621
www.dnr.state.wi.us

Notes on the trail: The trails are sometimes subject to flooding or damage and may be closed for these reasons. Be sure to call ahead to check the status. An annual or day-use motor vehicle sticker is required on state land as well as an annual or daily trail fee (see Land Status). These can be paid at the Pigeon Creek Campground office on any day of the week from Memorial Day weekend through Labor Day weekend and on weekends until November 1. At other times the fees must be paid at the Black River Falls DNR Service Center just south of the interchange of I-94 and WI 54.

The mainly one-way trails are well marked with brown signs with white mountain bike silhouettes and cross-country ski trail signs. From the south side of the Smreaker Trail parking lot, follow the East, Ridge, and North trails to the two-way link trail that crosses a paved road (North Settlement Road) to the Red Oak Trail, which you will pick up at the northwest side of the Red Oak Trail parking lot. Partway around the Red Oak Trail you will junction with another two-way link trail that will take you across a paved road (Shale Road) to the Wildcat Trail. Link trails are gated at road crossings. Return by the same links and follow the central loops on the Smreaker Trail to the trailhead.

RIDE 47 · Perry Creek Trail

AT A GLANCE

Length/configuration: 6 miles out-and-back (3 miles each way)

Aerobic difficulty: Low; only two short, steep sections will be encountered

Technical difficulty: Easy

Scenery: Deep pine and hardwood forest; nice views of Perry Creek near the southwest end

Special comments: Rides don't always have to be tough—take a leisurely ride on these wide forest trails to prove the point

This easy ride offers even the most novice rider a chance to enjoy the wooded scenery of the Black River State Forest on an almost entirely flat, nine-mile (total distance) out-and-back trail. The surface is mostly firm sand with a grassy cover. Some soft sand will be found near the north end, and some swampy, muddy spots will be encountered in the pine and aspen forest between East 7th Street and Cranberry Road. The trailhead is at Castle Mound Park. The view of Castle Mound, a half-mile long, parapet-like, 200-foot-high sandstone rock is shrouded by trees on most of the trail. When the leaves are off the trees, there is one fine view as you ride north just before crossing East 7th Street. From this spot you can see the mound's famous balancing rock, which seems to defy gravity. A hiking trail that also starts at the campground will lead you to a closer look on foot.

The trail's most scenic section, and the only part with any significant elevation change, is along Perry Creek. The trail rolls in this section as the stream winds along in a narrow gorge with numerous rapids through a pine, birch, and oak forest. Deer and numerous birds of prey are common sights throughout the forest.

General location: The trail starts at Castle Mound Area State Forest Campground, 2.2 miles south of the Interstate 94 and WI 54 interchange, Black River Falls exit.

Elevation change: Generally flat with two stream crossings that involve descents and climbs of 50' and an 80'.

Season: May 1 through November 1.

Services: All services, including bicycle retail and repair, are available in the city of Black River Falls.

Hazards: Although the trails receive regular maintenance, fallen trees or branches may be encountered at any time. The trail is open to hikers, though it is little used. For a short distance near Cranberry Road, the trail is shared with all-terrain vehicles.

Rescue index: Help is available at the Castle Mound Park, at the main Black River Falls DNR Service Center just south of the I-94 and WI 54 interchange, or in the city of Black River Falls.

Land status: Wisconsin State Forest. A daily or annual vehicle sticker ($5 daily/$18 annual for Wisconsin residents, $7 daily/$25 annual for out-of-state residents) is required to park in state forests. Bicyclists are not charged for visiting the forest, but a trail pass fee is required of bicyclists age 16 and older for riding the off-road trails ($3 daily/$10 annual). The trail pass also covers usages such as cross-country skiing, horseback riding, and bicycling on railroad-grade bike trails in other forests and parks.

Maps: A detailed map is available at the Castle Mound Park office.

Finding the trail: Exit I-94 at the WI 54, Black River Falls exit. Proceed west 1 mile and turn left on US 12/WI 27 as you enter the city of Black River Falls.

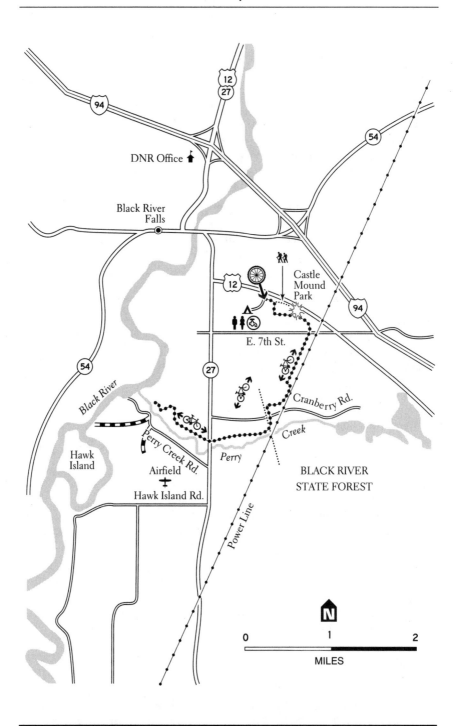

Perry Creek flows
through a mini-gorge
on its way to the
Black River.

Turn left on US 12 after 0.5 mile, where WI 27 continues straight. Follow US 12 for 0.7 mile to the entrance of Castle Mound Park on the right. Follow "Picnic Area" and "Parking" signs 0.2 mile to the "Perry Creek Mountain Bike Trail."

Sources of additional information:

Black River Area Chamber of
  Commerce
120 North Water Street
Black River Falls, WI 54615-1315
(715) 284-4658; (800) 404-4008
www.blackrivercountry.com

Black River State Forest
910 Highway 54 East
Black River Falls, WI 54615
(715) 284-4103

Wisconsin Department of Natural
  Resources
Bureau of Parks and Recreation
P.O. Box 7921
Madison, WI 53707-7921
(608) 266-2621
www.dnr.state.wi.us

Notes on the trail: An annual or day-use motor vehicle sticker is required to park on state land as well as an annual or daily per-person trail fee (see Land Status).

These can be paid at the Castel Mound Park office on any day of the week from Memorial Day weekend through Labor Day weekend, and on weekends until November 1. At other times, the fees must be paid at the Black River Falls DNR Service Center just south of the interchange of I-94 and WI 54.

From the Perry Creek Mountain Bike Trail trailhead at the Castle Mound Park picnic area parking lot, you will follow a route that is well marked in both directions by small brown signs with a white mountain bike silhouette. A parking lot at Perry Creek Pond is another possible spot for starting your ride.

RIDE 48 · Levis/Trow Mounds Trails

AT A GLANCE

Length/configuration: 7-mile loop, with 31 miles of trail available in the area

Aerobic difficulty: Moderate to high; trails either cover easy, rolling terrain or take on steep mounds

Technical difficulty: Easy to very challenging; the wide cross-country ski trails offer no technical difficulty, but the special mountain bike single-track will challenge any rider—expect to find soft surface, sidehill riding, tight switchbacks, extremely steep slopes, rocks, roots, and loose surface

Scenery: Beautiful pine and hardwood forest with scenic sandstone rock formations

Special comments: A real treasure for the extreme single-track aficionado; add interesting, but not technically challenging, cross-country ski trails and you've got an area with something for nearly everyone

Talk to anyone who has raced in the annual late-September madness called the Buzzard Buster and they'll tell you the single-track at Levis/Trow is as tough as it comes in the Midwest. The Wisconsin Off-Road Series (WORS) race has become the test to identify the riders who have the right combination of aerobic power (to motor on the double-track) plus technical skills (to master the tight stuff). And, if you're not too out of breath to enjoy it, the scenery is unsurpassed as well. The "mounds" are high sandstone rock formations that the trails wind around, over, and even under in places.

There are about 31 miles of trails total, with much of the distance on easy, double-track–width cross-country ski trails. A soft, sandy subsurface and some steep sections are all the challenge you'll find there. The 16.25 miles of single-track that snake through Levis and Trow are the flip side. Russell Park on Lake Arbutus three miles to the south makes a great base for your off-road adventures.

General location: 12 miles southwest of Neillsville and US 10.

RIDE 48 • Levis/Trow Mounds Trails

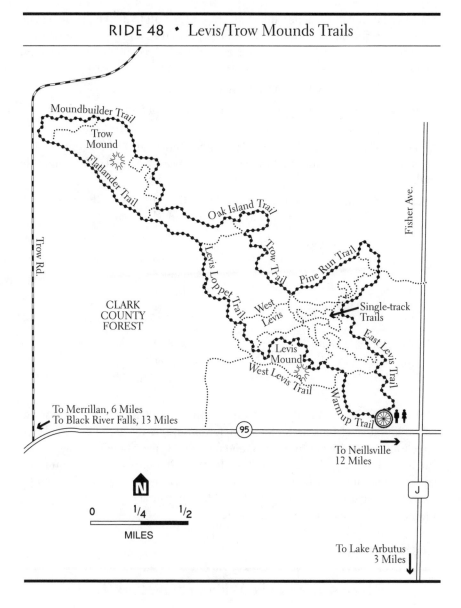

Moundbuilder Trail

Trow Mound

Flatlander Trail

Oak Island Trail

Trow Rd

Trow Trail

Levis Loppet Trail

Pine Run Trail

Fisher Ave.

CLARK COUNTY FOREST

West Levis

Single-track Trails

East Levis Trail

Levis Mound

West Levis Trail

Warmup Trail

To Merrillan, 6 Miles
To Black River Falls, 13 Miles

95

To Neillsville
12 Miles

J

N

0   ¹/₄   ¹/₂

MILES

To Lake Arbutus
3 Miles

Elevation change: From low point to high on the single-track is 170', which is broken up into many extremely steep climbs and descents. On the double-track, most moderate grades include climbs of about 100'; the easy sections roll over elevations of 30' to 40'.

Season: May through October.

Services: Camping, swimming, and a concession stand are found at Russell Park on Lake Arbutus, 3 miles to the south on County Road J. Pit toilets are available at the trailhead off WI 95. All services are available in Neillsville, and some are available in Merrillan and Hatfield.

Hazards: Windfall branches are typical hazards on all trails. The double-track trails have soft sand sections in spots, and you may find washouts on the steeper sections. On the single-track, anything goes. Rocks, roots, soft and loose surface, tricky turns, narrow passages, steep slopes—all can be hazardous to the unskilled.

Rescue index: Help is available at Russell Park, 3 miles south on CR J.

Land status: Clark County Forest. A daily trail fee of $3 for adults and $1 for children applies; season passes are available for $15.

Maps: An excellent trail map is available at the trailhead. The 7.5 series USGS quads for Merrillan and Hatfield show the terrain very well, but do not show the trails.

Finding the trail: Park in the trailhead lot near the junction of CR J and WI 95, 12 miles southwest of Neillsville and 6 miles east of Merrillan.

Sources of additional information:

Clark County Forest and Parks
Department
517 Court Street
Neillsville, WI 54456
(715) 743-5140

Neillsville Area Chamber of
Commerce
P.O. Box 52
Neillsville, WI 54456-0052
(715) 743-6444; (888) CLARK WI

Merrillan Lions Club
Merrillan, WI 54754
(715) 333-6901

Neillsville Area SingleTrack
Inhabitants
www.worba.org/nasti

Notes on the trail: A daily trail fee is required (see Land status). The wide, grassy double-track trails are well marked for mostly one-way travel in a clockwise direction with cross-country ski signs and periodic "you are here" map signs. The single-track is less well marked and the level of difficulty may make you think you've ridden much farther than you have. The close proximity of the double-track trails usually makes it possible to exit the single-track and find a map sign. I found the trail maps to be very accurate.

RIDE 49 · Lake Wissota State Park Trails

AT A GLANCE

Length/configuration: 5 miles on two loops connected by an out-and-back section

Aerobic difficulty: Low; the only workout comes from rolling, grassy trails

Technical difficulty: Easy

Scenery: Mixed open prairie and pine and birch woods

Special comments: A park with easy, grassy, "no surprises" trails and a nice swimming beach anyone can appreciate

Lake Wissota is actually a flowage on the great Chippewa River. It didn't exist naturally, and was created from water backing up behind a dam near the city of Chippewa Falls. When the first settlers arrived they found the area uninhabited. It was a no-man's land in the conflict between the Dakota (Sioux) based on the Mississippi and the Ojibwa (Chippewa) in northern Wisconsin. The last battle took place between Chippewa Falls and Eau Claire in 1854.

The five-mile route shown here covers most of the easy-riding mountain bike trails in the park. Initially, I had gotten a bit excited when I noticed the park's published mileage of trails for mountain biking had doubled recently. Unfortunately, there isn't much to get excited about. What happened was that someone decided the horse trails could also be used by bikers. These are worthless because the horses pulverize the sandy sub-base, making pedaling and steering exercises in futility. Stick to the hiking/biking trails, and leave the horse/biking trails to the nags.

The beach is the real attraction at Lake Wissota, and the campground is nicely placed near the lakeshore. Chippewa Falls has some interesting character. This old lumber town has a small zoo with a very healthy herd of buffalo, and the Leinenkugels Brewery, the state's oldest, can be toured by appointment.

An interesting development is the Old Abe State Trail, the south end of which is less than two miles west of the Lake Wissota State Park entrance. This rail-trail runs north along the Chippewa River to the town of Cornell. It was first developed for snowmobiling and is now surfaced with blacktop for biking. It is named after an eagle, captured and tamed in the area, which accompanied the 8th Wisconsin Regiment in 39 Civil War battles.

General location: 4 miles north of WI 29 near Chippewa Falls.

Elevation change: Virtually none.

Season: May through October.

Services: Water and flush toilets are at the swimming beach parking area. Water, flush toilets, and a playground are at the family campground. All services, including bicycle retail and repair, are available in Chippewa Falls, 8 miles to the west.

Hazards: Other than possible windfall branches, crossing horse trails, and sharing with the occasional hiker, the trails pose no threats.

Rescue index: Help and pay phones are available at the park office and swimming beach.

Land status: Wisconsin State Park. A daily or annual vehicle sticker ($5 daily/$18 annual for Wisconsin residents, $7 daily/$25 annual for out-of-state residents) is required to park in state parks. No trail pass fee is required of bicyclists at this time.

RIDE 49 • Lake Wissota State Park Trails

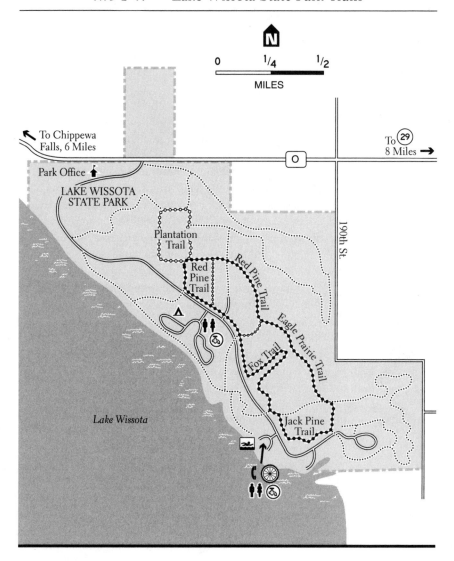

Maps: A trail map is available at the park office. The DeLorme book, *Wisconsin Atlas & Gazetteer*, shows local roads on page 61.

Finding the trail: From WI 29, follow the signs directing you to the Lake Wissota State Park on County Road K and County Road O. From the park entrance, follow the road to the beach parking lot.

Sources of additional information:

Chippewa Valley Convention and
    Visitors Bureau
3625 Gateway Drive, Suite F
Eau Claire, WI 54701
(715) 831-2345; (888) 523-3866
www.chippewavalley.net

Wisconsin Department of Natural
    Resources
Bureau of Parks and Recreation
P.O. Box 7921
Madison, WI 53707-7921
(608) 266-2621
www.dnr.state.wi.us

Notes on the trail: A daily or annual vehicle sticker is required (see Land status). The two-way trails are not terribly well signed, but everything in the park is quite compact, and with the aid of the map and the occasional trail-name sign, you can get around well. I only saw a couple of brown-and-white mountain bike silhouette signs to show the trails you can ride on, but the trails where biking is not allowed were pretty consistently marked with white-and-red no-biking signs. Biking is allowed on the horse trails, though I found them too soft and sandy.

From the beach parking lot, turn right (southeast) onto the park road. Ride about 3 blocks distance to the parking lot on the north side of the road at the entrance to the group camping area, and begin off-roading on the Staghorn Trail. At the first **T** intersection, the Staghorn Trail goes to the right and mountain biking is prohibited on it. Turn left onto the Jack Pine Trail at this point.

RIDE 50 · Lowes Creek County Park Trails

AT A GLANCE

Length/configuration: 4.5 miles for the outer trails of all loops; many loop combinations are possible

Aerobic difficulty: Low to moderate; most of the trails are on flat to gently rolling terrain, but you'll encounter moderately steep slopes while crossing the creek

Technical difficulty: Easy; trails are grassy or hardpack with occasional soft sand

Scenery: Open fields and hardwood forest with a pleasant stream crossing

Special comments: A nice introduction to off-roading for beginners or a fun, not-too-challenging ride for more seasoned mountain bikers; a compact network of grassy cross-country ski trails in a pleasant location

Except for the noise of semitrailer trucks roaring along on the long Interstate 94 grade, it's hared to believe the four lane is just a quarter mile from the

RIDE 50 • Lowes Creek County Park Trails

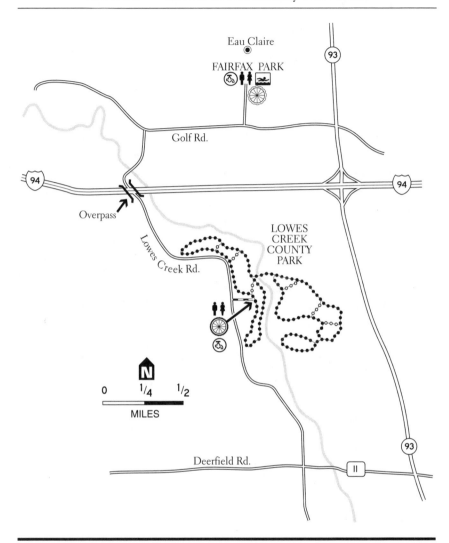

pretty Lowes Creek trails. While there is nothing overwhelming at this little park, you'll find some enjoyable riding on the three grassy loop trails that wind through woods and open areas.

As with all of the trails in this section, it is pretty easy to get to and from the I-Road. You might want to consider using Fairfax Park, on the south edge of the city of Eau Claire, as a base. The facilities there are very nice and include a swimming pool. Starting from Fairfax, you'd have a two-mile on-road warmup riding to Lowes Creek County Park.

General location: Just south of Eau Claire and I-94.

Elevation change: 50' to 60' crossing Lowes Creek and on the east-side loops.

Season: May through October.

Services: There are pit toilets and water at the Lowes Creek Park parking lot. Flush toilets, water, swimming, shelter, and a playground are available at Fairfax Park. All services, including many bicycle retail and repair options, are found in Eau Claire.

Hazards: Windfall branches may be encountered in wooded areas. There are soft sandy spots on some trail sections. Trails are also used by hikers.

Rescue index: Help is available at Fairfax Park or in Eau Claire.

Land status: Eau Claire County Park.

Maps: The 7.5 minute series USGS quad for Eau Claire East shows the terrain very well, but only shows some of the trails.

Finding the trail: Exiting I-94 at the WI 93 interchange, there are two choices for getting to the trails, each taking about three miles. You can head south on WI 93 to County Road II (Deerfield Road), turn west to Lowes Creek Road, then north to the park entrance. Or, you can head north on WI 93 a short distance and turn west on Golf Road to Lowes Creek Road, then south overpassing I-94 to the park entrance. Following this route you may want to consider basing at Fairfax Park on Golf Road, and riding on-road to Lowes Creek Park.

Sources of additional information:

Chippewa Valley Convention and
  Visitors Bureau
3625 Gateway Drive, Suite F
Eau Claire, WI 54701
(715) 831-2345; (888) 523-3866
www.chippewavalley.net

Eau Claire County Parks and Forests
  Department
227 1st Street West
Altoona, WI 54720
(715) 839-4738

Notes on the trail: The grassy, single-track, two-way cross-country ski trails have minimal marking, but the compact trails are hemmed in by the road and creek, making getting lost nearly impossible.

RIDE 51 · Chippewa River State Trail (Rail-Trail)

AT A GLANCE

Length/configuration: 24 miles one way, including the trail to Carson Park

Aerobic difficulty: Low; there is one steep grade into Carson Park, otherwise the ride is on a flat rail-trail

Technical difficulty: Easy

Scenery: Mixed woods and farmland with some fine views of the Chippewa River

Special comments: A nice family ride or high-speed cruise, with Carson Park and the Eau Claire at the trailhead; this paved trail attracts throngs near the city end and offers more solitude the farther away you get

Are you a baseball fan? Every crack of the bat that sounds at the small stone stadium at Carson Park is a reminder that this is where the all-time home-run king, Hank Aaron, began his professional career. A bronze statue of young Hank stands out front.

Carson Park is an excellent starting point for a ride on the Chippewa River State Trail. Other attractions include museums and a miniature steam train kids can ride. Besides, there is no parking other than on-street, down at Menomonie Street where the Chippewa River trail actually begins. One word of caution: There is a steep grade on the Carson Park trail. All riders should know how to control their speed with brakes before starting out.

If you are up for a real trek (no pun intended), the 24-mile Chippewa connects with the Red Cedar State Trail, which runs 14 miles up to the city of Menomonie. The first 9 miles of the Chippewa River trail are paved—except for a short stretch where flood water keeps rearranging it—and attract lots of bikes and in-line skaters. The farther you go, the lighter the traffic and the more isolated the trail gets. There is a nice wayside park at a big bend in the river and a country store at Caryville, but beyond that, nothing but quiet river bottom land.

Eau Claire makes up for the lack of services elsewhere. A spur trail running east along the north side of the river parallels Water Street in the University of Wisconsin Eau Claire area. They used to say that with the number of bars on the street you could get anything there but water. Today, it's a good place to find a bike shop or a microbrew. For a varied-terrain riding experience in the area, check out the Lowes Creek Trails (see Ride 50, page 167) nearby.

General location: Southwest of Eau Claire.

Elevation change: In Carson Park there is 80' of elevation change, but otherwise the route is flat.

Season: May through October.

Services: All services, including bicycle retail and repair, are available in Eau Claire. There are flush toilets and water at Carson Park, and water and clean pit toilets at the wayside park 5 miles down the trail. There is a country store at Caryville.

Hazards: There is a steep grade on the trail in Carson Park. The trail is shared with hikers and in-line skaters.

Rescue index: Help is available in Carson Park, Eau Claire, and Caryville.

Land status: Eau Claire city trails and Wisconsin State Park Trail. A trail pass fee is required for the Chippewa River State Trail for bicyclists age 16 and older

RIDE 51 • Chippewa River State Trail
RIDE 52 • Red Cedar State Trail

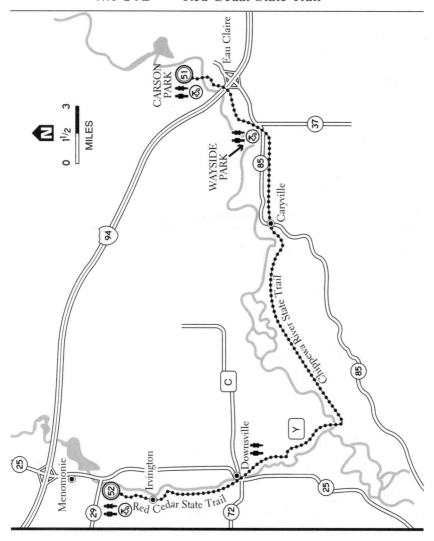

($3 daily/$10 annual). The trail pass also covers usages such as cross-country ski-ing, horseback riding, and bicycling on state mountain bike trails and other rail-trails.

Maps: A trail map is available from local information contacts and from the Wisconsin Department of Natural Resources. The DeLorme book, *Wisconsin Atlas & Gazetteer*, shows the rail corridor, all roads, and road names on page 60.

Finding the trail: For the eastern end of the Chippewa River State Trail, start at Carson Park, 1 mile north of Clairmont Avenue (US 12) in Eau Claire. Or, to start in the country park at the Wayside Park on WI 85, begin 2.5 miles west of the Interstate 94 WI 37/85 Eau Claire/Mondovi exit.

Sources of additional information:

Chippewa Valley Convention and
    Visitors Bureau
3625 Gateway Drive, Suite F
Eau Claire, WI 54701
(715) 831-2345; (888) 523-3866
www.chippewavalley.net

Wisconsin Department of Natural
    Resources
Bureau of Parks and Recreation
P.O. Box 7921
Madison, WI 53707-7921
(608) 266-2621
www.dnr.state.wi.us

Notes on the trail: An annual or day-use trail pass is required (see Land Status).

RIDE 52 · Red Cedar State Trail (Rail-Trail, On-Road)

AT A GLANCE

Length/configuration: 14.5 miles one way

Aerobic difficulty: Very low on the rail-trail or moderate on the adjacent on-road option

Technical difficulty: Easy

Scenery: Beautiful views of the Red Cedar River in many spots

Special comments: A great place to spot a bald eagle swooping down to pluck up a fish; this easy-riding, crushed-limestone trail visits the interesting village of Downsville

R olling down the Red Cedar State Trail takes you back in time to quieter, more peaceful days. From the bald eagles that soar over the river searching for fish to the sleepy village of Downsville, progress seems to have just left this valley alone.

The easy-riding, crushed-limestone 14.5-mile rail-trail officially ends in the Dunnville Bottoms after crossing the broad Chippewa River on a long stressed-iron bridge. I say officially because of its connection there to the recently developed Chippewa River State Trail (see Ride 51, page 170), which you can take 24 miles east to Eau Claire. For an aerobic workout, try abandoning the trail for a few miles (1.5 or 5.5 miles are options) for the paved roads that parallel the trail between Irvington and Downsville.

You won't find much in Irvington these days, but the character of its tavern makes up for quantity with quality. Have a brew and a few lines on the antique mechanical bowling machine. There are several taverns in Downsville, as well as the Empire in the Pines Museum, which preserves the lore of the rough-and-ready lumbering days in the valley. The major attraction in Downsville is the Creamery Restaurant, where you can enjoy food that would satisfy anyone in any era.

General location: South of Menomonie.

Elevation change: Virtually flat on the trail; 180' on the on-road option.

Season: May through October.

Services: All services, including bicycle retail and repair, are available in Menomonie. Flush toilets and water are at the trailhead depot in Menomonie, and there's a tavern in Irvington. There are taverns, a country store, a restaurant, and trailside restrooms in Downsville.

Hazards: The trail is also used by hikers.

Rescue index: Help is available in trail towns.

Land status: Eau Claire city trails and Wisconsin State Park Trail. A trail pass fee is required on the Chippewa River State Trail and Red Cedar Trail for bicyclists age 16 and older ($3 daily/$10 annual). The trail pass also covers usages such as cross-country skiing, horseback riding, and bicycling on state mountain bike trails and other rail-trails.

Maps: A trail map is available from local information contacts and from the Wisconsin Department of Natural Resources. The DeLorme book, *Wisconsin Atlas & Gazetteer*, shows the rail corridor, all roads, and road names on page 60.

Finding the trail: For the trail's north end, follow WI 29 west from Menomonie to the trailhead depot parking lot. For the mid-point, take WI 25 south from Menomonie to Downsville.

Sources of additional information:

Chippewa Valley Convention and
  Visitors Bureau
3625 Gateway Drive, Suite F
Eau Claire, WI 54701
(715) 831-2345; (888) 523-3866
www.chippewavalley.net

Red Cedar State Trail
Brickyard Road
Menomonie, WI 54751
(715) 232-1242

Wisconsin Department of Natural
  Resources
Bureau of Parks and Recreation
P.O. Box 7921
Madison, WI 53707-7921
(608) 266-2621
www.dnr.state.wi.us

Notes on the trail: An annual or day-use trail pass is required (see Land status).

WISCONSIN CENTRAL

This region name may not sound controversial, but it is. I could have called it by the generic-sounding "central Wisconsin." I chose not to, since two area cities, Stevens Point and Wausau, are duking it out over the right to refer to themselves and environs as "central Wisconsin," for whatever promotional value lies therein. So, I decided to flip-flop the words. You may note that it then becomes the same as the name of our famous, accident-prone regional railroad. Keep in mind that when you see the WC coming, the safest place to be may be on the tracks. Just kidding.

The area has some very enjoyable mountain biking and you should have no problem staying on track on these trails. At Hartman Creek State Park anyone can have an enjoyable trail ride and cool off in the clean waters of Hartman Lake afterward. Nearby, the Standing Rocks County Park Trails wait to challenge the aerobically fit, with a steep, rolling double-track network.

There is some easy family riding or high-speed cruising to be enjoyed on the recently opened Wiowash rail-trail. In the Wausau area, the Mountain Bay State Trail is another new rail-trail that junctions with the Wiowash Trail.

For a ride on the tougher side, the Nine Mile Forest Trails may be the place for you. Aerobically taxing double-track cross-country ski trails have been augmented recently with technically challenging single-track, making Nine Mile the most diverse compact trail system in the state. A few miles to the southeast you can enjoy the other side of the off-roading coin, and a refreshing swim too, on the easy trails at Big Eau Pleine County Park.

Also in the easy riding category, to the point of being a nice introduction to off-roading for little kids still on training wheels, are the trails at Council Grounds State Park. The park is also a nice camping stopover on the way up north.

RIDE 53 · Hartman Creek State Park Trails

AT A GLANCE

Length/configuration: 8 miles if all trails are ridden; the Glacial Trail loop is 3.3 miles; the Windfeldt Trail loop is 3 miles

Aerobic difficulty: Low to moderate; some hills will be encountered on the west ends of either loop

Technical difficulty: Easy; trails are wide and grassy for the most part

Scenery: Mixed open areas and hardwood and pine forest; small lakes add to the charm

Special comments: A good place to introduce newcomers to off-roading or for anyone to have an enjoyable ride; the out-and-back trail from the campground to the swimming beach is paved

Located on the edge of a jumbled terrain feature called recessional moraine, Hartman Creek offers riders a chance to mix some not-too-tough moraine riding (FYI: interlobate and terminal moraine is usually more difficult than recessional) with some flat, easy terrain.

The eight miles of trail include two loops that each take on the roller coaster moraine on their western sections, an out-and-back flat trail that was once a stagecoach route, and a flat paved trail that connects the campground area with a pleasant swimming beach on Hartman Lake.

The wonderful isolation of the park belies the fact that it's just a few miles west of the Waupaca Chain O'Lakes area, a popular summer tourism spot. If you get tired of cooking over a campfire, check out the restaurants there. You can access them via Rural and Whispering Pines roads.

General location: 6 miles west of Waupaca.

Elevation change: 110' on the west sections of the Glacial or Windfeldt loops.

Season: May through October.

Services: Showers, camping, water, flush toilets, and swimming can be found in the park. There is a country store in Rural, 3 miles east of the park on Rural Road. A number of restaurants and taverns are located in the Chain O'Lakes area to the east.

Hazards: Trails are well maintained, but windfall branches are always a possible hazard. Some loose surface and soft sand will be encountered. Trails are also used by hikers.

Rescue index: Help is available at the park office.

Land status: Wisconsin State Park. A daily or annual vehicle sticker ($5 daily/$18 annual for Wisconsin residents, $7 daily/$25 annual for out-of-state residents) is required to park in state parks. Bicyclists are not charged for visiting

RIDE 53 • Hartman Creek State Park Trails

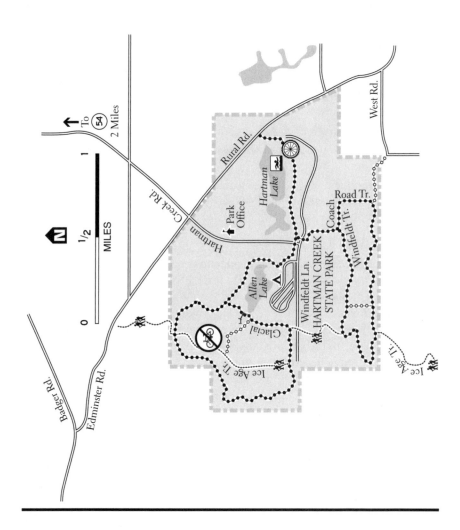

the park, but a trail pass fee is required of bicyclists age 16 and older for riding the trails ($3 daily/$10 annual). The trail pass also covers usages such as cross-country skiing, horseback riding, and bicycling on railroad-grade bike trails.

Maps: A detailed trail map is available at the park office or from the Wisconsin Department of Natural Resources. The 7.5 minute series USGS quad for King shows the terrain very well, but only shows some of the trails. The DeLorme book, *Wisconsin Atlas & Gazetteer*, shows all local roads on page 53.

Finding the trail: From WI 54, 6 miles west of downtown Waupaca, take Hartman Creek Road 2 miles south to the park entrance. Follow the park road to a **T**

intersection and turn east to the Hartman Lake Beach parking lot. The paved out-and-back trail can be picked up at the west end of the beach area.

Sources of additional information:

Hartman Creek State Park
N2840 Hartman Creek Road
Waupaca, WI 54981-9727
(715) 258-2372

Waupaca Area Chamber of
 Commerce
221 South Main Street
Waupaca, WI 54981
(715) 258-7343; (800) 417-4040
www.waupacaareachamber.com

Notes on the trail: An annual or day-use motor vehicle sticker is required to park on state land, as well as an annual or daily per-person trail fee (see Land status). The double-track width trails are well marked for mostly one-way travel by brown signs with white mountain bike silhouettes and cross-country ski signs. Two-way trails include the handle section of the Glacial Trail to Allen Lake, the Coach Road Trail, and the paved trail from the campground to the beach. Trails where riding is not allowed have white signs with a red slash through the silhouette.

RIDE 54 · Standing Rocks County Park Trails

AT A GLANCE

Length/configuration: 6.3 miles for the blue-signed outer loop

Aerobic difficulty: Moderate to challenging; though the maximum elevation change is not that great, slopes are often steep

Technical difficulty: Moderate; you must be able to climb steep slopes and have the confidence to handle downhill speeds

Scenery: Deep hardwood and pine forest with one nice overview from the downhill ski slope

Special comments: A favorite for riders looking for a good workout; the grassy, hardpack trails are easy to follow, and many shortcut options make for a nearly infinite combination of routes

Standing Rocks got its name from the abundance of rounded granite stones that dot the area. It seems there used to be a granite mountain somewhere northeast of the park before the relentless ice pancaked it. Some erratics are huge, the height of a person, and some are just nasty watermelon-sized buggers poking up out of the trail. In light-snow winters they cause skiers to nickname the place "Constant Rocks." In summer they make mountain bikers glad for the development of suspension forks.

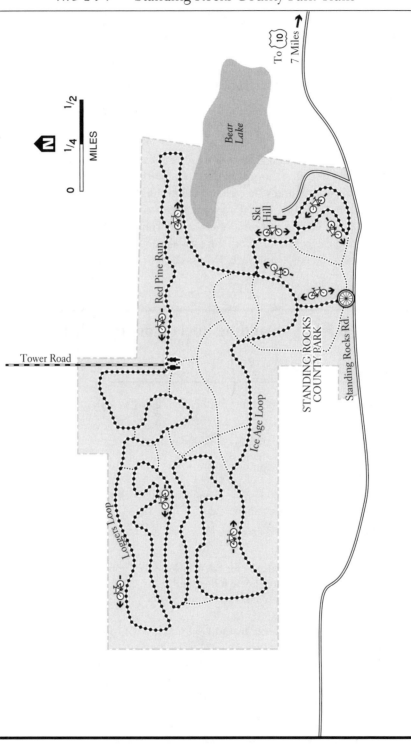

One of the few openings
on Standing Rocks'
wooded trails.

The 6.3-mile outer loop at Standing Rocks is a workout, but a fun one. With the exception of a short stretch of the graveled surface of Tower Road, the route is entirely on a one-way, double-track cross-country ski trail system running through a dense, mixed forest of pine, oak, and aspen. There is only about 100 feet of relief at the park, but you will make that amount of elevation in two separate, steady climbs. Otherwise the terrain is seldom the same grade for more than a few yards, and there are some real hero slopes that, while short, will test anyone's ability to stay on the bike. The trail surface is always firm and varies from hardpack to grassy surface. All of this makes Standing Rocks a moderately difficult ride that requires no great technical ability. There is a nice overlook of Bear Lake from the ski hill, and wildlife, particularly white-tailed deer, are abundant.

For those who like to ride rail-trails, an abandoned east-west corridor a mile north of the park is scheduled for development in the near future. It will be directly accessible from Tower Road.

General location: Standing Rocks County Park is 16 miles southeast of the city of Stevens Point.

Elevation change: Generally rolling with two steady 100' climbs.

Season: Officially open for mountain biking May through October, but may be closed due to excessively wet conditions.

Services: Food and gas are available in Amherst. All services are available in Waupaca, 18 miles to the east, or Stevens Point, 16 miles to the west. Bicycle repair and retail are available in Waupaca at Harbor Bike, and in Stevens Point at Campus Cycle & Sport Shop.

Hazards: Downed trees and branches may be found at anytime. Some trail sections are steep and rough.

Rescue index: The trails are patrolled at times, but if you are injured or have mechanical trouble your best chance of rescue will come if you make your way back to the trailhead and Standing Rocks Road.

Land status: Portage County Park. A trail pass must be purchased before riding. These are available as a $35 season pass or a $4 daily pass, and can be paid at a self-pay station at the park entrance on Standing Rocks Road or Tower Road. On weekdays, fees can be paid at the Portage County Parks Department (see contacts below).

Maps: A detailed map of the trails is available at trail pass purchase locations. "You are here" sign maps are posted frequently along trails. The 7.5 minute series USGS quad for Arnott shows the terrain very well, but only shows some of the trails.

Finding the trail: From US 10 at the town of Amherst, drive 4.5 miles west on County Road B. At County Road K turn south and drive 1 mile to Standing Rocks Road and turn west. Drive 1 mile to Standing Rocks County Park entrance.

Sources of additional information:

Portage County Parks Department
1462 Strongs Avenue
Stevens Point, WI 54481
(715) 346-1433

Stevens Point Area Convention and
    Visitors Bureau
340 Division Street North
Stevens Point, WI 54481-1153
(715) 344-2556; (800) 236-4636
www.spacvb.com

Waupaca Area Chamber of
    Commerce
221 South Main Street
Waupaca, WI 54981
(715) 258-7343; (800) 417-4040
www.waupacaareachamber.com

Notes on the trail: A trail pass must be purchased before riding (see Land status). Be sure to phone ahead to the parks department to make sure the trails are open, as they are sometimes closed to prevent damage due to excessive rainfall. From the roadside parking lot/trailhead, ride the mainly one-way route shown on the map by following the blue route marked by the frequent "you are here" cross-country ski trail signs. Mountain bikers are required to ride on the fine, crushed, red granite surface in the sections where it has been laid down.

RIDE 55 · Wiowash Trail (Rail-Trail)

AT A GLANCE

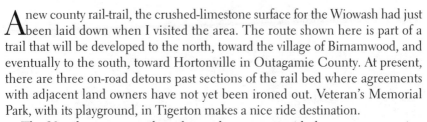

Length/configuration: 20 miles one way from Split Rock to Eland as currently configured, including several on-road detours

Aerobic difficulty: Low; typical rail-trail

Technical difficulty: Easy

Scenery: Mixed farm, marsh, and woodland

Special comments: A pleasant family ride or good high-speed cruise; this crushed-limestone rail-trail visits four small towns

A new county rail-trail, the crushed-limestone surface for the Wiowash had just been laid down when I visited the area. The route shown here is part of a trail that will be developed to the north, toward the village of Birnamwood, and eventually to the south, toward Hortonville in Outagamie County. At present, there are three on-road detours past sections of the rail bed where agreements with adjacent land owners have not yet been ironed out. Veteran's Memorial Park, with its playground, in Tigerton makes a nice ride destination.

The 20-mile one-way trail can be used to connect with the east-west running Mountain Bay State Trail at Eland (see Ride 57, 186). Towns are never very far apart, with the longest distance being nine miles between Tigerton and Wittenberg.

General location: Between Split Rock and Eland, paralleling US 45.

Elevation change: Virtually flat.

Season: May through October.

Services: There is a tavern in Split Rock. In Tigerton and Wittenburg are taverns, cafes, and groceries. The Community Park in Tigerton on Beech Street has water, flush toilets, and a playground. In Eland there is a tavern with a soft drink machine out front.

Hazards: Currently, to travel the entire length of the trail, some on-road detours must be taken, which entails several crossings of busy US 45. The trail is also used by hikers and all-terrain vehicles.

Rescue index: Help is available in trail towns.

Land status: Shawano County Trail.

Maps: The DeLorme book, *Wisconsin Atlas & Gazetteer*, shows all local roads and the abandoned rail bed on page 65.

Finding the trail: Near the south end at Split Rock on US 45, turn south on County Road SS (Split Rock Road) to the trail crossing. At the north end, the trail ends at County Road O in Eland, on the west side of US 45.

RIDE 55 • Wiowash Trail

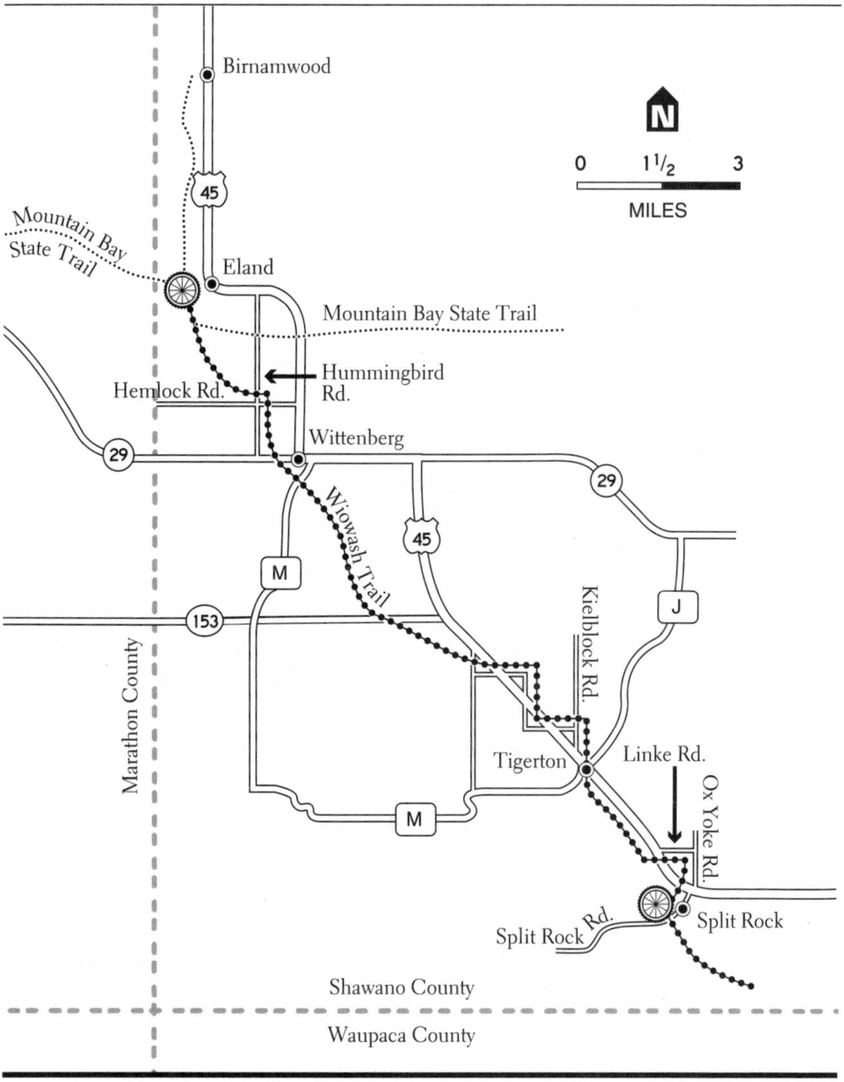

Source of additional information:

Tigerton Main Street, Inc.
P.O. Box 3
Tigerton, WI 54486
(715) 535-2110

Notes on the trail: Do not attempt to ride rural portions of the trail where on-road detours are indicated. Opposition from some adjacent land owners has been a bit wacko. Town roads are readily identified by on-trail signs at crossings.

From Split Rock you can take a 1.7-mile one-way jaunt to the southeast end of the trail, or ride northeast on CR SS to US 45, crossing onto Ox Yoke Road heading north. Eight-tenths of a mile later at Linke Road, you can turn west and rejoin the rail-trail after crossing US 45 again.

In Tigerton, as you travel northwest, the trail discontinues at a town street. Jog left, then make an immediate right onto Birch Street continuing northwest to Beech Street. Turn right (north) on Beech Street and follow it past the Community Park and across US 45, where it becomes Kielblock Road. After about 3 blocks distance turn left (west) on Morgenson Road, and cross US 45 where it becomes Hirt Road, which swings around to the north. Crossing US 45 again, Hirt Road becomes Breitrick Road. After about 6 blocks distance, Breitrick Road turns left and becomes North Townline Road. Crossing US 45 again, rejoin the rail-trail and continue northwest.

In Wittenburg, as you travel northwest, the trail discontinues in the parking lot for the Rainbow Apartments. Continue northwest to the lot exit, then jog to the left a half-block to Howard Street, and turn right on it for one block before jogging back a half-block to pick up the trail again. At Hummingbird Road, exit the trail and turn right (north) for about four blocks distance, then left (west) on Hemlock Road and rejoin the trail.

RIDE 56 · Mountain Bay State Trail—West (Rail-Trail)

AT A GLANCE

Length/configuration: 49 miles one way from Weston Town Hall to Shawano; this section is part of the complete 83-mile one-way trail from Weston (near Wausau) to Howard (near Green Bay)—see Ride 23, page 81, for the east end of the trail

Aerobic difficulty: Low; typical flat rail-trail

Technical difficulty: Easy

Scenery: Mixed farm and woodland

Special comments: A good family ride or high-speed cruise; the crushed-limestone rail-trail is unusually wide, so there is plenty of room for all types of users. The trail is asphalt paved within the city of Shawano

The west end of Wisconsin's mega–rail-trail butts up against the Wausau metro area. The city that straddles the Wisconsin River and lives in the shadow of towering Rib Mountain offers visitors many entertainment options not usually found in the northern half of the state. Good restaurants, museums, theaters, shopping districts, and yes, bike shops, are found there. The state park on top of Rib Mountain offers a terrific view of the river valley and city.

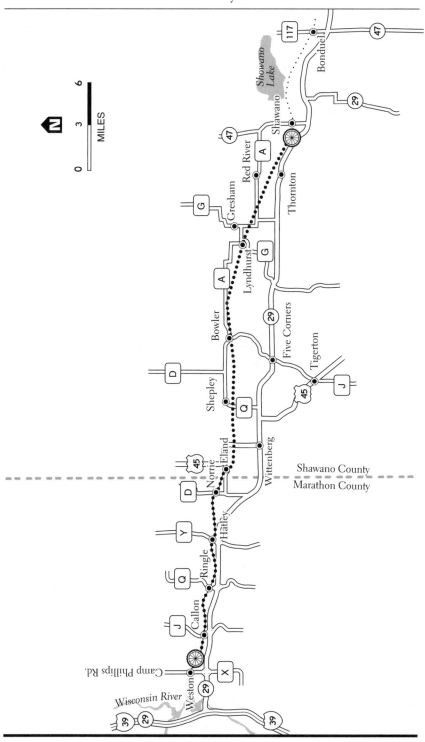

The trail begins in suburban Weston, and passes through four crossroads villages on the way to Eland and a junction with the Wiowash Trail (see Ride 55). These little communities seem to be slowly warming up to the idea of people in spandex stopping in for a snack or a drink. For a varied-terrain ride in the area, head for the Nine Mile Forest Trails (see Ride 57).

General location: Between Wausau and Eland, paralleling WI 29.

Elevation change: Virtually none; typical flat rail-trail.

Season: May through October.

Services: All services are available in Wausau and Shawano. Bicycle retail and repair is available at several locations in Wausau. Water and portable toilets are in the planning for the Weston trailhead. There is a tavern/restaurant in Callon and taverns in Ringle, Hatley, Shepley, Bowler, and Lyndhurst. Fast food and dining are available in Hatley.

Hazards: Use caution at frequent road crossings. The trail is also used by hikers.

Rescue index: Help is available in trail towns.

Land status: Wisconsin State Park Trail. A trail pass fee is required for the Mountain Bay State Trail for bicyclists age 16 and older ($3 daily/$10 annual). There is a self-pay station at the Weston trailhead. The trail pass also covers usages such as cross-country skiing, horseback riding, and bicycling on state mountain bike trails and other rail-trails.

Maps: A trail map is available from local information contacts and from the Wisconsin Department of Natural Resources. The DeLorme book, *Wisconsin Atlas & Gazetteer*, shows the rail line, all roads, and road names on pages 64 and 65.

Finding the trail: For the trail's west end, follow County Road X (Camp Phillips Road) north from WI 29 to Schofield Avenue, then go east 1 mile to the Weston Municipal Center. Turn north on Municipal Street and proceed one block to the trailhead parking lot. For the east end of the trail, park on the street at Memorial Athletic Park, at WI 22 (Main Street) and Lieg Avenue, and ride a block-and-a-half north on Main Street to the Mountain Bay Trail.

Sources of additional information:

Wausau-Central Wisconsin
  Convention and Visitors Bureau
10204 Park Plaza, Suite B
Mosinee, WI 54455
(715) 355-8788; (888) 948-4748
www.wausaucvb.com

Wisconsin Department of Natural
  Resources
Bureau of Parks and Recreation
P.O. Box 7921
Madison, WI 53707-7921
(608) 266-2181
www.dnr.state.wi.us

Notes on the trail: A trail pass fee is required (see Land status). In Ringle and Hatley, businesses are located on streets running parallel to the trail on its south side (2nd Avenue and Clark Street, respectively).

RIDE 57 · Nine Mile Forest Trails

AT A GLANCE

Length/configuration: 12.4-mile loop; many other trail combinations are possible; 10 miles of single-track trail are available

Aerobic difficulty: Moderate to high; depending on the combination of trails

Technical difficulty: Moderate to high; the double-track trails require climbing skill and confidence descending; the single-track includes similar steep grades plus narrow passages, tight turns, constant grade change, rocks, roots, and loose surface

Scenery: Deep pine and hardwood forest

Special comments: A great place for a workout; the recent single-track addition attracts many skilled riders to the area; the easy-to-follow grassy and forest floor trails offer an almost infinite variety of route combinations

Get serious and get your wheels over to Nine Mile. The trail system has been famous among cross-country skiers for years, and is the venue for the cross-country ski races of the Badger State Games. Now the trails draw enthusiastic mountain bikers to the tough terrain. Local riders have pioneered a number of new single-track sections that will test anyone's skill.

The only downside to the area is that the nice new trailhead building is only open during the winter. When you leave your trail fee donation, wrap it in a little note telling them you'd like to be able to use a bathroom or get water, at least on weekends.

Taking on the 12.4-mile loop shown here will give most riders a day's workout. The terrain is seldom the same grade for more than a few dozen yards, with plenty of steep grinds and fast descents. And, you won't run out of alternatives here. There are more than 30 miles of single-track and double-track trails at the site.

General location: 8 miles southwest of Wausau.

Elevation change: 140' from the low to high point. Many steep climbs are in the 60' to 80' range.

Season: May through October.

Services: All services, including bicycle retail and repair, are available in Wausau and surrounding communities.

Hazards: Trails are not particularly well maintained during the riding season and windfall branches are a possible hazard. Single-track trails are technically challenging with rocks, roots, and narrow passages.

Rescue index: Help is available in Wausau and surrounding communities.

RIDE 57 • Nine Mile Forest Trails

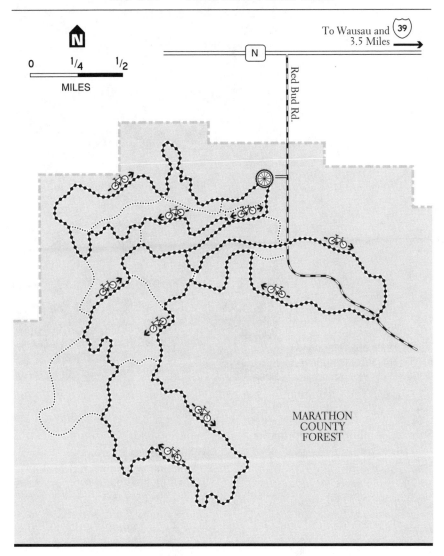

Land status: Marathon County Forest. A trail fee donation is requested and can be paid at a self-pay station at the trailhead.

Maps: An excellent cross-country ski trail map with topographical features is available from the Marathon County Forest Department.

Finding the trail: Exit US 51/Interstate 39 at the County Road N/Rib Mountain State Park interchange and head west on CR N to Red Bud Road; turn south to the trailhead parking area.

Wide cross-country ski
trails allow fast riding at
Nine Mile.

Sources of additional information:

Marathon County Forestry
    Department
500 Forest Street
Wausau, WI 54403
(715) 261-1550

Wausau-Central Wisconsin
    Convention and Visitors Bureau
10204 Park Plaza, Suite B
Mosinee, WI 54455
(715)355-8788; (888) 948-4748
www.wausaucvb.com

Notes on the trail: A trail fee donation is requested. The trails are well marked
with trail names and frequent "you are here" map signs. Most trail sections are
signed for one-way travel. Many loop combinations are possible.

RIDE 58 · Big Eau Pleine County Park Trails

AT A GLANCE

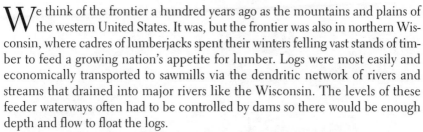

Length/configuration: 7-mile loop; several loop combinations are possible

Aerobic difficulty: Low; the terrain is nearly dead flat

Technical difficulty: Easy

Scenery: Mixed hardwood and pine forest with beautiful views of the Big Eau Pleine Flowage

Special comments: What a nice park! A peninsula in the Big Eau Pleine Flowage has been transformed into a fine place to visit, camp, and swim; it provides fun family or novice riding on wooded trails

We think of the frontier a hundred years ago as the mountains and plains of the western United States. It was, but the frontier was also in northern Wisconsin, where cadres of lumberjacks spent their winters felling vast stands of timber to feed a growing nation's appetite for lumber. Logs were most easily and economically transported to sawmills via the dendritic network of rivers and streams that drained into major rivers like the Wisconsin. The levels of these feeder waterways often had to be controlled by dams so there would be enough depth and flow to float the logs.

Today, the forest has regrown, and stately pines again give a primeval air to the north. Flowages, like the Big Eau Pleine, complement the woodlands to offer wonderful scenery and recreation. The seven miles of flat trails in the park won't tax anyone's riding strength or ability, but they will certainly show you a relaxing north-woods experience.

If the park trails aren't enough of a ride for you, try a lunar adventure by riding four miles east on Big Eau Pleine Road and Moon Road (gravel), to the crossroad village of Moon at the junction of County Road O. There is nothing there but a tavern, but you can say you've ridden to the Moon, or at least, to the only one in Wisconsin.

General location: 9 miles west of Mosinee and Interstate 39/US 51.

Elevation change: About 20' crossing the neck of the isthmus.

Season: May through October.

Services: All services are available in Mosinee and Wausau. Bicycle retail and repair are available in Wausau. Water, camping, pit toilets, and swimming are available in the park.

Hazards: Watch for windfall branches. Trails are also used by hikers.

Rescue index: Help is available at the park ranger station. There is a pay phone one-half mile east of the park on Eau Pleine Park Road.

RIDE 58 • Big Eau Pleine County Park Trails

Land status: Marathon County Park.

Maps: A trail map is available from the parks department. The DeLorme book, *Wisconsin Atlas & Gazetteer*, shows all roads and road names on page 64.

Finding the trail: From I-39/US 51, turn west on WI 153 and go 4.5 miles through Mosinee to Big Eau Pleine Park Road. Turn south, following signs to the park.

Take a break by the wooded shore of Big Eau Pleine.

Sources of additional information:

Marathon County Parks Department
Courthouse
Wausau, WI 54401-5568
(715) 261-1550

Wausau-Central Wisconsin
Convention and Visitors Bureau
10204 Park Plaza, Suite B
Mosinee, WI 54455
(715) 355-8788; (888) 948-4748
www.wausaucvb.com

Notes on the trail: The single-track, crushed-granite cross-country ski trail is easily picked up from either of the two boat-landing parking lots. Park roads and three cross-isthmus trail shortcuts make it easy to custom tailor your ride.

RIDE 59 · Council Grounds State Park Trails

AT A GLANCE

Length/configuration: 2-mile loop

Aerobic difficulty: Low; nearly dead flat

Technical difficulty: Easy

Scenery: Beautiful hardwood and pine forest with views of the Wisconsin River

RIDE 59 • Council Grounds State Park Trails

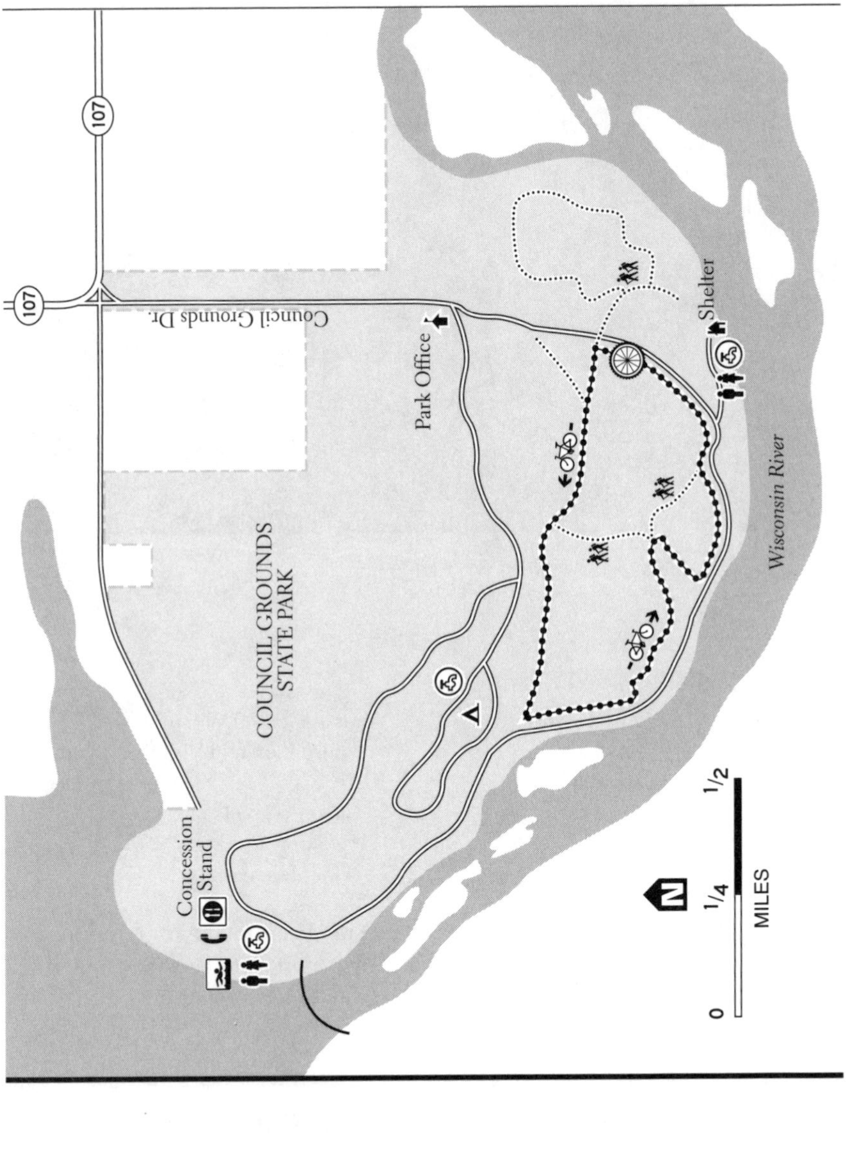

Special comments: A good, short family ride in a pleasant wooded park; well-marked grassy, pine needle–covered trails are easy to ride and follow

Looking for a nice camping stopover on your way north? How about trails where you can even take kids on training wheels? Location and easy-to-ride trails are both selling points for Council Grounds State Park. Just a bit north of Wisconsin's center, the park is a few miles off Interstate 39/US 51. Confined to a big bend in the Wisconsin River, the campground and trails are filled with the aroma of the pines.

Ride on a blanket of soft
pine needles.

The easy two-mile loop is a combination of off-road trails and park roads. Since both trails and roads are wide and one-way, they make for a safe riding experience. The trails have an exceptionally smooth surface, with a hardpack track over grass or fallen pine needles. You'll also pass through stands of oak, maple, and white paper birch. All this makes for a great place for family riding. The park personnel are super friendly too.

General location: 2 miles west of Merrill.

Elevation change: Virtually dead flat.

Season: May through October.

Services: All services, including bicycle retail and repair, are available in Merrill. Water, flush toilets, camping, and showers are available in the park.

Hazards: Trails are well maintained, but windfall branches may be encountered. Some portions of park roads open to motor vehicle travel must be ridden to cover the entire loop. Trails are also used by hikers.

Rescue index: Help is available at the park office.

Land status: Wisconsin State Park. A daily or annual vehicle sticker ($5 daily/$18 annual for Wisconsin residents, $7 daily/$25 annual for out-of-state residents) is required to park in state parks.

Maps: A detailed trail map is available at the park office. The DeLorme book, *Wisconsin Atlas & Gazetteer*, shows all local roads on page 76.

Finding the trail: Exit I-39/US 51 onto WI 64 and go west. At the junction of WI 107, follow WI 107 north to Council Grounds Drive, then follow signs to the park entrance. Park at the Krueger Pines Picnic Area parking lot.

Sources of additional information:

Council Grounds State Park
N1895 Council Grounds Drive
Merrill, WI 54452-8704
(715) 536-8773

Merrill Area Chamber of Commerce
720 East 2nd Street
Merrill, WI 54452-1265
(715) 536-9474; (877) 907-2757
www.merrillchamber.com

Notes on the trail: A daily or annual vehicle sticker is required (see Land status). From the Krueger Pines Picnic Area parking lot, turn north on the one-way park road (do not cross directly onto the Krueger Pines trails, as biking is not allowed), and make the first left onto the cross-country skiing/mountain bike trail. The double-track trail loop is well signed with green-and-white mountain bike silhouette signs for travel in a counterclockwise direction. Trails where riding is not allowed are marked with signs showing a bike beneath a red slash.

NICOLET FOREST

Wisconsin is blessed with two vast national forests. The Chequamegon (Sha-wa-ma-gun) is the better known of the two, thanks to the famous Fat Tire Festival of the same name. Its sister forest, the Nicolet (Nick-owe-lay) is also a terrific place to enjoy off-road riding. This section includes eight trails in the national forest and two others nearby that will show you the best the area has to offer.

The 19-mile section of the Oconto County Recreation Trail I recommend is an easy introduction to the north woods on an abandoned rail bed. It leads, with a few connecting town roads, to beautiful Chute Pond County Park. While this trail is also open to motorized all-terrain vehicles, usage is light, especially on weekdays. Nearby, the Lakewood Trails offer a tough, varied-terrain riding experience on ten miles one-way of wide, wilderness cross-country ski trail.

To the east, the Boulder Lake Trails are short and sweet for riders who like terrific scenery and single-track riding. The mile-and-a-half loop is so fine you'll want to do laps. The adjacent campground and lake are great spots to relax and swim.

There is a lot of solitude to be had in the Nicolet. I realize right now that during all my research, I didn't see a single other mountain biker and saw only a couple of hikers. Ed's Lake Trails is one of those attractive spots where you can have the whole place to yourself. A four-mile loop winds back through a dense maple, birch, and hemlock forest to a shelter overlooking its namesake lake. The trail could use some more people on it to roll in a hardpack, so saddle up all you intermediate and advanced riders.

To the east of the Nicolet Forest, the 3.4 miles of county trails at Gartzke Flowage offer intermediate and advanced riders a wide variety of terrain and scenery in a very compact area. The cross-country ski trails loop through sumac, pine, cedar, balsam fir, maple, and oak stands. A comfortable enclosed shelter with an inviting fireplace and a good stock of wood overlooks the trail bridge over the river.

At the Lauterman/Perch Lake Trails you can take on the challenge of a crazy mix of rocks and roots around Perch Lake, or tackle the technically easier but hillier loop circling Lauterman Lake. A few miles to the south, the 4.6-mile Ridge Trails take you to an overlook of the Pine River and up the back of a scenic glacial ridge. Camping and swimming at adjacent Lost Lake will make you glad you decided to get lost there.

The 7.1-mile loop on the Anvil Trails is another adventure in the primeval Nicolet. The Devil's Run single-track will test anyone's ability to stay on the bike. A connector trail runs east from the Anvil Trails to the Nicolet North Trails, where a 10.6-mile loop will challenge your aerobic capacity and show you some grand forest scenery to boot.

RIDE 60 · Oconto County Recreation Trail (Rail-Trail, On-Road)

AT A GLANCE

Length/configuration: 19.4 miles one way, including the 4-mile on-road section to Chute Pond Park

Aerobic difficulty: Very low; mostly on an abandoned rail bed

Technical difficulty: Easy

Scenery: Dense northern boreal forest mix of pine, birch, oak, and maple, with views of Chute Pond

Special comments: A family ride adventure for adults and older kids or a good high-speed cruise in a wilderness setting; this gravel rail-trail junctions with town roads that lead to picturesque Chute Pond County Park

The 19.4-mile route shown here includes a portion of the 30-mile length of the Oconto County Recreation Trail, which runs from Gillett on the southern end to Townsend in the north. It is one of the few rail-trails in the state that passes through a wild northern forest. While it is open to all-terrain vehicles, I found their usage to be light. Still, you might want to think twice about taking really young kids or beginning riders on it. The trail also follows the courses of both the north branch and south branch of the Oconto River, crossing the streams six times.

Spending a few miles riding quiet town roads, you can leave the rail bed and visit Chute Pond County Park. The pond is actually a flowage of the south branch of the Oconto River. In the park you can take hike a short two-thirds of a mile to a rock outcrop with a scenic overlook.

The crossroads villages of Lakewood and Mountain don't have much to offer other than a couple of taverns, and the Junction in Mountain serves food—but hey, this is the north woods. For a varied-terrain mountain bike ride try the nearby Lakewood Trails (see Ride 61).

General location: Between Lakewood and Mountain, paralleling WI 32.

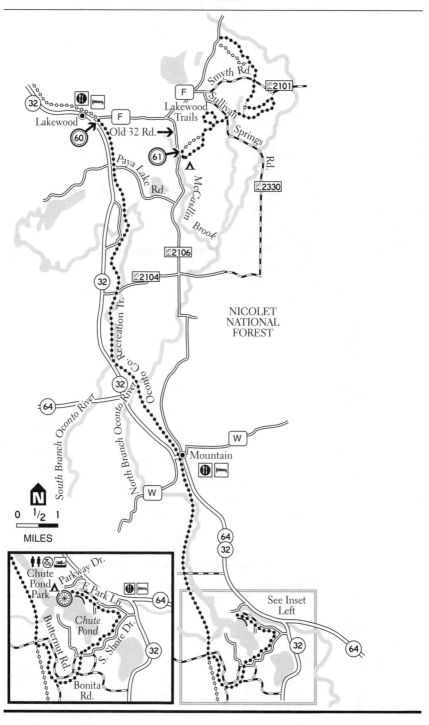

Elevation change: Virtually flat; typical rail-trail.

Season: Mid-May through September.

Services: Mountain has a motel, grocery, and restaurant; Lakewood offers a motel and bed-and-breakfast. There are taverns in both towns. Numerous resorts are located in the area. There are showers, camping, water, flush toilets, and swimming at Chute Pond County Park.

Hazards: The rail-trail is also open to all-terrain vehicle use. Sections of public roads open to motor vehicle traffic must be ridden to reach Chute Pond County Park.

Rescue index: Help is available in trail towns. There is a pay phone at Chute Pond County Park.

Land status: Oconto County Trail, public roadways.

Maps: The DeLorme book, Wisconsin Atlas & Gazetteer, shows all local roads and the rail bed on pages 78 and 79.

Finding the trail: From US 41/141, follow US 141 north to WI 22 and continue west to Gillett. For the south end of the trail, turn west off WI 32 onto Parkway Drive 3.5 miles south of Mountain, and follow the signs to Chute Pond Park. On the trail's north end, access is in Lakewood just east of WI 32 on County Road F.

Sources of additional information:

Oconto County Tourism
P.O. Box 43
Oconto, WI 54153-0043
(920) 834-6969; (888) 626-6862
www.ocontocounty.org

Notes on the trail: From Chute Pond County Park, cross the pedestrian walkway over the dam. Continue in the same direction along the path and gravel road (East Park Lane). Then follow Hillside Drive, South Shore Drive, Butternut Road (gravel) to the Oconto County Recreation Trail crossing and turn north. The rail-trail has not been specifically surfaced for bicycling, so it is best to use fat tires when riding it.

RIDE 61 · Lakewood Trails

AT A GLANCE

Length/configuration: 10.1 miles one way

Aerobic difficulty: High; there are very few level stretches and many steep climbs

Technical difficulty: Moderate; rocks, roots, windfalls, steep grades, and loose surface will be encountered

Scenery: Deep hardwood and pine forest

Special comments: A tough aerobic workout in a vast forest; this well-marked, grassy and forest floor surface trail can be ridden out-and-back or one-way, returning on adjacent roads

Look no further if you like your mountain biking tough and in a wilderness setting. The hills are nearly constant on the Lakewood Trail, and except for a couple road crossings, there are virtually no signs of civilization for ten miles. When you do come out onto the pavement of County Road F you'll feel like you've been shot out of a rocket.

The wide, grassy cross-country ski trail presents no real technical challenge other than windfall branches and a few deadhead rocks. It will tax your cardio-vascular system though. Expect to find steep climbs in the 80- to 100-foot range. The isolation of the beautiful maple and birch forest makes the effort worth-while. Several road crossings make bailing out to CR F possible if you find the going too difficult.

General location: 3 miles east of Lakewood, running roughly parallel to CR F.

Elevation change: There are several steep climbs of 80' on the southern section and 100' on the northern section.

Season: Mid-May through September.

Services: There are a motel, grocery, and restaurant in Mountain, motel and bed-and-breakfast in Lakewood, and taverns in both towns. Primitive campsites can be found along the creek just south of the trailhead. There are many resorts in the area, and the Prospect Lodge Resort and Restaurant is just northeast of the northern end of the trail on CR F.

Hazards: The trail receives little riding season maintenance and windfall branches will likely be encountered. Wide trail width helps riders avoid them. Iron gates are found across the trail at all road crossings. The trail is shared by hikers.

Rescue index: Help is available in Lakewood and at Prospect Lodge, just north-east of the north end of the trail.

Land status: Nicolet National Forest Trail.

Maps: A trail map is found in the Nicolet National Forest Trails booklet, avail-able from the forest service. The 7.5 minute series USGS quad for Wheeler Lake shows the terrain very well, but only shows some of the trails. The DeLorme book, Wisconsin Atlas & Gazetteer, shows all local roads on pages 78 and 79.

Finding the trail: From Lakewood on WI 32, go 2 miles east on CR F, turn south on Old 32 Road (Forest Service 2106), and go 1.3 miles to a parking pull-off on the west side of the road. The trail starts about 30 yards north of the pulloff, on the east side of the road.

The tough Lakewood Trails challenge cyclists.

Sources of additional information:

Nicolet National Forest
68 South Stevens Street
Rhinelander, WI 54501
(715) 362-1300
www.fs.fed.us/r9/cnnf

Oconto County Tourism
P.O. Box 43
Oconto, WI 54153-0043
(920) 834-6969; (888) 626-6862
www.ocontocounty.org

Notes on the trail: The wide skating and classic-width cross-country ski trail (wider than double-track) is well marked with blue posts and can be ridden in either direction. The trail's width alone makes it easy to follow. Occasionally, shortcut trails or trails with red signposts (narrower trails for classic skiing only) split off the blue trail. Iron gates stretch across the trail at all road crossings.

RIDE 62 · Boulder Lake Trails

AT A GLANCE

Length/configuration: 1.5-mile loop

Aerobic difficulty: Low to high; the yellow trail is low and the short green trail is high

Technical difficulty: Moderate to challenging; lots of rocks, roots, and loose surface on all trails, but these aspects combined with steep slopes make the green trail particularly challenging

Scenery: Beautiful forest, lake, and bog scenery

Special comments: The easy-to-follow trails are a good introduction to single-track riding on rock- and root-covered surfaces for riders with intermediate skills

What a find! I almost blew this one off because of the short distance. That would have been a mistake, because I had a wonderful ride on the single-track trails and would have put on some miles doing laps if I'd had more time. The Nicolet National Forest campground is in a beautiful setting on Boulder Lake. The only potential problem is the trail's close proximity to the campsites and the possibility of hiker-biker conflicts. Be careful and courteous. It would be a shame to lose this trail.

The trails offer a different type of scenery. For starters, you cross a tamarack bog on a boardwalk, and then circle another bog on the yellow trail. To me, bogs are wonders of nature and have a beautiful character found nowhere else. Tamaracks grow in an intriguingly random way. They look like pine trees, but loose their needles in the fall. Tamaracks are often the last trees in the forest to change color, and they turn a fantastic golden yellow. At an overlook of the bog on the yellow trail you can sit on a huge glacial boulder and soak up the scenery.

General location: 13 miles east of Mountain, off County Road W.

Elevation change: Steep grades of 40' in elevation are found on the green trail.

Season: Mid-May through September.

Services: There are a motel, grocery, tavern, and restaurant in Mountain. Camping, swimming, pit toilets, and water are available in the campground.

Hazards: Trails are well maintained, but windfall branches are always a possibility. All trails have rocks, roots, and loose surface. The green trail also has very steep slopes. Hikers also use the trails, and the closeness of the campsites makes surprise encounters possible.

Rescue index: Help is available from the campground hosts.

Land status: Nicolet National Forest Trails.

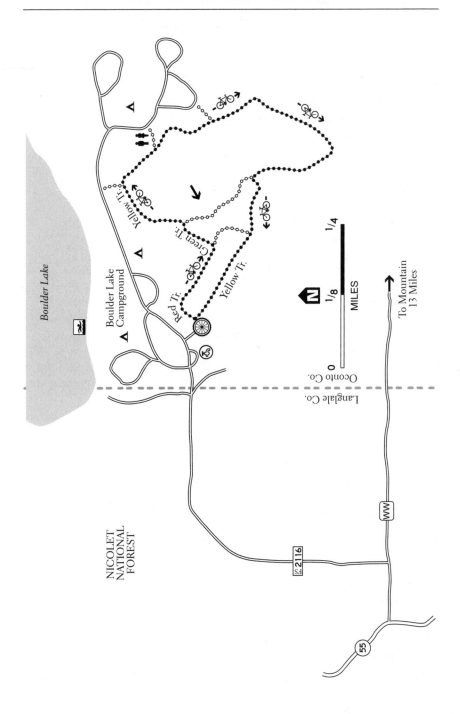

Try this narrow passage
on the Yellow Trail—
or go around.

Maps: A trail map is found in the Nicolet National Forest Trails booklet available from the forest service. The 7.5 minute series USGS quad for Langlade shows the terrain very well, but not the trails. The DeLorme book, Wisconsin Atlas & Gazetteer, shows all local roads on page 78.

Finding the trail: Drive 5 miles south of Langlade on WI 55 to CR WW, and follow the road east 0.5 mile to Campground Road (FR2166). From Mountain on WI 32, go west for 12 miles on CR W to reach Campground Road. Follow Campground Road north and park in the lot on the south side of the road, just past the information sign board.

Sources of additional information:

Nicolet National Forest
68 South Stevens Street
Rhinelander, WI 54501
(715) 362-1300
www.fs.fed.us/r9/cnnf

Oconto County Tourism
P.O. Box 43
Oconto, WI 54153-0043
(920) 834-6969; (888) 626-6862
www.ocontocounty.org

Notes on the trail: From the trailhead parking area, take the trail on the left (the red trail) that will be marked by red paint on trees or posts. The trails are well marked with paint blazes, and there are "you are here" map signs at intersections. Follow the red trail to the intersection with the green trail, and turn left onto it. After a short distance on this steep trail you will come to a **T** intersection with the yellow trail. Take it to the left and follow it around the bog until you have the option of going straight on the yellow trail or taking it to the left and uphill. Continue straight if you want to do some easy laps or head to the left to return to the trailhead.

RIDE 63 · Ed's Lake Trails

AT A GLANCE

Length/configuration: 4-mile loop; several loop combinations are possible

Aerobic difficulty: Moderate; two steep 70' climbs and a slow, soft forest floor also contribute to the difficulty

Technical difficulty: Easy to moderate; the only difficulty will be negotiating two steep climbs

Scenery: Beautiful deep hardwood forest with views of a pristine lake

Special comments: A neat place that just needs more riders to beat down a hardpack track; not to be missed if you like forest solitude on a not-too-challenging ride on wide, grassy, easy-to-follow trails

You know you're up in lake country when you find lakes with people's first names. I have no idea who Ed is or was, but he sure knew a nice body of water when he saw one. An Adirondack shelter on a rise above the shore is a fine place to enjoy the serenity of this small body of water with no development whatsoever on its shores.

Getting there will be half the fun on this four-mile, mostly easy riding loop through tall stands of maple, oak, hemlock, and birch. The only openings you see are a small field on Cutoff Route and at Ed's Lake. Along the way you'll find yourself riding through old railroad cuts where rotting ties can still be seen in the trail surface. In the lumberjack days, small gauge rail lines were often run into inaccessible areas to haul the logs out.

General location: Between Crandon and Wabeno on County Road W.

Elevation change: There are two 70' climbs.

Season: Mid-May through mid-October.

Services: All services are available in Crandon and Wabeno. There are pit toilets and water at the trailhead.

RIDE 63 • Ed's Lake Trails

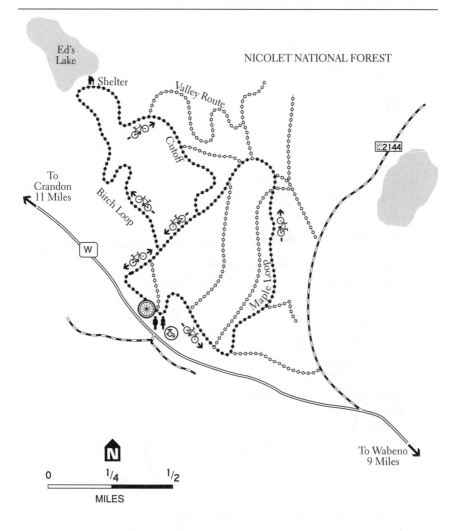

Hazards: Trails receive little riding-season maintenance so windfall branches may be encountered. Trails are also used by hikers.

Rescue index: Help is available in Crandon or Wabeno.

Land status: Nicolet National Forest trail.

Maps: A trail map is found in the Nicolet National Forest Trails booklet available from the forest service. The 7.5 minute series USGS quad for Roberts Lake shows the terrain very well, but not the trails. The DeLorme book, *Wisconsin Atlas & Gazetteer*, shows all local roads on pages 78 and 90.

Finding the trail: The well-signed trailhead is located directly off of CR W, 11 miles southeast of Crandon or 9 miles west of Wabeno.

Sources of additional information:

Crandon Area Chamber of
   Commerce
P.O. Box 88
Crandon, WI 54520-0088
(715) 478-3450; (800) 334-3387
www.crandonwi.com

Nicolet National Forest
68 South Stevens Street
Rhinelander, WI 54501
(715) 362-1300
www.fs.fed.us/r9/cnnf

Notes on the trail: The double-track, grassy, and forest floor surface trails are well signed with blue cross-country ski signs and periodic "you are here" map signs, for mostly one-way travel in a counterclockwise direction. From the trailhead, follow the easy Maple Loop to the right for a warmup, then take the Cutoff Route to the Birch Loop, returning on it to the trailhead.

RIDE 64 · Gartzke Flowage Trails

AT A GLANCE

Length/configuration: 3.4-mile double loop; several loop combinations are possible

Aerobic difficulty: Moderate to high; a slow roll on grassy and soft forest floor trails is moderate, and steep slopes on the valley sides make for the high difficulty

Technical difficulty: Easy to moderate; some climbing skills and descending confidence will be needed

Scenery: A mixed bag of pine, cedar, birch, balsam fir, and maple forest, with nice river views

Special comments: An interesting little trail system with a very nice shelter overlooking the channel of the Gartzke Flowage; wide, easy-to-follow, grassy and forest floor cross-country ski trails should be fun for intermediate-level riders

On a chilly day, the shelter alone makes it worth visiting this 3.4-mile easy- to-moderate double loop that lies in Langlade County just east of the Nicolet National Forest. Overlooking the bridge crossing the river, the enclosed building has an enticing fireplace and a good stock of wood. There is a lot of variety here for such a small trail system. Looping east from the parking lot, you'll pass through the tallest sumac grove I've ever seen and through a stand of Norway pine, and you'll see a ginseng farm to the left through the trees. If you don't know what one looks like, it's that lattice-covered structure over a field that's like some-

RIDE 64 • Gartzke Flowage Trails

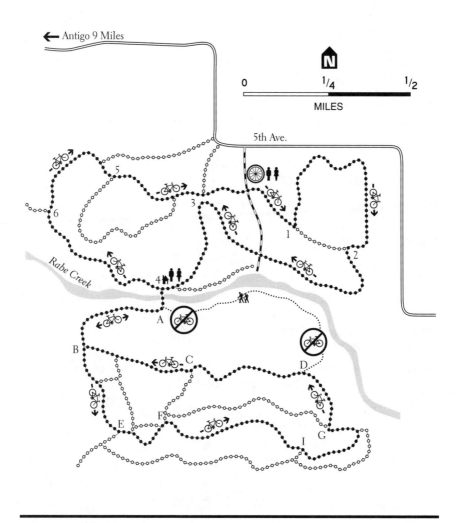

← Antigo 9 Miles

5th Ave.

thing you've never seen before. Although, it may not be there when you get to this trail, since ginseng can only be grown once on any piece of land.

The trail swings down onto a beautiful old logging road cut into the side of a wooded hill before heading up the valley side and down to the shelter and bridge. On the south side of the river your only option is to turn west (the trail to the east is signed "no biking"), where signs tell you to walk your bike. "Run your bike" is a better recommendation during mosquito season. Don't think you can make better time by ignoring the sign. The soft, boggy surface laced with cedar roots will stop you after a few feet anyway.

Soon you'll be looking at a very steep climb. At the top is something I've never seen on a cross-country ski trail before: A brass bell with a sign tells descending skiers to ring it, warning climbing skiers to look out. On top some wonderful terrain rolls through a dense hardwood forest, before a steep descent to the Cedar trail, which then traces the bottom edge of the slope back to the walk-your-bike section.

Back on the north side, you're in for some grassy trails and steep climbs to get back to the parking lot.

General location: 9 miles east of Antigo.

Elevation change: Four steep climbs of 50' elevation.

Season: Mid-May through September.

Services: All services, including bicycle retail and repair, are available in Antigo. There are pit toilets at the parking area and shelter house.

Hazards: Trails receive some riding-season maintenance, but riders must watch for windfall branches. Hikers also use the trails.

Rescue index: Help is available in Antigo.

Land status: Langlade County Forestry Department trail. A trail fee donation is requested and a self-pay station is located at the trailhead.

Maps: A trail map is available from the Langlade County Forestry Department. The 7.5 minute series USGS quad for Polar shows the terrain very well, but not the trails. The DeLorme book, *Wisconsin Atlas & Gazetteer*, shows all local roads on pages 77 and 78.

Finding the trail: Follow County Road F due east from Antigo to County Road S, and cross straight onto Fifth Avenue Road, which leads to the well-marked trailhead parking area.

Sources of additional information:

Antigo Chamber of Commerce
P.O. Box 339
Antigo, WI 54409-0339
(715) 623-4134; (888) 526-4523
www.newnorth.net/antigo.chamber/

Langlade County Forestry
Department
Box 460
Antigo, WI 54409
(715) 627-6236

Notes on the trail: A trail fee donation is requested at the trailhead. The grassy and forest floor double-track trails are well signed with blue-and-white mountain bike silhouette signs, a trail intersection numbering and lettering system, as well as periodic "you are here" map signs. The trail is maintained by a local group, The Antigo Bike and X-C Ski Club.

RIDE 65 · Lauterman/Perch Lake Trails

AT A GLANCE

Length/configuration: 5.4-mile double loop with an out-and-back section

Aerobic difficulty: Low to moderate; steep sections can be bypassed on the Lauterman Loop

Technical difficulty: Moderate to challenging; the narrow, relatively flat single-track around Perch Lake is covered with roots and rocks; it challenges handling skills on any day and is completely unrideable when wet; Lauterman Loop has rocks, roots, and steep slopes, but the greater width makes navigating easier

Scenery: Deep hardwood and pine forest with beautiful views of two wilderness lakes

Special comments: A variety of riding experiences in a wilderness setting; the single-track Perch Lake Trail will appeal to bikers with good handling skills, and the easier rolling Lauterman Trail can be enjoyed by anyone with intermediate or better ability

Trying to get away from it all? These trails are about as far as you can get. If you like wilderness riding without the risk of getting hopelessly lost, these trails are for you. The 5.4-mile route shown here breaks down into a 1.3-mile, narrow, technical single-track over rocks and roots around Perch Lake; a 0.5-mile out-and-back single-track connector; and a 3.1-mile single-track loop around Lauterman Lake with some steep climbs.

The Perch Lake Trail is a real challenge, despite being pretty flat. It is very grown-in, with lots of brush making for a narrow passage. The surface is a maze of rocks and roots that will test anyone's ability to stay on the bike.

You're in for some fine scenery on the Lauterman loop, with several boardwalk crossings in low spots and views of Lauterman Lake through the trees as you ride the high ground on the west side. You'll miss them if you take the easier bypasses that fork off to the right at the beginning of the two climbs. Intermediate to advanced riders will enjoy these loops. There is an Adirondack shelter at the south end of the lake.

Several miles to the south of the Lauterman loop are the equally appealing Ridge Trails (see Ride 66, page 212). You should be able to connect the two via Porkie's Trail at the south end of the Lauterman Trail, but I don't recommend trying this. I found it to be so poorly marked as to be impossible to follow.

General location: 12 miles west of Florence.

Elevation change: Perch Lake Trail is mostly flat. The connector has a climb of about 40' up to the road crossing. Elevation changes of 30' to 60' are found on the Lauterman Trail.

Season: June through September.

Boardwalks cross low spots at Lauterman Lake.

Services: All services are available in Florence. There are pit toilets and walk-in camping at Perch Lake and Lauterman Lake. Camping, pit toilets, swimming, and water are found at Lost Lake Campground to the south.

Hazards: Trails receive little riding-season maintenance and windfall branches are common. Rocks and roots are found on all trails, and the Perch Lake Trail is just littered with them. To ride the connector between the two loops you must cross WI 70. The trails are also used by hikers.

Rescue index: Help is available in Florence or from the campground host at Lost Lake Campground, adjacent to the Ridge Trail to the south.

Land status: Nicolet National Forest trails.

Maps: A trail map is found in the Nicolet National Forest Trails booklet available from the forest service. The 7.5 minute series USGS quads for Long Lake NE and Naults show the terrain very well, but only show some of the trails. The DeLorme book, *Wisconsin Atlas & Gazetteer*, shows all local roads on pages 90 and 91.

Finding the trail: 12 miles west of Florence, turn south on Forest Service Road 2154 for one-quarter mile to the parking lot on the east side of the road. The trails start on the west side.

Sources of additional information:

Florence County Chamber of
   Commerce
P.O. Box 410
Florence, WI 54121-0410
www.florencewisconsin.com

Nicolet National Forest
68 South Stevens Street
Rhinelander, WI 54501
(715) 362-1300
www.fs.fed.us/r9/cnnf

RIDE 65 • Lauterman/Perch Lake Trails
RIDE 66 • Ridge Trails

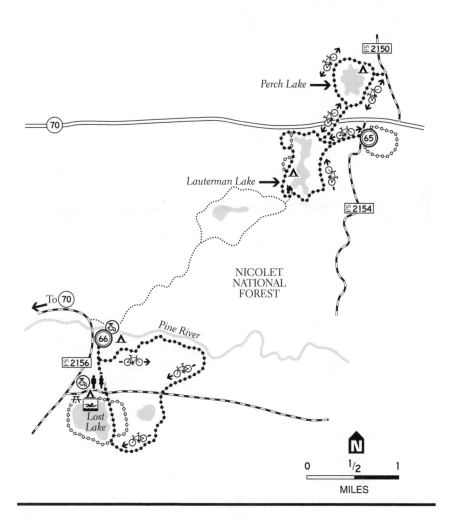

Notes on the trail: The single-track Lauterman Trail is marked for travel in a counterclockwise direction, with occasional "you are here" map signs and blue diamond blazes on trees. Riding west from the trailhead, follow the "best trail" sign to stay on course. You'll soon pass the connector trail running to the right toward Perch Lake Trail. At the south end of the Lauterman Trail loop, the Porkie's trail runs off to the south, but is not recommended. The two-way connector and Perch Lake Trail is not very well signed, but is still easy to follow.

RIDE 66 · Ridge Trails

AT A GLANCE

Length/configuration: 4.6-mile loop, including the out-and-back panhandle

Aerobic difficulty: Moderate to high; most of the distance is rolling, but several steep climbs and a slow rolling surface over much of the distance add difficulty

Technical difficulty: Moderate; the initial panhandle section from the trailhead to the loop is extremely rocky and root covered, but things get better on the loop

Scenery: Deep mixed hardwood and pine forest with an overview of the Pine River, and a ridge top ride among white birch trees

Special comments: The surface at the beginning is enough to turn anyone back, but the payoff view of the Pine River and the ridge-top ride make it worthwhile; the single-track varies greatly in surface type

Technically demanding trails are not for everyone, especially when the trickiest stretch comes right at the start. On the 4.6-mile Ridge Trail your reward will be a fine overview of the Pine River and, after a challenging climb, a ride along the back of a glacial esker. A steep, narrow ridge that falls away sharply on either side, an esker traces the course of a river inside a glacier, and this one has grown up with a magnificent hemlock and paper birch forest.

Farther on, the trail swings around to the north and passes scenic Lost Lake. You can spend some extra time in this tranquil spot by pitching a tent in the adjacent campground or taking time for a swim. Just north of the river, the Chipmunk Trail runs northeast, connecting with the Lauterman Trail (Ride 65). I don't recommend taking it at this point, due to poor signage.

General location: 20 miles west of Florence.

Elevation change: There is one very steep 70' climb.

Season: June through September.

Services: All services are available in Florence. Camping, pit toilets, swimming, and water are available at Lost Lake Campground.

Hazards: Trails receive little riding-season maintenance and windfall branches are common. Rocks and roots make the panhandle stretch from the trailhead to the loop hazardous for novice riders. There is an extremely steep descent from the esker ridge to the crossing of Forest Service Road 2417, and caution should be exercised. The trails are also used by hikers.

Rescue index: Help is available in Florence or from the campground host at Lost Lake Campground, adjacent to the Ridge Trail to the south.

Land status: Nicolet National Forest trails.

Maps: A trail map is found in the Nicolet National Forest Trails booklet available from the forest service. The 7.5 minute series USGS quads for Long Lake NE shows the terrain very well, but only shows some of the trails. The DeLorme book, *Wisconsin Atlas & Gazetteer,* shows all local roads on page 90.

Finding the trail: 17 miles west of Florence, turn south on Forest Service Road 2450. After another mile, just after the road turns to the west, turn south on Forest Service Road 2156 (Chipmunk Rapids Road), and follow it to the entrance road for the Chipmunk Rapid Campground, just south of the Pine River bridge. Turn east into the campground road and park in the parking area on the left side of the road. The Ridge Trail starts on the south side of the road between the parking area and FS 2156.

Sources of additional information:

Florence County Natural Resource
   Center
HCT, Box 83
Florence, WI 54121
(715) 528-5377

Nicolet National Forest
68 South Stevens Street
Rhinelander, WI 54501
(715) 362-1300
www.fs.fed.us/r9/cnnf

Notes on the trail: The single-track trail is signed for travel in either direction with brown-and-yellow signs and arrows. I recommend riding the loop in a clockwise direction.

RIDE 67 · Anvil Trails

AT A GLANCE

Length/configuration: 7.1-mile loop; several loop variations are possible

Aerobic difficulty: Moderate to high; while most of the distance is moderate, there are very tough climbs on Devil's Run

Technical difficulty: Moderate; trails are generally hardpack, but Devil's Run is covered with roots and rocks.

Scenery: Deep hardwood and pine forest

Special comments: A beautiful wilderness trail with a cozy shelter and fire pit along the way; a good ride for intermediate and better riders

The Nicolet National Forest Anvil Trails are perennial favorites for cross-country skiers. The deep maple forest and varied trails make for fun mountain biking, too. The 7.1-mile loop shown here ranks near the upper end of the moderate difficulty category for the average rider. Several options exist to make it shorter or easier. Trail surfaces vary greatly. You'll find firm double-track with grassy and hardpack earthen surface on the West and North Trails. You'll ride a

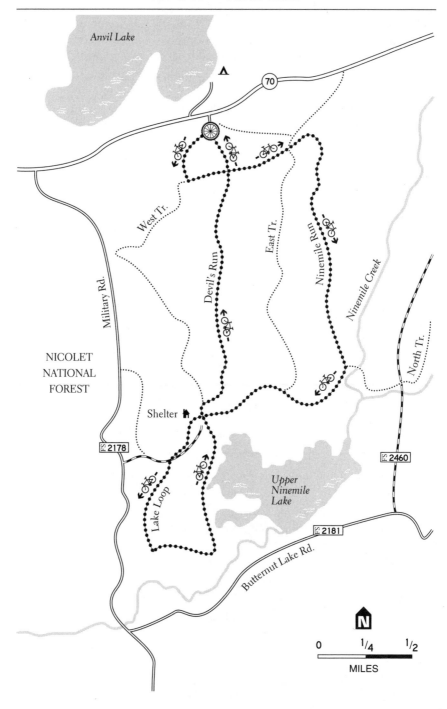

Anvil Lake

70

West Tr.

East Tr.

Devil's Run

Ninemile Run

Ninemile Creek

North Tr.

Military Rd.

NICOLET
NATIONAL
FOREST

Shelter

FS 2178

FS 2460

Lake Loop

Upper
Ninemile
Lake

FS 2181

Butternut Lake Rd.

N

0   1/4   1/2

MILES

Welcome to the Anvil Trails.

narrower cross-country ski trail with a bare forest floor and a rougher surface on Ninemile Run and Lake Loop. The Devil's Run is true single-track, rough from rocks and roots, with some very steep sections.

No matter where you are, the grade is never constant for more than a few yards. About halfway around you will find a small log cabin shelter with a fireplace and a good supply of wood, a nice stop for a break on a damp or chilly day. There is an overview of grassy Ninemile Lake near the end of the Lake Loop. No real technical ability is required except on Devil's Run, where the ability to weave among rocks and roots while climbing and then will bounce over the same going downhill is necessary.

You can make the Anvil Trail experience easier by taking the West Trail from the shelter to the trailhead, which cuts out the more difficult Devil's Run. Skipping the Lake Loop eliminates 1.8 miles of riding. If more is what you crave, you can take the 1.2-mile each-way connector trail to the east to the Nicolet North Trails (see Ride 68, page 217), and tack on another 10 miles of off-roading.

General location: 9 miles east of the town of Eagle River.

Elevation change: Terrain is nearly constantly rolling. Many steep pitches in the 20' to 40' range will be encountered, as well as several in the 70' range. The elevation difference between the high and low points on the trails is 120'.

Season: April through October. Insect populations are heavy from mid-May through July.

Services: There is a water pump at the trailhead. All services are available 9 miles west on WI 70 in the town of Eagle River, including bicycle retail and repair at Chain of Lakes Cyclery.

Hazards: The trails are very well maintained, but downed trees and branches may be found at any time. Single-track trails are rough from rocks and roots. All trails are also open to hiking.

Rescue index: Help is available in Eagle River. If you are injured or have mechanical problems, your best chance of rescue will come if you can make your way to WI 70 or Forest Service Road 2178 (Military Road).

Land status: Nicolet National Forest.

Maps: A detailed trail map is available from the Nicolet National Forest office. The 7.5 minute series USGS quad for Anvil Lake shows the terrain very well, but only shows some of the trails. The DeLorme book, *Wisconsin Atlas & Gazetteer*, shows all local roads on page 89.

Finding the trail: From the junction of US 45 and WI 70, just east of the town of Eagle River, travel eight miles and turn south at the Anvil Lake Trail sign.

Sources of additional information:

Nicolet National Forest Office
Eagle River-Florence Ranger District
P.O. Box 1809
Eagle River, WI 54521
(715) 479-2827
www.fs.fed.us/r9/cnnf

Eagle River Area Chamber of
    Commerce and Visitors Center
P.O. Box 1917
Eagle River, MN 54521-1917
(715) 479-6400, (800) 359-6315
www.eagleriver.org

Notes on the trail: The Anvil Trails are well marked with frequent "you are here" and trail-name signs. Most of the trails are one-way. From the trailhead follow the West Trail to the right. After 0.3 mile, at a **T** intersection, turn left on a connecting trail that runs to the east. Use caution at 0.9 mile, where the Ninemile Run trail begins. Forest Service trail signs are set at a low height and are brown with yellow lettering, not easily spotted in the deep forest where light may be low most of the time. The inclination at the Ninemile Run intersection is to go straight, which would take you to a gate out at WI 70. The correct turn turn is to the right onto the Ninemile Run, which is signed to the right on the trail itself.

At 2.5 miles turn right (southwest) onto the North Trail, a wider, grassy, rolling double-track ski trail. The trail that runs to the left (southeast) is the connector that goes to the Nicolet Nordic Trails.

At 3.5 miles you will arrive at a log cabin shelter and the intersection of the Devil's Run and West Trails. Follow the North Trail, which is a wide unimproved road at this point, to the left (south). After 0.3 mile turn left (south) on the Lake Loop. This will take you back to the shelter intersection where you will pick up the Devil's Run trail and ride it back to the trailhead.

RIDE 68 · Nicolet North Trails

AT A GLANCE

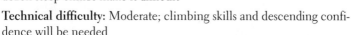

Length/configuration: 10.6-mile loop, including the out-and-back panhandle

Aerobic difficulty: High; while the terrain is mostly rolling, the resistance of soft grassy surface and a half-dozen steep climbs make it difficult

Technical difficulty: Moderate; climbing skills and descending confidence will be needed

Scenery: Deep northwoods wilderness forest with fine bog and lake views

Special comments: All things considered, Nicolet Nordic stacks up as a challenging day's riding; wide, grassy cross-country ski trails give it a slow roll, but the payoffs are some fine lake and bog views

Another favorite area for cross-country skiers, the Nicolet Nordic trails tie into private trails at Eagle River Nordic Ski Center on the east, where they probably test more skis during the winter months than any place this side of Scandinavia. The Nicolet National Forest trails are a fine place to put a mountain bike through its paces, too. The trails could use a few more riders to beat in a hardpack track, but even as they are, the trails are fun to ride and lead you to some real forest gems.

This 10.6-mile route allows a 1.4-mile warmup and cool down on paved Butternut Road from the recommended trailhead at the Franklin Lake boat landing. You'll be glad for the warm muscles when you hit the trails. Things are never the same grade for more than a few hundred yards on the double-track trails. Taking the Ash Meadow Trail, you'll pass through a tall maple forest where the leaf canopy blocks out the sun and little else can find enough light to grow. Riding south, the Pat Shay Trail skirts a picturesque pond and bog before making a steep switchback climb through a stunning stand of hemlock. Swinging east along the north shore of its namesake lake, the Pat Shay is called the Dow Jones here because of the constantly up-and-down terrain. Just after this stretch you can leave the Pat Shay Trail for the 1.3-mile each-way Hidden Lakes Trail that cuts southeast to Knapp Road. There is an interesting single-track stretch on it.

If a circuit at Nicolet Nordic isn't enough for you, take the 1.2-mile each-way Butternut Trail over to the Anvil Trails (Ride 67) for another 7.1-mile loop. If the ride has been plenty, just enjoy a relaxing dip in Franklin Lake.

General location: 15 miles east of Eagle River.

Elevation change: Very frequent climbs of 20' to 40' and a half dozen 60' to 80' climbs.

Season: June through September.

RIDE 68 • Nicolet North Trails

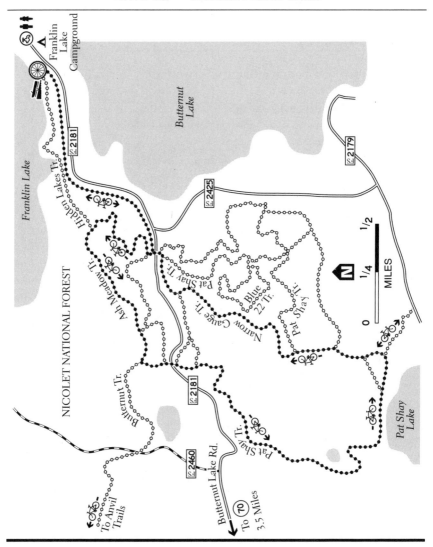

Services: Water and pit toilets are at the Franklin Lake boat landing trailhead. All services are available 9 miles west on WI 70 in the town of Eagle River, including bicycle retail and repair at Chain of Lakes Cyclery. Camping, swimming, water, and pit toilets are available at Franklin Lake Campground.

Hazards: The trails are very well maintained, but downed trees and branches may be found at any time. Single-track trails are rough from rocks and roots. All trails are open to hiking.

Riding through the Trees on the Nicolet North Trails.

Rescue index: Help is available in Eagle River. If you are injured or have mechanical problems, your best chance of rescue will come if you can make your way to WI 70 or Forest Service Road 2178 (Military Road).

Land status: Nicolet National Forest.

Maps: A detailed trail map is available from the Nicolet National Forest office. The 7.5 minute series USGS quad for Anvil Lake shows the terrain very well, but only shows some of the trails. The DeLorme book, *Wisconsin Atlas & Gazetteer*, shows all local roads on page 89.

Finding the trail: From the junction of US 45 and WI 70, just east of the town of Eagle River, travel 8 miles and turn south at the Anvil Lake Trail sign.

Sources of additional information:

Nicolet National Forest Office
Eagle River-Florence Ranger District
P.O. Box 1809
Eagle River, WI 54521
(715) 479-2827
www.fs.fed.us/r9/cnnf

Eagle River Area Chamber of
   Commerce and Visitors Center
P.O. Box 1917
Eagle River, MN 54521-1917
(715) 479-6400, (800) 359-6315
www.eagleriver.org

Notes on the trail: The double-track, grassy, and forest floor cross-country ski trails can be ridden in either direction, but these cues are for riding counterclockwise. Trail marking varies, but if you pay attention to these directions, you should be able to avoid getting lost. While the area is total wilderness, the up side is that it is completely surrounded by paved forest roads, so even if you're totally off-track, you should run into one eventually.

From the trailhead at the Franklin Lake boat landing parking lot, ride west on paved Forest Service Road 2181 (Butternut Lake Road) for 1.4 miles, passing Forest Service Road 2425 (Crossover Road) going off to the south. Look for the "trail crossing" sign as you ride west on FS 2181. Turn north just beyond the sign at the trail, and then make an almost immediate right turn to the east. This puts you on the Ash Meadow cross-country ski trail. As the trail junctions with other trails and swings around to the west, you will notice white diamond markers on trees. These will be your best and most constant trail guides until you pass Pat Shay Lake. The white diamonds will take you past the junction with the Butternut Trail, the connector that goes to the Anvil Trails, and to the south across FS 2181 onto the Pat Shay Trail. You'll be on the Pat Shay for a long distance. Just past Pat Shay Lake, a trail goes off to the south and is marked with the white diamond markers. This is the Hidden Lakes Trail, which goes to Knapp Road. Continue straight to stay on the Pat Shay and complete the loop.

Further on, the Pat Shay junctions with the Narrow Gauge Trail, which you should take to the left. It snakes around to the north and eventually junctions with the Pat Shay again at a T intersection. At this point take the Pat Shay to the right (northeast), and at the next intersection you will junction with the Mostly Up Trail, where you will turn left (northeast) to get back to FS 2181.

LAKE LAND

The title of this section says it all—lake and land. In Vilas and Oneida counties, it's almost a toss-up as to which you'll find more often. This is truly the land of lakes. There's even a town named Land O'Lakes. Vilas County has 346 lakes, accounting for 15 percent of its area. Add to that the marshes and bogs, and you've got about a quarter of the surface area that won't support foot or tread. Neighboring Oneida County isn't much different. On the face of the globe, only the boundary waters of Minnesota, Ontario, and parts of Finland compare.

There is plenty of terra firma left for good trails though. Since most vacation homes are built on lakeshores, much of the land is wilderness. Vast state and county forests cover the area. This means terrific trail riding with some wonderful lake views, except on the Washburn Trails and Razorback Ridges Trail.

This is also one of the most compact ride areas in this book. The ten trails are all located within a swath of land 15 miles wide and 35 miles long. Your choices are all close at hand once you've pitched your tent or checked in at a motel or resort. There is even an effort underway locally to join up a half dozen of these routes with off-road links on snowmobile trails.

Much of my research in the area was a process of picking and choosing. Vilas County alone claims a whopping 17 trail systems open to mountain biking, many of them in the Vilas County Forest. I found that most of the trails weren't worth your time or effort since little or no riding season maintenance was done (to the extent that windfall trees brought down over a year before by a big storm remained). Poor signage was another problem.

There may be some gold nugget of a trail out there that I missed, and there certainly is potential for good riding at many of these systems, but based on my work and advice from local riders, I'm fairly confident I have all of the trails worth visiting. Local riders are getting organized, the all-important step to ensuring continued use of the trails highlighted here and the opening of more systems in the future. Check locally for new possibilities. You won't be disappointed here no matter what your abilities or interests. There is something for everyone here, from rail-trail to technical single-track.

Let's start at the tough end of the scale at the Washburn Lake Trails near Rhinelander, where you'll find aerobically demanding double-track cross-country ski trails intertwined with awesome single-track, specially cut for mountain biking.

On the easier, scenic side of north woods riding, the McNaughton Trails double-track takes you over gently rolling terrain to scenic overviews of pristine lakes. Easier yet is the nearby Bearskin State Trail, a rail-trail that heads south from Minocqua in elegant style over long, scenic lake trestles. This is a fine family ride made even better by the location of Torpey Park near the north trailhead, where kids can swim in Lake Minocqua or frolic on the playground.

Just east of Minocqua are two sister trail systems with vastly different characters. The dark, mysterious Raven Trails lead riders of intermediate or advanced ability on double- and single-tracks to strikingly beautiful lakes. The Madeline Lake Trails are much more tame, and the grassy double-track loops are manageable even by novice riders.

Near Sayner, things get tough on the Razorback Trails, where the double-track trails traverse some steep terrain and the extensive, intertwining single-track can force all but the most expert riders to walk a stretch or two.

Farther north in the Boulder Junction area, two systems interconnect to create a potpourri of great scenery, potential wildlife encounters, and riding experiences, from family cruising on a paved trail, to gently rolling double-track, to stimulating, moderately-challenging single-track. The Escanaba Trails furnish the latter experience and take you past lovely lakes. The Boulder Area Trail System (BATS)/Lumberjack Trails are attainable even by novice riders, and offer the chance of spotting bald eagles catching a fish lunch on the Manitowish River. Also part of the BATS system is the gently rolling, paved trail that runs south from Boulder Junction to a picnic area on scenic Trout Lake.

The frosting on the cake for nature-loving riders is the Langley Lake Trails in the Eagle River area. The grassy, double-track trails visit a handful of pristine lakes and ponds where you may spot bounding deer or hear the slap of beaver's tails on the water.

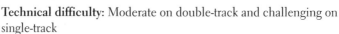

RIDE 69 · Washburn Lake Trails

AT A GLANCE

Length/configuration: 5.5-mile loop on cross-country trails interwoven with 3 miles of single-track; many loop combinations possible

Aerobic difficulty: High; constantly varying terrain with many steep climbs

Technical difficulty: Moderate on double-track and challenging on single-track

Scenery: Deep maple and birch forest

Special comments: A great place for a real aerobic workout on double-track trails, with the added challenge of newer single-track sections that will test bike handling skills; the grassy and forest floor surface trails are easy to follow and have a hardpack track ridden in

I rode the Washburn Trails with local cross-country skiing legend Mitch Mode. He showed me why the system is prized by both skiers and bikers looking for a workout. The constant up and down—often super-steep—even had him huffing and puffing.

Laid out on an assortment of old double-track logging roads and specially cut cross-country ski trails, the main loops make maximum use of the terrain. So do the new single-track sections that intertwine. You can expect the best of Midwestern single-track with all the fun of sudden and steep grade change, rocks, roots, narrow passages, and tight turns.

There is not much here for the novice rider, but if someone is aerobically fit and really wants to get an idea of what it is people love about the tough side of the sport, take them here. You might make another convert.

General location: 7 miles west of Rhinelander.

Elevation change: Extremes of 80' to 90' with many 30' to 50' climbs.

Season: Mid-May through mid-October.

Services: All services, including bicycle retail and repair at Mel's Trading Post, are available in Rhinelander, 8 miles to the east.

Hazards: Trails are well maintained, but windfall branches may be encountered. There is a cable gate across the trail at the bottom of a hill on the west loop. Deadhead rocks are common, and it's best to stick to the hardpack track on descents where they can be better seen. Rocks, roots, loose surface, extreme grades, and narrow passages between trees can be hazardous on the single-track. Carrying and knowing how to use a compass are advised. Trails are also used by hikers.

Rescue index: Help is available in Rhinelander.

Land status: Oneida County Forest.

Maps: A trail map is available from the information contacts. The 7.5 minute series USGS quads for McNaughton and Woodboro show the terrain very well, but only some of the trails.

Finding the trail: From US 8, 6 miles west of Rhinelander, turn north on Crescent Road, then almost immediately turn west on County Road N at a **T** intersection. Travel 0.75 mile to Washburn Lake Road and turn north. Travel 1.4 miles and look for the trailhead parking lot along the right side of the road after you pass Washburn Lake.

Sources of additional information:

Oneida County Forestry Department
Courthouse, Box 400
Rhinelander, WI 54501
(715) 369-6140

Rhinelander Area Chamber of
   Commerce
P.O. Box 795
Rhinelander, WI 54502-0795
(715) 365-7464; (800) 236-4386
www.rhinelanderchamber.com

RIDE 69 • Washburn Lake Trails

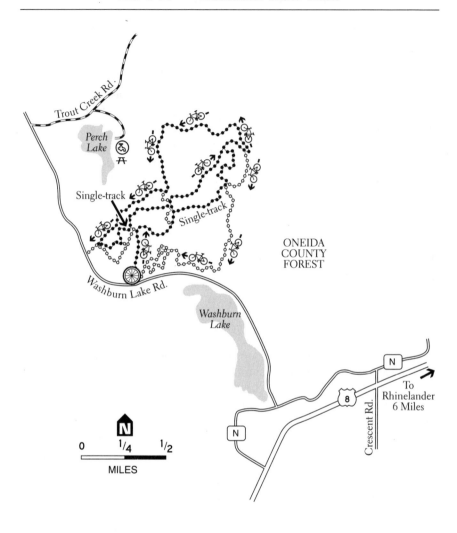

Notes on the trail: Double-track trails are well marked for one-way travel with brown-and-white mountain bike silhouette signs. To ride all of the double-track trail, you need to cover the first mile of trail (middle corridor) twice. Most single-track sections, which were not signed at the time I visited, can be picked up along this trail. The compact area of the trail system makes getting really lost unlikely. Trails are open seasonally. Please contact the Oneida County Department of Forestry for trail status.

RIDE 70 · McNaughton Trails

AT A GLANCE

Length/configuration: 7.4-mile loop; several loop combinations are possible

Aerobic difficulty: Low; most of the workout on these basically flat to gently rolling trails comes from a slow roll over soft trail surfaces

Technical difficulty: Easy; the greatest obstacle (walking is advised for novices) comes from logs laid parallel to the trail on short, soft, boggy stretches making for tricky wheel-grabbing riding, especially when wet

Scenery: Beautiful deep maple, birch, white pine, and hemlock forest with lake and bog views

Special comments: A nice beginner ride with a high aesthetic component; interconnecting, soft-surface trails are easy to follow

There are no big challenges on the McNaughton Lake Trails, other than coping with some logs laid over soft trail sections and the resident mosquito population. The 7.4-mile loop is an excellent place to bring beginners for a taste of just how pleasant and scenic off-road riding can be—at least in late summer and fall, when those nasty mosquitoes have retired for the season.

Multiple loops make many combinations of routes possible. The little lakes they pass are wonderful, peaceful spots. A boardwalk gives you a fine view of McNaughton Lake. Along the way you'll pass through tall stands of hemlock and white pine as you roll along trails made soft by a blanket of brown needles. Most of the lake views occur during the second half of the loop. An Adirondack shelter at the south end of Helen Lake makes a nice stop for lunch or a rest.

General location: 12 miles northwest of Rhinelander.

Elevation change: Basically flat to gently rolling, with about 30' of elevation on the west side of McNaughton Lake.

Season: June through mid-October.

Services: All services are available in Rhinelander and Minocqua. Bicycle retail and repair are available at Mel's Trading Post in Rhinelander and BJ's Sport Shop in Minocqua.

Hazards: Trails are well maintained, but windfall branches may be encountered. Trails are also used by hikers.

Rescue index: Help is available in Rhinelander and Minocqua.

Land status: Northern Highland—American Legion State Forest. A state trail pass fee is required of bicyclists age 16 and older for riding the off-road trails ($3 daily/$10 annual).

RIDE 70 · McNaughton Trails

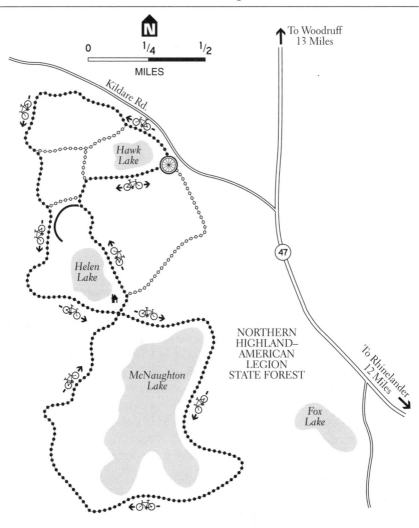

Maps: Trail maps are available from information contacts or from the Wisconsin Department of Natural Resources. The 7.5 minute series USGS quads for Lake Tomahawk and McNaughton show the terrain very well, but only some the trails.

Finding the trail: From WI 47, 12 miles northwest of Rhinelander or 13 miles southeast of Woodruff, turn west onto Kildare Road and travel 0.5 mile to the trailhead parking area on the south side of the road.

Sources of additional information:

Northern Highland—American
    Legion State Forest
8779 Highway J
Woodruff, WI 54568
(715) 385-2704

Rhinelander Area Chamber of
    Commerce
P.O. Box 795
Rhinelander, WI 54502-0795
(715) 365-7464; (800) 236-4386
www.rhinelanderchamber.com

Notes on the trail: A daily or annual state trail pass fee is required (see Land status). The grassy and forest floor double-track trails are well marked for mostly one-way travel with green-and-white mountain bike silhouette signs and "you are here" map signs at intersections.

RIDE 71 · Bearskin State Trail (Rail-Trail)

AT A GLANCE

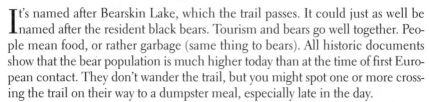

Length/configuration: 18 miles one way

Aerobic difficulty: Low; typical rail-trail

Technical difficulty: Easy

Scenery: Wonderful lake views from the trestle at the Minocqua trailhead, then deep northern forest

Special comments: Probably the most popular rail-trail in the north woods; a fun family ride or high-speed cruise based in the popular tourist town of Minocqua

It's named after Bearskin Lake, which the trail passes. It could just as well be named after the resident black bears. Tourism and bears go well together. People mean food, or rather garbage (same thing to bears). All historic documents show that the bear population is much higher today than at the time of first European contact. They don't wander the trail, but you might spot one or more crossing the trail on their way to a dumpster meal, especially late in the day.

A bear sighting might be the most exciting moment on a cruise of the 18-mile, crushed-granite Bearskin State Trail. It won't be the only highlight, however. Minocqua is the best place to begin and end your ride, as there is really nothing at the southern end. Right at the start you cross long railroad trestles with great views of Lake Minocqua and the town. Pleasure boats and jet skis zig-zag the waters on any nice summer day. Just north of the trailhead, along a city bike path, is Torpy Park, a wonderful spot on the lake with swimming, tennis courts, sand volleyball, picnic tables, grills, and a playground.

From Lake Minocqua you plunge into the deep northern forest and marshes that cast their wilderness spell on all city-weary visitors. About five miles south of

Minocqua, you can access the services of the crossroads community of Hazelhurst, along US 51 just east of the trail. The summer stage theater there is not something to ride to, but well worth an evening visit if you happen to be in the area. For those more interested in aerobics than aesthetics, the Raven and Madeline Lake trails are nearby (Rides 72 and 73).

General location: South of Minocqua, parallel to US 51.

Elevation change: Virtually none.

Season: May through mid-October.

Services: All services, including bicycle retail and repair at BJ's Sport Shop, are available in Minocqua. There are flush toilets, concessions, water, and swimming at Torpy Park. Food and lodging are available in Minocqua and Hazelhurst.

Hazards: The trail is also used by hikers.

Rescue index: Help is available in Minocqua and Hazelhurst.

Land status: Wisconsin State Park Trail. A trail pass fee is required for bicyclists age 16 and older ($3 daily/$10 annual). The trail pass also covers usages such as cross-country skiing, and bicycling on state mountain bike trails.

Maps: A trail map is available from local contacts or the Wisconsin Department of Natural Resources. The DeLorme book, *Wisconsin Atlas & Gazetteer*, shows the trail and all local roads and road names.

Finding the trail: For the trail's north end, from US 51 in Minocqua, turn west on Front Street and park in the municipal parking lot behind the post office. For the south end, from US 51 turn east on County Road K and go 0.75 mile to the trailhead parking lot on the north side of the road.

Sources of additional information:

Hazelhurst Information Center
P.O. Box 311
Hazelhurst, WI 54531-0311
(715) 356-7350

Minocqua-Arbor Vitae-Woodruff
 Area Chamber of Commerce
P.O. Box 1006
Minocqua, WI 54548-1006
(715) 356-5266; (800) 446-6784
www.minocqua.org

Wisconsin Department of Natural
 Resources
Bureau of Parks and Recreation
P.O. Box 7921
Madison, WI 53707-7921
(608) 266-2181
www.dnr.state.wi.us

Notes on the trail: A daily or annual state trail pass fee is required (see Land status). Services in Hazelhurst can be accessed via Oneida Street, which the trail crosses about 5 miles south of Minocqua.

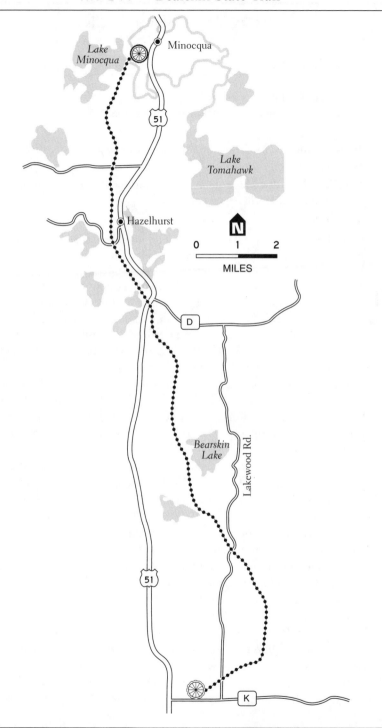

Lake
Minocqua

Minocqua

51

Lake
Tomahawk

Hazelhurst

N

0   1   2

MILES

D

Bearskin
Lake

Lakewood Rd.

51

K

RIDE 72 · Raven Trails

AT A GLANCE

Length/configuration: 4.9-mile loop, including the out-and-back panhandle; several loop combinations possible

Aerobic difficulty: Moderate; mostly rolling with several steep climbs

Technical difficulty: Moderate to challenging; loose surface on steep grades and soft sand will be encountered

Scenery: Superb north woods and lake scenery

Special comments: A real gem of a trail for intermediate and higher ability riders; the loop is easy to follow and wonderfully scenic

This is the one that almost got away. I remember how thrilled I was to find it when I first explored the area. Local riders told me it was the place to go, and I was richly rewarded with a primo riding experience. Then the Wisconsin Department of Natural Resources closed it to mountain biking. Seems there was some concern about erosion on a few steep sections, and conflicts with hikers due to riders venturing onto the verboten Nature Trail.

I was in Minocqua the week they shut down the Raven, and I hadn't been there a half-hour before I'd heard three riders gripe about what had happened. Sometimes, though, these things can have positive results. The locals got organized and pitched in with crews to deal with the erosion problems, so the Raven is once again open to bikers.

Good things don't have to last though, so if weather conditions are sloppy and you just have to ride, go to the grassy Madeline Lake Trails nearby (where the DNR was redirecting riders when they closed the Raven; see Ride 72, page 243). Don't skid your rear wheel on the steep downhills. If you can't handle the terrain, ride elsewhere. And don't ride on the Nature Trail, which is marked with the white-and-red no mountain biking signs.

The 4.9-mile route takes you past two pristine lakes. Clear Lake is just what it says. It's a good idea to take a close look at it to remind yourself that this is what water is supposed to look like. Little Inkpot Lake, however, is no less clear. It must have gotten its name solely from its tiny size and shape.

This loop is at the low end of challenging on the rating scale, and is a great place for an introduction to steep, technical, single-track riding. Over half the distance is single-track characterized by short, steep plunges and climbs in the 20- to 30-foot range, on a surface made rough by roots and rounded cobbles. The run-outs are nearly all straight and you can really bomb them, particularly if you have suspension.

On the less radical scale, the single-track is a good place to learn weight shift, proper braking, and uphill techniques for weaving through the rocks and keep-

RIDE 72 • Raven Trails

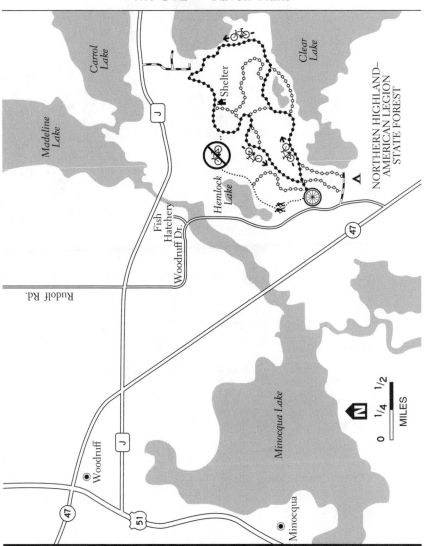

ing momentum going. It's fun for riders, and there's nothing that will make you scream, "My God, I'm gonna die!" Less experienced riders may want to lower the saddle a bit to make weight shifting easier. The single-track is broken up by gently rolling sections on grassy, double-track cross-country ski trails. There are a number of places you can get airborne on the single-track, including a 70-foot downhill that seems to head straight for the lake with a whoop-de-do at the end where you can catch some major air—if you want to.

Too much talk about the biking might make you think that this is what the Raven Trail experience is all about. Really though, the aesthetic component is at

Don't let the "lack of snow" keep you off the Expert Loop.

least as vital as the riding. The north woods magic begins at the trailhead, where a stand of tall white pines has covered the rooted trail with soft, coppercolored needles. The white pines soon give way to a dense canopy of birch, maple, and Norway pine. The trees grow close to the trail, and glimpses and views of the lakes through the trees are frequent.

Several short side trails run down to their shores. As you turn away from Clear Lake you'll climb remnant sand dunes and a steep hogback ridge on your way to the cross-country ski shelter. The open shelter faces south to catch the sun, and you can enjoy the heat from an elevated stone fire ring in chilly weather. You can ignore the "Expert Loop closed due to lack of snow" sign, but you might want to think about coming back when the skiing is good.

General location: 6 miles east of Minocqua/Woodruff.

Elevation change: The terrain is almost constantly rolling. Short, steep pitches of 20' to 30' are common. The greatest elevation difference is 70', and there are several climbs and descents in that range.

Season: May through October.

Services: There is a water pump at the trailhead. All services are available in Woodruff and Minocqua, including bicycle retail, rental, and repair at BJ's Sport Shop in Minocqua.

Hazards: The trails are very well maintained, but downed trees and branches may be found at anytime. Single-track trails are very rough from rocks and roots. If speed is not moderated it is possible to get airborne. All trails are open to hiking.

Rescue index: Help can be summoned at the State Fish Hatchery or the Woodruff DNR station, located opposite one another 1 mile south of CR J on Woodruff Drive. Although the trail is popular with hikers and riders, your best chance of rescue will come if you make your way to Woodruff Drive or to County Road J.

Land status: Northern Highland–American Legion State Forest. Wisconsin trail pass fees do not apply.

Maps: A basic trail map is available from the DNR. A topographical map titled *Minocqua and Tomahawk Chain*, which uses 7.5 minute USGS maps as its base, is available from Northwoods Nature at the Boardwalk Shops, 8528 A Highway 51 N, Minocqua, WI 54548; (715) 356-4884 or (800) 656-4884. It shows most of the Raven Trails.

Finding the trail: From US 51 at the Minocqua/Woodruff town line, turn east on CR J. After 1.9 miles, turn south onto Woodruff Drive. After 3.9 miles, turn left into the parking area for the State Forest Nature Trail & Hiking Trail.

Sources of additional information:

Minocqua-Arbor Vitae-Woodruff
Area Chamber of Commerce
P.O. Box 1006
Minocqua, WI 54548-1006
(715) 356-5266; (800) 446-6784
www.minocqua.org

Northern Highland–American
Legion State Forest Headquarters
4125 Highway M
Boulder Junction, WI 54512
(715) 385-2727

Wisconsin Department of Natural
Resources
Bureau of Parks and Recreation
P.O. Box 7921
Madison, WI 53707-7921
(608) 266-2181
www.dnr.state.wi.us

Notes on the trail: The Raven Ski Trail is well marked with frequent "you are here" maps and cross-country ski trail signs. The Nature Trail is marked with white-and-red "no biking" signs. From the trailhead follow the Red Trail, the expert outer loop. Many of the trails are marked for one-way travel. Most of the Red Trail is on rough single-track, but at points it will merge with wider, grassy, less-steep double-track trails. At 3.4 miles, at the ski shelter, you will get on wider trails that continue to the end. A short distance beyond the Red Trail, the path splits off to the right and is marked with a "no biking" sign (it leads to the Nature Trail). Ignore the "do not enter" sign and follow the wider trail to the left, which will lead you back to the trailhead.

RIDE 73 · Madeline Lake Trails

AT A GLANCE

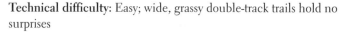

Length/configuration: 5.5-mile loop including a half-mile panhandle; several loop combinations are possible

Aerobic difficulty: Low; the terrain is mostly flat to gently rolling with only two hills of any significance

Technical difficulty: Easy; wide, grassy double-track trails hold no surprises

Scenery: Resurging new-growth forest

Special comments: Madeline is the rather sad sister of the nearby Raven Trails, and isn't a bad place to introduce novice riders to varied-terrain off-roading; the grassy double-track trails are tame and fairly easy to follow

It seems strange to say this, but there aren't a lot of reasons to ride the Madeline Trails other than the fact that you can. One of the three designated mountain bike trails in the Northern Highland–American Legion State Forest (Lumberjack and McNaughton are the others, and all require the state trail pass), Madeline is the least interesting, aesthetically. There will be glimpses of several small ponds and bogs, but you never see its namesake lake. Much of the route travels through regrowth forest that lacks the compelling beauty of mature tree stands.

So why is it in this book? Well, as I said, it is legal to ride here. Also, it's an okay experience for beginning riders, since trails are laid out on practically-domesticated, grassy old logging roads and the terrain is flat to gently rolling. Most importantly, it is an alternative to the Raven Trails. Madeline is the place to go when wet weather might foster trail damage at the Raven. The grassy, less-used trails at Madeline can take it.

General location: 2.5 miles east of Minocqua/Woodruff.

Elevation change: The terrain is mostly flat to gently rolling, with a few 20' to 30' climbs.

Season: May through October.

Services: All services are available in Woodruff and Minocqua, including bicycle retail, rental, and repair at BJ's Sport shop in Minocqua. Camping is available at the Northern Highland–American Legion State Forest campground at Carroll Lake, 1.5 miles east of Rudolph Road on County Road J.

Hazards: The trails are very well maintained, but downed trees and branches may be found at anytime. All trails are open to hiking.

Rescue index: Help can be summoned at the State Fish Hatchery or the Woodruff DNR station, located opposite one another 1 mile south of CR J on Woodruff Drive.

RIDE 73 • Madeline Lake Trails

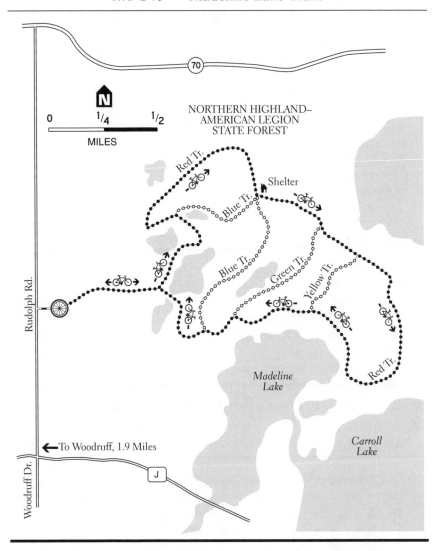

Land status: Northern Highland–American Legion State Forest. A trail pass fee is required for bicyclists age 16 and older ($3 daily/$10 annual). The trail pass also covers usages such as cross-country skiing, and bicycling on state mountain bike trails.

Maps: A basic trail map is available from the Wisconsin Department of Natural Resources or Forest Headquarters. A topographical map titled *Minocqua and Tomahawk Chain* that uses 7.5 minute USGS maps as its base, is available from Northwoods Nature at the Northwood Boardwalk Shops, 8528 A Highway 51 N,

Minocqua, WI 54548; (715) 356-4884 or (800) 656-4884. It shows some of the Madeline Lake Trails.

Finding the trail: From US 51 at the Minocqua/Woodruff town line, turn east on CR J. After 1.9 miles, turn north on Rudolph Road (Woodruff Drive goes off to the south at this intersection). After 1.25 miles, turn east into the trailhead parking area.

Sources of additional information:

Minocqua-Arbor Vitae-Woodruff
Area Chamber of Commerce
P.O. Box 1006
Minocqua, WI 54548-1006
(715) 356-5266; (800) 446-6784
www.minocqua.org

Northern Highland–American
Legion State Forest Headquarters
8770 Highway J
Woodruff, WI 54568
(715) 356-5211

Wisconsin Department of Natural
Resources
Bureau of Parks and Recreation
P.O. Box 7921
Madison, WI 53707-7921
(608) 266-2181
www.dnr.state.wi.us

Notes on the trail: A daily or annual state trail pass fee is required (see Land status). The double-track trails are fairly well signed for travel in a clockwise direction, with blue cross-country ski signs and periodic "you are here" map signs.

RIDE 74 · Razorback Ridges Trails

AT A GLANCE

Length/configuration: 7.7 miles for the double-track loop (numerous single-track segments intertwine)

Aerobic difficulty: High, though some low-difficulty short loops can be pieced together; the double-track loop shown here and the single-track sections will tax your cardiovascular system

Technical difficulty: Easy for the double-track trails, and challenging on the single-track, where you can expect rocks, roots, loose surface, constant grade change, extremely steep slopes, and narrow passage

Scenery: Deep hardwood and pine forest

Special comments: A great place for a workout, especially with the expansion of single-track sections and improved signage; the presence of McKay's Corner Store at the trailhead is a real plus for the carbo-depleted

Any rider can enjoy a cruise through the deep maple, pine, and birch forest on the Razorback Ridges cross-country ski trails. The 7.7-mile Long Rider Loop garners a challenging rating because of its length and some very steep pitches. But, with numerous shortcut options and a smooth, wide, grassy or bare ground surface, riding at Razorback can be recommended to even novice off-roaders.

More seasoned riders will love Razorback. There are more trails here than can possibly be depicted on this map, and many of them are intriguing single-track. Signing is much improved on the double-track trails and on the single-track trails, where it was non-existent on my first visit. Recently I rode the 1.1-mile Ridge Tail single-track segment and was impressed with how challenging and fun it was. Snaky hardly begins to describe it. Add lots of rock, roots, loose surface, and two really nasty hills, and you've got a riding experience that can be both humbling and thrilling.

There's no question that the trails are popular with local riders. The trails are the site of the annual WORS (Wisconsin Off-Road Series) Ridge Rider race in late August. You can have a great ride on the main trails and, if you have enough time and technique, you can take on some of the single-track loops.

General location: 2 miles west of the town of Sayner.

Elevation change: Most of the terrain is constantly rolling with the exception of a short, flat, warm-up and cool-down stretch and a longer section about half way around the Long Rider Loop. Elevation changes will be in the range of 30' to 60'.

Season: Mid-May through September. Insect populations are heavy from mid-May through July.

Services: There is a water pump and ice cream stand at the trailhead. Food, drink, and gasoline are available at McKay's Corner Store. All services are available in Sayner and the Woodruff/Minocqua area, including bicycle retail, rental, and repair at BJ's Sport shop in Minocqua.

Hazards: The trails are very well maintained, but downed trees and branches may be found at anytime. Single-track trails are rough from rocks and roots. It is a good idea to carry a compass. All trails are open to hiking.

Rescue index: Help can be summoned at McKay's Corner Store at the trailhead. While the trails are very popular, your chance of on-trail rescue is not great, and you should seek the shortest route to the trailhead.

Land status: Northern Highland–American Legion State Forest. Wisconsin trail pass fees do not apply, but donations are welcomed. Trails are maintained by the Sayner–Star Lake Lions Club.

Maps: A trail map is available at McKay's Corner Store or the Sayner–Star Lake Chamber of Commerce. A topographical map titled *Boulder Junction*, which uses 7.5 minute USGS maps as its base, is available from Northwoods Nature at the Northwood Boardwalk Shops, 8528 A Highway 51 N, Minocqua, WI 54548;

RIDE 74 • Razorback Ridges Trails

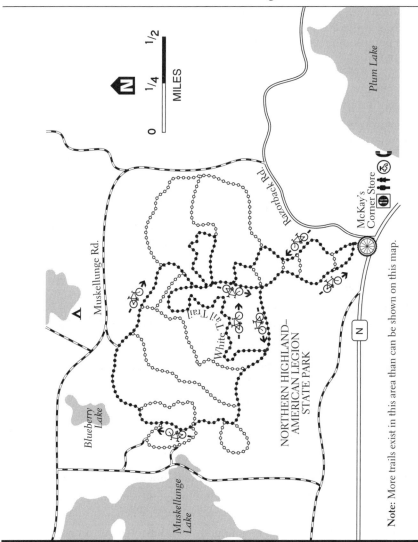

(715) 356-4884 or (800) 656-4884. It shows the terrain in the Razorback area, but not the trails.

Finding the trail: From the Woodruff/Minocqua town line on US 51 at County Road J, travel 5.7-miles north and turn northeast onto County Road M. After 2.4-miles, turn east on County Road N. After 6.7 miles, turn left onto Razorback Road at McKay's Corner Store. Watch for the sign "Razorback Ridges Trails Cross-Country Parking."

The trail tunnels through
tall birch trees.

Sources of additional information:

Northern Highland–American
  Legion State Forest Headquarters
4125 Highway M
Boulder Junction, WI 54512
(715) 356-5211

Sayner–Star Lake Chamber of
  Commerce
P.O. Box 191
Sayner, WI 54560-0191
(715) 542-3789

Wisconsin Department of Natural
  Resources
Bureau of Parks and Recreation
P.O. Box 7921
Madison, WI 53707-7921
(608) 266-2181
www.dnr.state.wi.us

Notes on the trail: Wisconsin trail pass fees do not apply, but donations are welcomed. The main trail loops are marked with frequent "you are here" signs and arrows for specific trail loops. Single-track loops running off of the main loops are signed with blue mountain bike silhouette signs with trail names on them. Follow signs for the Long Rider loop, which is indicated by a green line.

RIDE 75 · Escanaba Lake Trails

AT A GLANCE

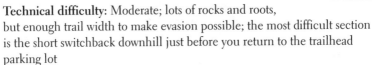

Length/configuration: 6.7-mile loop as described here
(the red outer loop would be 9 miles)

Aerobic difficulty: Moderate; mostly rolling with a few
steep climbs

Technical difficulty: Moderate; lots of rocks and roots,
but enough trail width to make evasion possible; the most difficult section
is the short switchback downhill just before you return to the trailhead
parking lot

Scenery: Deep northern forest with beautiful lake views

Special comments: It's hard to find, but great for an intermediate level or
better rider; the Escanaba Trails are considered among the primo trails in
the area (along with the Raven and Razorback systems)

This is one of those places the intermediate-ability local riders love to tackle.
At the same time this mixed system of single-track and double-track cross-country ski trails is out-of-the-way enough not to be overused. The Escanaba
Trails are what mountain biking was meant to be: a perfect blend of beautiful
surroundings and fun riding.

For starters, there's the tall maple forest that keeps down the ground vegetation
and makes for long sight lines in the woods. I suppose that the trail is so named
because it circles Escanaba Lake, although the wonderful lake views on the route
are of two other lakes, Pallette Lake and Lost Canoe Lake. You'll cruise along their
shores and between the lakes. If the situation hasn't been remedied, you'll tiptoe
along the edge of a flooded stretch of trail, using your partially submerged bike for
balance as you get by the handiwork of the ubiquitous north woods beavers. These
critters just love to create little lakes where none existed before.

Next comes your biggest vertical challenge, a 90-foot-high glacial esker ridge
overlooking the waters of Lost Land Lake. Diving off the end of the ridge, a
three-mile spur trail runs off to the right to a parking lot on County Road K, and
ultimately to the Boulder Area Trail System (BATS)/Lumberjack Trails (see
Ride 77, page246). Link up the two and you'll have a good day's off-roading.

Continuing on the Escanaba Trail you soon have a choice of taking either a
2.5-mile trail back to the trailhead or one that is just 2 miles. Take the shorter trail
if you want a more challenging run on single-track, as well as a glimpse of Mystery
Lake through the trees. The chance for a view of Escanaba Lake comes at a little
vista on the lake's bay. It must be overgrown now, since I couldn't see much on my
visit. The biggest challenge on the trail is yet to come. There is a really steep down-hill blast as the trail turns away from Nebish Road back to the trailhead parking lot.
If this seems like too much, walk it or bail out to the road at the vista spot.

RIDE 75 • Escanaba Lake Trails
RIDE 76 • BATS/Lumberjack Trails

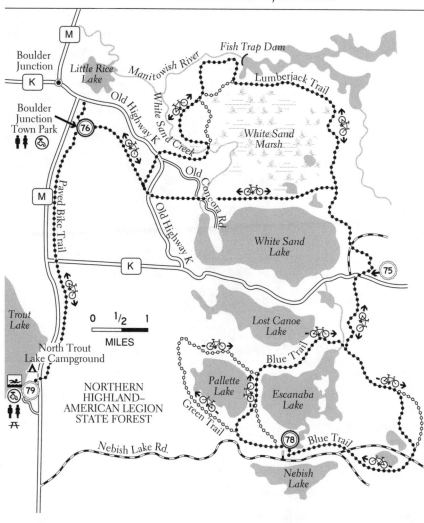

General location: 7 miles southeast of Boulder Junction.

Elevation change: Mostly moderate rolling terrain with a few really steep sections, including a 90' climb and descent on a glacial ridge.

Season: Mid-May through September.

Services: All services, including bicycle retail and repair, are available in Boulder Junction.

Riders love the challenge
at Escanaba Lake.

Hazards: Trails are well maintained, but windfall branches are possible hazards. The trail is also popular with hikers.

Rescue index: Help is available in Boulder Junction and at the Trout Lake Northern Highland–American Legion State Forest headquarters, which can be accessed opposite Nebish Road at County Road M.

Land status: Northern Highland–American Legion State Forest.

Maps: A trail map is available from the Wisconsin Department of Natural Resources or information contacts. A topographical map titled *Boulder Junction*, which uses 7.5 minute USGS maps as its base, is available from Northwoods Nature at the Northwood Boardwalk Shops, 8528 A Highway 51 N, Minocqua, WI 54548; (715) 356-4884 or (800) 656-4884. It shows the terrain in the Escanaba area, but not the trails.

Finding the trail: From Boulder Junction travel 4 miles south on CR M to Nebish Road and turn east. Travel about 3 miles east and turn north into the trailhead parking area. An alternative trailhead is the parking lot on the north side of County Road K, about 3.5 miles east of CR M and just past Nixon Road.

This lot is on the connector trail that links the Escanaba Trails with the BATS/Lumberjack Trails.

Sources of additional information:

Boulder Junction Chamber of
  Commerce
P.O. Box 286
Boulder Junction, WI 54512-0286
(715) 385-2400; (800) 466-8759
www.boulderjct.org

Northern Highland–American
  Legion State Forest Headquarters
4125 Highway M
Boulder Junction, WI 54512
(715) 356-5211

Wisconsin Department of Natural
  Resources
Bureau of Parks and Recreation
P.O. Box 7921
Madison, WI 53707-7921
(608) 266-2181
www.dnr.state.wi.us

Notes on the trail: The forest floor surface and sometimes grassy single-track and double-track cross-country ski trails are well marked, with blue-and-white cross-country ski trail markers and periodic "you are here" map signs, for travel in a clockwise direction.

RIDE 76 · Boulder Area Trail System (BATS)/ Lumberjack Trails

AT A GLANCE

Length/configuration: 10.4 miles for the outer loop on the unpaved cross-country ski and snowmobile trail route; 3.5 miles for the paved trail to North Trout Lake campground and picnic area

Aerobic difficulty: Low; mostly flat or gently rolling with a few short steep grades; some challenging riding on the 3-mile connector trail to the Escanaba Trails

Technical difficulty: Easy; some technically challenging riding on the 3-mile connector trail to the Escanaba Trails

Scenery: Deep northern forest, a wonderful view crossing White Sand Creek; a side trip to Fish Trap Dam offers a good chance to sight eagles; and a side trip to White Sand Lake offers a fine overview of the water through a pine forest

Special comments: A terrific combination of trails that will appeal to novice bikers, families, and even more experienced riders who love wildlife and scenery

Boulder Junction—where boulders meet? Who knows how it got its name, enough massive granite chunks around the forest make a rock rendezvous a definite possibility. What Boulder Junction has a lot of these days is bike trails. This pleasant crossroads tourist town has a 3.5-mile paved trail that runs south, following the contour of the land along County Road M down to the State Forest campground and picnic area at Trout Lake. A playground at the town park trailhead makes this a very nice family ride.

The 10.4-mile loop on the Lumberjack double-track cross-country ski trails and snowmobile trails also starts at the town park. These easy-riding, grassy or forest floor surface with hardpack track trails are flat to gently rolling, and are extremely well signed by the Boulder Area Trail System (BATS) with bright arrow signs and their bat-bike logo. Throughout the loop portion you will travel on little slivers of land that rise above the lakes and bogs.

The Lumberjack Trail takes you to a little wooden bridge across White Sand Creek with a beautiful view of the vast flowage to the east. Further on you can take a short side trip to Fish Trap Dam on the Manitowish River. When I stopped, I spotted two bald eagles looking for a fish lunch.

Swinging south, you'll hit the most challenging section, a few 40-foot climbs, before passing by a chain gate and intersecting with the snowmobile trail that heads back west to the trailhead. Appropriately, the snowmobile trail is guarded against intruding four-wheel-drive vehicles by big granite boulders. On the way back you'll pass close to lovely Nellie Lake. To take on the more challenging Escanaba Trails (see Ride 75, page 240), jog to the east a few yards at the T intersection on the snowmobile trail, and you'll see a blue cross-country ski trail sign on a trail running uphill to the south. This 3.5-mile connector single-track trail also offers a chance for a short half-mile side trip to a fine overlook of White Sand Lake through a pine forest. Or, for an even greater challenge, take it a mile-and-a-half out to the County Road K parking lot.

If hedonism is also on the agenda, microbrew fans should check out the Boulder Beer Bar, where you can get it, whatever it is, as long as it has hops, barley, and comes in a bottle. The food's not bad either.

General location: South and east of Boulder Junction.

Elevation change: Mostly flat to gently rolling with changes in the 20' to 30' range. There are a few 40'-plus, somewhat steep climbs on the eastern section.

Season: Mid-May through September.

Services: All services, including bicycle retail and repair, are available in Boulder Junction.

Hazards: Trails are well maintained, but windfall branches are possible hazards. The trail is also popular with hikers.

Rescue index: Help is available in Boulder Junction or at the Trout Lake Northern Highland–American Legion State Forest headquarters, which can be accessed opposite Nebish Road at County Road M.

Tranquility along Old
Concora Road.

Land status: Northern Highland–American Legion State Forest. A state trail pass fee is required on the Lumberjack portion of the trail for bicyclists age 16 and older ($3 daily/$10 annual). The trail pass also covers usages such as cross-country skiing, horseback riding, and bicycling on state mountain bike trails.

Maps: A good trail map is available from the Boulder Junction Chamber of Commerce. A topographical map titled *Boulder Junction*, which uses 7.5 minute USGS maps as its base, is available from Northwoods Nature at the Northwood Boardwalk Shops, 8528 A Highway 51 N, Minocqua, WI 54548; (715) 356-4884 or (800) 656-4884. It shows the terrain in the Boulder Junction area, but not many of the trails.

Finding the trail: Both the paved trail and natural-surface trail begin at the Boulder Junction Public Park on CR M, also the location of the Chamber of Commerce office. The paved trail swings around the ballpark outfield, and the natural-terrain trail can be picked up beyond right field. An alternative trailhead is the parking lot on the north side of CR K about 3.5 miles east of CR M and just past Nixon Road. This lot is on the connector trail that links the Escanaba Trails with the BATS/Lumberjack Trails.

Sources of additional information:

Boulder Junction Chamber of
Commerce
P.O. Box 286
Boulder Junction, WI 54512-0286
(715) 385-2400; (800) 466-8759
www.boulderjct.org

Northern Highland–American
Legion State Forest Headquarters
4125 Highway M
Boulder Junction, WI 54512
(715) 356-5211

Wisconsin Department of Natural
Resources
Bureau of Parks and Recreation
P.O. Box 7921
Madison, WI 53707-7921
(608) 266-2181
www.dnr.state.wi.us

Notes on the trail: A daily or annual state trail pass fee is required on the Lumberjack portion of the trail (see Land status). The paved trail swings around the ballpark outfield at the Boulder Junction Town Park and is easily identified. Near its south end the trail crosses CR M and junctions with the North Trout Lake Campground sanitary station road. Follow this a short distance to the intersection with the park drive, and turn west to get to the picnic area on Trout Lake.

The natural terrain trail begins from the paved trail at right field. The trails are very well marked for two-way travel, with orange squares with yellow arrows for travel in a clockwise direction, and green squares with yellow arrows for riding counterclockwise.

RIDE 77 · Langley Lake Trails

AT A GLANCE

Length/configuration: 5.5-mile loop, including a short panhandle; many loop combinations are possible

Aerobic difficulty: Moderate; mostly gently rolling, but a few steep hills will be encountered; a slow roll on grassy surfaces adds difficulty

Technical difficulty: Easy; slow rolling, grassy, double-track trails contain few surprises

Scenery: Mixed forest of aspen, birch, white pine, and jack pine dotted with beautiful tiny lakes

Special comments: A loop not to be missed by nature lovers; the nontechnical, grassy, double-track leads to a handful of pristine little lakes harboring wild critters

Langley Lake is out of the way and out of this world. The 5.5-mile loop on grassy, double-track cross-country ski trails doesn't get ridden much (there is

RIDE 77 • Langley Lake Trails

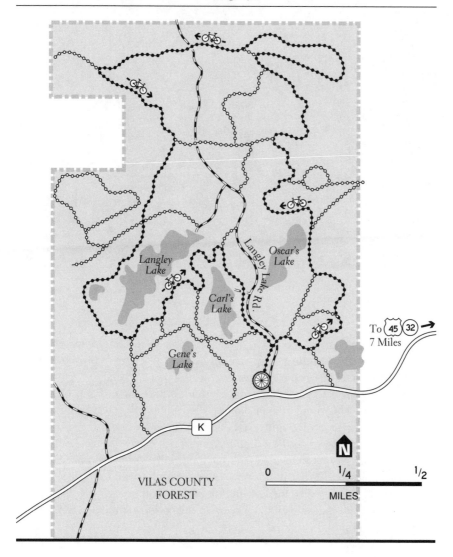

no hardpack track), but the rewards for taking them on are wonderful. Besides tiny Langley Lake, the largest, there are a handful of other lakes that are hardly bigger than ponds. Some of these are named after Gene, Carl, and Oscar—I'd guess the lakes were probably their favorite fishing holes.

There is just enough elevation change to give you a workout and take you to some fine overviews of the lakes. As I passed Langley Lake, a surprised doe decided to bound across it at a narrow reedy spot. She tapped into her ability to speed from

A placid beaver pond shimmers through paper birch.

zero to forty in an instant, and hit the water full force. It was amazing to watch how her body responded to the energy-sapping water—all effort went into forward motion. In a matter of seconds she was on the far shore and gone.

Farther on, the trail passes close by a nameless little pond that is home to a clan of beavers. The sound of their slapping tails told me they had seen me coming and dove for cover. Partially gnawed aspen trees lay about the shore. The pond is down in a bowl, and these industrious critters have cleared out all the aspen on its sides. I was amazed to see what looked like hardpack mountain bike tracks running straight up the sides, when I'd seen no rolled-in track along the trails. A closer look revealed tracks with little beaver footprints all over them. The little buggers were traipsing all the way up to the trail to get more aspen. I don't suppose they'd mind if you tried the grade on your bike.

If you are basing out of the Eagle River area, also check out the Anvil and Nicolet North trails (Rides 67 and 68) to the east of town.

General location: 16 miles northwest of Eagle River.

Elevation change: Mostly gently rolling with a few climbs in the 40' to 50' range.

Season: Mid-May through September.

Services: All services, including bicycle retail and repair at Chain of Lakes Cyclery, are available in Eagle River, 16 miles to the southeast. Snacks are available at the Star Lake Store, 3.5 miles west on County Road K.

Hazards: Trails receive little riding-season maintenance, and windfall trees and branches are commonly encountered. Carrying and knowing how to use a compass are advised. Trails are open to hikers.

Rescue index: Help is available in Star Lake, 3.5 miles to the west on CR K.

Land status: Vilas County Forest trails.

Maps: Trail maps are available at the Star Lake Store or from information contacts. The 7.5 minute series USGS quad for Star Lake shows the terrain very well but only some of the trails.

Finding the trail: Coming from the east, turn west off US 45/WI 32 onto CR K and travel 7 miles. Look for a "Cross-Country Skiing" sign at Langley Lake Road, on the north side of CR K. Coming from the west, travel 3.3 miles east on CR K from its junction with County Road N at Star Lake, and look for the same sign mentioned above.

Sources of additional information:

Eagle River Area County Chamber
of Commerce
P.O. Box 1917
Eagle River, WI 54521-1917
(715) 479-6400; (800) 359-6315
www.eagleriver.org

Sayner–Star Lake Chamber of
Commerce
P.O. Box 191
Sayner, WI 54560-0191
(715) 542-3789

Notes on the trail: The grassy, double-track trails are well marked with blue cross-country ski signs most easily followed by traveling in a counterclockwise direction. There is a central dirt road running north from the trailhead parking lot and "you are here" map signs are at all trail crossings. There are a great many intersecting trails in the area, and it's important to remember to follow the cross-country ski trail signs carefully to avoid getting lost or riding out of the area. Bring a compass and, having noted which side of the central dirt road you're on, make your way either east or west to locate it if you become lost or confused.

THE GREAT NORTHWEST

What makes the northwest great? This is where the Wisconsin wilderness begins. It's the transition zone between farmland and woodland. Fields become spottier and stands of tall trees become denser. The character of the forests changes too. The oaks, maples, and birch are mixed with white pine, Norway pine, and hemlock. The trails listed here, for the most part, make off-road pedaling playgrounds out of these lovely places. To the down-state mountain biker, this means north-woods riding an hour or two closer to home.

The area is hardly an excuse for a wilderness either. In Rice Lake, the small city near five of the rides in this section, people laughingly recount how a couple of years ago kids got on a school bus to go home and found a black bear sleeping in the back. The driver was caught totally unaware and thought the kids were pulling his leg. Leaving your car windows rolled up while you're out biking is a good idea.

Your not-so-far-north woods riding experience begins at the top with the Timms Hill Loop Trails. Timms is the highest point in the state; a compact little trail system will take you there, as well as past several pristine lakes. Also in the area are the Timms Hill Spur/Pine Line Trails, which, pieced together with a couple of beautiful town roads, make the longest loop in this book. Included are the rough Timms Hill National Trail, Ice Age Trail, RR #1, and the Pine Line, a flat rail-trail.

Looking west from the city of Rice Lake you can see the silhouette of a series of rugged hills with a bluish hue in the distant haze. These are the Blue Hills, remnants of an ancient mountain range. Sister double-track cross-country ski trail systems offer two different riding experiences in this beautiful forest. The eastern trails are as tough as anything you'll find in the state, while the western loop is a moderately difficult jog past woods and bogs.

North of Rice Lake, the Tuscobia State Trail is a rail-trail with a twist. The trestles were removed before the trail was developed and new bridges were placed near stream level, making it the only rail-trail around with climbs and descents. Nearby, the Sawmill Lake Tour on-road loop follows gravel and paved roads past gorgeous lake and bog scenery, and visits its namesake park. Just north of the loop lie the Nordic Woods Trails, a cross-country ski trail loop through the same beautiful country that's easy enough for any rider to try.

Touching the scenic St. Croix River Valley at either end of its route, the Gandy Dancer State Trail is a new rail-trail that strings nine towns together.

Interstate State Park, at the southern end, is one of the most scenic in Wisconsin. The trail also comes near Forts Folle Avoine, a living history museum of the fur trade era. At Frederic, along the trail's route, the compact, steep, double- and single-track cross-country ski trails at Coon Lake Park will give you a chance to test your skills and your gears.

RIDE 78 · Timms Hill Loop Trails

AT A GLANCE

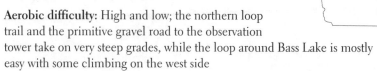

Length/configuration: 2.7-mile double loop with an internal out-and-back segment; other loops exist in the area for the more adventurous

Aerobic difficulty: High and low; the northern loop trail and the primitive gravel road to the observation tower take on very steep grades, while the loop around Bass Lake is mostly easy with some climbing on the west side

Technical difficulty: Moderate to easy; the northern loop requires climbing skills and downhill confidence, while the southern loop is easy

Scenery: Deep hardwood and pine forest, and a vast overlook of the woods and surrounding lakes from an observation tower

Special comments: Intermediate and advanced riders will enjoy the scenic, forest-floor surface, single-track hiking and cross-country ski trails, and a chance to climb to the highest point in the state

Many people don't know about Timms Hill. Until about forty years ago, Rib Mountain, overlooking WI 51 and the city of Wausau, was thought to be the highest point in the state. Then up crops out-of-the-way, 1,951-foot Timms Hill, a whopping 3 nose-bleeding feet higher than Rib. The people in Price county know where the highest point is, though, and they've turned it into a real nice county park.

The 2.7 miles of trails here offer several experiences in a compact area. The northern loop is hilly—Timms hilly. You'll find a very steep climb up the back side of Timms Hill on single-track cross-country trails (the blue-signed loop) and the park road. You can take the hill head-on, riding up a primitive gravel road to the observation tower. A climb up to the tower will reward you with a great view of the vast forest and lake country.

To the south of the observation tower, you'll see Bass Lake and a chalet-style resort on its shore. This is the lovely Catch a Dream Lodge, and I guarantee it's where you'll want to stay if you're spending some time in the area. The loop around Bass Lake takes you on easy and moderate hiking trails linked with Rustic Road 62, which takes you right past the lodge.

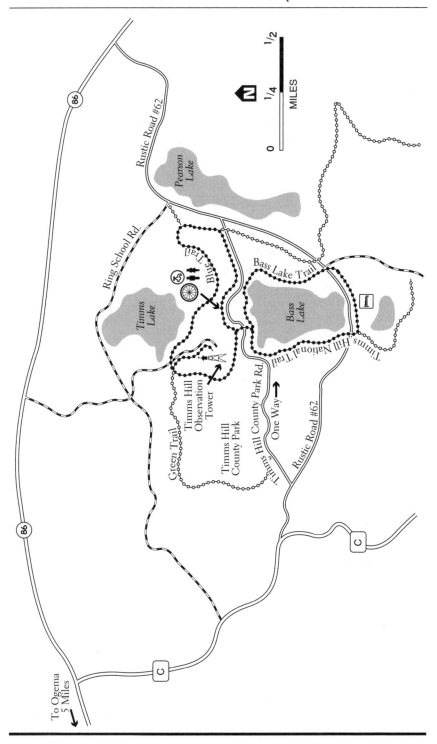

The view from the state's highest point.

There are a number of other ski trail loops in the area, as well as the Timms Hill Spur/Pine Line Trails (see Ride 80, page 258). I found the other ski trails to be covered with high grass on a soft surface, so I'm not recommending them here. If you feel you've got the endurance though, you can take on an additional six miles of trails.

General location: 7 miles east of Ogema and WI 13.

Elevation change: 100' climbs up Timms Hill, on either the ski trail loop or primitive gravel road.

Season: Mid-May through September.

Services: There are pit toilets and water at the park trailhead. There are taverns in Ogema.

Hazards: Windfall branches may be encountered. Trails are open to hikers.

Rescue index: Help is available in Ogema or at Catch a Dream Lodge.

Land status: Price County Park.

Maps: The Price County Cross-country Ski Trails brochure available from Price County Tourism shows all the loops. The 7.5 minute series USGS quad for Timms Hill shows the terrain very well, but only some of the trails.

Finding the trail: From WI 86, turn south on County Road C. Travel 0.9 mile to RR 62 and turn east. After about a block's distance, turn north onto the narrow, one-way Timms Hill Park Road, and follow it to the parking lot.

Sources of additional information:

Price County Tourism Department	(715) 339-4505; (800) 269-4505
126 Cherry Street	www.pricecounty.com
Phillips, WI 54555-1249	

Notes on the trail: For the northern loop on the Highpoint Ski Trails, from the trailhead parking lot follow the narrow, one-way, paved park road out of the park to the east, about three blocks distance to the green-and-blue ski trail crossing. Turn north on the trail. This means you'll be traveling in a counterclockwise direction, which is the wrong way for ski travel signage, but it keeps you going the right way on the paved park road where motor vehicles might be encountered. As the trail nears the stream exiting Timms Lake, take either the primitive gravel road (there will be a gate from the other direction) up to the observation tower or take the left ski trail that begins to climb immediately. The ski trail will take you back to the park road to complete the loop or pick up the Bass Lake Trail.

For the southern loop on the Bass Lake Trail, ride very carefully counter to traffic flow on the park road downhill a short distance, to a point where you can access the trail between the road and the shore of Bass Lake. Ride in a clockwise direction until you reach the paved RR 62. Turn west, going past Catch a Dream Lodge, and pick up the Timms Hill National Trail to the north, just past the Bass Lake shore.

RIDE 79 · Timms Hill Spur/Pine Line Trails

AT A GLANCE

Length/configuration: 37-mile loop or out-and-back sections of various lengths

Aerobic difficulty: Low to high: the Pine Line Trail rail section is dead flat; town and county roads are rolling; the Ice Age and Timms Hill trails have steep sections

Technical difficulty: Easy to moderate

Scenery: Deep hardwood and pine forest with beautiful lake views

Special comments: A real northern adventure for those who are fit enough to take on the whole loop, or a high-speed cruise or family ride by doing an out-and-back on the town roads or Pine Line rail-trail

If this loop isn't a day's worth of riding I don't know what is. Take in 16 miles of rugged terrain on the Ice Age and Timms Hill trails, 12 rolling miles on town and county roads, and 9 miles on the Pine Line rail-trail. If 37 miles at once is too much for you, chop it up into out-and-back sections of your own choosing.

No matter how you do it, this ride will be a total immersion into one wild part of the state. You're in the land of Ice Man Ugh, the town of Rib Lake's mythical

RIDE 79 • Timms Hill Spur/Pine Line Trails

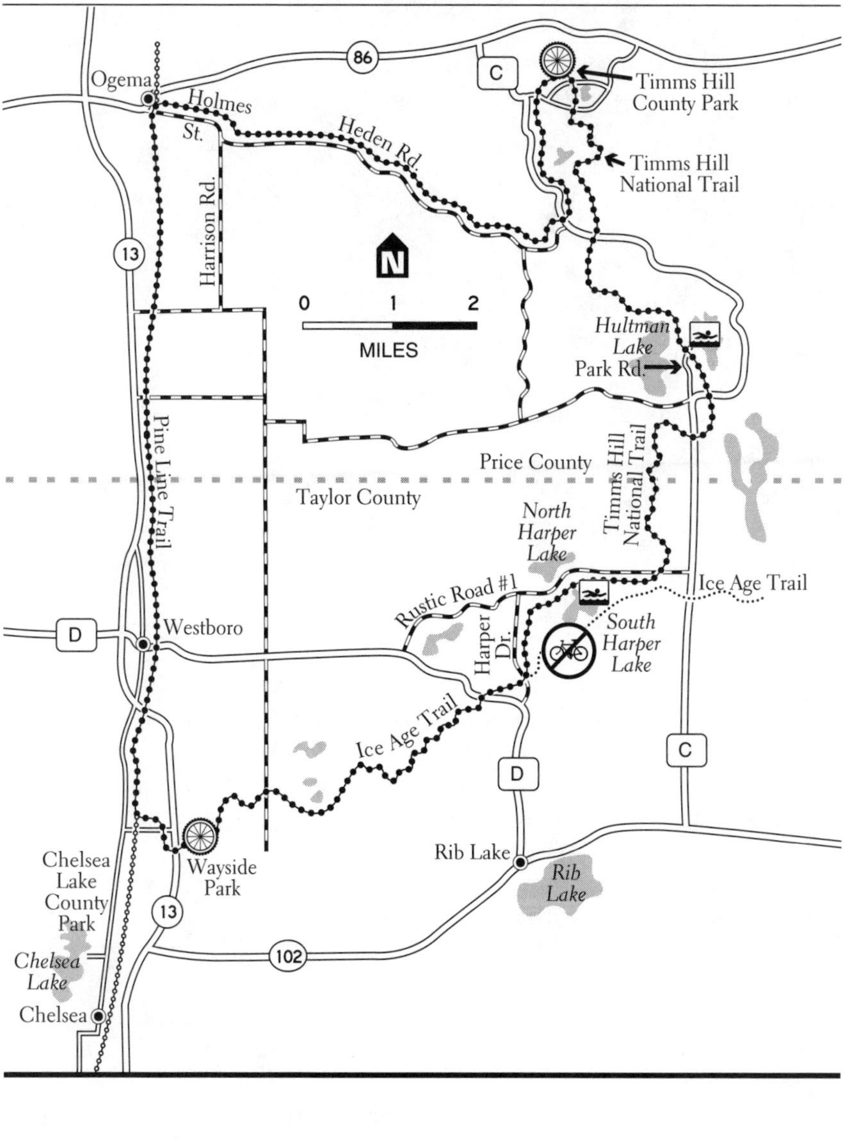

Paleolithic mascot and symbol of the area's ice age heritage. This is where the Chippewa and Wisconsin Valley ice sheets got nasty with each other. After the big meltdown, the leftovers were typical of the great-riding interlobate terrain that mountain bikers love to hate at sites of other ice sheet altercations, such as the Kettle Moraine State Forest and the Chequamegon National Forest.

The varied-terrain off-road sections are double- and single-track segments of the Ice Age and Timms Hill trails. The former is part of a cross-state trail that traces the edge of the Wisconsin Glacier, the most recent and dramatic of the continental ice

A cavern in the deep maple forest.

sheets. The latter is a spur of the Ice Age Trail that goes to Timms Hill, the highest point in the state (see Ride 78, page 251). These grassy and forest floor graded trails celebrate the best scenery and terrain the area has to offer. Constantly rolling with some really steep climbs, the trails aren't ridden enough in most sections to have a hardpack track worn in. They will take you to some magical places though. Lakes, bogs, and flowing springs are all part of the picture.

Due to easement restrictions on a section of the Ice Age Trail, you get to link to the Timms Hill National Trail via Harper Drive and Rustic Road 1, the first scenic road in the state, protected from development in 1975. Just west of Harper Drive on the Ice Age Trail is the Deutsches Wiedervereinigkeits Brucke—say that three times fast—or in English, the German Reunification Bridge. The little wooden structure was built in 1989 to commemorate the historic event and is appropriately signed.

The Pine Line rail-trail runs through Ogema, Westboro, and if you push a couple of miles south of the loop, to Chelsea. Uninspiring is not too unkind a description of these little burgs, where taverns are the main, and nearly only, attractions. However, Little Chelsea Lake County Park is a very pleasant spot.

General location: Between Ogema and Rib Lake.

Elevation change: The Pine Line Trail is dead flat. Expect numerous steep climbs in the 50' to 80' range on the Ice Age and Timms Hill trails, plus many more shorter ones.

Season: Mid-May through September.

Services: All services are available in Rib Lake. There is a public campground in town and a private campground 7 miles north on WI 102. There are taverns and a grocery in Ogema, and taverns in Westboro. You'll find water, shelters, and pit toilets at Timms Hill and Chelsea Lake county parks. There is a flowing spring at an active beaver pond, just east of the Timms Hill National Trail junction with RR 1. A swimming beach and pit toilets can be found along RR 1 at South Harper Lake and at Stone Lake Park, just north of Timms Hill National Trail on Park Road. There is a flowing spring there as well.

Hazards: Windfall branches may be encountered on the Ice Age and Timms Hill trails. These trails and the Pine Line Trail are also open to hikers. Public roadway sections are shared with motor vehicles.

Rescue index: Help is available in Ogema, Westboro, Chelsea, and Rib Lake.

Land status: Price and Taylor county trails and forest, and public roads.

Maps: The 7.5 minute series USGS quads for Ogema, Timms Hill, Westboro, and Rib Lake show the terrain very well, but only some of the trails. The DeLorme book, *Wisconsin Atlas & Gazetteer*, shows the rail bed and all local roads and road names on page 75.

Finding the trail: Several trailheads are possible. The Ice Age Trail starts at a wayside park on WI 13, 1.25 miles north of WI 102. The Pine Line Trail is easy to find in Ogema, Westboro, or from Chelsea Lake County Park, all readily accessible from WI 13.

Timms Hill County Park is a good northern jumping-off point: From WI 86, turn south on County Road C. Travel 0.9 mile to Rustic Road 62 and turn east. After about a block's distance, turn north onto the narrow, one-way, Timms Hill Park Road and follow it to the parking lot.

The town of Rib Lake may be a convenient starting point since it has the most services available in the area. The loop can be accessed by traveling 2 miles north on County Road D.

Sources of additional information:

Rib Lake Village Hall
P.O. Box 205
Rib Lake, WI 54470
(800) 819-LAKE

Taylor County Tourism Council
P.O. Box 172
Medford, WI 54451-0172
(715) 748-4729; (800) 682-9567
www.medfordwis.com

Notes on the trail: The route can be ridden in either direction. Public roads are signed with road-name signs. The Timms Hill National Trail and the Ice Age Trail are well marked with red paint dots on trees and three-sided Ice Age Trail signs. There is an extensive cross-country ski trail system intertwining with the Ice Age Trail between RR 1 and Harper Drive. Due to easement restrictions, mountain biking is not allowed on these trails.

RIDE 80 · Blue Hills East Trails

AT A GLANCE

Length/configuration: 8.1-mile loop with a panhandle; many loop combinations are possible

Aerobic difficulty: High; certainly some sections are easier than others, but I don't think it's possible to avoid some of the steepest, longest climbs in the state

Technical difficulty: Moderate; climbing skills and confidence on downhills are required

Scenery: Deep maple forest

Special comments: This is one tough trail system; determined intermediates and advanced riders will get their fill here; gravel road sections give time for a necessary warm-up and cool-down

A day of mountain biking is a cure for the blues, and a day in the Blue Hills is a cure for anything. Geologists say that once the mountainous peaks of the region towered over 20,000 feet high, but are now a mass of tough hills rounded over by eons of erosion. The challenging 8.1-mile loop shown here should test the aerobic capacity of any rider.

The tougher of two sister trail systems (see Ride 81, page 261), these are the cross-country trails that skiers like to hammer on to get ready for the annual American Birkebeiner marathon, one of the toughest in the world. It's a great training ground too. You won't find longer, steeper terrain anywhere in the state. The trails are wide double-track, designed to accommodate both the skating and traditional striding cross-country ski technique. This reduces the technical challenge for mountain biking, but, hey, you will not be bored here. The challenge will come in trying to maintain your momentum while keeping the front wheel on the ground on the climbs, and seeing how much velocity your nerves can handle heading downhill.

There are a tremendous number of riding options beyond the route shown here. I'd say pedal 'til you drop, but that might not be good advice here. It could be a long walk out. Better to bite off smaller and smaller loops if you want to extend the workout.

General location: 23 miles east of the city of Rice Lake.

Elevation change: 310' maximum, with many 100'-plus climbs.

Season: May to mid-October.

Services: All services are available in Rice Lake. Bicycle retail and repair are available at River Brook Bike and Ski in Spooner, 24 miles north of Rice Lake on US 53. There are campsites, pit toilets, water, and a playground at Audie Flowage Recreation Area.

RIDE 80 • Blue Hills East Trails
RIDE 81 • Blue Hills West Trails

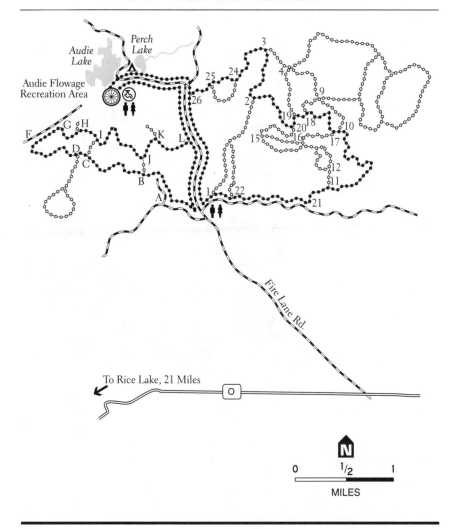

Hazards: Trails receive little riding-season maintenance and windfall branches are common. Public road sections are open to motor vehicle traffic. Trails are also used by hikers and horseback riders.

Rescue index: Help is available in Rice Lake.

Land status: Rusk County Forest. A $2 trail fee donation at the trailhead is requested.

Maps: Trail maps are available from information contacts. The 7.5 minute series USGS quads for Bucks Lake and Becky Creek show the terrain very well,

The mirrored
surface of Audie Lake.

but only few of the trails. The DeLorme book, *Wisconsin Atlas & Gazetteer*, shows the all local roads and road names on page 85.

Finding the trail: From the city of Rice Lake, follow County Road C east. At the Rusk County line it becomes County Road O. Continue east for another 9.5 miles to Fire Lane Road (gravel) and turn northwest where a sign says "Blue Hills Trail 2 miles, Audie Flowage Recreation Area." Pass the Blue Hills Trail parking area, continue on another 2 miles and turn west on Perch Lake Road, following signs to Audie Flowage Recreation Area. Park in the picnic area.

Sources of additional information:

Rice Lake Area Chamber of
  Commerce
37 South Main Street
Rice Lake, WI 54868-2226
(715) 234-2126; (800) 523-6318
www.rice-lake.com

Rusk County Visitor Center and
  Depot Museum
205 West 9th Street South
Ladysmith, WI 54848-2902
(715) 532-2642; (800) 535-RUSK
www.ruskcounty.org

Notes on the trail: The wide double-track trails are well signed for travel in either direction, with intersection numbers and arrows pointing to the next numbered intersection.

RIDE 81 · Blue Hills West Trails

AT A GLANCE

Length/configuration: 7.8-mile loop with an out-and-back panhandle; many loop combinations are possible

Aerobic difficulty: Moderate; you'll find a slow roll on soft grassy trails and a few steep slopes

Technical difficulty: Moderate; some rocks and loose surface on slopes will be encountered, as well as several small stream crossings

Scenery: Resurgent aspen forest along with old hardwoods and pond and bog views

Special comments: A not-too-tough ride with enough terrain and scenery to keep things interesting; Audie Lake Flowage Recreation Area makes a pleasant jumping-off point.

The Blue Hills West Trails are less humbling than their sister trails to the east (see Ride 80, page 258). The relief comes from about one-fourth the elevation. That doesn't mean the west trails are flat. They are constantly rolling, but they won't beat you down as much. Along the way you'll find pleasant scenery. Several interconnecting trails make a number of loop options possible. If you combine these trails with the loop to the east, you can make a real day of riding covering more than 13 miles.

The only downside to riding the west trails is the somewhat vague trail markings. When I was there the letter signs at intersections were all down. I was able to get around alright because arrows pointing to the next lettered intersection were painted on the signposts. These were quite faded and required me to stop for a closer look. This could be a problem in low light.

Audie Lake is a nice place to relax a bit. As you gaze over its tranquil waters you may or may not see a small island with a few tamarack trees on it. I say may not, because this region is famous for its not-always-visible floating island, made of masses of sphagnum moss that even support trees. Several decades ago, on Lake Chetek, twenty miles to the west, a larger version of a floating island drifted up against the shore of some lakefront homes. After a few weeks of having the view blocked, a powerboat posse was formed. Seventeen boats tugged with all their might, but couldn't budge the errant island. Then one day it just floated off.

General location: 23 miles east of the city of Rice Lake.

The only tough climb on the west trail.

Elevation change: 60' maximum, with many 30'-plus climbs.

Season: May through mid-October.

Services: All services are available in Rice Lake. Bicycle retail and repair are available at River Brook Bike and Ski in Spooner, 24 miles north of Rice Lake on US 53. There are campsites, pit toilets, water, and a playground at Audie Flowage Recreation Area.

Hazards: Trails receive little riding-season maintenance and windfall branches are common. Inspect all signposts carefully for directions to other intersections. Carrying and knowing how to use a compass is advised. Public road sections are open to motor vehicle traffic. Trails are also used by hikers and horseback riders. The far western link between intersections G and F, which is a primitive road, appears to be used by all-terrain vehicles.

Rescue index: Help is available in Rice Lake.

Land status: Rusk County Forest. A $2 trail fee donation at the trailhead is requested.

Maps: Trail maps are available from information contacts. The 7.5 minute series USGS quad for Bucks Lake shows the terrain very well, but few of the trails. The DeLorme book, *Wisconsin Atlas & Gazetteer,* shows all the local roads and road names on page 85.

Finding the trail: From the city of Rice Lake, follow County Road C east. At the Rusk County line it becomes County Road O. Continue east for another 9.5 miles to Fire Lane Road (gravel), and turn northwest where a sign says "Blue Hills Trail 2 miles, Audie Flowage Recreation Area." Pass the Blue Hills Trail parking area, continuing on another 2 miles, and turn west on Perch Lake Road, following signs to Audie Flowage Recreation Area. Park in the picnic area.

Sources of additional information:

Rice Lake Area Chamber of
  Commerce
37 South Main Street
Rice Lake, WI 54868-2226
(715) 234-2126; (800) 523-6318
www.rice-lake.com

Rusk County Visitor Center and
  Depot Museum
205 West 9th Street South
Ladysmith, WI 54848-2902
(715) 532-2642; (800) 535-RUSK
www.ruskcounty.org

Notes on the trail: The double-track trails are signed for travel in either direction with intersection signposts. The problem is, the signs identifying the intersections are missing (or were at the time of my riding). You can still deduce where you are by looking at the faded arrows painted on the posts that point to the direction of other intersections. Problems are somewhat minimized by the lack of other trails that might lead you off the system. The exception is the far western link between intersections G and F, which is a primitive road that continues beyond the system. It may connect to Audie Lake Recreation Area on the north end, though I have no evidence that it does.

RIDE 82 · Tuscobia State Trail (Rail-Trail)

AT A GLANCE

Length/configuration: 17.5 miles one way from Birchwood to Couderay

Aerobic difficulty: Low to moderate; basically a flat rail-trail punctuated by steep slopes down to stream bridges

Technical difficulty: Easy to challenging; the flat rail-bed portions are easy, while the steep slopes on the sides of stream crossings are challenging due to grade and loose surface; significant differences in the level of the bridges and trail surface add to the difficulty

Scenery: Deep hardwood and pine forest with many stream crossings

Special comments: An unusual rail-trail—the normally flat riding is broken up by steep descents and climbs at stream crossings; an interesting family ride for the slightly more experienced or a high-speed cruise with occasional challenges

An interesting wrinkle in rail-trail riding. The 17.5 mile-segment shown here is part of the 74-mile state trail from Park Falls in the east to Tuscobia in the west. Brought on-line in the early hey-days of trail development in the 1970s, the Wisconsin Department of Natural Resources did not acquire the right-of-way before the stream trestles were removed. In an economy move, these were replaced with new, shorter bridges down near stream level. This made the trail virtually worthless for riding in the days of skinny-tired bikes.

Today, the Tuscobia Trail offers a unique riding opportunity for the mountain biker. The flat rail-bed ride is interrupted by nine stream crossings between Birchwood and Couderay. Steep slopes on either end of the bridges are difficult to descend or climb, thanks to loose surface (the all-terrain vehicle use doesn't make this any better). And, don't think that if you're a hot-shot down-hiller you can just let it all hang out. There is typically a large step between the ground and the bridge level.

So why would you want to ride here? Well, it's the only rail-trail in the area. More advanced riders can enjoy high-speed cruising with periodic stream slope challenges. Less experienced riders can always walk up or down. The first stream crossing is 4 miles east of Birchwood, so family riders can do a mod-est out-and-back ride without the challenge. Most attractive of all is the chance to plunge deep into the wild forest environment.

For an interesting on-road return route, work your way west on town roads and take County Road F along the shore of Lake Chetac back to Birchwood. Or, check out the nearby on-road Sawmill Lake Tour (see Ride 83, page 266) or off-road Nordic Woods Trails (see Ride 84, page 268).

You won't be the first to be mesmerized by the vast forest along the trail. It has been home to Native Americans since time immemorial. The village of Coud-eray is a phonetic spelling of nearby Lac Courte Oreilles, and the Ojibwe Reser-vation of the same name. In 1659 Pierre Esprit Radisson and his uncle Grosseilliers, the first French to visit, wintered in the village there. Overcrowded with refugees from the Iroquois wars, the natives and French faced starvation during a hard winter. They were saved by "racquettes" when the snow crusted over. These snowshoes that resembled French tennis equipment allowed them to easily catch deer whose sharp hoofs broke through the crust. Radisson proba-bly thought: "I knew there was something I liked about that game."

General location: Between Birchwood and Couderay.

Elevation change: Mostly flat, with periodic 30' to 60' drops to stream crossings.

Season: Mid-May through Mid-October.

Services: All services are available in the city of Rice Lake. Bicycle retail and repair are available at River Brook Bike and Ski in Spooner, 24 miles north of Rice Lake on US 53. All other services are available in Birchwood, and there are showers, camping, water, and flush toilets at Doolittle Park on the north side of town. There are taverns and a country grocery in Couderay.

RIDE 82 • Tuscobia State Trail

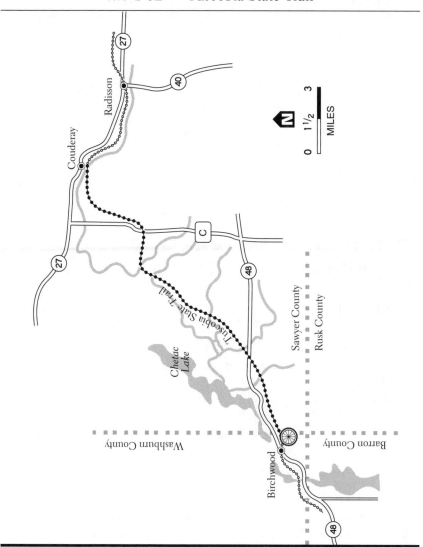

Hazards: The trail is also open to hikers and all-terrain vehicles.

Rescue index: Help is available in Birchwood and Couderay.

Land status: Wisconsin State Park Trail.

Maps: A trail map is available from the DNR and other information contacts. The DeLorme book, *Wisconsin Atlas & Gazetteer*, shows the trail and all local roads and road names on pages 84 and 85.

Finding the trail: The trail is easily accessible in either Birchwood or Couderay. Take County Road D north from WI 48 into Birchwood, to the trail crossing. In Couderay, look for the trail parallel to and on the south side of WI 27/70.

Sources of additional information:

Birchwood Area Lakes Association
P.O. Box 9
Birchwood, WI 54817-0009
(715) 354-7846; (800) 236-2252
www.birchwoodwi.com

Wisconsin Department of Natural
  Resources
Bureau of Parks and Recreation
P.O. Box 7921
Madison, WI 53707-7921
(608) 266-2181
www.dnr.state.wi.us

Notes on the trail: The wide, gravel-surface rail-trail has periodic descents and climbs at stream crossings.

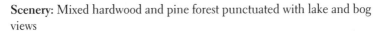

RIDE 83 · Sawmill Lake Tour (On-Road)

AT A GLANCE

Length/configuration: 18.8-mile loop

Aerobic difficulty: Low; gently rolling terrain provides slight difficulty

Technical difficulty: Easy; paved and gravel roads are easily handled

Scenery: Mixed hardwood and pine forest punctuated with lake and bog views

Special comments: A scenic high-speed road cruise; a rest stop at Sawmill Lake is a bonus

Take on this scenic, quiet ride on paved and gravel roads and you'll be cruising kettle moraine country north-woods style. This time the ice sheets in question are the Chippewa and Superior lobes of the Wisconsin ice sheet. While less severe terrain-wise to terrain other areas of kettle moraine, this region is dotted with more kettle lakes and bogs than you can shake an icicle at. The roadside scenery is entrancing.

Sawmill Lake Campground is a pleasant place to base your ride from or to hit for an on-route rest stop. You can combine your on-road ride with some off-roading by taking on the Nordic Woods Trails (see Ride 84, page 268) at the north end of the loop, or a rail-trail cruise on the Tuscobia State Trail (see Ride 82, page 263) at nearby Birchwood.

General location: 6 miles north of Birchwood.

Elevation change: Rolling terrain with changes in the 30' to 50' range.

RIDE 83 • Sawmill Lake Tour
RIDE 84 • Nordic Woods Trails

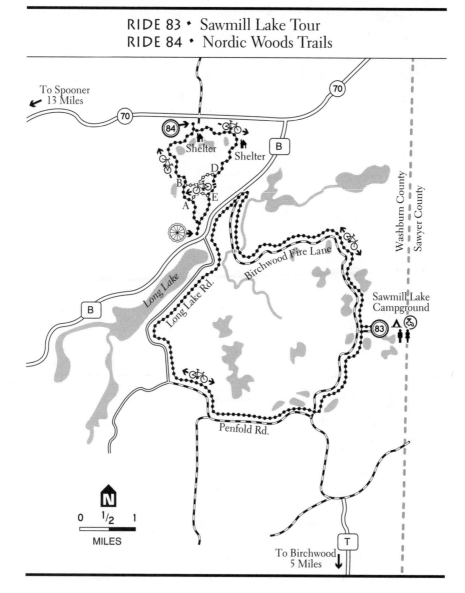

Season: Mid-May through mid-October.

Services: All services are available in the city of Rice Lake. Bicycle retail and repair are available at River Brook Bike and Ski in Spooner, 24 miles north of Rice Lake on US 53. All other services are available in Birchwood, and there are showers, camping, water, and flush toilets at Doolittle Park on the north side of town. Bobby Schmidt's Resort, where lodging and beverages are available, is located just off the route to the southwest on County Road B.

Hazards: The roads are shared with motor vehicles.

Rescue index: Help is available in Birchwood and at Bobby Schmidt's Resort.

Land status: Public roadways.

Maps: The DeLorme book, *Wisconsin Atlas & Gazetteer*, shows all local roads and road names on page 84.

Finding the trail: From Birchwood, take County Road D north to County Road T and travel north to Birchwood Fire Lane (gravel) and Sawmill Lake Campground.

Sources of additional information:

Birchwood Area Lakes Association
P.O. Box 9
Birchwood, WI 54817-0009
(715) 354-7846; (800) 236-2252
www.birchwoodwi.com

Riverbrook Bike and Ski
102 East Maple Street
Spooner, WI 54801

Washburn County Forestry
(715) 635-4490

Notes on the trail: This gravel and paved on-road route is well signed for travel in either direction, with street-type road name signs at intersections. Nearby single- and double-track trails pose greater technical difficulty. For details on the condition of other area trails consult local riders, such as the folks at Riverbrook Bike and Ski.

RIDE 84 · Nordic Woods Trails

AT A GLANCE

Length/configuration: 6.6-mile loop (add 1.2 miles if starting and finishing at the south parking lot); several loop combinations are possible

Aerobic difficulty: Moderate; terrain is gently rolling, but a soft surface adds to the difficulty

Technical difficulty: Easy; a few soft, boggy spots are the only difficulty

Scenery: Beautiful deep forest of maple, birch, and pine, with trailside views of tiny lakes and bogs

Special comments: A magical trail system that will charm riders of any ability with its scenery; the double-track grassy and forest floor trails are very easy to follow

What a wonderful spot! Sometimes I question if my reaction to different trails has more to do with my particular mood than to the experience I find there. Not at Nordic Woods. A solid shot of woods and lake scenery is always good for what ails you, and you won't get a better dose than on this 6.6-mile loop. The terrain is easy enough for any rider to take on, and shortcut trails are options

Water, woods, and sky on
Nordic Woods Trail.

that should keep even beginners from getting overextended. There are several
Adirondack shelters, ideal for scenic rest stops, along the route.

There are two trailhead choices. The north-end parking lot is most easily
accessible from the town of Spooner. For the south end, you can park in the trailhead lot off County Road B or across the road at Bobby Schmidt's Resort, where
lodging and beverages are available. This south parking lot is also close to the
Sawmill Lake Tour loop (see Ride 83, page 266), if you'd like to try an on-road
cruise as well.

General location: 13 miles east of Spooner on WI 70.

Elevation change: Mostly gently rolling terrain, with climbs in the 30' range.

Season: Mid-May through mid-October.

Services: All services, including bicycle retail and repair (at River Brook Bike
and Ski), are available in Spooner. All other services are available in Birchwood,
and there are showers, camping, water, and flush toilets at Doolittle Park on the
north side of town. Bobby Schmidt's Resort, where lodging and beverages are
available, is located just off the route to the northeast on CR B.

Hazards: The trail is also open to hikers.

Rescue index: Help is available in Spooner, Birchwood, and at Bobby Schmidt's Resort.

Land status: Washburn County Forest.

Maps: Trail maps are available from information contacts. The 7.5 minute series USGS quads for Potato Lake and Stone Lake show the terrain very well, but show few of the trails. The DeLorme book, *Wisconsin Atlas & Gazetteer*, shows all local roads and road names on page 84.

Finding the trail: For the north trailhead, travel east from Spooner on WI 70 for 13 miles to the Nordic Woods Ski Trail parking lot on the south side of the highway at DuBois Road. For the south trailhead, continue east past the north parking lot for another 1.6 miles, then turn south on CR B. Travel another 3.25 miles to the Nordic Woods Ski Trail parking lot on the west side of the road, or park at Bobby Schmidt's Resort on the east side.

Sources of additional information:

Birchwood Area Lakes Association
P.O. Box 9
Birchwood, WI 54817-0009
(715) 354-7846; (800) 236-2252
www.birchwoodwi.com

Spooner Chamber of Commerce
P.O. Box 406
Spooner, WI 54801-0406
(715) 635-2168; (800) 367-3306
www.washburncounty.com

Washburn County Forestry
(715) 635-4490

Notes on the trail: The grassy-surface double-track trails are well signed for travel in a clockwise direction, with lettered "you are here" map signs at all intersections.

RIDE 85 · Gandy Dancer State Trail (Rail-Trail)

AT A GLANCE

Length/configuration: 47 miles one way between St. Croix Falls and Danbury; from Danbury an additional 51-mile section continues through Minnesota, then back into Wisconsin to the city of Superior

Aerobic difficulty: Low; typical flat rail-trail

Technical difficulty: Easy

Scenery: Mixed woods and farmland south of Frederic, with deep woods and many lake views to the north

Special comments: A relatively new rail-trail, the Gandy Dancer is part of a two-state link that connects St. Croix Falls with Superior; a fine family ride with frequent small towns and parks, and also a good high-speed cruise

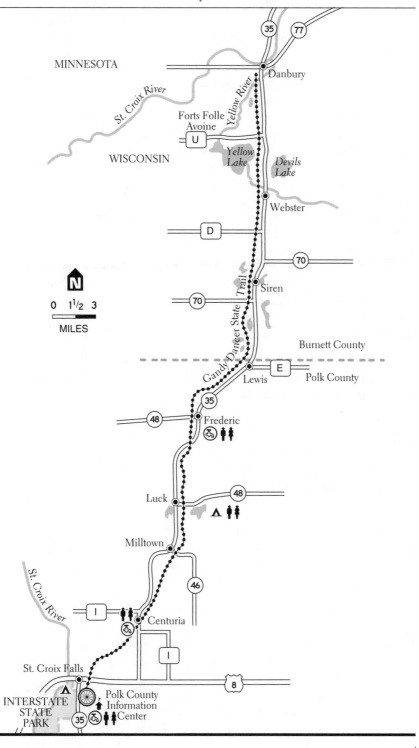

With the opening of the 47-mile Gandy Dancer, northwest Wisconsin finally got a great rail-trail that is fully developed for bicycling. Cutting across a broad curve of the St. Croix National Scenic Riverway, it connects the towns of St. Croix Falls at the south end with Danbury at the north. Seven more small towns are strung between these anchors, so services are always just around the bend. For a varied-terrain riding experience in the area, check out the Coon Lake Park Trails in Frederic (Ride 86).

The Gandy Dancer takes its name from the crews who kept the rails in shape by prying, pulling, and perhaps even pirouetting with railroad implements from the Gandy Tool Company. The many parks along the way are a big attraction for family riders. There are seven, many with playgrounds and swimming beaches. Most impressive is Interstate State Park, connected to the Polk County Information Center by a spur trail. The glacial legacy of the St. Croix Valley is explained there at an excellent interpretive center, and you can visit the river shore to watch rock climbers take on sheer lava cliffs.

Just a couple of miles west of Webster on County Road U is Forts Folle Avoine, a living museum on the actual site of the North West Company's trading post, which was built in 1802 during the last hurrah of the fur-trade era. The trade between French Canadian voyageurs and Native Americans lasted for more than 150 years. It was an interaction between European and American cultures that allowed them to learn and benefit from one another.

General location: Between St. Croix Falls and Danbury, parallel to WI 35.

Elevation change: Dead-flat rail-trail, except for a connector trail from the southern trailhead that climbs 140'.

Season: April through November.

Services: All services are available in St. Croix Falls, Luck, Frederic, Siren, and Danbury. Bicycle retail and repair are available in Webster at Hayes Pro Bike & Ski; repair is also available at the Wissahickon Bed-and-Breakfast in St. Croix Falls. There are cafes in Milltown and Webster. Taverns are in all trail towns. Swimming is available at Interstate State Park, Butternut Lake Park in Luck, Crooked Lake Park off the trail in Siren, and Ralph Larrabee Park just south of Danbury. Playgrounds are at Milltown, Luck, Frederic, and Siren. Camping is available at Interstate State Park, Coon Lake Park in Frederic, Luck Village Park, and Crooked Lake Park in Siren. All parks have either pit or flush toilets.

Hazards: The trail is also used by hikers.

Rescue index: Help is available in trailside towns.

Land status: Wisconsin State Park Trail. A trail pass fee is required for bicyclists age 16 and older ($3 daily/$10 annual). The trail pass also covers usages such as cross-country skiing, horseback riding, and bicycling on state mountain bike trails.

Maps: An excellent trail map is available from information contacts. The DeLorme book, *Wisconsin Atlas & Gazetteer*, shows the trail and all local roads and road names on pages 70, 83, and 92.

Finding the trail: At St. Croix Falls, at the Polk County Information Center on WI 35, just south of the US 8 intersection.

Sources of additional information:

Burnett County Department of
Tourism and Information
7410 County Road K #112
Siren, WI 54872
(715) 349-7411; (800) 788-3164
www.mwd.com/burnett/

Polk County Information Center
710 Highway 35 South
St. Croix Falls, WI 54024
(715) 483-1410; (800) 222-POLK
www.polkcountytourism.com

Notes on the trail: A daily or annual state trail pass fee is required (see Land status).

RIDE 86 · Coon Lake Park Trails

AT A GLANCE

Length/configuration: 3.3-mile loop; several loop variations are possible

Aerobic difficulty: High; they don't call it Cardiac Climb for nothing

Technical difficulty: Moderate; climbing skills and descending confidence are needed

Scenery: Deep forest of maple, birch, and pine overlooking Coon Lake

Special comments: A neat little trail system that gives intermediate and advanced riders a good workout; grassy single- and double-track trails cover steep, scenic terrain

Wouldn't the world be a wonderful place if every little town had a trail like Coon Lake? The people of Frederic not only have these trails for cross-country skiing, hiking, and biking, they have the Gandy Dancer State Trail running through town as well (see Ride 85, page 270).

The 3.3-mile loop is short but sweet, depending on your definition of sweet. The first uphill is called Cardiac Climb, and it's a steady grind up 90' of elevation before a rocket-sled ride down to a hairpin turn. Back at the access road, the loop snakes back and forth up the side of the big hill in a series of low gear tests before setting off on the gentler northern leg of the loop.

If the big hill is too much, you can just avoid it by continuing north from the parking lot on the access road and taking the first trail to the right just beyond the boulder barricade.

General location: On the east side of Frederic.

RIDE 86 · Coon Lake Park Trails

Elevation change: 90' of steady climbing on the south loop, plus several steep, shorter climbs.

Season: May through October.

Services: All services are available in Frederic. Bicycle retail and repair are available 16 miles north in Webster, at Hayes Pro Bike & Ski. There are flush toilets, camping, and water at Coon Lake Park.

Hazards: Trails receive little riding-season maintenance and windfall branches are often encountered. Trails are also used by hikers.

Rescue index: Help is available in Frederic.

Land status: Frederic town park.

Maps: A trail map is available from the information contacts below. The 7.5 minute series USGS quad for Frederic shows the terrain very well, but not the trails.

Finding the trail: In Frederic, turn east on Ash Street and travel just past the shore of Coon Lake, making an immediate left turn into the trailhead parking area.

Sources of additional information:

Frederic Community Association
P.O. Box 250
Frederic, WI 54837-0250
(715) 327-4294

Polk County Information Center
710 Highway 35 South
St. Croix Falls, WI 54024
(715) 483-1410; (800) 222-POLK
www.polkcountytourism.com

Notes on the trail: The grassy double-track trails have minimal signage, but are easy to follow due to limited complexity in a compact area. It is best to ride them in a counterclockwise direction. A gravel road running north from the trailhead parking area is part of the return loop. It also allows access to the easier, northernmost trails. To ride the entire outer loop, ride north from the parking area on the gravel road, and turn right on the first off-road trail. After scaling the long climb and descending back down, the loop returns to the gravel road, and steep loops swing back up the hillside. The last loop branches off to the right immediately after passing large stone barriers on the gravel road.

CHEQUAMEGON FOREST

The Chequamegon (pronounced Sha-wa-ma-gun) has become legendary among off-roaders thanks to a pioneering off-road event called the Chequamegon Fat Tire Festival. This weekend of mountain bike races and games was the first off-road competition in the Midwest when it began in 1983. Today, it features one of the largest off-road races in the nation, attracting 2,500 riders to the Chequamegon 40 and the 16-mile Short & Fat, which run concurrently.

There are more reasons than a weekend of racing to pay a visit to the Chequamegon. The people who live there and ride there know this, and several years ago they formed the Chequamegon Area Mountain Bike Association (CAMBA), which in a remarkably short time mapped and marked more than 300 miles of mountain bike routes. A recent study of the economic impact of mountain biking tourism in the area showed that the sport was bringing in 1.2 million dollars annually.

The area's wild terrain is mostly interlobate glacial moraine, formed between the Superior and Chippewa lobes. It is similar to the kettle moraine of southern Wisconsin. It simply can't be beaten for fun mountain biking. And, the Ojibwe reservation at Lac Court Oreilles (La-coo-ter-ray) has the best listener-sponsored radio station in the Midwest: WOJB. From blues to country, you'll hear music on 88.9 FM that most stations ignore or have forgotten.

The CAMBA routes, eleven of which are included here, are favorites among local riders. Good signage makes them accessible to visitors who needn't fear getting lost in the vast forest. There are no fees for riding the trails, but the Forest Service does charge for parking at some trailheads. CAMBA sells packets of detailed maps and encourages riders to join the organization.

At the southern end of the CAMBA system, Trail Descente introduces riders to the mix of forest and logging roads that characterize so much of the mountain biking network, and also tosses in some miles on the famous American Birkebeiner Ski Trail, known for testing the cross-country skiing stamina of thousands in the annual ski marathon of the same name.

A bit to the north, the Frost Pocket Tour is an easy paved road, forest road, and snowmobile trail route based in the small sport- and lumber-oriented community of Seeley. Starting at the halfway rest cabin on the Birkebeiner Trail, the Winding

Pine Trail leads riders through gorgeous woodlands and offers the option of a tough climb up the Seeley Fire Tower Hill. Nearby, the Lake Helane Tour is a moderately difficult ride on forest roads that pass by the shores of two scenic lakes.

The Short and Fat is a challenging point-to-point route that follows the Chequamegon Fat Tire Festival race course and some of the toughest hills on the north end of the Birkebeiner Trail. A challenging glacial feature is the highlight of a ride on the Esker Trail, which starts and finishes at Telemark Lodge.

At Rock Lake, riders can take on a challenging loop on cross-country ski trails that pass through a towering forest and past pristine lakes. The mix of scenery and single-track has made this route a favorite with off-roaders for years. Also in the area is the Namekagon Trail, which takes on easier terrain on forest roads and snowmobile trails.

To the north, the Drummond Trails offer a moderate ride that follows some single-track on the North Country Trail and leads to a scenic swimming beach. The Delta Hills Trails are a challenging slice of deep woods beauty through a land of lakes and white paper birch. On the Cisco/Pigeon/Star Lake Tour, any rider can enjoy a cruise through the beautiful Chequamegon National Forest scenery on gravel and paved roads.

RIDE 87 · Trail Descente

AT A GLANCE

Length/configuration: 8.6 miles made of three loops strung between out-and-back sections; several loop combinations possible

Aerobic difficulty: High; even higher if you add more Birkie Trail sections

Technical difficulty: Moderate; climbing skills and descending confidence are needed, as well as the ability to negotiate soft surfaces

Scenery: Deep forest of pine, aspen, and maple

Special comments: An excellent introduction to the variety of CAMBA trail riding for intermediate and advanced riders; the grassy double-track trails are easy to follow

The southern anchor of the extensive CAMBA trail system, Trail Descente takes in a plunge or two. Incorporating segments of the famous Birkebeiner cross-country ski trail (technically the Sawyer County Recreation Trail), famous for rising and falling like the waves of the sea, the route also takes in some tough terrain on old logging roads and an easier-riding fire lane road. The route is also the closest CAMBA trail to the resort town of Hayward. Tourism is the town's lifeblood, encompassing everything from muskie fishing to lumberjack shows.

RIDE 87 • Trail Descente

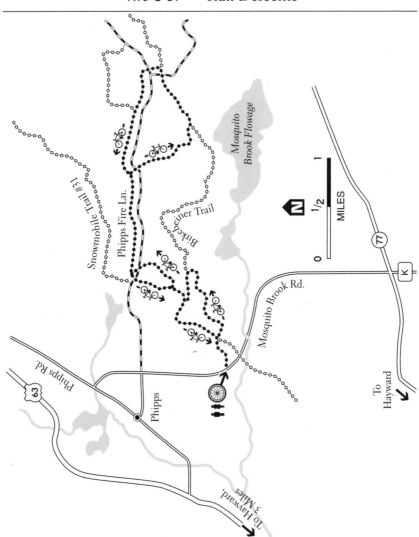

The route also incorporates or accesses several other CAMBA trails in the area, including the Whitetail Trail, Plantation Trail, and Bar Stool Trail. If you were to continue riding north on the Phipps Fire Lane for several miles, you'd junction with the Frost Pocket Tour (see Ride 89, page 283). Another option to keep in mind is a retuen to the trailhead via the Birkebeiner Trail.

General location: 7 miles northeast of Hayward.

Elevation change: Several steep 80' climbs and numerous ones in the 30' to 50' range.

Season: Early-May through October.

Services: All services, including bicycle retail and repair at New Moon Ski & Bike, are available in Hayward. There are pit toilets at the Mosquito Brook trailhead.

Hazards: Watch for windfall branches. Trails are also used by hikers. The Phipps Fire Lane is shared with motor vehicles.

Rescue index: Help is available in Hayward or Phipps.

Land status: Sawyer County Forest. A $5 daily or $30 annual vehicle parking fee is required at the Mosquito Brook trailhead.

Maps: The CAMBA maps include detailed route and topographical information. The map for this route is available at the trailhead. A complete set of detailed maps for all CAMBA trails and an overview map are available for $6.50 by writing CAMBA at the address listed below. The overview map locates the trail clusters and mountain bike–friendly businesses in the area. CAMBA individual memberships, which include a map set, voting privileges, and frame sticker, are available for $20.

Finding the trail: From Hayward, drive east 4.8 miles on WI 77 to the junction with County Road K. Turn north on Mosquito Brook Road (opposite CR K), and travel 2.3 miles to the CAMBA trailhead parking area. Several other CAMBA trails can be accessed from this trailhead.

Sources of additional information:

Chequamegon Area Mountain Bike
  Association (CAMBA)
P.O. Box 141
Cable, WI 54821
(715) 798-3599; (800) 533-7454
www.cambatrails.org

Hayward Area Chamber of
  Commerce
P.O. Box 726
Hayward, WI 54843-0726
(715) 634-8662; (800) 724-2992
www.haywardlakes.com

Notes on the trail: An annual or daily vehicle parking fee is required at the trailhead (see Land status). The grassy double-track trails are very well signed, with blue CAMBA markers and arrows as well as frequent "you are here" map signs, for two-way travel on the out-and-back sections and counterclockwise travel on the three loop sections. Trail Descente is contiguous with the Whitetail Trail for some distance and junctions with the Plantation and Barstool trails at the east end. A riding option would be to take the wide, hilly Birkebeiner Trail back to the trailhead instead of the Phipps Fire Lane and other trails.

RIDE 88 · Frost Pocket Tour (On-Road)

AT A GLANCE

Length/configuration: 10.5-mile loop with a panhandle

Aerobic difficulty: Moderate; flat sections are combined with one fairly steep climb and several easier ones

Technical difficulty: Easy; all you will have to deal with is a little loose surface

Scenery: Dense pine and hardwood forest with occasional openings

Special comments: A terrific paved- and gravel-road tour that riders of any ability can handle; the trailhead is at a pleasant park with a swimming hole

This easy 10.5-mile loop with a handle takes you deep into the north woods and past the strange feature that gave the route its name. The frost pocket is a geographical feature unique to terrain formed between two lobes of the continental glacier in northern latitudes. Melting blocks of ice formed pockets, or kettles, as they are also known. In an area where night temperatures are cool even in summer, these pits fill with cold air so many nights of the year, that little besides tough grasses and lichens will grow in them. They are also called sunbowls because they offer openings to the sky in the dense woods.

This route follows paved and improved gravel roads as well as several unimproved roads that serve as snowmobile trails in winter. All could be negotiated by a four-wheel-drive vehicle. This ride is rated as easy, and is a good one for novice mountain bikers or a nice tour for riders of any ability. No technical riding skill is necessary other than braking ability on a short, steep section with loose surface on snowmobile trail #5.

Silverthorn Park is a pleasant spot for the trailhead. The local baseball team, the Seeley Loggers, play there, and the small, clean lake has a nice swimming beach. The village of Seeley offers a mix of local color that includes the rough-and-ready chainsaw types and cross-country skiers and bicyclists. The Sawmill Saloon caters to all with food and drink. Just beyond Seeley on CAMBA County Road OO and Old OO, you'll pass by the Uhrenholt Memorial State Forest, which preserves a majestic stand of white pine and gives an idea of what the area was like before commercial logging began a hundred years ago.

General location: Silverthorn Park, 1 mile north of the village of Seeley.

Elevation change: The route begins and ends in the Namekagon River Valley on a flat stretch. The rest of the terrain tends to be rolling, with about 180' of total elevation difference, which includes one steep 120' climb on Old OO.

Season: Early-May through October.

Services: All services are available in Hayward, including bicycle rental, repair, and retail at New Moon Ski & Bike. Food and drink are available in Seeley, as well as bicycle rental, repair, and retail at Seeley Hills Ski and Bike.

RIDE 88 • Frost Pocket Tour

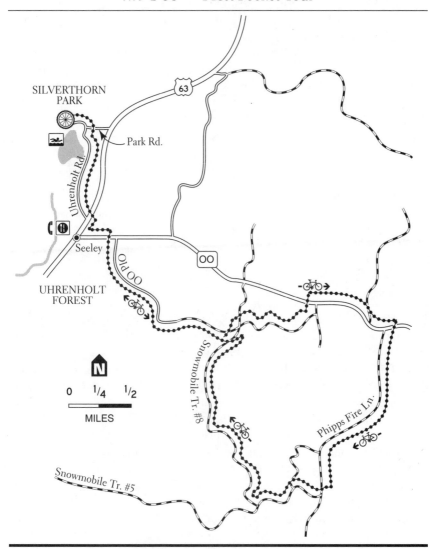

Hazards: Roads are kept clear, but downed trees and branches may be encountered at any time. Sandpit washouts at the bottom of steep hills on trails and roads are common. County and forest roads, and even snowmobile trails, are used by local two-wheel-drive vehicles and logging trucks. Hunting season begins in mid-September.

Rescue index: Help is available at Seeley. While the forest road and the snowmobile trails are traveled, your best chance for rescue will come if you can make your way back to CAMBA CR OO.

Land status: Public roads through private and public land, and snowmobile trails through Sawyer County Forest.

Maps: The CAMBA maps include detailed route and topographical information. The map for this route is available at the trailhead. A complete set of detailed maps for all CAMBA trails and an overview map are available for $6.50 by writing CAMBA at the address listed below. The overview map locates the trail clusters and mountain bike–friendly businesses in the area. CAMBA individual memberships, which include a map set, voting privileges, and a frame sticker, are available for $20.

Finding the trail: From the village of Seeley, drive 0.5 mile north on US 63, and turn west on Park Road heading toward Silverthorn Town Park. Several other CAMBA trails can be accessed from this trailhead.

Sources of additional information:

Chequamegon Area Mountain Bike Association (CAMBA)
P.O. Box 141
Cable, WI 54821
(715) 798-3599; (800) 533-7454
www.cambatrails.org

Hayward Area Chamber of Commerce
P.O. Box 726
Hayward, WI 54843-0726
(715) 634-8662; (800) 724-2992
www.haywardlakes.com

Notes on the trail: The route can be ridden in either direction, but the CAMBA trail signs and these directions indicate riding in a clockwise direction. It is well marked with blue-and-white CAMBA trail markers and "you are here" signs. From the Silverthorn trailhead follow the CAMBA signs that lead you in the direction of US 63 on the remnant of an old road. After a short distance you will pass through a vehicle barricade. This places you on Grandis Road, which turns into Uhrenholt Road as you ride south. Turn right at a **T** intersection onto US 63, which has a paved shoulder. At the village of Seeley turn left on CAMBA CR OO. Ride 0.3 mile and turn right on Old OO (CAMBA markers begin at this point), which begins as a paved road and becomes a gravel road. Near the top of the hill the pavement begins again, and Frint Road (a dead-end) goes off to the right. Pass Frint Road and at a **T** intersection, turn right on CAMBA CR OO. Ride 0.6 mile and turn right onto the Phipps Fire Lane (note that a short loop veers off to the left at this point and returns to CAMBA CR OO). After riding 1.5 miles, turn right on snowmobile trail #5 and use caution on the steep, loose downhill surface (snowmobile trails are marked with orange diamonds and arrows). Ride 0.5 mile and turn right on snowmobile trail #8 (the frost pockets are along this section). At a **T** intersection turn left, which will put you back on Old OO. Retrace your route to the trailhead.

RIDE 89 · Winding Pine Trails

AT A GLANCE

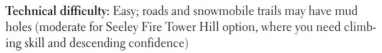

Length/configuration: 8.5-mile loop with an out-and-back panhandle (add another 2.5 miles for the Seeley Fire Tower Hill option)

Aerobic difficulty: Moderate; mostly rolling terrain with some flat sections (challenging if taking the Seeley Fire Tower Hill option)

Technical difficulty: Easy; roads and snowmobile trails may have mud holes (moderate for Seeley Fire Tower Hill option, where you need climbing skill and descending confidence)

Scenery: Deep mixed hardwood and pine forest with a gorgeous run on snowmobile trail #8

Special comments: A relatively short route that should be fun for riders of any ability; the Seeley Fire Tower Hill option adds difficulty

Winding Pine. The name sounds so alluring. As it should, since the twisting course of Snowmobile Trail #8 through tall white and Norway pines will cement any rider's bond with the forest. This 8.5-mile ride on gravel forest roads and dirt trails should be easy for just about any rider, and if they're adventurous, beginners can sample the wide, grassy Birkebeiner Trail, or add a loop and step up to the Seeley Fire Tower Hill.

When I say step up, I mean step up, especially if you choose to ride the extra 2.5-mile Fire Tower loop counterclockwise. Going that way, you'll be climbing the 210 feet in a series of four steps. This is the same direction the Chequamegon 40 race route follows, and though the average grade is one-in-ten (you gain one foot of elevation for every ten feet of travel), the steep pitches make you understand why the first rider over the top is often the winner. To make the climb easier and take on the steps as a downhill challenge, ride the loop clockwise. The climb is reduced to 150 feet at a one-in-twenty average grade. Either way, the view on top is grand.

General location: 3 miles east of US 63 and the village of Seeley.

Elevation change: You will only find about 100' of elevation difference along the route. However, there are several very steep, uphill and downhill pitches of around 80'. The Seeley Fire Tower Hill climb is 210' from the south and 150' from the west.

Season: Early-May through October.

Services: Shelter, water, and pay telephones are available at the CAMBA County Road OO trailhead. No services whatsoever will be found en route. All services are available in Hayward, including bicycle retail, rental, and repair at New Moon Ski & Bike. Food and drink are available in Seeley, along with bicycle retail, rental, and repair at Seeley Hills Ski and Bike.

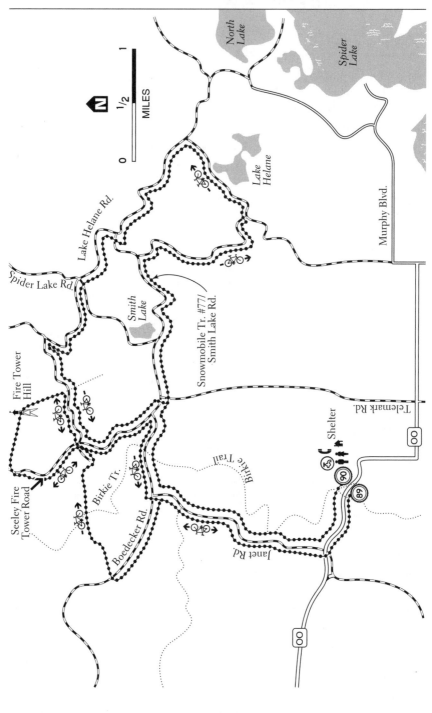

Hazards: Trails and roads are kept clear, but downed trees and branches may be encountered at any time. On steep slopes, loose stones and large embedded rocks may be present, requiring technical riding skill. Some downhills are extremely steep. Sandpit washouts at the bottom of steep hills on trails and roads are common. Forest roads are used by local two-wheel-drive vehicles and logging trucks. Hunting season begins in mid-September. Carrying and using a compass is recommended.

Rescue index: Help is available at Seeley or can be summoned by phone from the CAMBA CR OO trailhead. If you are unable get back to the trailhead, your best chance of rescue will come by making your way to Spider Lake Road or south off the route to Murphy Boulevard.

Land status: Public forest roads and logging trails through private and public Sawyer County Forest land. A $5 daily or $30 annual vehicle parking fee is required at the CAMBA CR OO trailhead.

Maps: The CAMBA maps include detailed route and topographical information. The map for this route is available at the CAMBA CR OO trailhead. A complete set of detailed maps for all CAMBA trails and an overview map are available for $6.50 by writing CAMBA at the address listed below. The overview map locates the trail clusters and mountain bike–friendly businesses in the area. CAMBA individual memberships, which include a map set, voting privileges, and a frame sticker, are available for $20.

Finding the trail: Drive 3 miles east of US 63 at the village of Seeley on CR OO, to the CAMBA CR OO trailhead at the Birkebeiner cross-country ski trail rest cabin. Several other CAMBA trails use this trailhead.

Sources of additional information:

Chequamegon Area Mountain Bike
Association (CAMBA)
P.O. Box 141
Cable, WI 54821
(715) 798-3599; (800) 533-7454
www.cambatrails.org

Hayward Area Chamber of
Commerce
P.O. Box 726
Hayward, WI 54843-0726
(715) 634-8662; (800) 724-2992
www.haywardlakes.com

Notes on the trail: An annual or daily vehicle parking fee is required at the trailhead (see Land status). The grassy double-track trails are very well signed, with blue CAMBA markers and arrows as well as frequent "you are here" map signs, for two-way travel on the out-and-back sections and clockwise travel on the Winding Pine loop section.

The optional Seeley Fire Tower loop can be ridden in either direction, but is only partially signed as an official CAMBA trail. To ride it clockwise, follow the CAMBA Fire Tower Trail signs (the route is contiguous with the Winding Pine up to the Seeley Fire Tower Road) to the north on the Seeley Fire Tower Road, to the spur road that takes you to the top of the Fire Tower Hill. To descend the extremely steep downhill, continue straight over the top and down a dirt logging road. At a cross intersection where the terrain levels out, turn west on a better logging road (also called Snowmobile Trail #8) and follow it back to the Seeley Fire Tower Road.

To ride in a counterclockwise direction, turn north on Seeley Fire Tower Road off of the Winding Pine Trail, and immediately veer off to the right on a level logging road (a continuation of Snowmobile Trail #8). Travel east for about a half-mile watching for CAMBA map sign S 17. At this point, turn north and begin an immediate steep climb up the Seeley Fire Tower Hill.

RIDE 90 · Lake Helane Tour (On-Road)

AT A GLANCE

Length/configuration: 14.5-mile loop with an out-and-back panhandle

Aerobic difficulty: Moderate; just enough climbs to get your heart rate up a few times

Technical difficulty: Moderate; several steep, rocky downhill sections

Scenery: Superb, deep north woods and pristine lakes

Special comments: A terrific high-speed cruise with hard-to-match scenery for riders of intermediate ability or above; mostly gravel forest roads skirt the edges of two beautiful lakes

This 14.5-mile ride to Lake Helane will take you through the Sawyer County Forest on scenic two-wheel-drive forest roads and four-wheel-drive logging roads. En route, you will pass two pristine north-woods lakes. It is a moderately difficult ride due to steep, rocky downhill sections on Smith Lake Road and Lake Helane Road that require technical riding skill.

The ride's namesake, Lake Helane, is an example of nature's pure poetry, and is a fine spot to stop for a rest, perhaps spot an eagle plummeting from the sky to catch a fish, or hear the call of the loon. Smith Lake is a much smaller sister lake, and is a scenic surprise after a tense, rocky downhill on snowmobile trail #77. You'll skirt the very tip of Smith Lake, and you may find yourself splashing through shallow water on the firm road surface when the lake level is high. This is another gorgeous forest spot ringed with pine trees.

In the 1930s, Smith Lake was the site of a Civilian Conservation Corp (CCC) camp. The CCC was a program created in the depths of the Great Depression by the Roosevelt administration to deal with overwhelming unemployment and to provide useful public works. In this area, the CCC men reforested a landscape that had been left as barren as the face of the moon by the lumber barons. The CCC also created the excellent system of forest roads riders enjoy today.

The steep climb
from Smith Lake.

An interesting alternative route on the way back to the trailhead is to ride the section of the Birkebeiner Trail that parallels Janet Road. This wide, grassy trail, known as the Birkie, is the route followed by more than 7,000 cross-country skiers in the annual American Birkebeiner race held the last weekend of February, and is often used as part of the route for the Chequamegon 40 mountain bike race, held in mid-September.

General location: 3 miles east of US 63 and the village of Seeley.

Elevation change: You will only find about 100' of elevation difference along the route. However, there are several very steep uphill and downhill pitches of around 80'.

Season: Mid-May through September.

Services: Shelter, water, and pay telephones are available at the CAMBA CR OO trailhead. No services whatsoever will be found en route. All services are available in Cable and Hayward. Food and drink are available in Seeley. Bicycle retail, rental, and repair are available at Seeley Hills Ski and Bike and at New Moon Ski & Bike in Hayward.

Hazards: Trails and roads are kept clear, but downed trees and branches may be encountered at any time. On steep slopes, loose stones and large embedded rocks may be present, requiring technical riding skills. Some downhills are extremely steep. Sandpit washouts at the bottom of steep hills on trails and roads are common. Forest roads are used by local two-wheel-drive vehicles and logging trucks. Hunting season begins in mid-September. Carrying and using a compass is recommended.

Rescue index: Help is available at Seeley or can be summoned by phone from the CAMBA CR OO trailhead. If you are unable to get back to the trailhead, your best chance of rescue will be making your way to Spider Lake Road or south off the route to Murphy Boulevard.

Land status: Public forest roads and logging trails through private and public Sawyer County Forest land. A $5 daily or $30 annual vehicle parking fee is required at the CAMBA CR OO trailhead. There is a self-pay station at the trailhead.

Maps: The CAMBA maps include detailed route and topographical information. The map for this route is available at the trailhead. A complete set of detailed maps for all CAMBA trails and an overview map are available for $6.50 by writing CAMBA at the address listed below. The overview map locates the trail clusters and mountain bike–friendly businesses in the area. CAMBA individual memberships, which include a map set, voting privileges, and a frame sticker, are available for $20.

Finding the trail: Drive 3 miles east of US 63 from the village of Seeley on CAMBA CR OO to the CAMBA CR OO trailhead at the Birkebeiner cross-country ski trail rest cabin. Several other CAMBA trails use this trailhead.

Sources of additional information:

Cable Area Chamber of Commerce
P.O. Box 217
Cable, WI 54821
(800) 533-7454
www.cable4fun.com

Chequamegon Fat Tire Festival
P.O. Box 267
Cable, WI 54821
(715) 798-3594
www.cheqfattire.com

Chequamegon Area Mountain Bike
  Association (CAMBA)
P.O. Box 141
Cable, WI 54821
(715) 798-3599; (800) 533-7454
www.cambatrails.org

Notes on the trail: An annual or daily vehicle parking fee is required at the trailhead (see Land status). From the CAMBA trailhead at the Birkebeiner Ski Trail rest cabin, ride 0.5 mile west on CAMBA CR OO toward Seeley, then turn right on Janet Road. The route is marked with blue-and-white CAMBA trail markers for two-way travel on Janet and Boedecker roads, and for counterclockwise travel on the loop section. At a T intersection, turn right on Boedecker Road. At a stop sign (an unmarked intersection with Spider Lake Road), go straight. After 0.5 mile, as the road swings to the left, use extreme caution as you follow the

CAMBA arrow to the right onto the steep, rocky snowmobile trail #77. Slow down for this one; you may be lulled into complacency by the fast, easy ride on the gravel roads. A sand washout at the bottom of the hill along Smith Lake may be difficult to negotiate. This section will be followed by a steep, rocky uphill and a steep, rocky, and often rutted downhill, just before a **T** intersection at which you will turn right. There is one more rocky downhill just before Lake Helane. At a **T** intersection a short distance past Lake Helane, turn left onto Lake Helane Road. After 1.4 miles turn right, and in 0.5 mile you will junction with Spider Lake Fire Lane. Turn left, and after 0.2 mile turn right onto Horseshoe Bend Road (unmarked). After 0.6 mile you are at the horseshoe, and must turn left. After another 0.5 mile you are at the intersection of the Seeley Fire Tower climb, the infamous 0.3 mile grind in the Chequamegon 40 mountain bike race. The route goes straight here, but if you want to take on the challenge you can climb to a fine overview of the forest. At 0.5 mile, turn left at the junction of a slightly better road (unmarked Seeley Fire Tower Road). After another 0.8 mile, turn right on an improved gravel road (unmarked Boedecker Road) and return to the trailhead by retracing the route or taking the Birkebeiner Trail.

RIDE 91 · Short & Fat Trails

AT A GLANCE

Length/configuration: 16 miles one way, point-to-point

Aerobic difficulty: High, due to very steep climbs on the Birkebeiner Trail

Technical difficulty: Moderate; climbing skills and descending confidence will be needed

Scenery: Beautiful hardwood and pine forest

Special comments: A chance for advanced and determined intermediate riders to ride the Short & Fat race course on a mix of gravel roads, wide cross-country ski trails, and logging roads

When the Chequamegon Fat Tire Festival was looking at adding a shorter distance race to complement their annual premier Chequamegon 40 event, the name they chose was a real no-brainer. Short & Fat is a good description for this course. It gives people a chance to enjoy fat-tire competition that is more attainable than the 40-mile main event. About a thousand riders compete annually in the Short & Fat. Its course has varied over the history of the Chequamegon Fat Tire Festival, but the current course has been so popular the Chequamegon Area Mountain Bike Association (CAMBA) has signed it for recreational use.

The 16-mile route gives you a fine sampling of riding experiences. You begin with an easy roll out of town on a paved road that becomes a gravel forest road.

Note: More trails exist in this area than can be shown on this map.

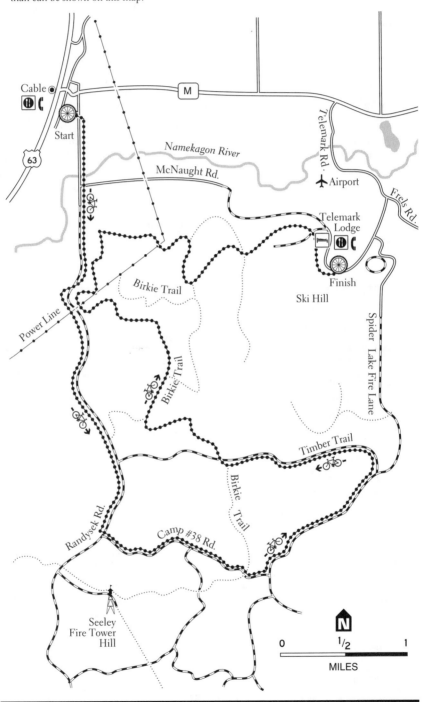

Cable

Start

63

Namekagon River

McNaught Rd.

M

Telemark Rd.

Airport

Frels Rd.

Telemark Lodge

Finish

Birkie Trail

Ski Hill

Power Line

Birkie Trail

Spider Lake Fire Lane

Timber Trail

Birkie Trail

Randysek Rd.

Camp #38 Rd.

Seeley Fire Tower Hill

N

0   1/2   1

MILES

Then you follow a snowmobile trail and more gravel forest roads to the American Birkebeiner (Birkie) Ski Trail. This is where things get serious, as you take on the steep grades that challenge thousands of skiers each winter. The very wide, grassy trail gives way to narrower double-track cross-country ski trails on the Telemark Lodge property. The route merits a challenging rating due to the toughness of the Birkie Trail, but unless washouts are encountered, no real technical skill is needed other than the ability to handle a bike on steep uphills and downhills.

The Short & Fat course is a one-way route through Bayfield and Sawyer County forests and Telemark property. The deep woods are a mix of pine, maple, aspen, birch, and oak. You won't see any sign of habitation between the start and finish. There are two options for riding back to the Cable trailhead. You can follow the pavement on Telemark Road and County Road M (which has a paved shoulder), or take the shorter but sandy McNaught Road.

There are other riding possibilities on-route. For more adventure you can deviate from the route by continuing south on Randysek Road, and taking the side road up to the Seeley Firetower Hill for a grand overview of the forest. You can also pick up more Birkie trail off of Randysek or Camp #38 Road. If you want to bail out, Spider Lake Fire Lane is an easy way back to Telemark. Another bail-out option entails hopping back on Randysek Road where the power line crosses the Birkie Trail and taking the road back to Cable.

General location: The village of Cable.

Elevation change: The route is generally rolling, but will climb steadily 270' to Camp #38 Road. On the Birkie Trail there are extremely steep grades of 50' to 100'.

Season: Mid-May through September.

Services: All services are available in Cable. Lodging and dining are available at Telemark Lodge. Bicycle retail and repair are found in Seeley at Seeley Hills Ski and Bike.

Hazards: Trails and roads are kept clear, but downed trees and branches can be encountered at any time. Winter frost continually heaves large glacial stones out of the ground. These rocky surfaces may be encountered anywhere and can be hidden by grass. Washouts may be found on forest roads. Forest roads are used by local two-wheel-drive vehicles and logging trucks. Hunting season begins in mid-September. Hikers may be encountered on ski trails; horseback riders use some ski trails on Telemark property. CAMBA trail marking is excellent, but vandalism of signage does happen, so it's a good idea to carry a compass.

Rescue index: Help is available at Telemark Resort and in Cable. If you are injured or have mechanical problems, make your way to Randysek, Spider Lake, Timber Trail, or McNaught Road for the best chance of rescue.

Land status: Public roads and ski trails through Bayfield or Sawyer County forests, and private ski trails on Telemark Resort property.

Maps: The CAMBA maps include detailed route and topographical information. The map for this route is available at the Telemark trailhead. A complete set of detailed maps for all CAMBA trails and an overview map are available for

$6.50 by writing CAMBA at the address listed below. The overview map locates the trail clusters and mountain bike–friendly businesses in the area. CAMBA individual memberships, which include a map set, voting privileges, and a frame sticker, are available for $20.

Finding the trail: From US 63 turn east on CR M in the village of Cable. After one block turn right on First Street (unsigned), travel past the post office, and take the first left onto First Avenue (unsigned). Travel a half block, and find the CAMBA trailhead in the old grade school parking lot on the left.

Sources of additional information:

Cable Area Chamber of Commerce
P.O. Box 217
Cable, WI 54821
(800) 533-7454
www.cable4fun.com

Chequamegon Fat Tire Festival
P.O. Box 267
Cable, WI 54821
(715) 798-2594
www.cheqfattire.com

Chequamegon Area Mountain Bike
  Association (CAMBA)
P.O. Box 141
Cable, WI 54821
(715) 798-3599; (800) 533-7454
www.cambatrails.org

Notes on the trail: The route is well marked with blue-and-white CAMBA trail signs and periodic "you are here" maps, as well as some street-type road signs and cross-country ski trail signs. From the Cable trailhead, turn east on First Avenue and after a half-block turn right (south) on Randysek Road. At about 4 miles, turn left onto Camp #38 Road (unmarked). Follow it to a T intersection and turn left onto Spider Lake Fire Road (unmarked). As the road finally levels out after a long downhill run, turn left onto Timber Trail Road. Turn right after about a mile-and-a-half onto the American Birkebeiner Ski Trail, the only extremely wide, grassy trail in the forest. At the power line take a sharp left, following the CAMBA arrows onto a narrower forest trail. Follow it to Telemark Resort.

RIDE 92 · Telemark/CAMBA Single-Track Trails

AT A GLANCE

Length/configuration: 9.1-mile loop

Aerobic difficulty: High; several climbs are long and steep, many short climbs are very steep

Technical difficulty: Challenging; steep grades, loose surface, tight corners, and narrow passages will test anyone's skills

Scenery: Deep woods of pine, birch, and maple

RIDE 92 • Telemark/CAMBA Single-Track Trails

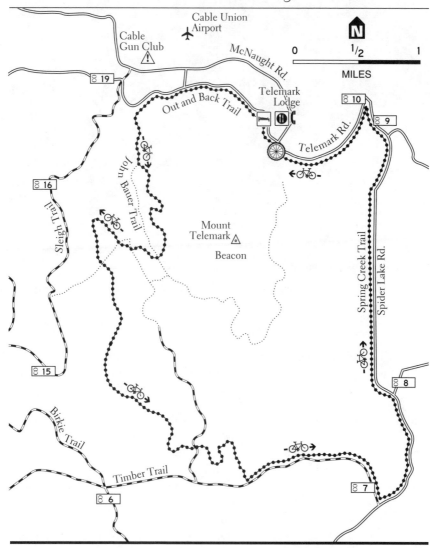

Special comments: In response to a growing demand for true single-track trails, the Chequamegon Area Mountain Bike Association (CAMBA) has created two new trails on the Telemark Resort property and adjacent Bayfield County Forest land. Riders who want a real test of their bike handling skills can try the 1.5-mile Telemark Terrain Park loop on the Mt. Telemark ski hill, while those interested in a tough, but less aerobically-demanding trail on more moderate terrain can take on the 9.1-mile loop described here. Advanced-skill riders will love the challenge of these single-track trails.

The Telemark/CAMBA Single-Track Trails offer a mix of woods and forest openings.

CAMBA, under the direction of local trail guru Ron Bergin, has gone great guns creating new single-track trails. The terrain around Telemark has always been aerobically challenging for cross-country skiers and mountain bikers, with most of the area's mountain biking done on cross-country ski trails, snowmobile trails, forest roads, and logging roads. A look at the CAMBA topographic trail maps show that the pocked glacial landscape has a lot more to offer. There is hardly any level ground.

The trail described here is new and a name hasn't been finalized yet. And, the 4.3 miles of single-track on this loop is just the start. More trail, four times the distance of the present single-track, is planned for the future. Eventually the trail will make a complete loop of over 20 miles.

The ride starts on double-track cross-country ski trails and finishes on dirt, gravel, and paved forest roads. At 1.4 miles, you leave the John Bauer ski trail and turn left onto the single-track, which is also signed as the Ojibwe Snowshoe Trail at this point. The trail is narrow and twisty, with a very uneven surface. Some smoothing can be expected as more mountain bikers ride the trail. After 1.2 miles, the single-track trail crosses the John Bauer Trail. If the single-track has been too difficult, you can bail out at this point. There is more difficult riding to come. Soon the trail works its way up onto a ridge and crosses a section of World Cup cross-country ski trail aptly named "The Wall." The next 1.5-mile stretch is equally tough. Then the terrain becomes a bit more moderate. The rocks, roots, twists, turns, and sudden short but steep sections just keep coming though. This trail requires total concentration.

You will be amazed at how easy the riding seems when you leave the single-track for the packed dirt on Timber Trail road. Spider Lake Fire Lane, which is a wide, well-traveled gravel road is an easy, if sometimes bumpy, roll back to paved Telemark Road.

General location: Telemark Resort, three miles east of the village of Cable and US 63.

Elevation change: The total elevation difference of 120' is gained and lost in nearly constant bites of 15' to 50' in the single-track sections. The gravel and paved road sections are rolling to gently rolling with elevation changes in the 30' range.

Season: Mid-May through September.

Services: All services are available in Cable. Lodging and dining are available at Telemark Lodge. Bicycle retail and repair can be found in Hayward at the New Moon Ski Shop.

Hazards: Trails and roads are kept clear, but downed trees and branches may be encountered at any time. Roots and glacial stones may be encountered any-where. The trail is new and the surface, nearly always soft, is very loose in places. The passage between trees is often very narrow. Some downhills are extremely steep and require technical ability. Forest roads are used by local two-wheel-drive vehicles and logging trucks.

Rescue index: Help is available at Telemark Resort and in Cable. While the CAMBA trails are popular by north-woods standards, don't count on other riders coming along. If you are injured or have a mechanical failure, you should make your way to the trailhead, or at least out to Spider Lake Fire Lane or Timber Trail Road, as best you can.

Land status: Private land and Bayfield County Forest.

Maps: The CAMBA maps include detailed route and topographical informa-tion The map for this route is available at the Telemark trailhead. A complete set of detailed maps for all CAMBA trails and an overview map are available for $6.50 by writing CAMBA at the address listed below. The overview map locates the trail clusters and mountain bike–friendly businesses in the area. CAMBA individual memberships, which include a map set, voting privileges, and frame sticker, are available for $20.

Finding the trail: From U.S. 63 turn east on County Road M in the village of Cable. Proceed east two miles to Telemark Road and turn south. This takes you to Telemark Lodge. You can park in the lower parking lot on the right side of the road, between the lodge and the alpine ski hill. The Telemark trailhead is directly across Telemark Road from the parking lot. Several other CAMBA trails use this trailhead.

Sources of additional information:

Cable Area Chamber of Commerce
P.O. Box 217
Cable, WI 54821
(800) 533-7454
www.cable4fun.com

Chequamegon Area Mountain Bike
Association (CAMBA)
P.O. Box 141
Cable, WI 54821
(715) 798-3599; (800) 533-7454
www.cambatrails.org

Notes on the trail: From the lower parking lot CAMBA Trailhead follow signs for "Out & Back Trail" and "Sleigh Trail" to the right (signs for the "Telemark Terrain Park" single-track point left). After 1.1 miles, turn left on the John Bauer ski trail. At 1.4 miles, turn left onto the single-track marked as the Ojibwe Snowshoe Trail. By the time you have a chance to use this trail it will certainly have its own name and be well marked with CAMBA signs, as all the other trails are. There are many intersecting trails en route, so it is recommended that you ride with a compass and bicycle odometer.

RIDE 93 · Rock Lake Trails

AT A GLANCE

Length/configuration: 9.9-mile loop; several loop variations are possible

Aerobic difficulty: High; big hills become more frequent the farther you get into the loop

Technical difficulty: Moderate; climbing skills and descending confidence will be needed

Scenery: Beautiful mixed pine and hardwood forest

Special comments: Ask any local which CAMBA trail is the most beautiful and most fun to ride, and they'll say Rock Lake; the challenging grassy and forest floor surface single-track trail won't disappoint determined intermediate or advanced riders

Once you've ridden the Rock Lake Trail you'll have a common bond with hundreds of other mountain bikers who have enjoyed this 9.9-mile single-track, cross-country ski trail system. This is the kind of trail where indelible mountain bike memories are made. You'll be inside the deep woods of the Chequamegon National Forest for the entire distance. This woodland character made the Rock Lake area an ideal location for the Chequamegon Fat Tire Festival to hold its mountain bike orienteering contests during the event's early years. What better place to chase through the woods with a map and compass?

The Rock Lake Trail is a good ride for people interested in a challenging route. It's a nice transition trail for riders wanting to move up from moderate

RIDE 93 • Rock Lake Trails
RIDE 94 • Namekagon Trails

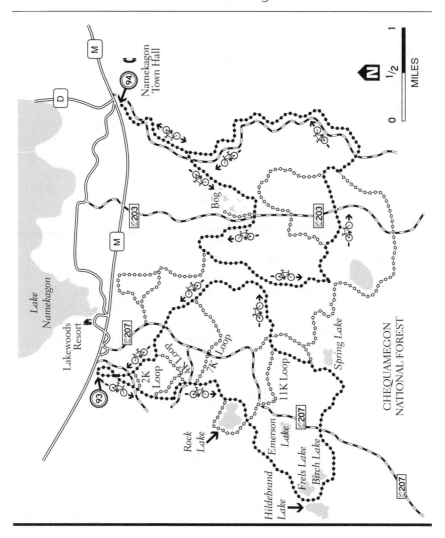

trails. Trail surfaces are mainly grassy with a hardpack track. On steep slopes you will find some loose rock, but no sharp turns. Technical ability is required to stay on the bike on many steep upgrades and to handle the bike on rough descents. The loop follows a cross-country ski trail wide enough for an all-terrain vehicle, and occasionally follows sections of four-wheel-drive roads. The terrain is almost constantly rolling, and you will rarely find the same grade for more than a few yards.

The forest is so dense that the trail often tunnels through the trees. When you come upon Rock Lake it is a wonderful scenic surprise. Several other small lakes can be accessed or seen from the trail. Wildlife is abundant, but not easily spotted unless on the trail itself or on a lake. Look for bald eagles and loons on Rock Lake, and broad-winged hawks on the trails.

General location: 7 miles east of US 63 and the village of Cable.

Elevation change: The terrain is almost constantly rolling, and steep grades of 30' to 60' are common. A few climbs and descents of 80' to 100' will be found.

Season: Mid-May through September.

Services: Food and lodging are available at Lakewoods Resort, a short distance from the trailhead. Gasoline, groceries, and lodging are found in Cable.

Hazards: The trails are regularly maintained by CAMBA and the U.S. Forest Service, but windfall trees and branches may be encountered at anytime. Washout ruts may be found on steep slopes. Trails are open to hikers, but beyond Rock Lake encounters will be rare. Although closed to motor vehicle traffic and signed for one-way riding, people may be riding in the opposite direction. The trail crosses Forest Service Road 207 (known as Rock Lake Road) several times, and caution must be exercised at this well-traveled road.

Rescue index: Help is available at Lakewoods Resort. While this trail is popular with off-road riders, the chances of on-trail rescue are slim. If injured or mechanically disabled, your best option is to make your way to well-traveled FR 207 or County Road M.

Land status: Chequamegon National Forest. A vehicle parking fee is required for the Rock Lake Trails parking lot ($2 daily/$8 annual). There is a self-pay station at the trailhead.

Maps: CAMBA maps include detailed route and topographical information. The map for this route is available at the trailhead. A complete set of detailed maps for all CAMBA trails and an overview map are available for $6.50 by writing CAMBA at the address listed below. The overview map locates the trail clusters and mountain bike–friendly businesses in the area. CAMBA individual memberships, which include a map set, voting privileges, and a frame sticker, are available for $20.

Finding the trail: The CAMBA Rock Lake trailhead is located on CR M, 7 miles east of the village of Cable and US 63. Several other CAMBA trails use this trailhead.

Sources of additional information:

Cable Area Chamber of Commerce
P.O. Box 217
Cable, WI 54821
(800) 533-7454
www.cable4fun.com

Chequamegon Area Mountain Bike
    Association (CAMBA)
P.O. Box 141
Cable, WI 54821
(715) 798-3599; (800) 533-7454
www.cambatrails.org

Rock Lake Trails
are among CAMBA's
most popular.

Chequamegon National Forest
Service
Great Divide Ranger District
604 Nyman Avenue or P.O. Box 896

Hayward, WI 54843
(715) 634-4821
www.fs.fed.us/r9/cnnf

Notes on the trail: From the CAMBA Rock Lake trailhead follow the blue-and-white CAMBA trail signs. Forest Service roads are marked with small, low, brown signs with yellow lettering. The trail is signed for one-way travel for mountain biking and for cross-country skiing. Light-blue diamond signs are cross-country trail markers. Frequent "you are here" signs for skiing and mountain biking will reassure you of your location. Be sure to follow the CAMBA signs for the Rock Lake Trail, as the route also intersects with CAMBA's Glacier Loop Trail. The ski trail system features four shortcut loops that may be used as bailout options or to access FR 207. While the signage is excellent, it is still a good idea to carry a compass.

RIDE 94 · Namekagon Trails

AT A GLANCE

Length/configuration: 10-mile loop including the out-and-back panhandle

Aerobic difficulty: Moderate; the toughest climb will come in the first mile

Technical difficulty: Easy; trails and gravel roads are easily negotiated

Scenery: Deep boreal forest with side-trip overviews of marshes and bogs

Special comments: A wonderful high-speed cruise for the fit, or a not-too-demanding tour for intermediate riders; gravel roads and snowmobile trails are easy to follow

The name of this ride recalls the legend of Chief Namekagon's treasure. It seems the aging Ojibwe chief had the habit of paying for everything in pure silver, which people conjectured he was chipping off some gigantic nugget hidden in the forest. He never revealed the secret of his source, so the bonanza may still be out there.

You can look for treasure as much as you want, but your real reward on this 10-mile journey is a chance to revel in the beauty of northern forest and bog. The rolling, but not-too-tough, mix of gravel roads, double-track snowmobile trails, and single-track on overgrown logging roads will take you through some lovely country.

As you cross Forest Service Road 203 on the first leg of the ride, take a short side trip on it for just a couple of blocks distance to the north. There, looking to the east, you'll have a fantastic overview of a huge bog. Bogs are marvelous places, where sphagnum moss covering the cold waters teems with rare flora such as wild orchids and insect-eating pitcher plants.

At the southernmost tip of the loop you can try another side trip. Continuing south for a half-mile on the double-track trail beyond the route's sharp turn to the northeast will take you to a beautiful overview of wilderness forest and bog.

General location: 10 miles east of US 63 and the village of Cable.

Elevation change: The terrain is almost constantly rolling, and steep grades of 30' to 60' are common. A few climbs and descents of 80' to 100' will be found.

Season: Mid-May through September.

Services: Food and lodging are available at Lakewoods Resort, 2 miles west of the trailhead, or Garmish Resort, due north of FS 203 on Lake Namekagon.

Hazards: The trails are regularly maintained by CAMBA and the U.S. Forest Service, but windfall trees and branches may be encountered at any time. Washout ruts may be found on steep slopes. Forest roads are open to motor vehicle traffic.

A moo-ving machine on the Namekagon Trails.

Rescue index: Help is available at Lakewoods Resort or the Birches Bar at the County Road M and County Road D intersection opposite the town hall. There is a pay phone at the town hall. While the trail is popular with off-road riders, the chances of on-trail rescue are slim. If injured or mechanically disabled, your best option is to make your way to FS 203 or CR M.

Land status: Chequamegon National Forest.

Maps: CAMBA maps include detailed route and topographical information. The map for this route is available at the trailhead. A complete set of detailed maps for all CAMBA trails and an overview map are available for $6.50 by writing CAMBA at the address listed below. The overview map locates the trail clusters and mountain bike–friendly businesses in the area. CAMBA individual memberships, which include a map set, voting privileges, and a frame sticker, are available for $20.

Finding the trail: The CAMBA Namekagon Town Hall trailhead is located on CR M, 10 miles east of the village of Cable and US 63. The Patsy Lake Trail also uses this trailhead.

Sources of additional information:

Cable Area Chamber of Commerce
P.O. Box 217
Cable, WI 54821
(800) 533-7454
www.cable4fun.com

Chequamegon Area Mountain Bike
Association (CAMBA)
P.O. Box 141
Cable, WI 54821
(715) 798-3599; (800) 533-7454
www.cambatrails.org

Chequamegon National Forest
Service, Great Divide Ranger
District
604 Nyman Avenue or P.O. Box 896
Hayward, WI 54843
(715) 634-4821
www.fs.fed.us/r9/cnnf

Notes on the trail: From the CAMBA Namekagon Town Hall trailhead, follow the blue-and-white CAMBA trail signs. Forest Service roads are marked with small, low, brown signs with yellow lettering. Most of the trail is signed for one-way travel. Frequent "you are here" signs for skiing and mountain biking will reassure you of your location. Be sure to follow the CAMBA signs for the Namekagon Trail as the route is also at times contiguous with, and in other places intersects with, CAMBA's Patsy Lake Trail.

RIDE 95 · Drummond Trails

AT A GLANCE

Length/configuration: 12.9-mile loop and out-and-back route; many variations are possible

Aerobic difficulty: Moderate; easier on the north end with a few long climbs on the south end

Technical difficulty: Moderate if the single-track section is included, otherwise the route is technically easy

Scenery: Deep north woods with several lake views and a visit to ancient white pine and basswood trees

Special comments: A fine introduction to the joys of north-woods riding on paved roads and single- and double-track trails, including a visit to inspiring remnants of the once virgin forest and a stop at a wonderful swimming beach

Covering this 12.9-mile route will give you a fine taste of the beauty and history of the Chequamegon National Forest. The trailhead itself is in a beautiful setting on the shore of Lake Drummond. The slap of a beaver's tail may be the most startling surprise to occur at this peaceful spot. This trailhead is also the jumping-off point for the Cisco/Pigeon/Star Lake Tour (see Ride 97, page 311).

RIDE 95 • Drummond Trails

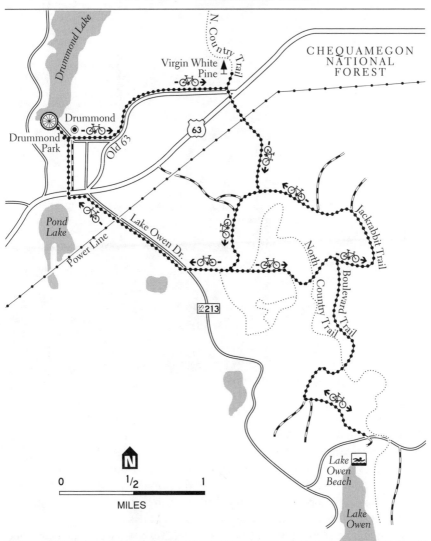

There are 2.8 miles of on-pavement riding on the Drummond Trails route, roughly divided into warm-up and cool-down stretches. In between, you'll be treated to a manageable section of the North Country Hiking Trail, the easy riding Jackrabbit cross-country ski trails, and the more demanding Boulevard Ski Trail, giving this ride an overall rating of moderate difficulty.

A short 0.2-mile excursion to the north on the North Country Trail at the start of your off-pavement ride will take you past a virgin basswood tree, a living virgin white pine, and the stump of a monstrous white pine that died in the late 1970s.

Rocks and roots along North Country single-track.

White pine was pay dirt before the appetite of the big mill in Drummond left these hills completely barren in the early part of the century. Despite the trees' value, they chose to spare a few for our benefit. This part of the North Country Trail, and the section south of US 63, give a good introduction to north-woods single-track riding. Rocks and roots abound on the firm, earthen trail, but none of the grades are too long and they don't include tight downhill corners.

The Jackrabbit loop is an easy roll on wide, grassy ski trails that were once logging roads. A hardpack track is worn in on the Jackrabbit, and to a lesser degree on the slightly narrower Boulevard Trail. Both run through a deep forest canopy comprised of birch, aspen, pine, hemlock, and maple trees. The perfume of the deep woods may make you dizzy. The big difference between the two cross-country ski trails comes from the more severe terrain on the Boulevard, which will necessitate use of the low gears for most riders. Still, the trail shows what fun riding these old logging roads can be. And there is nothing to scare you, unless you chance upon one of the area's residents—the black bear. Once they hear you, these fascinating creatures will take off, with more speed than you'd imagine such a large animal to be capable of. Just don't get between a mother bear and her cubs.

Your destination on this ride is the Lake Owen beach and picnic area, an idyllic spot and a great place to take a break or a dip. This ride presents many options. You could cruise back to the trailhead on the smooth pavement of Lake Owen Drive. If you liked the North Country Trail, you might want to ride more of it. I'll warn you, however, that it gets rougher the farther south you get off the Jackrabbit loop, and the fun factor starts to wear off. If you want to really take it easy, you can just cruise down Lake Owen Drive to the entrance road to the Drummond Ski Trail and make the Jackrabbit loop your entire ride.

General location: In the village of Drummond off of US 63.

Elevation change: Almost constantly rolling, with changes of 25' to 50' on the northern section and 75' to 100' on the southern section.

Season: Mid-May through September.

Services: Limited food and lodging are available in the village of Drummond. The Chequamegon Saloon is a gathering place for the local bike club. There is a water pump at the Lake Owen Picnic Area.

Hazards: Trails and roads are kept clear, but downed trees and branches may be encountered at any time. Due to the density of the forest cover and the serpentine character of the trails, a compass is an important safety asset. Forest roads are used by local two-wheel-drive vehicles and logging trucks. Hikers may be encountered on any of the trails, but particularly on the North Country Trail.

Rescue index: Help is available in Drummond. If you are injured or have mechanical failure, make your way to US 63 or to Lake Owen Drive for the best chance of rescue.

Land status: Public roads and trails in the Chequamegon National Forest.

Maps: CAMBA maps include detailed route and topographical information. The map for this route is available at the Drummond trailhead. A complete set of detailed maps for all CAMBA trails and an overview map are available for $6.50 by writing CAMBA at the address listed below. The overview map locates the trail clusters and mountain bike–friendly businesses in the area. CAMBA individual memberships, which include a map set, voting privileges, and a frame sticker, are available for $20.

Finding the trail: From US 63 turn north on Wisconsin Avenue (at the junction of Lake Owen Drive at the location of the Black Bear Inn) into the village of Drummond. At a T intersection turn left onto Superior Street and follow it downhill to Drummond Park, site of the CAMBA trailhead. Several other CAMBA trails can be accessed from this trailhead.

Sources of additional information:

Cable Area Chamber of Commerce
P.O. Box 217
Cable, WI 54821
(800) 533-7454
www.cable4fun.com

Chequamegon Area Mountain Bike
  Association (CAMBA)
P.O. Box 141
Cable, WI 54821
(715) 798-3599; (800) 533-7454
www.cambatrails.org

Chequamegon National Forest
  Service, Washburn Ranger District
113 East Bayfield Street or
P.O. Box 578
Washburn, WI 54981
(715) 373-2667
www.fs.fed.us/r9/cnnf

Notes on the trail: From the CAMBA trailhead in Drummond Park retrace your route up the hill and follow Superior Street (not signed as a CAMBA route in this direction) east through the village of Drummond. At Old 63 turn left and follow it to the North Country Trail, crossing just before the junction with US 63. Turn left on the North Country Trail, taking care to negotiate—or dismount and walk—the short flight of steps. At the bottom of the steps turn right. Ride 0.2 mile to the giant white pine stump and return by the same route.

From the trailhead, cross US 63 to the south and follow the North Country Trail (marked with blue symbols) 0.8 mile to a wide, grassy trail and turn right. You will be on the Jackrabbit cross-country ski trail loop, and can follow the blue-and-white CAMBA trail signs in a counterclockwise direction to the Boulevard trail. Follow the Boulevard Trail to the paved road (Lake Owen Drive) and cross it, following the CAMBA arrows to the Lake Owen Picnic Area and swimming beach.

Follow the Boulevard Trail back to the Jackrabbit loop and turn right (east) onto it. Follow the Jackrabbit loop counterclockwise to a **T** intersection, and turn right following the directions to the parking lot. At the paved road (Lake Owen Drive, FS 213) turn right. Forest Service roads are marked with small, low, brown signs with yellow lettering. At US 63 turn left, taking care to watch for traffic. Ride on the paved shoulder 0.2 mile and turn right on an unmarked gravel road following the CAMBA markers. At a **T** intersection, turn left and follow the paved street (Superior Avenue) downhill to Drummond Park.

RIDE 96 · Delta Hills Trails

AT A GLANCE

Length/configuration: 15.8 miles if the Wanoka Lake Trailhead is used; 19.2 miles if the Delta Lake Park Trailhead is used; several loop variations are possible

Aerobic difficulty: High; enough long, steep climbs to keep any aerobic animal happy

Technical difficulty: Challenging; loose surface on steep slopes will test climbing and descending skills

Scenery: Beautiful stands of white paper birch in the south and pine forest in the north with occasional lake and bog views

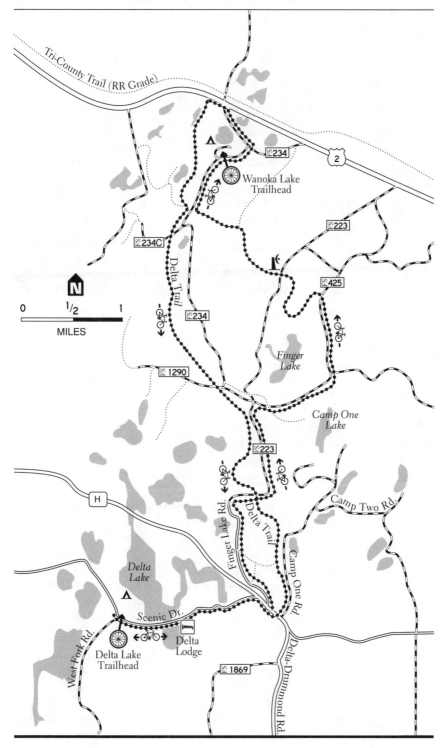

A bog view along Delta Hills Trail.

Special comments: A great day's riding for advanced riders or determined intermediates; easy-to-follow mix of paved and gravel roads and snowmobile trails

If you are up for taking on as much as the north woods can dish out, the 23.6-mile Delta Hills Trails loop is your meat. The term "hills" implies that it's not flat and, while the climbs and descents will only be in the 40- to 100-foot range, they will be constant. There is only about a mile of relatively flat off-roading on the route. This is a very challenging ride for the average bicyclist. Many grades are extremely steep, and some are subject to rutting from heavy rain. Several options allow you to shorten the route, but the very challenging rating would still apply due to the technical ability needed to handle the grades. Several forest roads also provide bail-out options.

The southbound portion of the route is on the Delta Lake Trail. Don't worry about the signs on the forest road gates that say "Trail closed April 1 to December 1"—you can ignore them. They're for the snowmobilers who use the trail in winter, the only time of the year the white paper birch forest may be even more striking than it is in summer and fall. The southern section of the loop has large stands of the stunning birch mixed with pine, oak, and maple. The birch throughout the region have been dying in recent years from a period of drought that left them vulnerable to certain insects and a virus. This has been true in the Delta Hills area, but the stands are so vast that the decimation doesn't seem as great. On the northern parts of the loop, where the soil is sandier, the birch give way to Norway pine and jack pine.

There are more rewards to taking on the Delta Hills. Frequent lakes and bogs are a treat for the eyes. The route uses some sections of paved roads near the trailhead and portions of graveled forest roads on the northbound section. The trails are wide with a firm, sandy-soil base covered with light grass and often moss. Given a choice between riding on a suspension bike or on a mossy trail, take the moss. It's like rolling on a velveteen cushion.

The Wanoka Lake campground near the north end invites you to make this ride a two-day trip or at least to take a swimming break. You'll be far from civilization on most of this route, but the Delta Lodge near the trailhead offers the kind of end-of-ride north-woods hospitality off-roaders love.

General location: 12 miles north of the village of Drummond.

Elevation change: The terrain is constantly rolling. Steep grades in the 40' range are common, and some are 70' to 100'.

Season: Mid-May through September.

Services: Food, drink, and lodging are available at Delta Lodge. There is a water pump at the Delta Lake Campground near the Delta Lake trailhead. Other pumps will be found just west of the Scout Camp Cutoff intersection and at the Wanoka Lake trailhead. All services, except bicycle, are available in the small village of Drummond, or in the town of Iron River, which is 7 miles west of the Wanoka Lake trailhead on US 2.

Hazards: Trails and roads are kept clear, but downed trees and branches may be encountered at any time. Rocky surfaces may be encountered anywhere and may be hidden by grass. Some downhills are extremely steep and have sandy, rocky washouts. Forest roads are used by local two-wheel-drive vehicles and logging trucks. Hunting season begins in mid-September. Hikers may be encountered.

Rescue index: Help is available at Delta Lodge. Your chances of on-trail rescue are slim. If you're in need of help, you should make your way to one of the forest roads or paved highways.

Land status: Chequamegon National Forest.

Maps: The CAMBA maps include detailed route and topographical information. The map for this route is available at the Delta and Wanoka Lake trailheads. A complete set of detailed maps for all CAMBA trails and an overview map are available for $6.50 by writing CAMBA at the address listed below. The overview map locates the trail clusters and mountain bike–friendly businesses in the area. CAMBA individual memberships, which include a map set, voting privileges, and a frame sticker, are available for $20.

Finding the trail: From US 63 at the village of Drummond travel 10 miles north on Delta-Drummond Road. At County Road H turn northwest, and after a half-mile turn west on Scenic Drive. The Delta Lake Park trailhead will be on the right, at 1.5 miles. The Wanoka Lake trailhead can be reached by turning south on FS 241 off US 2, 6 miles east of the town of Iron River. However, the trail notes are for riding from Delta. Several other CAMBA routes begin at the Delta Lake Park trailhead.

Sources of additional information:

Cable Area Chamber of Commerce
P.O. Box 217
Cable, WI 54821
(800) 533-7454
www.cable4fun.com

Chequamegon Area Mountain Bike
  Association (CAMBA)
P.O. Box 141
Cable, WI 54821
(715) 798-3599; (800) 533-7454
www.cambatrails.org

Chequamegon National Forest
  Service, Washburn Ranger District
113 East Bayfield Street or
P.O. Box 578
Washburn, WI 54981
(715) 373-2667
www.fs.fed.us/r9/cnnf

Notes on the trail: Excluding the paved roads, the route is well marked for one-way travel with blue-and-white CAMBA trail signs and arrows and periodic "you are here" map signs. Forest Service roads are marked with small, low, brown signs with yellow lettering. From the Delta Lake Park trailhead, travel east for 1.5 miles and turn south on County Highway H. At CR H turn left and make an immediate right onto Finger Lake Road (FS 223).

You will pass a fork after the pavement turns to gravel, but continue on FR 223 for a total of 2.6 miles until you intersect FS 425. Take a right on the dirt double-track and follow the wooded trail for almost 2 miles to pass through a clear-cut area before veering left (west) onto grassy single-track. Watch for low hanging limbs and brush. At 0.3 mile, bear left and climb back to Finger Lake Road. Turn left and follow the road south for 0.4 mile, then turn left on a dirt road. Pass the radio tower and climb to a clearcut area where you can enjoy the view before climbing to a single-track stretch of trail. Watch the trail carefully on the ensueing downhill.

The trail ends at FS 234. Take a right and ride north to an intersection with a dirt road. Turn left and ride 0.5 miles to the Wanoka Lake trailhead. From there, follow the trail parallel to Highway 2 and turn left onto a snowmobile trail. Pass two gates on a hilly stretch of trail, then pass an intersection with FS 234C and two more gates. After more hills, intersect FS 1290, Tube Lake Cut-off Trail, which leads back to FS 223 to the left. Continue on the snowmobile trail past another pair of gates and up a steep hill. Ride through an intersection with FS 223 and continue on the hilly snowmobile trail. After making a sharp left, you'll emerge onto Camp One Road.

After returning to CR H via Camp One Road, turn northwest on CR H, then after 0.5 mile turn west on Scenic Drive to return to the trailhead.

RIDE 97 · Cisco/Pigeon/Star Lake Tour (On-Road)

AT A GLANCE

Length/configuration: 20-mile loop

Aerobic difficulty: Low; gently rolling terrain will tax your cardiovascular system only if you hammer

Technical difficulty: Easy; gravel and paved roads present no technical challenges

Scenery: Beautiful northern forest with occasional lake views

Special comments: A great leisurely tour or high-speed cruise through fine Chequamegon Forest scenery on paved or gravel roads

This easy 20-mile route is a combination of several CAMBA gravel-road loops running north and west of Drummond. For riders just getting used to mountain biking or the more proficient who want an easy tour or high-speed cruise, this loop offers the kind of scenery that bonds people to the Chequamegon Forest.

The views of Drummond Lake from the trailhead and along Delta Drummond Road are inspiring, as is Cisco Lake to the north. More experienced riders may want to toss a few miles of single-track riding on the North Country National Scenic Trail into the tour mix. Just north of Cisco Lake you can take the North Country to the west for two miles to Delta Drummond Road, covering some rugged terrain and skirting Overby, Esox, and Mirror lakes. Continuing west of Delta Drummond Road, the North Country runs over easier terrain another mile-and-a-half to Forest Service Road 392.

General location: North and west of Drummond.

Elevation change: 80' is the greatest change along County Road N. Most change is in the range of 20' to 40'.

Season: Early-May through October.

Services: Limited food and lodging are available in the village of Drummond. The Chequamegon Saloon is a gathering place for the local bike club. There is a water pump at the Lake Owen Picnic Area.

Hazards: All roads on this route are shared with motor vehicles.

Rescue index: Help is available in Drummond. If you are injured or have mechanical failure, make your way to CR N or Delta Road for the best chance of rescue.

Land status: Public roads in the Chequamegon National Forest.

Maps: CAMBA maps include detailed route and topographical information. The map for this route is available at the Drummond trailhead. A complete set of detailed maps for all CAMBA trails and an overview map are available for $6.50 by writing CAMBA at the address listed below. The overview map locates

RIDE 97 • Cisco/Pigeon/Star Lake Tour

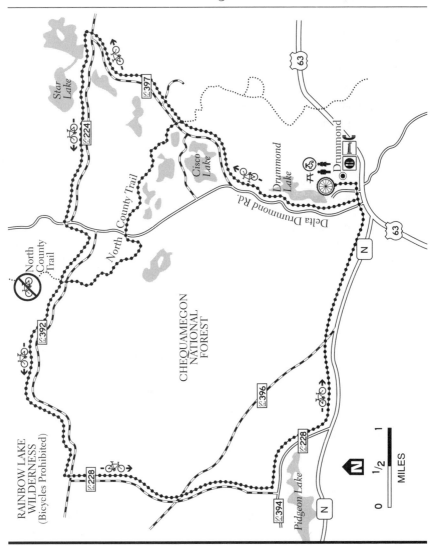

the trail clusters and mountain bike–friendly businesses in the area. CAMBA individual memberships, which include a map set, voting privileges, and a frame sticker, are available for $20.

Finding the trail: From US 63 turn north on Wisconsin Avenue (at the junction of Lake Owen Drive at the location of the Black Bear Inn) into the village of Drummond. At a **T** intersection turn left onto Superior Street, and follow it downhill to Drummond Park, site of the CAMBA trailhead. Several other CAMBA trails can be accessed from this trailhead.

Wide gravel roads lead from lake to lake.

Sources of additional information:

Cable Area Chamber of Commerce
P.O. Box 217
Cable, WI 54821
(800) 533-7454
www.cable4fun.com

Chequamegon Area Mountain Bike
    Association (CAMBA)
P.O. Box 141
Cable, WI 54821
(715) 798-3599; (800) 533-7454
www.cambatrails.org

Chequamegon National Forest
    Service, Great Divide Ranger
    District
604 Nyman Avenue or P.O. Box 896
Hayward, WI 54843
(715) 634-4821
www.fs.fed.us/r9/cnnf

Notes on the trail: The route is marked with blue-and-white CAMBA trail signs, periodic CAMBA "you are here" map signs, county and town road signs, and Forest Service road signs. The route can be ridden in either direction, but these cues are for riding counterclockwise.

From the CAMBA trailhead in Drummond Park, retrace your route up the hill to the intersection of Superior Street and turn right on the unmarked gravel road heading south. At this point you are on the CAMBA routes for the Cisco Lake and Star Lake routes. At the **T** intersection with US 63, turn west and travel a block's distance on the paved shoulder to the Delta Drummond Road where you will turn to the north.

After skirting Cisco Lake, the CAMBA Cisco Lake Trail splits off of FS 397 to the west. Continue straight on FS 397 following the CAMBA Star Lake Trail. Just a block's distance north of this intersection the North Country National Scenic Trail crosses FS 397. You may wish to try this more rugged single-track trail, which rejoins the route on FS 392 3.5 miles to the west. Riding the North Country to the southeast is not recommended due to swampy spots, and riding north of FS 392 is strictly forbidden, as this is the Rainbow Lake Wilderness Area where wheeled travel is not permitted.

After the Star Lake Trail rejoins the Delta Drummond Road and heads south for about a half-mile, it junctions with FS 392. Turn to the west at this point to follow the route to Pigeon Lake. You will actually be riding the reverse direction on the CAMBA Reynard Lake Trail until you join the Pigeon Lake Trail on FS 228. Follow the Pigeon Lake Trail back to the trailhead at Drummond.

LAKE SUPERIOR

When you go as far north as possible in Wisconsin this is where you end up. Superior is the name of the Great Lake that forms part of the state's northern border. It also describes the quality of outdoors experience you'll find there and the reason many people choose to live in this part of the world.

Superior country is also a land of rocks and minerals. Lava flows once welled up from fissures in the earth's crust. These lines of trap rock, as it is called, are now barriers to flowing waters, creating beautiful waterfalls. Ancient geologic events also formed mountain ranges that have since eroded to rugged hills, where iron mines spawned boomtowns. Today the mines are history, but the terrain makes for some great mountain biking.

At Copper Falls State Park, riders have the choice of challenging single-track trails or a flat trail easy enough for family rides. Great scenery is a big payoff in this park. A short hike from the trailhead leads to several entrancing waterfalls.

I don't know if the term hurly-burly inspired the naming of the old mining town of Hurley. If it did, it was appropriate — in the past at any rate. The town once had 200 bars, but that was during Prohibition when drinking was illegal. Things are more subdued today and other types of recreation, including mountain biking, are promoted. On the Gile Falls Tour you can take an easy ride to a historic mine site. Riding Trail #6 will be an experience of another type. Tracing the rugged spine of the Penokee Range, it is probably the toughest ten-mile stretch in the state.

Two sister cross-country ski trail systems in the middle of the Bayfield Peninsula offer different experiences. The tough Valkyrie Trails lead to a beautiful sunbowl, an opening in the forest. The neighboring Teuton Trails are less challenging, but no less enjoyable.

The Apostles Tour has plenty of variety. On the mainland you can ride a loop that gains more than 500 feet of elevation. On Madeline Island many routes are possible, all easy enough to leave time to enjoy the island's unique ambiance.

Finally, the Osaugie/Tri-County Trails give family riders, novices, or those interested in a high-speed cruise a chance to take in the sites of a major harbor on Lake Superior and ride to scenic waterfalls.

RIDE 98 · Copper Falls State Park Trails

AT A GLANCE

Length/configuration: A 2.3-mile loop, a 2.2-mile loop and/or a 1.8-mile (each way) out-and-back; several loop combinations are possible

Aerobic difficulty: High; with the exception of the flat North Country National Scenic Trail segment between the park and Mellen

Technical difficulty: Moderate; the ability to handle rock- and root-covered trails, climb skillfully, and descend with confidence will be needed

Scenery: Superb hardwood and pine forest with beautiful lake and river views plus a walk-in side trip to see waterfalls

Special comments: A not-to-be-missed scenic park that keeps getting better and better for mountain biking; if you ride everything you'll cover 16.5 miles (13.3 off-road), take on some challenging single-track, and cruise into the town of Mellen on a trail suitable for family riding

Copper Falls is an extraordinary state park with an interesting variety of off-roading opportunities. There are two single-track loops on cross-country ski trails on either side of the park road, a connector trail on the west side that runs south to another ski trail loop where mountain biking is tentatively allowed, and an out-and-back segment of the North Country National Scenic Trail that runs into the town of Mellen. This adds up to 13.3 miles of off-roading (16.5 miles total with on-road connections).

The Takesin Ski Trail has some fine single-track riding despite its short 2.3-mile length. Add another 0.5-mile out-and-back on pavement from the lower parking lot trailhead and you have a total of 3.3 miles. Your reward on the outer part of the off-road loop is a fantastic overview of a radical bend in the Bad River, 80 feet below the trail as the stream courses toward the cascade of Copper Falls.

The trail is constantly rolling and the surface varies from rough-but-firm grass and earthen surface, with frequent roots and occasional rocks, to hardpack through clover and moss. The technical skill needed to negotiate the rough trail surface and some short, steep grades make this a ride of moderate difficulty, and a good introduction for those with some off-road experience who want to take on some single-track through the dense canopy of a maple forest.

On the east side of the park road, the 2.2-mile Vahtera Ski Trail traverses similar terrain with slightly more gradual climbs. There is currently more off-road riding at Copper Falls than the trails officially signed for mountain biking. A 1.3-mile (each way) connecting cross-country ski trail will take you to the tough, 1.8-mile figure-eight loop, Red Granite Ski Trail. These trails are in off-road limbo with riding being allowed on an experimental basis.

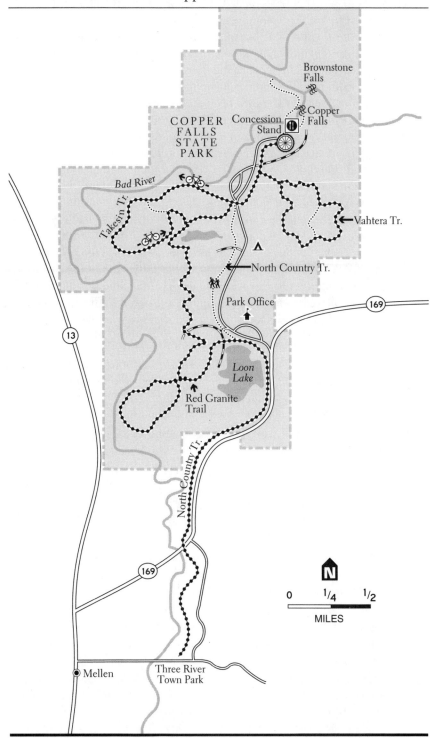

The Red Granite Trail is designated as a hiking trail, but is little used as such, and the connector trail is seldom hiked since it parallels the in-park section of the North Country National Scenic Trail (where riding is absolutely not allowed). To this point the results have been good, with only one hiker complaint in three years according to the park superintendent, so be courteous and help this excellent riding opportunity to remain open.

A 1.8-mile long section of the North Country National Scenic Trail is being sanctioned for joint hiking and mountain biking use between the park (access is on the west side of the park road between the Visitor Entry Station and WI 169) and Mellen. The trail is quite flat and, despite its close proximity to WI 169, has a secluded feel. This trail can be recommended for family riding if the kids are beyond the training wheel stage. Three River Town Park at the south end has some playground equipment.

The main attractions at the park are the waterfalls, which are easily accessible via a footbridge and trails created in the 1930s by the Civilian Conservation Corps. The park's namesake, Copper Falls, splits into two cascades and drops 29 feet over black lava rock. A short distance further, where Tylers Fork joins the Bad River, Brownstone Falls plunges 30 feet over red lava. The fractured lava is called trap rock, meaning it flowed up from fissures in the earth's crust. As the rivers eroded, their courses met these walls of tough rock and the falls were created.

General location: 2 miles north of the town of Mellen.

Elevation change: The Takesin Ski Trail is rolling, and it has one steady, steep, 70' climb. The eastern ski trail has 70' of change gained in moderate climbs. The Red Granite Ski Trail is on higher ground, with the high point being 180' above the trailhead elevation. The North Country Trail into Mellen is basically flat.

Season: May through October. Trails may be closed at anytime due to wet conditions.

Services: Camping, water, and showers are available in the park. Snacks are available at the park concession stand at the trailhead parking lot. All services, except bicycle retail and repair, are available in the small town of Mellen. Bicycle retail and repair are available in Ashland at Bay City Cycles, 26 miles to the north on WI 13.

Hazards: Trails are regularly maintained and clear, but fallen trees and branches may be encountered at any time. Hikers may be encountered on all trails. Despite the signage and small confines of the riding area, using a compass is a good idea.

Rescue index: Help is available at the park headquarters or in Mellen. In case of injury, making for the park headquarters, concession stand, or paved roadways is recommended.

Land status: Wisconsin State Park and public roads. A daily or annual vehicle sticker ($5 daily/$18 annual for Wisconsin residents, $7 daily/$25 annual for out-of-state residents) is required in state parks.

Copper Falls spills over black lava rock.

Maps: Maps of the trails are available at Copper Falls State Park Headquarters. The USGS 7.5 minute Mellen quadrangle map gives excellent information on the terrain, but doesn't show the mountain bike trails.

Finding the trail: Turn east onto WI 169 from WI 13 at the north edge of the town of Mellen. Travel 1.5 miles to the entrance road of Copper Falls State Park and follow it all the way to the parking lot at the end.

Sources of additional information:

Copper Falls State Park
Box 438
Mellen, WI 54546
(715) 274-5123

Mellen Area Chamber of Commerce
P.O. Box 193
Mellen, WI 54546-0193
(715) 274-2330
www.mellenwi.org

Wisconsin Department of Natural Resources
Bureau of Parks and Recreation
P.O. Box 7921
Madison, WI 53707-7921
(608) 266-2181
www.dnr.state.wi.us

Notes on the trail: The trails are sometimes subject to flooding or damage and may be closed for these reasons. Be sure to call ahead to check on the status. A daily or annual vehicle parking sticker is required to park in the state park (see Land status).

The one-way mountain bike trails are signed with green markers bearing a white bike silhouette, as well as blue cross-country ski trail markers, for mainly one-way travel. The two-way connector trail from the Takesin Ski Trail to the Red Granite Trail is marked only with blue cross-country ski trail markers, as is the one-way Red Granite Trail itself. The two-way North Country National Scenic Trail section between the park and Mellen is marked with three-sided North Country Trail symbols.

From the trailhead, ride south on the road back toward the park entrance. After 0.3 mile you will see the entrance to the ballfield parking lot on the east side of the road. This is also the start for the Vahtera Ski Trail.

After 0.5 mile south on the park road from the trailhead, you will pass the exit road for the north campground on the right (marked "do not enter"). Immediately beyond the road on the right is Takesin Ski Trail, the beginning of the off-road portion of the route.

A trail splitting off to the left of the Takesin Ski Trail just after the start is marked with the blue symbol of the North Country Hiking Trail, and biking is not allowed on it. At 0.7 mile you have the option of turning left on a shortcut. If you take it, you will miss the overview of the Bad River. At 1.9 miles, just before a small lake on the right, you can turn right on a cross-country ski trail that connects the Takesin Trail with the Red Granite Trail. The connector and the Red Granite Trail are not signed for mountain biking, but riding has been allowed on them on an experimental basis. Be sure to check on their status at the park office. To exit the Takesin Trail, follow the arrow directing you to the parking lot.

Access to the North Country National Scenic Trail segment into Mellen is on the west side of the park road between the Visitor Entry Station and WI 169 (riding on other North Country segments in the park is not allowed). In Mellen the trailhead is at the corner of Tyler Avenue and Butler Street, three blocks east of WI 13.

RIDE 99 · Gile Falls Tour (On-Road)

AT A GLANCE

Length/configuration: 5.2 miles one way (10.4 miles round-trip)

Aerobic difficulty: Low; the few grades that exist are gradual

Technical difficulty: Easy; mostly on paved streets and gravel roads

Scenery: Old mining towns, mine sites, and a picturesque little waterfall

Special comments: A nice tour of old mining country; the easy-to-follow route on paved and gravel roads and a snowmobile trail should be fun for intermediate riders

Around the turn of the twentieth century, mining built these range towns strung out between the highlands of the Penokee Range. The steep, slanting rock layers of the Penokees are evidence that they were once the core of an ancient mountain range. And the core is where the precious minerals are.

From the trailhead in Montreal you'll see the first evidence of mining history—towering piles of tailings, the waste product of ore extraction. Soon you'll be at pleasant little Gile Falls, and a bit further at Gile Park, on the vast flowage lake of the same name.

Heading west, you'll trace the streets and back roads of the valley. Passing through Montreal you'll notice rows of houses that all look alike. These were cookie-cutter mining company houses built to house employees. The Inn on Wisconsin Avenue is a wonderful bed-and-breakfast located in the stately old company headquarters building.

Leaving Pence, you'll take on the interesting snowmobile trail #77. This is where the challenge comes in on this ride. It starts on a rail-bed grade, but then climbs through the woods on a rough old logging road. All-terrain vehicle use churns up the surface pretty badly. After crossing WI 77 you're a short distance via gravel roads to the Plummer Mine Headframe, the last structure of its kind still standing in Wisconsin. The 80-foot high steel girder frame once lifted miners and ore from thousands of feet below the surface. The incline angle of the frame conforms to the slope of the ore-bearing rock layers.

General location: Between Montreal and Iron Belt, along WI 77.

Elevation change: Gradual climbs take you 160' higher than the trailhead.

Season: Anytime snow is not on the ground, which could only be July and August. Realistically though, May through September are a fairly safe bet.

Services: All services are available just east of the route in Hurley. Bicycle retail and repair are available at Trek & Trail in Hurley's sister city, Ironwood, Michigan. Lodging and taverns are in Montreal; lodging, a cafe, and taverns can be found in Iron Belt; and taverns are open in Upson and Pence. There are flush toilets, water, swimming, and a playground at Gile Park.

Hazards: All of the roads are shared with motor vehicles. It is necessary to ride a short distance on WI 77 and cross it several times. Parts of the route are also used by all-terrain vehicles.

Rescue index: Help is available in Montreal and Pence.

Land status: Public roadways and easements across private land.

Maps: A useful Pines and Mines trail map is available from information contacts. The USGS 7.5 minute Iron Belt and Ironwood quadrangle maps give excellent information on the terrain. The DeLorme book, *Wisconsin Atlas & Gazetteer*, shows the rail bed and all local roads and road names on page 96.

Finding the trail: The trailhead is at Montreal City Hall on WI 77.

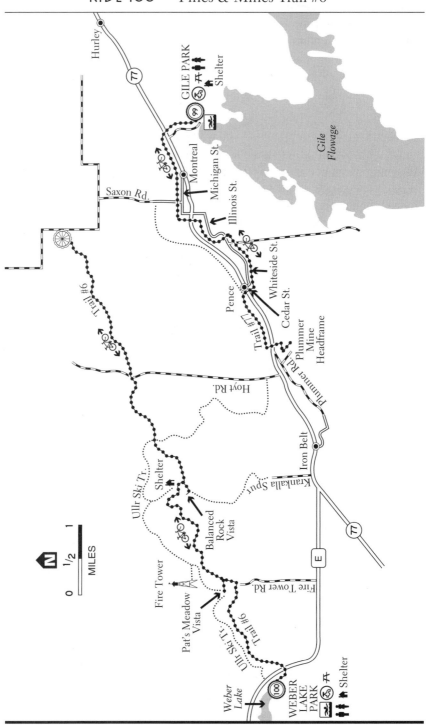

Sources of additional information:

Hurley Area Chamber of Commerce
316 Silver Street
Hurley, WI 54534-1254
(715) 561-4334
www.hurleywi.com

Pines and Mines
Iron County Development Zone
P.O. Box 97
Hurley, WI 54534-0097
(715) 561-2922

Notes on the trail: Only parts of this route are signed with blue-and-white Pines and Mines mountain bike signs, as it is pieced together from several of their routes. From the trailhead follow Pines and Mines signs east a short distance to a gravel road, turn right, and make an almost immediate right again onto a dirt road to visit Gile Falls. Return to the gravel road and go right then right again a short distance later to go to Gile Park.

The route must be followed carefully from Pence to the Plummer Mine Headframe. After crossing WI 77 to the north in Pence, turn west on an abandoned railroad bed (snowmobile trail #77) and travel about 3 blocks distance. At that point, bear left onto an old logging road that climbs up to WI 77 and a junction with Plummer Road (gravel) veering off on the south side of WI 77.

RIDE 100 · Pines & Mines Trail #6

AT A GLANCE

Length/configuration: 10 miles one way

Aerobic difficulty: Very high; you'll face constant steep climbs

Technical difficulty: High; the trail is wide, but loose surface, deadhead rocks, and mud holes will test your skills and your intuition for the right line

Scenery: Deep hardwood and pine forest with several fantastic overviews of surrounding lowlands

Special comments: Not for the faint-hearted! Trail #6 is the most difficult 10 miles in Wisconsin—the wide, easy-to-follow trail has too many steep, rocky climbs to count, and you'll probably want to ride it point-to-point

Squeek just laughed at us as we sat in his bar on WI 77. My friend Will and I had just told him we were going to mountain bike Trail #6 along the spine of the Penokee Range. "You'll never make it," he said. Hours later as we struggled up another in the endless series of rock-strewn slopes and bounced down into equally endless mud holes, we wondered if he'd been right. The all-terrain vehicles bomb into these mud holes, obliterating any firm earth right up to the trailside trees.

We did make the 10-mile run though, despite several bail-out opportunities. It took us three hours and we were off the bike almost as much as on. Whenever we questioned if anyone in their right mind would do this, all we had to do was look at the mountain bike tread tracks ahead of us. They were no testimony to sanity, but did show that others had gone before us.

Trail #6 took us to two wonderful vista spots via steep spur trails. The first from the west is Pat's Meadow Vista, a beautiful view of the marshland along Sullivan Creek. The second is Balanced Rock Vista, where, near a balanced boulder, you view the broad valley between the Penokee ridges, with the village of Iron Belt on the far rim. No one would call you a wimp if you just turned around at these points or bailed out on the roads and trails that run south from each vista.

For Will and I, when the going got tough, the tough started whining. But, we did press on all the way to Saxon Road. Back at Squeek's tavern, mosquito-bitten and covered with mud, everyone knew we were nuts. It was then that Squeek told us that 30 culverts would be laid down that summer to drain the low spots. That was good for another of Squeek's belly laughs.

General location: Between Upson and Montreal, north of and parallel to WI 77.

Elevation change: At the vista overlook, 300' from low to high points, with constant climbs of 40' to 100'.

Season: May through September.

Services: All services are available just east of the route in Hurley. Lodging and taverns are in Montreal; lodging, a cafe, and taverns in Iron Belt; and taverns in Upson and Pence. Bicycle retail and repair are available at Trek & Trail in Hurley's sister city, Ironwood, Michigan. There are pit toilets, camping, water, and swimming at Weber Park.

Hazards: All of the roads are shared with motor vehicles. It is necessary to ride a short distance on WI 77 and cross it several times. Parts of the route are also used by all-terrain vehicles.

Rescue index: Help is available in Montreal and Pence.

Land status: Iron County Forest land and easements on private land.

Maps: A useful Pines and Mines trail map is available from information contacts. The USGS 7.5 minute Saxon, Iron Belt, and Ironwood quadrangle maps give excellent information on the terrain but don't show the mountain bike trails. The DeLorme book, *Wisconsin Atlas & Gazetteer*, shows all local roads and road names on page 96.

Finding the trail: The western trailhead is at Weber Park, 3.5 miles north of the village of Upson and WI 77, via WI 122 and County Road E. To access the trail at the east end, take Saxon Road 2.3 miles north from WI 77 in Montreal. Look for a pull-out parking area on the west side of the road.

Sources of additional information:

Hurley Area Chamber of Commerce (715) 561-4334
316 Silver Street www.hurleywi.com
Hurley, WI 54534-1254

Pines and Mines   Hurley, WI 54534-0097
Iron County Development Zone   (715) 561-2922
P.O. Box 97

Notes on the trail: The trail can be ridden in either direction. Signage is adequate, with blue-and-white Pines and Mines mountain bike signs, orange snowmobile trail signs, and direction and trail names signs to the vistas and junctioning trails.

From Weber Lake Park, travel about 4 blocks distance to the southeast on CR E, and look for Trail #6 climbing sharply to the east. Bail-out options south to CR E or WI 77 include Fire Tower Road (gravel), contiguous with the route and leaving it just west of the Pat's Meadow Vista spur trail; the Krankalla Spur, crossing the route just east of the Balanced Rock Vista spur; and the Ullr Ski Trail, crossing the route in a low area just east of an Adirondack shelter.

RIDE 101 · Valkyrie Trails

AT A GLANCE

Length/configuration: 6.4-mile loop; several loop variations are possible

Aerobic difficulty: High; climbs get progressively longer and steeper toward the north end of the loop

Technical difficulty: Moderate; mainly due to stretches of soft sand

Scenery: Deep forest of maple, oak, birch, and pine, with an overview of a huge clearing

Special comments: A challenging ride through a beautiful forest leading to an interesting feature called a sunbowl

Sunbowl is actually a generic term. No, it has nothing to do with football. Sunbowls are a glacial feature—basically, kettles—as in kettle moraine. Where two massive ice sheets ground against each other, as the Superior and Chippewa lobes did here, huge ice blocks were buried in the churned earth. When the ice sheets receded these giant ice cubes melted, leaving a crater-like feature. In many other parts of the state lakes and bogs formed in these low spots. Here the soils are very sandy and drain well. What these pits do hold is cold air. At this latitude, the temperature in the bottom drops below freezing 330 days of the year. The usual forest flora cannot survive.

The sunbowl you'll visit on this route is the biggest one in the forest. About 140' deep and as long as six football fields, the pit lets the sun shine into the otherwise dark, deep forest. In the bottom, lichens grow on the ground amidst wiry grasses and a few scrubby trees.

RIDE 101 • Valkyrie Trails
RIDE 102 • Teuton Trails

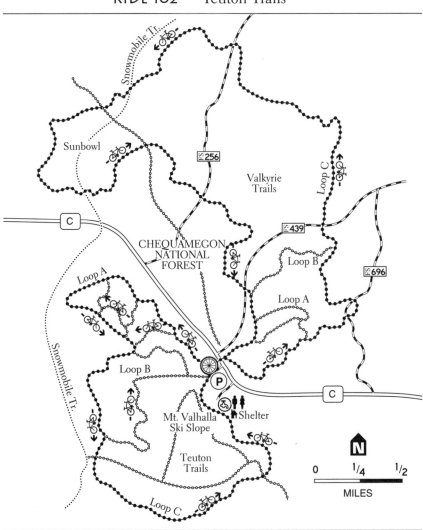

This 6.4-mile loop will challenge fit riders as they climb longer and steeper slopes leading to the sunbowl. A sandy subsurface is mostly stabilized by grasses, mosses, and tree roots, providing a firm, if rough, roll. Horses also use these trails, and though such use is low, their impact is apparent on steep slopes where their hooves have broken the surface cover and churned up the sand.

For a look at real destruction, check out the snowmobile/all-terrain vehicle trails that lace the area. At the sunbowl overview they run up the side of the crater and have cut down ten feet into the lip. The all-terrain vehicle riders have now

ATVs have eroded the sunbowl near Valkyrie Trails.

abandoned this route, cut another one five feet deep, and are working on damaging a third. Even on the flat these things have totally pulverized the surface. For some unknown reason, these all-terrain vehicle trails have been signed for mountain bike use with red and white silhouettes. You could put Ned Overend in a plutonium supporter and even he couldn't make it fifty yards through that stuff.

Certainly the Valkyrie Trails could suffer from overuse by mountain bikers as well. Their remoteness and challenging nature probably preclude that, but from a trail ethics standpoint, it's hard to consider discouraging riders from visiting this wonderful area when horse riders and all-terrain vehicles have such free reign.

General location: 8 miles west of Washburn on County Road C.

Elevation change: If you venture off route into the sunbowl, 140'; other climbs are in the range of 80' to 120'.

Season: June through September.

Services: All services are available in Washburn. There are pit toilets and water at the south corner of the trailhead parking lot, near the downhill ski area shelter. Bicycle retail and repair are at Bay City Cycles in Ashland, 16 miles to the south.

Hazards: Windfall trees and branches may be encountered. Hitting soft sand stretches at high speed is not a good idea. Trails are also used by horses and hikers. There are a number of crossings of all-terrain vehicle trails.

Rescue index: Help is available in Washburn.

Land status: Chequamegon National Forest. A vehicle parking fee is required for the Mt. Valhalla parking lot ($3 daily/$10 annual). There is a self-pay station at the trailhead.

Maps: Good trail maps are available at the trailhead self-pay station or from information contacts. The 7.5 minute series USGS quad for Mt. Valhalla shows the terrain very well, but few of the trails.

Finding the trail: From Washburn and WI 13, drive west 8 miles on CR C to the Mt. Valhalla Winter Sports Area parking lot on the south side of the road.

Sources of additional information:

Chequamegon National Forest
1170 4th Avenue South
Park Falls, WI 54552
(715) 762-2461

Washburn Area Chamber of
Commerce
204 West Bayfield Street
Washburn, WI 54891-0074
(715) 373-5017; (800) 253-4495
www.cheqnet.net/~washburn/

Notes on the trail: From the Mt. Valhalla Winter Sports Area parking lot, ride out to CR C and turn northwest a short distance to pick up the Valkyrie Trail on the opposite side of the road. The double-track trails are well-signed with blue and white cross-country ski markers and "you are here" map signs at intersections. To complete this route you will follow Loop C. Several drastic shortcuts are possible by taking loops A or B. You can exit Loop C to CR C via a sandy all-terrain vehicle trail at the south end of the sunbowl.

RIDE 102 · Teuton Trails

AT A GLANCE

Length/configuration: 4.1-mile loop; many loop variations are possible

Aerobic difficulty: Moderate; climbs are long but gradual

Technical difficulty: Easy; fairly smooth trails are readily negotiated

Scenery: Deep hardwood and pine forest

Special comments: A beautiful forest ride that should be fun for intermediate and advanced riders; trails are easy to follow and have a firm surface

The Teuton Trails are the sweet sister to the Valkyrie. Although they lead up to similar elevations at the north and south ends of the system, the climbs are

much steadier and more gradual. The character of the trails is different too. The double-track is less wide, and the maple, birch, and pine forest seems closer in. The trail surface is more consistently firm, approaching hardpack.

The greatest challenge, or the most fun depending on how you look at it, comes on the southern end of the loop as you complete the circuit of the Mt. Valhalla downhill ski slope. The run down toward the trailhead is exhilarating. Every ride should end like this.

General location: 8 miles west of Washburn and WI 13 on County Road C.

Elevation change: 120' at both the north and south ends of the loop.

Season: June through September.

Services: All services are available in Washburn. Pit toilets and water are at the south corner of the trailhead parking lot near the downhill ski area shelter. Bicycle retail and repair are available at Bay City Cycles in Ashland.

Hazards: Windfall trees and branches may be encountered. Hitting soft sand stretches at high speed is not a good idea. Trails are also used by horses and hikers. There are a number of intersections with all-terrain vehicle trails.

Rescue index: Help is available in Washburn.

Land status: Chequamegon National Forest. A vehicle parking fee is required for the Mt. Valhalla parking lot ($2 daily /$8 annual). There is a self-pay station at the trailhead.

Maps: Good trail maps are available at the trailhead self-pay station or from information contacts. The 7.5 minute series USGS quad for Mt. Valhalla shows the terrain very well, but few of the trails.

Finding the trail: From Washburn and WI 13, drive west 8 miles on CR C to the Mt. Valhalla Winter Sports Area parking lot on the south side of the road.

Sources of additional information:

Chequamegon National Forest
1170 4th Avenue South
Park Falls, WI 54552
(715) 762-2461

Washburn Area Chamber of
  Commerce
204 West Bayfield Street
Washburn, WI 54891-0074
(715) 373-5017; (800) 253-4495
www.cheqnet.net/~washburn/

Notes on the trail: From the northern corner of the Mt. Valhalla Winter Sports Area parking lot, follow the signs for Loop C (Loops A and B offer shortcuts). The firm, double-track trails are well signed for travel in a counterclockwise direction, with blue-and-white cross-country ski markers and "you are here" map signs at trail intersections. If in doubt, always take the right-most trail to complete this route.

RIDE 103 · Apostles Tour (On-Road)

AT A GLANCE

Length/configuration: 8.8-mile loop on the mainland, possibilities of 34.3-, 27.1-, 18.2-, and 11-mile routes on Madeline Island

Aerobic difficulty: High on the mainland, low on Madeline Island

Technical difficulty: Easy; entirely on paved or gravel roads

Scenery: Wonderful Lake Superior and island views

Special comments: Get ready for the beauty and sense of adventure only the Apostle Islands can offer

You need to ride these routes, and not just for a workout either. This is a wonderful part of the world, and the best way to explore it is by mountain bike. There are enough gravel roads to make fat tires the preferred tread.

If you've never been here, give yourself a full day, or better two. If you start slamming microbrews—or the ever popular Huber Bock special—at Tom's Burned Down Cafe on Madeline Island, you'd better give yourself a week. Either way, you'll come away with an understanding of the appeal of the Apostles. There is too much to tell you in this narrative. You'll notice I have offered plenty of ride options. Maybe you need a workout, but more likely you need to just kick back and enjoy.

The mainland loop will make anyone sweat. The climb is over 500 feet, most of it coming in the first couple of miles. The island is much easier. Get your workout over with and head for the ferry dock. The lure of the island is timeless. Once the center of the Ojibwe culture, Madeline attracted thousands each summer to enjoy its climate and take part in the fur trade. The book "Kitchi-Gami" by Johann Georg Kohl, a German who spent a summer on the island in the mid–nineteenth century, is a fascinating account. Life on the island was wonderful then too.

La Pointe is an interesting little village by itself. The above-mentioned Tom's Burned Down Cafe is the Margaritaville of the north. The Madeline Island Historical Museum is worth a visit to view artifacts of the past. Go there before Tom's. Actually, get in your ride before Tom's. For a nominal fee you can shower there afterwards (no beer bottles in the shower please).

Heading north out of La Pointe, you can follow the long loop or the shortcut on Black Shanty Road. If you take the long way, you may want to try finding Hidden Beach (see Notes on the trail), a wonderful spot the locals love. Returning on South Shore Road, the Big Bay Town Park is a pleasant rest stop. Further on, I strongly recommend a side trip to Big Bay State Park. There is a beach there too, but swimming anywhere in the cold lake waters is for the brave. Better to hike over the soft mossy trails to the rock formations on the point.

RIDE 103 • Apostles Tour

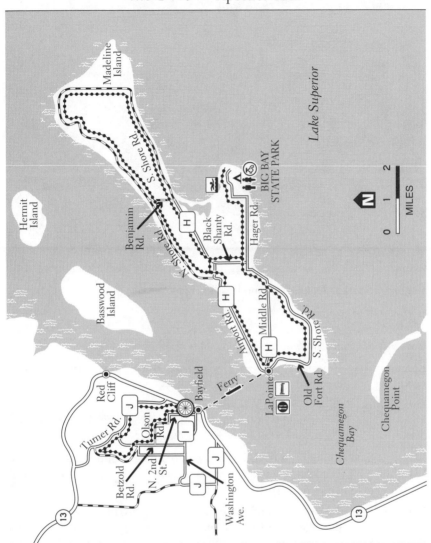

For a sea kayak adventure, check out the tours at Trek and Trail Outfitters in Bayfield. There are many fascinating ways to enjoy the Apostles.

General location: Bayfield on the mainland and La Pointe on Madeline Island.

Elevation change: On the mainland route, 520'; there is 80' of change on Madeline Island, but most of the routes are flat to gently rolling.

Season: May through September.

Services: All services are available in Bayfield and La Pointe. Bicycle retail and repair is available at Bay City Cycles in Ashland, 20 miles south on WI 13.

The State Historical Society Museum showcases Madeline Island's past.

Hazards: All routes are on public roads shared with motor vehicles.

Rescue index: Help is available in Bayfield, La Pointe, and at Big Bay State Park.

Land status: Public roads and Wisconsin State Park. A daily or annual vehicle sticker ($5 daily/$18 annual for Wisconsin residents, $7 daily/$25 annual for out-of-state residents) is required to park to park in Big Bay State Park.

Maps: A good map of the islands is available from the Apostle Islands National Lakeshoret. The DeLorme book, *Wisconsin Atlas & Gazetteer,* shows all local roads and road names on page 103.

Finding the trail: The mainland route can be accessed via town streets in Bayfield. To access the Madeline Island routes, take the ferry from Bayfield to La Pointe and begin riding there. Ferry schedules are available from information contacts, and times become less frequent in shoulder seasons outside of the Memorial Day to Labor Day high season. For day trippers, it's cheaper to take the crossing with just your bike and leave the motor vehicle on the mainland.

Sources of additional information:

Bayfield Chamber of Commerce
P.O. Box 138
Bayfield, WI 54814-0138
(715) 779-3335; (800) 447-4094
www.bayfield.org

Madeline Island Chamber of
Commerce
P.O. Box 274
La Pointe, WI 54850-0274
(715) 747-2801

Notes on the trail: The mainland and island routes can be ridden in either direction, but the cues here are for riding clockwise.

On the mainland in Bayfield, ride north on North 2nd Street. This becomes a gravel road as it levels out and is named Olson Road. At a **T** intersection with Betzold Road turn north. A half-mile later Betzold ends at County Road J. Turn west at this point; travel a quarter-mile and turn north on Torbick Road, a gravel road that splits off where CR J turns to the south. Torbick becomes Weidinger Road and ends at a **T** intersection with Turner Road (paved). Turn south at this point and follow Turner Road to CR J, where a turn to the east will take you on a long, fast downhill run to WI 13.

In La Pointe on Madeline Island, turn left (north) at the end of the drive to the ferry dock. This will put you on County Road H, which is Airport Drive. At North Shore Road go straight rather than turning right on CR H if you want to complete the long loop around the island. To find Hidden Beach, travel 7.7 miles on North Shore Road from this point and look for a sandy vehicle pull-out in a on the right side of the road. The trail to the beach is opposite this point. Use caution if riding down the trail, as there was a forehead-high windfall tree across the trail when I was there. When North Shore Road swings around to the south it becomes South Shore Road. At Benjamin Road it junctions with CR H, onto which you should go straight. This is also the location of Big Bay Town Park. At the junction of CR H and Black Shanty Road, turn south on Black Shanty Road. A mile later at the junction with Hager Road, you have the option of turning east for a 3.4-mile each-way trip to Big Bay State Park. To continue on the long loop, turn west on CR H. A mile later, South Shore Road splits off to the left. Follow it to Old Fort Road and turn north to complete the loop.

RIDE 104 · Tri-County/Osaugie Trail (Rail-Trail)

AT A GLANCE

Length/configuration: 2.5 miles each way for the Osaugie Trail and 10.3 miles each way for the Tri-County Trail to Amnicon Falls State Park

Aerobic difficulty: Low; with a few gradual grades on the Osaugie Trail, but the Tri-County Trail is a typical rail-trail

Technical difficulty: Easy

Scenery: Wonderful views of Superior Bay, the Twin Ports harbor, and scenic cascades at Amnicon Falls State Park

Special comments: A terrific family ride or high- speed cruise; the Twin Ports harbor teems with ships from all over the world.

Dates of some historic events are unforgettable. Depending on your generation, you probably remember exactly where you were when President Kennedy was assassinated or when the space shuttle Challenger exploded. The Twin Ports of Duluth and Superior are a place where people remember exactly where they were on November 10, 1975, when word came that the Edmund Fitzgerald had gone down with all hands. The Edmund Fitz had left the harbor with a load of taconite ore, and some locals still get a bit misty-eyed when they recall the storm that took the modern freighter and 29 crewmen to the bottom of the bay in an instant.

The sister cities of Duluth, Minnesota, and Superior, Wisconsin, are tied to the lake in history and spirit. Thanks to the new 2.5-mile paved Osaugie Trail, you can soak up the maritime history and scenery in Superior in a traffic-free environment. The trail junctions at its east end with the Tri-County Trail, a multi-use gravel trail that runs all the way to Ashland, 60 miles away. For your purposes, it can take you another 10.3 miles east to Amnicon Falls State Park, a wonderful spot to relax to the sound of water cascading toward Lake Superior.

On its west end, the Osaugie Trail begins in Superior at Harbor View Park at the intersection of US 2 and US 53 (Harbor View Drive and Belknap Street). A modern playground in the nearby Harborview Park makes it a great spot for kids. A short distance to the east on the trail, a road crosses to Barker's Island, where you can see a sleek-looking, black-hulled freighter with white wedding cake–like superstructures. This is the S.S. Meteor, a maritime museum, and the brainchild of Alexander McDougall. He had the idea that the secret to mastering the fierce lake was to build iron boats (lake freighters are never called ships, no matter how large) with the lines of a leviathan. The Meteor, launched in Superior in 1896, is the last of these vessels (which came to be known as whalebacks). While a step forward in nautical engineering, the whalebacks were no more invulnerable than the Edmund Fitz, and several went down to watery graves.

There are still ships in the harbor though. Ocean-going ships from all continents come here via the St. Lawrence Seaway to load up with the bounty of the Great Plains. Cargos are often part of our foreign aid program. Ships parade past the Osaugie trail to pass in and out of the channel through the sandbar that encloses the harbor.

Further east on the Osaugie Trail you'll see a huge ore dock, Loonfoot Landing, jutting out into the harbor. This marks the end of the Osaugie and the beginning of the Tri-County Trail. Shared with all-terrain vehicles, the Tri-County Trail may have limited appeal to motor-shy kids and novices. It is very wide and I didn't see a single all-terrain vehicle when I rode it, albeit on a weekday evening. The Tri-County leads to Amnicon Falls State Park, and it would be a shame to miss that.

I couldn't come up with a varied-terrain trail in the area to associate with these flat trails. There are mountain trails at Jay Cooke State Park, west of Duluth in Minnesota (see *Mountain Bike! the Great Lakes States* by this author and Jack McHugh, also published by Menasha Ridge Press).

RIDE 104 • Tri-County/Osaugie Trail

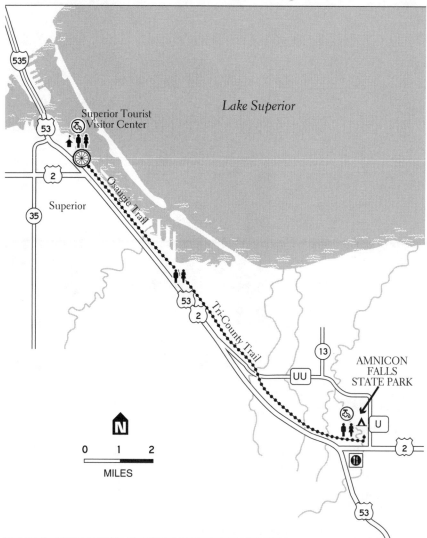

Another diversion among the many attractions of Superior and Duluth are sea kayak tours of the harbor. These programs are offered through the Canoe and Kayak Institute at the University of Minnesota, Duluth. Trade in your pedals for a paddle and get up close and personal with the huge vessels that ply the lakes. No experience is necessary.

General location: Running east from Superior on the north side of US 2.

Elevation change: Nearly flat, mostly on a rail-trail.

One of the small but fascinating falls at Amnicon Falls State Park.

Season: May through October.

Services: All services, including bicycle retail and repair, are available in Superior and Duluth. There are restrooms, water, and a playground at Harbor View Park at the Osaugie Trail trailhead. There are pit toilets and a playground at the Moccasin Road crossing on the Tri-County Trail. There is a tavern/restaurant between the trail and US 2 near Amnicon Falls State Park. At Amnicon Falls State Park you will find pit toilets, camping, and water.

Hazards: The Osaugie Trail is also used by walkers and in-line skaters. It is not entirely flat, and children riding it should have the skill to moderate speed with their brakes. Street crossings are few, but watch for them. The Tri-County Trail is also used by hikers, horseback riders, and all-terrain vehicles. It is necessary to ride a short distance on County Road U to connect the Tri-County Trail to Amnicon Falls State Park.

Rescue index: Help is available in Superior and at Amnicon Falls State Park.

Land status: Superior City trail, Douglas County trail, Wisconsin State Park, and public roadway. A daily or annual vehicle sticker ($5 daily/$18 annual for Wisconsin residents, $7 daily/$25 annual for out-of-state residents) is required to park in Amnicon Falls State Park.

Maps: Maps are available from information contacts. The DeLorme book, *Wisconsin Atlas & Gazetteer,* shows the railroad grade, all local roads, and road names on pages 100 and 101.

Finding the trail: For the west end of the Osaugie Trail, locate the trailhead at the juction of US 2 and US 53. The Tri-County Trail can be accessed from Amnicon Falls State Park via CR U.

Sources of additional information:

Superior & Douglas County
   Visitors Center
906 East 2nd Street
Superior, WI 54880
(800) 942-5313; (715) 392-2773
www.visitdouglascounty.com

Wisconsin Department of Natural
   Resources
Bureau of Parks and Recreation
P.O. Box 7921
Madison, WI 53707-7921
(608) 266-2181
www.dnr.state.wi.us

Notes on the trail: Both trails are easily followed. At the west end of the Osaugie Trail, the trail comes out into a parking area. To the east, a passage under an ore dock marks the beginning of the Tri-County Trail. A daily or annual vehicle sticker is required to park in Amnicon Falls State Park (see Land status).

GLOSSARY

This short list of terms does not contain all the words used by mountain bike enthusiasts when discussing their sport. But it should serve as an introduction to the lingo you'll hear on the trails.

ATB	all-terrain bike; this, like "fat-tire bike," is another name for a mountain bike
ATV	all-terrain vehicle; this usually refers to the loud, fume-spewing three- or four-wheeled motorized vehicles you will not enjoy meeting on the trail—except, of course, if you crash and have to hitch a ride out on one
blaze	a mark on a tree made by chipping away a piece of the bark, usually done to designate a trail; such trails are sometimes described as "blazed"
blind corner	a curve in the road or trail that conceals bikers, hikers, equestrians, and other traffic
blowdown	see "windfall"
buffed	used to describe a very smooth trail
catching air	taking a jump in such a way that both wheels of the bike are off the ground at the same time
clean	while this may describe what you and your bike won't be after following many trails, the term is most often used as a verb to denote the action of pedaling a tough section of trail successfully
combination	this type of route may combine two or more configurations; for example, a point-to-point route may integrate a scenic loop or an out-and-back spur midway through the ride; likewise, an out-and-back may have a loop at its farthest point (this configuration looks like a cherry with a stem attached; the stem is the out-and-back, the fruit is the terminus loop); or a loop route may have multiple out-and-back spurs

and/or loops to the side; mileage for a combination route is for the total distance to complete the ride

cupped   a concave trail; higher on the sides than in the middle; often caused by motorcycles

dab   touching the ground with a foot or hand

deadfall   a tangled mass of fallen trees or branches

diversion ditch   a usually narrow, shallow ditch dug across or around a trail; funneling the water in this manner keeps it from destroying the trail

DNR   Wisconsin Department of Natural Resources, the agency of the state government responsible for maintaining state parks, forests, and many of the trail systems in this book.

double-track   the dual tracks made by a jeep or other vehicle, with grass, weeds, or rocks between; mountain bikers can ride in either of the tracks, but you will of course find that whichever one you choose, and no matter how many times you change back and forth, the other track will appear to offer smoother travel

dugway   a steep, unpaved, switchbacked descent

endo   flipping end over end

feathering   using a light touch on the brake lever, hitting it lightly many times rather than very hard or locking the brake

four-wheel-drive   this refers to any vehicle with drive-wheel capability on all four wheels (a jeep, for instance, has four-wheel drive as compared with a two-wheel-drive passenger car), or to a rough road or trail that requires four-wheel-drive capability (or a one-wheel-drive mountain bike!) to negotiate it

game trail   the usually narrow trail made by deer, elk, or other game

gated   everyone knows what a gate is, and how many variations exist upon this theme; well, if a trail is described as "gated" it simply has a gate across it; don't forget that the rule is if you find a gate closed, close it behind you; if you find one open, leave it that way

Giardia   shorthand for Giardia lamblia, and known as the "back-packer's bane" until we mountain bikers expropriated it; this is a waterborne parasite that begins its life cycle when swallowed, and one to four weeks later has its host (you) bloated, vomiting, shivering with chills, and living in the

	bathroom; the disease can be avoided by "treating" (purifying) the water you acquire along the trail (see "Hitting the Trail" in the Introduction)
gnarly	a term thankfully used less and less these days, it refers to tough trails
grated	refers to a dirt road that has been smoothed out by the use of a wide blade on earth-moving equipment; "blading" gets rid of the teeth-chattering, much-cursed washboards found on so many dirt roads after heavy vehicle use
hammer	to ride very hard
hammerhead	one who rides hard and fast
hardpack	a trail on which the dirt surface is packed down hard; such trails make for good and fast riding, and very painful landings; bikers most often use "hardpack" as both a noun and adjective, and "hard-packed" as an adjective only (the grammar lesson will help you when diagramming sentences in camp)
hike-a-bike	what you do when the road or trail becomes too steep or rough to remain in the saddle
jeep road, jeep trail	a rough road or trail passable only with four-wheel-drive capability (or a horse or mountain bike)
kamikaze	while this once referred primarily to those Japanese fliers who quaffed a glass of sake, then flew off as human bombs in suicide missions against U.S. naval vessels, it has more recently been applied to the idiot mountain bikers who, far less honorably, scream down hiking trails, endangering the physical and mental safety of the walking, biking, and equestrian traffic they meet; deck guns were necessary to stop the Japanese kamikaze pilots, but a bike pump or walking staff in the spokes is sufficient for the current-day kamikazes who threaten to get us all kicked off the trails
loop	this route configuration is characterized by riding from the designated trailhead to a distant point, then returning to the trailhead via a different route (or simply continuing on the same in a circle route) without doubling back; you always move forward across new terrain, but return to the starting point when finished; mileage is for the entire loop from the trailhead back to trailhead
off-camber	a trail that slopes in the opposite direction than one would

	prefer for safety's sake; for example, on a side-cut trail the slope is away from the hill—the inside of the trail is higher, so it helps you fall downhill if your balance isn't perfect
ORV	a motorized off-road vehicle
out-and-back	a ride where you will return on the same trail you pedaled out; while this might sound far more boring than a loop route, many trails look very different when pedaled in the opposite direction
point-to-point	a vehicle shuttle (or similar assistance) is required for this type of route, which is ridden from the designated trailhead to a distant location, or endpoint, where the route ends; total mileage is for the one-way trip from the trailhead to endpoint
portage	to carry your bike on your person
quads	bikers use this term to refer both to the extensor muscle in the front of the thigh (which is separated into four parts) and to USGS maps; the expression "Nice quads!" refers always to the former, however, except in those instances when the speaker is an engineer
runoff	rainwater or snowmelt
scree	an accumulation of loose stones or rocky debris lying on a slope or at the base of a hill or cliff
side-cut trail	a trail cut on the side of a hill
signed	a "signed" trail has signs in place of blazes
single-track	a single, narrow path through grass or brush or over rocky terrain, often created by deer, elk, or backpackers; single-track riding is some of the best fun around
slickrock	the rock-hard, compacted sandstone that is great to ride and even prettier to look at; you'll appreciate it even more if you think of it as a petrified sand dune or seabed (which it is), and if the rider before you hasn't left tire marks (from unnecessary skidding) or granola bar wrappers behind
snowmelt	runoff produced by the melting of snow
snowpack	unmelted snow accumulated over weeks or months of winter—or over years in high-mountain terrain
spur	a road or trail that intersects the main trail you're following
stair-step climb	a climb punctuated by a series of level or near-level sections

switchback	a zigzagging road or trail designed to assist in traversing steep terrain: mountain bikers should not skid through switchbacks
technical	terrain that is difficult to ride, due not to its grade but to its obstacles—rocks, roots, logs, ledges, loose soil…
topo	short for topographical map, the kind that shows both linear distance and elevation gain and loss; "topo" is pronounced with both vowels long
trashed	a trail that has been destroyed (same term used no matter what has destroyed it . . . cattle, horses, or even mountain bikers riding when the ground was too wet)
two-wheel-drive	this refers to any vehicle with drive-wheel capability on only two wheels (a passenger car, for instance, has two-wheel-drive); a two-wheel-drive road is a road or trail easily traveled by an ordinary car
waterbar	an earth, rock, or wooden structure that funnels water off trails to reduce erosion
washboarded	a road that is surfaced with many ridges spaced closely together, like the ripples on a washboard; these make for very rough riding, and even worse driving in a car or jeep
whoop-de-doo	closely spaced dips or undulations in a trail; these are often encountered in areas traveled heavily by ORVs
wilderness area	land that is officially set aside by the federal government to remain natural—pure, pristine, and untrammeled by any vehicle, including mountain bikes; though mountain bikes had not been born in 1964 (when the United States Congress passed the Wilderness Act, establishing the National Wilderness Preservation system), they are considered a "form of mechanical transport" and are thereby excluded; in short, stay out
windchill	a reference to the wind's cooling effect upon exposed flesh; for example, if the temperature is 10 degrees Fahrenheit and the wind is blowing at 20 miles per hour, the windchill (that is, the actual temperature to which your skin reacts) is minus 32 degrees; if you are riding in wet conditions things are even worse, for the windchill would then be minus 74 degrees!
windfall	anything (trees, limbs, brush, fellow bikers…) blown down by the wind

APPENDIX

Bicycle Federation of Wisconsin
106 east Doty Street
Madison, WI 53703
(608) 251-4456
www.bfw.org

IMBA (International Mountain Bicycling Association)
P.O. Box 7578
Boulder, CO 80306-7578
(303) 545-9011; (888) 442-4622
www.imba.com

RIDE (Recreation for Individuals Dedicated to the Environment)
208 South LaSalle, Suite 1700
Chicago, IL 60604
(312) 853-2820
www.bike-ride.com

WORBA (Wisconsin Off-Road Bicycling Association)
P.O. Box 1681
Madison, WI 53701
(608) 222-5608; (414) 297-9616 (Milwaukee Metro Hotline)
www.worba.org

WORS (Wisconsin Off-Road Series)
3292 Soo Marie Drive
Stevens Point, WI 54481
(715) 341-3267
www.wors.org

INDEX

ABOUT THE AUTHOR

Phil Van Valkenberg has written seven books on bicycling in Wisconsin and the Midwest. Recently he worked as a consultant with the Wisconsin Department of Tourism to produce the *Wisconsin Biking Guide*. He has been involved in bicycle route mapping since 1972. In 1974 he began riding off-road in the Chequamegon National Forest, and his account of this—at that time unusual—bike experience, was published in *Bike World Magazine* in 1977. In 1983, with a group of friends, he founded the Chequamegon Fat Tire Festival, the nation's largest mountain bike event. He continues his love of off-roading by racing occasionally and exploring every new trail system he can find.